ETHICS, AGING, AND SOCIETY

The Critical Turn

Martha B. Holstein, PhD, has served as a Research Scholar at the Park Ridge Center for the Study of Health, Faith, and Ethics in Chicago, where her focus was on practical ethics, particularly as related to aging. She holds a PhD from the Institute for the Medical Humanities at the University of Texas Medical Branch and was formerly on the staff of the Hastings Center, Associate Director of the American Society of Aging. Committed to interdisciplinary work, she has been interested in the bridge between theory and practice; and the social sciences and the humanities. She has been involved in aging-related issues since 1973 and situates herself in the "camp" of critical and feminist gerontology. Dr. Holstein writes, teaches part-time in the Department of Philosophy at Loyola University, lectures, and conducts training on the subject of ethics and aging. She has edited two books, most recently *Ethics and Community-Based Elder Care* (with Phyllis Mitzen), has published in journals such as *The Gerontologist, The Journal of Aging Studies, Academic Medicine,* and frequently contributes chapters on ethics and aging to books and anthologies. She is a member of the American Society on Aging and the Gerontological Society of America.

Jennifer A. Parks, PhD, is Associate Professor in the Department of Philosophy and Director of the Bioethics Minor Program at Loyola University in Chicago. She has been interested in ethical issues in aging since the 1990s, when she first received her training and began working as a home health aide. It was this "frontline" care work with mostly elderly female clients that led her to work in the area of aging and ethics. She is the author of a book on home health care, *No Place Like Home? Feminist Ethics and Home Health Care* (2003), as well as coeditor (with Victoria Wike) of *Bioethics in a Changing World* (2009), and coauthor (with David Ingram) of *The Complete Idiot's Guide to Understanding Ethics* (2010). She has published a number of articles in journals such as the *Hastings Center Report, Bioethics, Hypatia,* and *Theoretical Medicine and Bioethics.* She is also a member of the American Society for Bioethics and Humanities (ASBH) and Feminist Ethics and Social Theory (FEAST).

Mark H. Waymack, PhD, is Associate Professor in the Philosophy Department of Loyola University Chicago. He is also an Adjunct Associate Professor in Loyola University's Neiswanger Institute for Bioethics and Policy, as well as an Adjunct Associate Professor in Northwestern University's Feinberg School of Medicine, in the Program for Medical Humanities and Bioethics. He is the coauthor, with George Taler, MD, of *Medical Ethics and the Elderly* (1988), and the author of numerous articles in bioethics, ethics and aging, and the history of ethics. He has been an active member of the American Society for Bioethics and Humanities, receiving its "Distinguished Service Award" in 2006, and has also been a member of the American Society for Aging.

Ethics, Aging, and Society
The Critical Turn

MARTHA B. HOLSTEIN, PhD

JENNIFER A. PARKS, PhD

MARK H. WAYMACK, PhD

SPRINGER PUBLISHING COMPANY

NEW YORK

Springer Publishing Company, LLC
11 West 42nd Street
New York, NY 10036
www.springerpub.com

Acquisitions Editor: Sheri W. Sussman
Senior Editor: Rose Mary Piscitelli
Cover design: Steven Pisano
Project Manager: Nick Barber
Composition: Techset Composition Ltd.

ISBN: 978-0-8261-1634-5
E-book ISBN: 978-0-8261-1635-2

10 11 12 13/ 5 4 3 2 1

The author and the publisher of this Work have made every effort to use sources believed to be reliable to provide information that is accurate and compatible with the standards generally accepted at the time of publication. The author and publisher shall not be liable for any special, consequential, or exemplary damages resulting, in whole or in part, from the readers' use of, or reliance on, the information contained in this book. The publisher has no responsibility for the persistence or accuracy of URLs for external or third-party Internet Web sites referred to in this publication and does not guarantee that any content on such Web sites is, or will remain, accurate or appropriate.

CIP data is on file at the Library of Congress

Special discounts on bulk quantities of our books are available to corporations, professional associations, pharmaceutical companies, health care organizations, and other qualifying groups.

If you are interested in a custom book, including chapters from more than one of our titles, we can provide that service as well.

For details, please contact:
Special Sales Department, Springer Publishing Company, LLC
11 West 42nd Street, 15th Floor, New York, NY 10036-8002
Phone: 877-687-7476 or 212-431-4370; Fax: 212-941-7842
Email: sales@springerpub.com

Printed in the United States of America by Gasch Printing

Contents

Acknowledgments

To make a book like this happen requires one part idea, one part perseverance, one part the pleasures of collaborative work, one part the support of friends and family, and one part the loyal support of one's publisher. We have been lucky in all these ways. We had an idea that we brought to Sheri Sussman, our editor at Springer, who supported this project from the beginning. Whenever we slipped behind schedule, often for reasons that were truly beyond our control, Sheri stood by us. We thank her most gratefully. We also have had the privilege to work in a true interdisciplinary partnership with much laughter, food, as well as dogged work. We have come to appreciate the differences between our disciplines and the value of bringing them together in a full-length volume. We have also been gratified by our colleagues' close and critical readings of several chapters. For this, we thank Marty Martinson, Madelyn Iris, Phyllis Mitzen, Karen Nisely Long, Larry Polivka, and LuMarie Polivka. We also thank Bryan Kibbe, a star doctoral student in the Philosophy Department at Loyola University, for enthusiastically taking on the chapter on natural disasters, thus helping us to address a topic rarely covered in the ethics and aging literature.

Introduction

THE CRITICAL TURN AND ITS MEANING

This book reflects the commitment of two philosophers and a critical gerontologist to bring together in one place critical reflections on ethics, aging, and society. In the spirit of interdisciplinary scholarship and in appreciation of the work of our friends and colleagues in both philosophy and gerontology, we have conceptualized this book in ways that we hope will be both intellectually challenging and practically useful. We see this book as entering into a dynamic stream of thought in both gerontology and philosophy, where old certainties are being rethought and new possibilities are opening up. Hence, we think of this book as an adventure that not only marries disciplines but opens many rich possibilities for improved care in health and social service settings and for growing old with pride no matter one's physical or mental health or one's economic or social status. We find it particularly exciting that intellectual ferment can contribute to making lives better.

Achieving these ends calls for a critical perspective that we have sought to incorporate in each section of this book. This perspective, in harmony with a growing trend in bioethics, values and uses the insights of empirical research and multiple sources of moral knowledge. Consider how a morally complex play, novel, or poem provides insights and ideas that a more rule-like approach would not reveal (see Nussbaum, 1990). These contextual and narrative sources do not rely on moral expertise nor honor the rules of impartiality and universality. In fact, they often leave us with feelings of moral uncertainty; yet, we argue that from such sources we gain a rich understanding of the moral domain and its possibilities.

As we think this book will make apparent, we have also found that more empirical disciplines such as psychology, sociology, and anthropology add immeasurably to our understanding of ethics. Empirical research helps us to understand how revered values actually work in practice. We see this clearly when anthropologists (Drought & Koenig, 2002; Kaufman, 2000) raise important challenges to the cherished beliefs in control at the end of life or when sociologists (Aronson, 2006) expose how older women experience the public home care system's limited ability to provide and reflect what they most care about. We can see, in practice, how the commitment to "client-centered" care in these home care systems dissolves the relational core of care and applies the thinnest conception of autonomy as morally sufficient.

If we are to hold people accountable for meeting their moral commitments, it is important to know what kind of selves we are and what it is possible for us to do. Here, too, empirical research is a guide. Philosophy, when joined with psychology, sociology, and the cognitive sciences, tells us much about the nature of the self. In recent years, they have pointed to the social or relational self and how that understanding reshapes our moral commitments. They tell us, for example, that self-respect is not something that we attain on our own; it is a communal product and, as such, an achievement gained through relationships with others. These disciplines help us to understand that obligations are not always voluntary and that we have critical relational obligations to others, especially to those who are vulnerable. An understanding of the relational self does what conventional ideas about the self cannot do—helps us to conceptualize what counts in our moral relationships with people who need help to manage day-to-day life. This view of the self helps us to appreciate that the realization of autonomy is very nearly impossible in the absence of a social or economic foundation to support its exercise. This understanding, of the self, gains strength from its interdisciplinary confirmation.

Given the social nature of the self, it is not surprising that the critical perspective we reflect is also attuned to context. Social relationships help make us who we are but they also sustain us and our identities. Thus, supportive social and cultural contexts are essential for developing richly formed identities that are worthy of respect and allow us to speak in our own voice. But social contexts are often not supportive in this way, especially for people who are not privileged. It is often a struggle to claim their voice. This means that women, old people, those who are poor, and racial and ethnic minorities do not gain the support that they need from the broad contexts in which they live. With other feminist scholars, we hold that if our values, perceptions, concepts, and identities are in large measure social products then the social world must be as important to ethicists and gerontologists as it is to the individual.

Context also calls attention to our particularity. As very particular people, many of us do not find an easy fit the normative values that suit the more privileged. While we would hope that the cultural practices, beliefs, and values can be modified to be more hospitable to people at the margins, we look to smaller communities of meaning as sites where people find support for their identities, meanings, and self-worth. These communities can also be sources of practical and moral knowledge that help to inform practices of care.

Other contextual features of our lives are more directly important. The received view of ethics does not take into account the conditions that older people need to make self-affirming decisions. Inhospitable structural conditions, economic insecurity, social disregard along with illness, disability, suffering, and death all impede our ability to speak in our own voice. We see this graphically displayed in hospitals and nursing homes but also in conditions of elder abuse and neglect.

The policy environment is another critical contextual feature of our lives. It deeply influences the kind of life we can lead and the choices that are available to us. Hence, we have a dual interest in policy. First, we want to reveal how the values that support it are not neutral: for example, people not well served by the market are victims of the prevailing neo-liberal ideology. And, second, we want to suggest policy alternatives that rely on other normative values that can ground policy choices that take into account such concerns as gender, justice, and care. To introduce new and different normative ideals for policy development calls for an activist engagement with the world. It is not enough to notice problems; it is also essential to try to do something about them.

Our critical perspective also means that we reject standard approaches to ethical thinking. This rejection, however, does not mean that we support relativism. With Margaret Walker (1998), we believe that certain actions and practices are infinitely better than others, but that the way to determine best action is not through the application of principles and theoretical ideas. Rather, we achieve our best ends though narrative and communicative approaches, in which the integrity of each individual, and of the group, both count. We are not suggesting that we abandon principled knowledge; we simply recognize that such principled knowledge is merely the beginning and not the end point of moral engagement (Walker, 1993).

We write this book for several rather different audiences: philosophers, ethicists, gerontologists, social workers, physicians, nurses, attorneys and others who, as scholars, teachers, or practitioners, are committed to understanding how the conditions of old age are worth detailed moral inquiry. We hope that by bringing together different ways of thinking, we will provide an enriching and provocative reading experience. We write from the "edge" of both philosophy and gerontology. While respecting and learning from our more mainstream colleagues, we write specifically from the critical perspective we have just briefly described. In gerontology, for example, this perspective has been represented by critical gerontology, an interdisciplinary approach utilizing the humanities and political and moral economy to raise questions about "what everyone knows." This approach allows us to seek the often hidden values that support research agendas and dominant discourses; to specifically call attention to the ways in which class, gender, and race affect us as we age; and to probe for the voices at the margins that rarely command notice and that lack social and epistemological power (Baars, Dannefer, Phillipson, & Walker, 2006; Minkler & Estes, 1999).

When critical gerontologists consider ethical issues and aging (Holstein, 2010) the canvas extends beyond client-professional issues, with its focus on client autonomy that has long dominated scholarship. While concerned with those issues—especially with an eye to enlarging how we think about them—critical gerontology has also been interested in such areas as normative implications of cultural images, tropes and metaphors and the ways in which social and public policy can as constrain choices for older people. Critical gerontology also takes embodiment as a morally important feature of old age. A woman with severe osteoporosis experiences the world very differently from a young and well-conditioned marathon runner.

In philosophical ethics, provoked, in part, by the publication of Carol Gilligan's *In a Different Voice* (1982), to be at the "edge" has meant exploring the moral relations between intimates or between people in legitimate relationships of dependency. This has meant moving beyond individual autonomy, assumed to be a characteristic possessed by most moral agents, to a consideration of a more complex understanding of autonomy that understands the self as necessarily ensconced in relationships of care. It suggests that the preoccupations with individual rights as the grounding of obligation to older people who need care are inadequate. Moral claims, Eva Kittay (1999) suggests, arise "out of the relationship between one in need and one who is situated to meet that need" (p. 55). We thus reiterate that this view of the self means that our lives are filled with necessary obligations that we ignore at peril to our self-respect. But it also means that our response to these obligations calls for support so that women, who are the primary caregivers in our society, do not face exploitation as a result of this responsiveness.

To honor autonomy, in our view, calls for a focus on the external conditions that support or impede its exercise. Context, including practical matters such as economic insecurity, physical limitations, threats of abuse, or life in a nursing home setting, all come between "real and apparent desires" (Meyers, 1989). Thus, part of the responsibility of professionals working with elders is to start with awareness about the autonomy-constraining features of these contexts and to then work with persons to reveal their values and desires. This path to reaching an authentic voice is best done through narrative, which has the capacity to reveal what matters most to elders. It also has the ability to allow us to re-story our lives by letting us break free of master narratives (Lindemann Nelson, 2001; Ray, 2007) so that it opens more paths to living in ways that support identity. Narrative, based on a communicative or dialogic approach, is the way most of us make important decisions and reflect upon our lives. We urge its further practice in work with older people. Once again, we affirm that much of the important communicative work involved in developing emancipatory narratives and defining our core values, beliefs, needs, and identities, occurs in smaller communities of meaning where older people are free to define themselves in a safe environment.

A GLANCE AT THE CHAPTERS

In Chapter 1, we present the received view of ethics that has informed a great deal of work on aging, a view that we believe does violence to the realities of aging and old age. This approach, which takes respect for autonomy to be the ultimate concern, faces many challenges because it ignores factors such as institutional power, compromised autonomy, and the degree to which our selves are socially situated and socially constituted.

As we argue, the principle of autonomy is problematic when we are considering people of advanced age, who cannot maintain a facade of being independent and self-sufficient. In addition, the principle is not helpful within the context that a large number of older adults find themselves: nursing homes or assisted-living care centers. The conditions of old age and the living conditions one finds in long-term care facilities are not conducive to the principle of autonomy as it has traditionally been understood. In this chapter we call for the rethinking of autonomy, how we understand it, and the ways in which it applies to older adults, in order to ensure that people are not unduly harmed by it.

Chapter 2 explores how new ways of thinking about autonomy can significantly expand our understanding of ethics and aging. As we note in Chapter 1, in its common understanding autonomy continues to mean self-directing action, which is symbolized and enacted by the process of informed consent. This view, however, is far "thinner" than what a robust approach to aging requires. Autonomy is often reduced to making choices, with no consideration of the impediments that make such choice difficult if not, in some cases, impossible. Without an availability of options, the ability to pay for those options, or the presence of meaningful life choices, we fail to provide for our elderly in ways that are significant and meaningful for them. Respect for autonomy thus means more than removing barriers to and honoring choice: personal autonomy requires much more than uncoerced choice.

As we argue in Chapter 2, our goal is not to eliminate autonomy from ethics and aging, but to alter the understanding of autonomy that is typically invoked in connection to the elderly. Respect for the choices and values of older persons are important, especially in the face of a culture that has largely denigrated the elderly and reduced them to the status of children. The way in which autonomy is defined and understood, however, affects our treatment of these individuals. If a concept of autonomy is to serve such persons, then it must be couched in a moral language that finds some "fit" with their actual experiences and capacities. For this reason, we advocate a relational conception of autonomy that is rooted in feminist ethics. When understood as "relational," autonomy is divested of both the social contract model (human exchange conducted among equals), and the concept of self as detached and self-interested. Instead, we suggest that human beings should be viewed as beings-in-relationship—as being *necessarily* and not only contingently ensconced in relationships of care. Chapter 2 sets out the feminist, narrative and communicative ethic frameworks by which we argue that we can achieve significant change in how we think about ourselves in relation to others.

In Chapter 3, we explore old women's embodiment through cultural, moral, and biological lenses. Our intent is to show why embodiment and body image matter in our social practices and in the moral life more generally. In this chapter, we integrate biological understandings of the aging body with social constructionist views that take bodily experiences to be a socially determined phenomenon. In so doing, we suggest that both biological *and* social understandings constitute what it means to have an aging or aged body.

How we experience our aging bodies is thus complex, influenced by structural, institutional, and cultural forces and the myriad interactions that occur in the overlapping and discrete contexts in which we live. Our embodied selves shape and are shaped by these forces and interactions. We do not argue that aging and aged women ought to be entirely free from cultural judgements concerning their bodies: for, as we recognize, as social being, the body is partly physical phenomenon and partly social construct. Rather, we reject the ubiquitous negative understanding of the aging body, which denies the very possibility of an authentic experience of it.

In Chapter 3 we argue for the need to open up meanings of aging that contribute to older women's sense of self-worth and personal identity, finding the opportunity to do so within the micro-communities within which aging and aged women socialize and live.

Chapter 4 offers a sustained critique of emerging normative ideas about what one ought to be and do in the "third age," that period after retirement and prior to the experience of serious physical and cognitive limitations. These normative ideals, captured in such expressions as successful aging, productive aging, and civic engagement, envision an elder population that is relatively affluent and in good health who *ought* to use that status to contribute actively to the community. While we have no objections to creating opportunities for continued participation, indeed find it a good thing, our objections are based on the normative qualities that infuse these ends. These cultural ideals reflect a privileged view that upholds for all older people a way of life that may be possible for only a relatively few. Given the importance of images, tropes and other cultural ideals as ingredients in shaping and evaluating one's identity, we see these ideals as potentially damaging to those who cannot live up to them or who do not wish to do so. If we do not see ourselves in these master narratives, our ability to interact with the larger community may be constrained along with our freedom to act as we might wish to. We argue that it is critical to see how the paths to old age are deeply shaped by social location with some locations providing the foundation for a "successful" old age while others make it very difficult especially for lower income women and people of color.

Instead of these broad narratives of what is good and desirable in old age—both for individuals and for society—we turn once again to small communities as places where older people will find the resources to develop their ideas of what it means to live in ways that confirm their self-worth and support identity even when they are no longer able to do what once confirmed who they were. In these communities they have a chance to re-story their lives so they are not bound by the conventional story lines, whether those stories are the old ones of decline and loss or the newer ones of an extended middle age that have infused society.

In Chapter 5, Anti-aging Medicine, we grapple with the idea of anti-aging medicine. A commonly discussed concern is whether or to what extent there is any validity to the claims put forward by enthusiasts of anti-aging medicine. Despite the enthusiasm of the anti-aging proponents, we express some skepticism about the likelihood of technological success in this endeavor. Additionally, one can speculate about the likely effects upon society and social structures if anti-aging medicine were to become a reality: Would we truly enjoy such vastly extended life spans? What would happen to such social institutions as marriage and family? And what kind of pressures might this put upon such social arrangements as retirement, Social Security, and so forth. But there are very present social justice issues that have received considerably less attention. In particular, we would like to raise the question of how the enterprise of anti-aging medicine in its current form—whether it ever proves technologically successful or not—has adverse effects upon the elderly. Specifically, we argue that the whole enterprise of "anti-aging" medicine perpetuates and even exacerbates negative stereotypes of aging. These negative stereotypes devalue those who are elderly in our society, and cause harm through this devaluation and the accompanying loss of self-esteem. In short, far from being positively beneficial, or even just neutral, the enterprise of anti-aging medicine is actually harmful.

In this chapter, we will argue that ethics can importantly contribute to policymaking while being mindful of the serious impediments to constructing effective bridges. We argue for the importance of exposing the values that are the foundation for policy choices so that they can be interrogated and assessed. We also argue that while justice is a distributive issue it is also about who sits at the table as needs are identified and intervention proposed. Because our commitment throughout this book is to counter a privileged view perspective, we will argue for broad participation in policymaking.

To lay the foundations for the alternative normative values that we will propose, we describe and critique the ideology known as neoliberalism, which endangers the well-being of people of all ages who are not well served by the market. We argue for a value foundation for policy that supports both families and elders so that individuality and interconnectedness can thrive without the gender and class exploitations that are now so prominent. It will argue for social, economic, and institutional supports that permit freedom commensurate with physical and cognitive abilities. This alternative value foundation rests on a relational ontology and commitments to personal and social interdependence and solidarity, dignity, and gender justice. This chapter is one step in an act of resistance to those politics, ideologies, and individualistic moral values that disregard context and the conditions of possibility for people of different kinds.

In Chapter 7, we open by affirming the vitally important role that "home" plays in all our lives. As our bodies become more uncertain, the more we need what is familiar and identity confirming. To stay at home, for so many elders, means having the support of others—usually a family member, most often a woman. Since caregiving is not employment at will, we critique the common assumption that family members, primarily women, are able and willing, with minimal support, to give care to their elders.

This chapter reminds us that giving and receiving care are essential to the continuity of human life. This fact is visible "proof" that the self in relationship is a more apt descriptor of who we are than the independent self that is upheld as morally commendable. This view of the self that we have integrated into all of our work opens the way for a more penetrating analysis of the moral problems encountered in home care. The situations that occur there, so often problems of living in the face of loss and social devaluation, are not susceptible to standard approaches to decision-making. Because they also involve deeply intimate parts of our lives, they are fraught with sensitivities and the inevitable need to negotiate what to do and how to do it. Hence, in home care, we argue for justice-based commitments to the care provider, who should not suffer immediate and long-term harms because of her response to need. But we also argue for a communicative approach to addressing the problems that arise since this is the clearest way to respect not only the individuals but the relationships that are so sustaining.

In Chapter 8, The Nursing Home: Beyond Medicalization, we confront the social descendant of America's "poor house." We, as a society, harbor a loathing of these underfunded and understaffed institutions. Placement in a nursing home stands as an explicit judgment that the individual has failed at a central American value: independence. And while Americans are deeply averse to the idea that we ourselves will become residents in one of these facilities, many of us do wind up living out our last years in just such a nursing home. We argue that de-medicalizing our understanding of the nursing home—and nursing home care—and emphasizing instead a sense of caring for persons in what has effectively become their home will be a far better way of supporting and benefiting nursing home residents than happens in the typical contemporary nursing facility. We also argue that true nursing home reform will ultimately require a revaluation of American's obsessive fixation on independence and aversion to dependence in any form. Accordingly, from our critical perspective, we call for a reconceptualization of the physical and organizational environment of the nursing home, de-emphasizing the medical-acute-care flavor of so many institutions today, and arguing instead for the nursing home as a humane, environmentally enriched place to live where persons are cared for, not bodies in beds.

Chapter 9 addresses a sampling of relational issues that arise within the long-term care setting. The issues we consider include confidentiality, power, boundaries, bias, and conflicts of interest. We examine these issues as they emerge in different settings, both in the community and within institutions. In particular, we incorporate the new approaches to doing ethics that we discuss in previous chapters. We consider a case study that highlights a commonly occurring relational dilemma in the nursing home setting—the development of romantic relationships between nursing home residents and the conflicts those relationships may cause.

As Chapter 9 argues, an appeal to traditional autonomy is not responsive to the rich and complex relational issues that arise between caretakers and the elderly in long term care. By taking seriously the relational autonomy approach detailed in Chapter 2, we can more effectively address the complex social relationship issues that arise in the long term care setting. We argue that a feminist conception of relational autonomy best characterizes the relationships between care takers and care recipients and recognizes the unique features of each relationship. If human beings are, as this view claims, interdependent beings, and if our very identities come out of the relationships in which we are involved, then we ought to judge the ethical nature of long-term care by the quality of the relationships in question, not by the degree to which individual autonomy is respected.

Chapter 10 addresses the painful questions associated with elder abuse, neglect, and self-neglect. While recognizing that the etiologies and the probable interventions in these situations are very different, our interest is in exploring how the "critical turn" in ethics can open new possibilities for addressing the ethical problems these situations create. For health and social service professionals, much hinges on questions of decisional capacity since that determination helps to govern the actions that are deemed morally acceptable. The chosen actions then support either autonomy or beneficence/paternalism. These are seen as oppositional. One cannot respect autonomy at the same time that one acts paternalistically. This approach takes these core values as determinative—the beginning and the end of ethical deliberations—even when professionals continue to feel dissonance between their wish not to trample the right to choose with their sense of obligation to protect elders from harm, when protection is possible. To respond to this dilemma, we argue for a sustained effort to detect, through narrative, re-storying, and varied communicative strategies, what the abused, neglected, or self-neglecting elder cares most about. It aims to help her to recover or discover her authentic voice (Meyers, 2002) that is so often hidden even from herself by reasons that are social, cultural, familial, and economic in origin. We further adopt Kittay's (2006) concept of the "transparent self" as the most congenial means to reach that end. We suggest that this dissolves the opposition between autonomy and paternalism since both (or all) people involved have a common aim—helping this elder have what she most cares about met. This approach, we know, is a difficult one in the time and resource constrained environment in which many professionals work. It is also complicated by the long histories of families and how they relate to one another and is further complicated by the disturbing fact that violence is probably not eliminable. We, nonetheless, argue for this approach as the most likely way to meet professional responsibilities at the same time that we try to meet the elder's genuine autonomous wishes.

In Chapter 11, Alzheimer's Disease and an Ethics of Solidarity, we argue that prevailing cultural and philosophical norms of personhood and dignity come together to radically devalue that individual with Alzheimer's disease. The obsession in Western culture with highly individual, fully rational autonomy, by focusing on only one facet of personhood, obscures and devalues all other aspects of being a person. Yet, Alzheimer's (and such dementias in general), might be thought of as an extreme challenge to the notion of personhood. As cognition is interrupted and memory fades, in what sense can personal identity—selfhood—remain? And, in our "hypercognitive" culture, when we gaze upon those individuals with dementia, we see inherently compromised and diminished persons: They become less and they count for less. We argue that understanding persons as relational rather than as isolated both helps explain how self can be sustained through dementia and what kind of care is of greatest value for those with dementia.

In Chapter 12, we take on the task of looking at end-of-life care from a vantage point similar to that we adopted in other chapters, that is, by raising questions about the "taken for granted," by using empirical research to raise questions about "ideal" formulations of what is good at the end of life, and then considering an enlarged scope of approaches to such care. We describe efforts, such as advance care planning and hospice that are designed to "tame" death and then critique the commitment to control as a central goal for end-of-life care. We argue that control relies on problematic assumptions about what it is that people most want, their willingness and ability to rationally plan for their own dying, and the inattention to the medical culture that strongly influence the possibilities open to many people. We worry that over reliance on rational planning erases the vulnerable, hurting, emotional self in favor of the rational, cognitive self and that the individualistic focus of so much advance care planning denigrates the continued concern for others that people who are dying continue to express. Fear of burden signals, once again, the central place of relationships in our lives.

While supportive of hospice and palliative care and efforts to improve advance care planning, we argue for a broader range of interventions that lessen the importance of individual treatment choices that ease the burden of decision making, and address the caring needs of patients and families. We look to "bottom up" ideas directed at the still stubbornly resistant problem—how to ease the transition from life to death in ways that respect individuals and the significant relationships of which they are a part.

Chapter 13, Aging and Disasters: Facing Natural and Other Disasters, is an effort to tell a consistent and compelling story about the elderly amidst catastrophic disaster, and to then develop an ethical analysis and practical strategy for addressing their unique situation. In the first portion of our chapter we make the case that the elderly are routinely overlooked amidst catastrophic disasters, and thereby often suffer disproportionately relative to the general population. More than being just a vulnerable population of people, elders are susceptible to additional and compound harms. A failure to recognize their special needs will consistently lead to their marginalization in disaster response efforts. Therefore, in the second section of the chapter, we emphasize our ethical obligations to (1) responsible planning prior to the occurrence of a disaster and also to (2) promote and maintain effective communication and collaboration both in planning for and responding to a major disaster. These two elements seek to address the particular situation of older people relative to major disasters.

To further specify and make meaningful these broad commitments, we introduce an ethics of placeholding, arising out of work by Lindemann (2009) and Young (1997), as an important framework for analysis and assessment. In the final portion of the chapter, we offer some concrete recommendations for a renewed approach to disaster planning and response that is conscious of the elderly amidst catastrophic disasters.

CONCLUSION

As you engage this text, we invite you to join us in the spirit of communicative ethics—with an open mind and a willingness to settle in for a conversation about matters of practical and intellectual importance. We hope that bringing together these various elements of a critical ethics, we have entered into and advanced on ongoing conversation about ethics, aging, and society. Since both ethics and gerontology are historically situated practices, we anticipate that what we have done in this book will unlikely be the end of this process of edging conversation in newer directions. As readers, you start the process of revisioning, adopting what makes sense to you and rejecting what does not. We feel fortunate that we have had the chance to speak to you in what we consider our authentic voices.

REFERENCES

Aronson, J. (2006). Silenced complaints, suppressed expectations: The cumulative effects of home care rationing. *International Journal of Health Services, 36*(3), 335–356.

Baars, J., Dannefer, D., Phillipson, C., & Walker, A. (Eds.) (2006). *Aging, globalization and inequality: The new critical gerontology.* Amityville, NY: Baywood Publishing.

Drought, T., & Koenig, B. (2002). Choice in end-of-life decision making: Researching fact or fiction? *The Gerontologist, 42*(Special Issue III), 114–128.

Gilligan, C. (1982). *In a different voice: Psychological theory and women's development.* Cambridge, MA: Harvard University Press.

Holstein, M. (2010). Ethics and aging: Retrospectively and prospectively. In T. Cole, R. Ray, & R. Kastenbaum (Eds.), *A guide to humanistic studies in aging.* Baltimore: Johns Hopkins University Press.

Kaufman, S. (2000). Senescence, decline, and the quest for a good death: Contemporary dilemmas and historical antecedents. *Journal of Aging Studies, 14*(1), 1–23.

Kittay, E. F. (1999). *Love's labor: Essays on women, equality, and dependency.* New York, NY: Routledge.

Kittay, E. F. (2006). Beyond autonomy and paternalism: The caring transparent self. In T. Nys, Y. Denier, & T. Vandervelde (Eds.), *Autonomy and paternalism: Beyond individualism and good intentions* (pp. 1–29). Leuven: Peeters.

Lindemann, H. (2009). Holding one another (well, wrongly, clumsily) in a time of dementia. *Metaphilosophy, 40*(3&4), 462–474.

Lindemann Nelson, H. (2001). *Damaged identities, narrative repair.* Ithaca, NY: Cornell University Press.

Meyers, D. (1989). *Self, society and personal choice.* New York, NY: Columbia University Press.

Meyers, D. (2002). *Gender in the mirror: Cultural imagery and women's agency.* New York, NY: Oxford University Press.

Minkler, M., & Estes, C. (1999). *Critical gerontology: Perspectives from political and moral economy.* Amityville, NY: Baywood Pub. Co.

Nussbaum, M. (1990). *Love's knowledge: Essays on philosophy and literature.* New York, NY: Oxford University Press.

Ray, R. (2007). Narratives as agents of social change: A new direction for narrative gerontologists. In M. Bernard, & T. Scharf (Eds.), *Critical perspectives on ageing societies* (pp. 59–72). Bristol, UK: Policy Press.

Walker, M. (1993). Keeping moral spaces open. *Hastings Center Report, 23(2)*, 33–41.

Walker, M. U. (1998). *Moral understandings: A feminist study in ethics*. New York, NY: Routledge.

Young, I. M., & Princeton, N. J. (1997). *Intersecting voices (House and home: Feminist variations on a theme)*. Princeton, NJ: Princeton University Press.

SECTION I

Approaches to Ethical Thinking

CHAPTER 1

Ethics and Aging

Challenges to the Received View

INTRODUCTION

As individuals and members of families, in work environments, communities, and nations, we develop moral understandings that fundamentally inform how we live and act. These understandings are most often implicit, requiring attention only when they cease working effectively, or when they come into clash with differing world views (Walker, 2007). They are deeply influenced by culture, power relationships, values, and professional norms that are often taken for granted, if noticed at all. At times, however, new situations, issues, and problems arise for which we have few, if any, moral understandings. At other times, scholars or practitioners bring different experiences and training to an area, leading to alternative perceptions and responses to what once may have appeared unproblematic. Such changes provide opportunities for rethinking and lead to what has been called the "critical turn" in ethics (McCullough, 2005). In gerontology and ethics, for example, the evolution of feminist thinking called attention to the ways in which gender operates in our moral practices and beliefs so that generalizations and idealizations most often reflected conditions that certain people are more likely to meet than others. Feminists and other scholars have also introduced ways to think about ethics that are based less on theory and abstract rules and principles than on, in Margaret Walker's (2007) terms, an "expressive–collaborative" model of decision-making that is context sensitive.

Most often, ethical dilemmas can be framed in "right versus right" terms when one can defend two or more choices on the basis of held values (Kidder, 2003). Problems such as those posed by chronic illness, for example, are painful to face and even harder to resolve. How shall we care for an aging parent who has Alzheimer's disease, while also caring for our immediate family and ourselves? How ought responsibilities for such care be distributed among individuals, families, and the public sector? End-of-life care is another such example. While respecting a person's right to make treatment choices, when do cognitive changes so impair judgment that others must decide? How might biases influence such decisions? How ought safety and risk be balanced when an old woman lives alone in a dangerous neighborhood but insists on leaving the door unlocked so neighbors can drop in? Questions such as these, which are just a small sample of the pressing concerns we face, call for ethical analyses that yield justifiable actions when we cannot do everything and when no answers are perfect.

Because ethics is a disciplined and systematized reflection on our moral practices (Walker, 2007), it can raise questions about our conventional moral values and judgments, and also reveal how relationships of power influence moral practices. Who does what for whom, and on what basis? The gendered nature of caregiving, often effaced by the language of "family care," is one example. Similarly, the historic subject matter of ethics—relationships among equal strangers in the public sphere—is suggestive of the hidden power that has determined what ethical issues received attention. Moral philosophy, until the past 20 years or so, paid almost no attention to the private sphere and so to issues that directly affected the lives of women and legitimate relationships of dependency.

In this book, we will defend an approach to ethics that we argue is far more applicable to issues in aging than the current received view. The approach for which we are advocating, fleshed out fully in Chapter 2, is intersubjective, interdisciplinary, and methodologically diverse; it takes emotions seriously as sources of moral knowledge and moral value, and rather than treating ethics as the concern for "experts," it embeds ethics in the everyday social worlds in which we live and work. As Barry Hoffmaster has rightly claimed, "Moral experience does not have the clarity, precision, and rigor, or the constancy and consistency that a moral theory requires, and those demands cannot be imposed on moral experience without substantial loss and distortion" (2001, p. 223). We learn about our esteemed moral values in the practices of individuals and communities, and these moral values help to ground further reflections (Kuczewski, 1999; Walker, 2007). "Doing" ethics, then, is much more messy and complex than abstract principles and theories would suggest.

In what follows in this chapter, we will lay out the received view of ethics that has informed a great deal of work on aging, a view that we believe does violence to the realities of aging and old age. This approach, which takes respect for autonomy to be the ultimate concern, faces many challenges because it ignores factors such as institutional power, compromised autonomy, and the degree to which our selves are socially situated and socially constituted.

A SHORT HISTORY OF ETHICS AND AGING

For the last two decades, scholarly writing on ethics and aging has placed certain substantive values at the forefront of our thinking: for example, values about keeping confidences, telling the truth, and respecting older people as important decision-makers about their own lives. First among equals, however, has been the principle of autonomy. In the early years of biomedical ethics (the 1970s and 1980s), it was common to think of bioethics as "applied ethics." In other words, familiar theories—utilitarianism, Kantianism, and the social contract—were applied in practice settings. This approach emerged because philosophers, mostly male, and mostly American, came to dominate bioethics; unsurprisingly, they transferred what was well established in the academic setting to the practice one. Hence, the idea held sway that moral thinking is (and should be) detached, universal, and impartial. This perspective, intended to ascertain that personal feelings, biases, and preferences would not "muddy" moral analysis, seemed to define the ethical enterprise.

This received view has a long-standing and well-respected philosophical history. For example, in his work *On Liberty* (originally published in 1859), John Stuart Mill produced a liberal theory which has, at its core, the notion that "Over himself, over his own body and mind, the individual is sovereign" (1956, p. 13). On Mill's account, the only grounds on which an individual or society may interfere with the desires, choices, or actions of others is self-protection. He claims:

> The only freedom which deserves the name is that of pursuing our own good in our own way, so long as we do not attempt to deprive others of theirs, or impede their efforts to obtain it. Each is the proper guardian of his own health, whether bodily, or mental and spiritual. Mankind are greater gainers by suffering each other to live as seems good to themselves, than by compelling each to live as seems good to the rest.
>
> —Mill, 1859, pp. 16–17

Mill's definition of individual autonomy is clear: it is the freedom of choice or guardianship over our own minds and bodies, without the coercive influence of other parties. He puts forth a notion of self-rule such that an individual is free from the interferences of others: this does not entail the freedom to do certain things, but simply freedom from outside interference.

Autonomy is significant on Mill's theory because it is characteristic of liberal society. Simply put, where we have the freedom to think and choose rationally, we have a liberal society; where there is no protection against the "tyranny of the prevailing opinion and feeling," and where society does not protect against the imposition of its own ideas and practices as rules of conduct on the rational individual, there is often unwarranted despotism (p. 13). Self-government is central for Mill, then, because it is basic to his conception of a liberal society.

Although Immanuel Kant's deontological moral theory vastly differs from Mill's utilitarian approach, he shares with Mill a concern for respecting and protecting the will and autonomy of the individual. Kantian moral theory views our moral lives in the context of duties, obligations, and right behavior. It claims that we act morally when we perform actions that are right—that are required by the moral law or duty.

According to Kant, one duty to which we are required to adhere unconditionally and universally is the imperative to "Act only according to that maxim whereby you can at the same time will that it should become a universal law without contradiction" (1785, p. 30). By this he means that an action is moral only if it recognizes the dignity, the intrinsic value, and the autonomy of persons. Persons are not things, and though we may inevitably use people as means to our own ends, we must always do so with the knowledge and recognition that other persons are intrinsically valuable and equally worthy of respect. Given that persons have autonomy, there are ways of acting toward them that will always be unacceptable, such as manipulating them, lying, or using coercion or blackmail to get them to act as we wish. Respect for persons, and recognition of individual autonomy, is a central value in Kant's deontological theory.

Built into this notion of respect for persons is a deep responsibility on the part of each individual rational agent. For example, it means that one must always be her own person, acting as a rational, autonomous chooser. It also means that one has to behave independently of prejudices, preferences, personal relationships, or self-serving motives. Part of what it means to have reason and will is to be autonomous—to be self-governing, or in charge of one's own life. By using others for our own ends or failing to live up to our own potentialities, we violate this autonomy and treat others (and ourselves) as objects or mere things.

These philosophical conceptions of autonomy have contributed in significant ways to our current understandings of autonomy in bioethics generally, and ethics and aging in particular. As some critics have pointed out, the practice of bioethics has been largely informed by the work of philosopher-ethicists, who hew closely to the conception of the autonomous, rational agent that comes out of the philosophical canon (Devries & Subedi, 1998). Much to the detriment of bioethics, these critics claim, we have inherited this conception of the autonomous individual: as a fallout, we see "stick-figure" depictions of ethical dilemmas in medicine that have little to do with the actual lives and experiences of individuals.

THE EVOLUTION OF THE "FOUR PRINCIPLES" APPROACH TO BIOMEDICAL ETHICS

In an attempt to avoid the failings of these highly theoretical approaches to ethics, and to identify principles that would be of common value in bioethics, Tom Beauchamp and James Childress introduced the *Principles of Biomedical Ethics* (1979). In it, Beauchamp and Childress identify four basic principles of respect for autonomy, beneficence, nonmaleficence, and justice. These four principles have played a major role in the evolution of bioethics, and indeed have been formative in the development of ethics and aging. By asking us to weigh and balance these mid-level principles when we encounter an ethical conundrum in biomedicine, this approach gives a structure to moral intuitions and captures prevailing ideas about what ought to count when making medical care decisions. This method for addressing ethical problems in medicine adopts these four principles as "general norms that leave considerable room for judgment in many cases" (Beauchamp & Childress, 2001, p. 13). These rules are substantive, such as confidentiality; procedural, such as rules for organ distribution; and about authority, such as who decides. In practice settings, clinicians, social workers, and other practitioners repeatedly invoke them when facing ethical dilemmas in which two (or more) conflicting actions can be defended on ethical grounds.

This explicit four-principle approach was first used in the clinic or the hospital intensive care unit and later transferred to the nursing home and community care settings. Hence, "doing" ethics was organized around the notion of a "dilemma," where values conflicted and the possibility of a solution was promised (Jennings, 2007). Ethical analysis focused on "patient competency and self-determination, on the nature and limits of caregiver obligation, on threats posed by professional paternalism, institutional self-interest, and the imperatives of high tech medicine" (Collopy, Dubler, & Zuckerman, 1990, p. 7). The patient, and later the long-term care client, was the decision-maker unless incompetent or unable to make decisions. While efforts were made to address the demands placed on others as the result of patient or client choices (Blustein, 1993; Collopy et al., 1990), in practice client choice reigned relatively unchallenged.

As experience would show, this impartial, universal approach to "doing" ethics was generally unable to satisfactorily address, for example, the "household" issues that arose in work with older people. Problems such as who was to care for whom, what to do when family members disagreed, or when the responsibility for care fell completely on one person seemed to need something beyond principles to guide individuals, families, and professionals as they sought to make wise choices in the face of loss and other elements of the aging condition. Nonetheless, the mindset that called for applying abstract principles and rules carried a particular authority, an authority that defines what it means to do an ethical analysis: "There is a certain logic to a procedure that asks us to order, weigh, or reconcile the differing values and interests of morally autonomous, rational, and competent individuals" (Cole & Holstein, 1996, p. 482).

Because this practice emerged in the American context, where individualism is central to national self-identity, *principlism*, as it came to be known, quickly elevated autonomy, understood as self-direction, to the first principle among equals, a place that it still holds. As a result, the individual has generally taken priority over the collective—the focus has less often been on changing the context, such as the public policies that help define the possibilities actually available to older people, or even defining the context, than on using individual strategies for bettering conditions (Capitman & Sciegaj, 1995; Lloyd, 2004). Thus, the absence of social or economic conditions that made autonomy very nearly impossible for a large number of older people received far less attention than individual choice, however limited those choices may have been in practice.

Another difficulty was the "self" that came to dominate thinking: individuals who are detached and free of unchosen obligations became the "subject" of ethics. This view of the self did not fit either with the older person, whose infirmities and complicated life created many of the problems that called for attention, or with the life-world of the caregiver, whose responsibilities severely constrained her or his ability to choose. By limiting ethical thinking to people who were free, independent, and at least putatively equal to one another, ethics was unable to satisfactorily account for people who were legitimately dependent because of age, ill health, or other features of their lives. Because moral theorizing assumed a certain kind of person, it was inadequate when faced with moral concerns that arose in situations of legitimate dependency and vulnerability. Instead, the theoretical concepts developed for people engaged in symmetrical, equal relationships were applied to other, very different relationships where they had little relevance (Walker, 2007). This effort obscured "the moral significance of our day-to-day relationships which are frequently involuntary and unequal and thus [we have] failed to see how those attributes apply in the ... wider society" (Held, 2006, p. 13). Considering all the unequal relationships that persist in our hierarchical and class-based society, it might be argued that sustained analysis of their moral elements might make a difference for all who are involved.

By the mid-1980s, the principle of autonomy was extended to people who lacked the capacity to make decisions for themselves. Authorized proxy decision-makers were instructed to decide as that person would have decided had they been able to act for themselves. Acting benevolently—or in an elder's best interests—was a distinct second best. The focus on individual autonomy often led health professionals to view families skeptically, as less than trustworthy transmitters of the interests of their loved ones (Levine & Zuckerman, 1999).

Although autonomy commits us to an acceptance of advance care planning for disability, not all questions about proxy decision-making are settled. Consider the person with Alzheimer's disease, who cannot speak a coherent sentence but laughs and smiles a great deal: she develops a massive infection that requires intravenous antibiotics. Which view should count: the one she expressed in her advance directive that she wrote when she was of sound mind, indicating she did not want to live in this condition, or her current experiential state, which suggests that she derives some pleasure from her existence (Dresser, 1995; Dworkin, 1993)? What happens in the presence of family disagreement even if there is an appointed proxy?

In the United States, the Retirement Research Foundation's initiative "Enhancing Autonomy in Long-Term Care," launched in 1984, almost single-handedly defined the work to come in subsequent years. This development created a critical mass of individuals who, for the first time, focused concentrated attention on ethics as they applied to older persons in need of long-term care services. It also supported empirical work that revealed the limited choices available in such settings. Researchers, for example, uncovered multiple ways in which nursing homes disregarded client/patient autonomy (Agich, 1990; Lidz, Appelbaum, & Meisel, 1988), while Bart Collopy (1988) contributed a conceptual analysis of autonomy, recognizing that the inability to act on our choices does not mean denying the right to choose. In what remains a classic account of autonomy in long-term care, Collopy called attention to issues that are still inadequately addressed, such as the interrelation between competency (or incapacitated choice) and autonomy, the right to be left alone against the need for positive action that makes real choice possible, and the distinction between short-term and long-term autonomy.

American nursing homes now post a "Patient Bill of Rights." They less often address the companion piece—responsibilities of living in a closed community. Admissions agreements are improved (Ambrogi & Leonard, 1988) and patients are invited to participate in "care planning." In community-based care, autonomy is also the most frequently articulated value. This commitment sets the stage for common ethical conundrums such as individual choice versus safety, causing Levin and Kane (1998) to ask how one avoids interfering with life goals while meeting one's professional obligation to promote health and safety. As they observe, "the rights of a consumer to take informed risks are modified by the moral, legal, and regulatory responsibilities of health professionals and care organizations" (1998, p. 79). In an effort to address these concerns, strategies for assessing risk have been developed (Fireman, Dornberg-Lee, & Moss, 2001), while negotiated risk agreements (Levin & Kane, 1998) permit facilities, usually assisted living, to protect themselves from litigation, while granting considerable freedom to individuals.

By the early 1990s, the new discipline of bioethics framed discourse on aging and ethics (Moody, 1992). With minimal changes to the medical context and the policy apparatus that supported hospitals and medical care, ethical shifts still occurred, most significantly in the one-to-one relationships between physician and patient and between social service professionals and clients. Informed consent became the central enactment of autonomy in the medical setting. Later, as language transformed the patient into the consumer and then the customer, without analysis of the moral significance of these changes, medicine began to be viewed as a contractual relationship between putative equals. Unfortunately, this contractual model did not account for the actual situation in hospitals: unrecognized and unacknowledged power relationships permitted its effects to go unaddressed. This model also permitted busy hospital or nursing home staff or community-based social workers to adopt a "minimalist ethics" (Fox & Swazey, 1988) that suited their training time constraints and their professional codes.

In their studies of autonomy in nursing homes, Kane and Caplan (1990) found that residents worry less about major decisions, like termination of treatment, than the opportunity to make private phone calls or to preserve private space for either visitors or themselves. Agich (1990) reinforced the observation that what really matters to people in long-term care settings is the ability to live in habitual ways which allow them, as much as possible, to preserve a sense of self in spite of loss. Care providers can play a significant role in this effort to make everyday life a source of self-preservation, which Agich describes as "interstitial" or "actual" autonomy. This means "acknowledg[ing] the essential social nature of human development" (Agich, 1990,

p. 12), a point that has been further developed by feminist philosophers (Kittay, 1999; Parks, 2003; Tronto, 1993). This view of autonomy understands individuals as concrete and not as generalized others for whom choice is not an abstractly given right, but rather a meaningful reflection on their identity. Given this understanding of actual autonomy, to respect individuals means that we "attend to their concrete individuality, to their affective and personal experiences" while also learning "how to acknowledge their habits and identifications" (Agich, 1990, p. 14). It means, to start with, that we offer not merely choice to people, but *meaningful* choice. These enlarged ethical obligations and the practical demands on carers affirm the notion that the good precedes the right. The right to choose is meaningless in the absence of an idea of the good and the possibility to realize that good. Yet, for people in long-term care settings, rights are granted without any assurance that they will be able to live in ways that they would consider good, despite their limitations.

That we live our lives purposefully and coherently matters at any age. For many older people, the effects of chronic illness and the social devaluation that accompanies frailty and inactivity threaten their self-respect and what Charles Taylor (1984) calls "horizons of meaning." Both are critical. In Taylor's view, dignity, in terms of "commanding (attitudinal) respect" (1984, p. 15), grounds self-respect. Social devaluation threatens our dignity at its most fundamental level. But, along with our profound need to feel respected is a need for a framework that shapes our conception of the good in the absence of which our life is "spiritually senseless" (1984, p. 18). It is this sense of making qualitative distinctions—that some way of life is infinitely higher than others—that becomes increasingly difficult when we become old in societies as diverse as the ones in which we live. Extant cultural norms give little or no guidance once we become frail or "not young." Yet, this search for a viable self, for recognizing and having goods that express who we are, even in conditions of frailty and dependency, is essential for remaking our identity when so much that has been familiar is eroding. Morality is thus far more demanding than granting individual rights to make choices that may not have any connection with their deeply held values or beliefs.

WHY AUTONOMY?

The principle of respect for autonomy, captured in ideas of negative liberty and noninterference, has a particular appeal in the United States, which is founded on the belief that all people have the right to live as they choose. Autonomy is a formative notion on which U.S. culture and our system of health care delivery is largely based. Indeed, it has become the foundational principle of health care. Such a preoccupation with autonomy obscures the fact that we ultimately lack control over aging, illness, disability, suffering, and death. To admit this lack of autonomy is to admit that the human condition is beyond our control; to relinquish autonomy is to acknowledge our deep vulnerability, especially as we age.

Furthermore, this preoccupation with autonomy relates to independence, since a person's independence and her ability to live independently of others is symbolic of her autonomy. Within the United States, dependence has been strongly associated with weakness, incapacity, neediness, and a lack of dignity; insofar as individuals are able to resist dependency, they are able to maintain their dignity and self-respect. But this strong emphasis on autonomy as independence has had a very negative impact on aging and aged persons, who find themselves increasingly in need of assistance to bathe, go to the bathroom, dress, eat, and get about. It is seen to be shameful and embarrassing to admit that you can no longer perform all these tasks unassisted, and as a result many older adults will refuse for as long as possible to ask for help; instead, they struggle or simply go without their baths or meals rather than ask for assistance.

An appeal to traditional autonomy also fits nicely with the acute care model that guides our approach to medicine and health care in the United States. The language of autonomy and control is used so freely within medical and social discourse and is so integral to our culture that it leads to our cultural fixation on controllable, acute medical emergencies. Indeed, as many authors have noted, although chronic illness is a primary health problem in North America, especially among the aged, our health care model remains focused on acute medical emergencies (Hinton-Walker, 1993; Moros, Rhodes, Baumrin, & Strain, 1991; Roth & Harrison, 1991). As a result, chronic care and palliative care are not satisfactorily represented in medicine because such models of care admit to the realities of human aging, disability, illness, and our lack of control over our health and our bodies. Current medical practice—and the focus on acute care measures— thus conceals the extent to which many individuals live with chronic health problems and/or disability.

Acute care is characterized by the high-tech monitoring of acute illnesses, complex diagnostic procedures, and treatable conditions: the medical problem is definable, recognized (both medically and socially), and controllable at the acute stage. Victims in acute care situations present medical problems that are immediately recognizable and treatable. Chronic care—the kind of care that best characterizes treatment of the elderly—is, by contrast, marked by an uncertainty of condition and outcome, no social and often no medical recognition of the problem, and the inability to control or eliminate the medical condition.

It is the very possibility of treatment, diagnosis, and control in acute medical situations that leads to our paradigm of acute care. This care paradigm supports the social emphasis we place upon control, health, and personal autonomy. As Susan Wendell claims, "However alienating it may be, the scientific third-person perspective on the body fosters the illusion of control" (1996, p. 121). Thus, our health care system focuses on acute care, given the possibilities in acute medical treatment for saving lives, curing illnesses, and maintaining the false illusion of control that is so important to our culture. The main goal of medicine thus comes to be, as it is in wider society, to control the body. This is not often possible in chronic care situations, and it is worse in palliative care where the goal is to ease individuals into death. Since these care models admit to the frailty of the human body and life in general, they fail as medical paradigms, despite the large number of individuals who are (or will be) chronically ill, disabled, or dying.

Acute care is also paradigmatic because of the autonomous self it presupposes, that is, one that is free from external limits or constraints, including bodily ones. Controllable, acute medical emergencies allow health care practitioners to return the patient to a state of health such that the body does not limit the autonomy of the individual. In this way, the autonomous self is disembodied such that one's corporeal state is not understood as being integrated with one's sense of self. Indeed, as Bruce Jennings, Daniel Callahan, and Arthur Caplan state, "The first component of the autonomy paradigm is a particular interpretation of the meaning of illness and the goal of medicine: illness is seen as an alien threat to the self, and the goal is to defend and restore the self by curing or compensating for the illness" (1988, p. 12). The "true self" according to this autonomy paradigm is the self unencumbered by a disabled, chronically ill, or vulnerable body. The natural bodily state, then, is that of the normalized body, which does not interfere with the desires or ends of the self. On this view, one's autonomy, identity, and personal ends are prior to and independent of one's experience of illness; illness becomes merely a physical state that interferes with the autonomy and self-identity of the ill or frail person's life; thus, if we can overcome illness through technology, we can preserve the unencumbered, autonomous self with which we all supposedly identify.

What we fail to acknowledge with our paradigms of health, control, acute care, and autonomy is that these are not absolute states. Health varies in degree and can mark some areas of a person's life but not others. One can be healthy, for example, while experiencing the limitations imposed by a 90-year-old body; one can be physically healthy, yet live with paraplegia. Furthermore, patients may survive an acute medical emergency only to remain chronically ill thereafter. Alternatively, a doctor can preserve lives in acute situations without providing cure. The bright lines drawn between health and illness or disability are recognized by some bioethicists as highly problematic, since doctors may act to save a life but not provide a "cure" for the patient's ailments. In short, the medical world cannot be cleanly divided into acute versus chronic care or curative versus noncurative treatment (Moros et al., 1991).

The acute care paradigm allows us to treat a patient's acute medical problem without the attendant mental and social components that constitute chronic care. A patient in an acute medical crisis is assumed to need only *medical* attention: the medical condition can be controlled such that the patient can ultimately be returned to her prior autonomous and fully functioning state. Older persons who require long-term care services, on the other hand, are not in such a situation, and their particular problems usually have complex social and psychological facets. The acute care paradigm thus allows medicine to sidestep many socio-medical and relational issues that arise within long-term chronic care, such as loneliness, depression, poverty, lack of social support, nutrition concerns, the navigation of chronic pain and psychic suffering, and, perhaps most importantly, the fact of seriously compromised autonomy.

So the principle of autonomy is arguably problematic when we are considering people of advanced age who cannot maintain a facade of being independent and self-sufficient. In addition, though, the principle is not helpful within the context that a large number of older adults find themselves in: nursing homes or assisted-living care centers. As George Agich (1990) points out, the conditions of old age and the living conditions one finds in long-term care facilities are not conducive to the principle of autonomy as it has traditionally been understood. We need to rethink autonomy, how we understand it, and the ways in which it applies to older adults, in order to ensure that people are not unduly harmed by it.

AUTONOMY IN THE LONG-TERM CARE SETTING

The particular conditions that create the need for long-term care raise ethical issues that differ from those that occur in acute care. In long-term care, an elder's basic survival needs requires assistance from others. In these situations, decision-making rarely involves a single or brief event— such as whether or not a person wants a certain form of chemotherapy or a surgical intervention. Decision-making is generally dynamic and ongoing and may not result in visible action or change. Decisions almost always intimately involve others and address topics such as finances, places of residence, and division of caregiving responsibilities; these areas often merge and interact (Kane, 1995). Many decisions turn on questions of capacity, but that is rarely an "either/or" condition. An individual may be able to make some decisions even far into the dementia process yet be unable to make other decisions. Yet decisions, however they are made, have wide-ranging consequences.

Many older people, who need long-term care services, encounter problems of biographical discontinuity, threats to their adult status, and compromised identity and selfhood (Charmaz, 1993; Kaufman, 1987). While such threats may also temporarily affect ill adults or younger people, because they are short-term limitations, they usually do not threaten to dissolve former sources of meaning. Because of these threats to selfhood that people with long-standing chronic illness experience, their relative frailty, their necessary reliance on others, and the continuous nature of what must be done to maintain well-being, the most ordinary human acts assume weight and significance. Focusing primarily on autonomy as making self-directed choices is an impoverished view of our moral obligations to elders in this situation. Quotidian acts like bathing, dressing, or preparing meals—compounded by history, a foreshortened future, loss, and the necessity for trust and mutuality—must be included in our understanding of ethics and aging. Ethics is inscribed in every facet of daily living. When faced with the need to make decisions, "sensitivity, flexibility, discretion, and improvisation to find precisely what responds to the very particular case" are called for. Attention to the "histories of relationships and the understandings specific to these histories are needed to determine what responses between these particular people mean" (Walker, 1992, pp. 28–29). For example, a husband and wife may have regularly communicated by shouting or cursing; for this couple, that pattern is habitual and not a signal of abuse. So ethics in long-term care requires attention to expanded notions of autonomy and attention to the everyday features of daily life that are the sources of identity and thus also the grounding for autonomy. The basic givens of long-term care—conditions of dependency, limited options, forced intimacy, unequal power relationships, and the bureaucratization of care in conditions of cost constraints—all challenge the standard framework that has governed ethics and long-term care for the past 15 years.

Long-term care thus exposes the limits of traditional notions of autonomy and encourages us to challenge the hegemony of existing value systems, an opening that expands the possibilities for ethical action. What other values count? Is it morally permissible not to take others, like one's adult children or spouse, into account? How is identity linked to choice? Context, the moral status of others as caregivers, and the elder's need for a familiar identity that grounds self-respect and self-esteem thus call for an enlarged concept of what is morally important in long-term care. To neglect other important features of the moral life reduces individuals to their choices and cannot support well-being. Philosopher Own Flanagan reminds us, "It may be that our shared conception of moral life . . . undervalues many goods which play important roles in the moral lives of many individuals . . . the question . . . arises as to how long the publicly underestimated and undervalued aspects of moral life can survive without recognition and sustenance" (1991, p. 195). Yet one problem, as we shall see, is that autonomy is a relatively easy moral value to support; other moral values are more demanding and so harder to put in place in a resource-constrained environment.

Thus, while we do not oppose making choices, sanction paternalistic interventions, or insist that individuals can function only within a set of commonly endorsed background conditions as many communitarian thinkers would hold, we are worried about the moral poverty that a singular emphasis on the language of autonomy suggests. It cannot capture what a textured and robust understanding of ethics can do when a lack of options and threats to self-respect and self-esteem are often the major source of ethical problems. It cannot expose how oppressive systems of ideology and power instruct older people about what they ought to value and it does not focus sharply on achieving the morally fulfilling lives that are possible, even in a context of old age. Yet, we are heartened because ethical practices in long-term care are far richer than the rhetoric that describes them; these practices might be even better if there was a moral language that gave voice to these practices and the wider moral world they reflect.

Individual choice is not *the* necessary condition for self-respect. Writing an advance directive or giving informed consent is only a fragment of what it takes to know one's dignity is respected. While there is reason to applaud the achievements that this focus on autonomy helped to create, there are equally compelling reasons to note its limits and propose alternative or perhaps complementary ways to think about ethics and long-term care. The effects of such altered thinking—and the behaviors it calls for—reside in the good it can bring to patients but also to all participants in the caregiving context.

In the next chapter, we will offer a different and, we believe, better way of understanding autonomy, one that derives from feminist, narrative, and discourse ethics approaches. These approaches do not minimize or set aside autonomy, but reinterpret it in light of an understanding of humans as interdependent beings who are closely linked by relationships of care and concern. They also share a commitment to the importance of context and individual stories in order to best address the needs of the individuals in question. As we will argue, within the arena of ethics and aging it is especially important to redefine autonomy so that we can avoid its pitfalls as identified in this chapter.

REFERENCES

Agich, G. J. (1990). Reassessing autonomy in long term care. *Hastings Center Report,* 20(6), 12–17.

Ambrogi, D., & Leonard, F. (1988). The impact of nursing home admissions agreements on resident autonomy. *The Gerontologist,* 28, 82–89.

Blustein, J. (1993). Doing what the patient orders: Maintaining integrity in the doctor–patient relationship. *Bioethics,* 7(4), 289–314.

Capitman, J., & Sciegaj, M. (1995). A contextual approach for understanding individual autonomy in managed community long-term care. *The Gerontologist,* 34(4), 533–540.

Charmaz, K. C. (1993). *Good days, bad days: The self and chronic illness in time.* New Brunswick, NJ: Rutgers University Press.

Cole, T. R., & Holstein, M. (1996). The evolution of long-term care in America. In R. H. Birnstock, L. E. Cluff, & O. von Mering (Eds.), *The future of long-term care.* Baltimore, MD: Johns Hopkins University Press.

Collopy, B. J. (1988). Autonomy in long term care: Some crucial distinctions. *The Gerontologist,* 28, 10–17.

Collopy, B., Dubler, N., & Zuckerman, C. (1990). The ethics of home care: Autonomy and accommodation. *Hastings Center Report,* Special Supplement, 20(2), 1–16.

DeVries, R., & Subedi, J. (Eds.) (1998). *Bioethics and society: Constructing the ethical enterprise.* Englewood Cliffs, NJ: Prentice-Hall.

Dresser, R. (1995). Dworkin on dementia: Elegant theory, questionable policy. *Hastings Center Report,* 25(6), 32–38.

Dworkin, R. (1993) *Life's dominion: An argument about euthanasia and abortion.* New York, NY: Knopf.

Fireman, D., Dornberg-Lee, S., & Moss, L. (2001). Mapping the jungle: A proposed model for ethical decision making in geriatric social work. In M. B. Holstein & P. B. Mitzen (Eds.), *Ethics in community-based elder care* (pp. 145–165). New York, NY: Springer Publishing Company.

Flanagan, O. (1991). *Varieties of moral personality: Ethics and psychological realism.* Cambridge, MA: Harvard University Press.

Fox, R., & Swazey, J. (1988). Medical morality is not bioethics—Medical ethics in China and the United States. In R. Fox (Ed.), *Essays in medical sociology* (pp. 645–671). New Brunswick, NJ: Transaction Books.

Held, V. (2006). *The ethics of care: Personal, political, and global.* New York, NY: Oxford University Press.

Hinton-Walker, P. (1993). Care of the chronically ill: Paradigm shifts and directions for the future. *Holistic Nursing Practice, 8*(1), 56–66.

Hoffmaster, B. (2001). *Bioethics in a social context.* Philadelphia, PA: Temple University Press.

Jennings, B. (2007). Autonomy. In B. Steinbock (Ed.), *The Oxford handbook of bioethics* (pp. 72–89). New York, NY: Oxford University Press.

Jennings, B., Callahan, D., & Caplan, A. (1988). Ethical challenges of chronic illness. *Hastings Center Report*, Special Supplement, *18*(1), 1–16.

Kane, R. A. (1995). Expanding the industry while keeping the vision. *Assisted Living Today, 2*(2), 32–33.

Kane, R. A., & Caplan, A. L. (Eds.) (1990). *Everyday ethics: Resolving dilemmas in nursing home life.* New York, NY: Springer Publishing.

Kant, I. (1993). *Grounding for the metaphysics of morals* (J. W. Ellington, trans.) (3rd ed.). Indianapolis, IN: Hackett Publishers. (Original work published in 1785.)

Kaufman, S. (1987). *The ageless self: Sources of meaning in late life.* Madison, WI: University of Wisconsin Press.

Kidder, T. (2003). *Mountains beyond mountains.* New York, NY: Random House.

Kittay, E. F. (1999). *Love's labor: Essays on women, equality, and dependency.* New York, NY: Routledge.

Kuczewski, M. (1999). *Fragmentation and consensus: Communitarian and casuist bioethics.* Washington, DC: Georgetown University Press.

Levin, C., & Kane, R. A. (1998). Who's safe? Who's sorry? The duty to protect the safety of clients in home- and community-based care. *Generations, 22*(3), 76–81.

Levine, C., & Zuckerman, C. (1999). The trouble with families. *Annals of Internal Medicine, 130*, 148–152.

Lidz, C. W., Appelbaum, P. S., & Meisel, P. (1988). Two models of implementing informed consent. *Archives of Internal Medicine, 148*(6), 1385–1389.

Lloyd, L. (2004). Mortality and morality: Ageing and the ethics of care. *Aging and Society, 24*, 235–256.

McCullough, L. B. (2005). The critical turn in clinical ethics and its continuous enhancement. *The Journal of Medicine and Philosophy, 30*(1), 1–8.

Mill, J. S. (1859). Chapter 1: Introductory. In C. V. Shields (Ed.), *On liberty* (1956). Indianapolis, IN: Bobbs-Merrill Educational Publishing.

Moody, H. R. (1992). *Ethics in an aging society.* Baltimore, MD: The Johns Hopkins University Press.

Moros, D., Rhodes, R., Baumrin, B., & Strain, J. (1991). Chronic illness and the physician–patient relationship: A response to the Hastings Center's 'Ethical challenges of chronic illness.' *Journal of Medicine and Philosophy, 16,* 161–181.

Parks, J. A. (2003). *No place like home? Feminist ethics and home health care.* Indianapolis, IN: Indiana University Press.

Roth, P., & Harrison, J. (1991). Orchestrating social change: An imperative in the care of the chronically ill. *Journal of Medicine and Philosophy, 16,* 343–359.

Taylor, C. (1984). *Growing on: Ideas about aging.* New York, NY: Van Nostrand Reinhold.

Tronto, J. C. (1993). *Moral boundaries: A political argument for an ethic of care.* New York, NY: Routledge.

Walker, M. (1992). Feminism, ethics, and the question of theory. *Hypatia, 7*(3), 23–38.

Walker, M. (2007). *Moral understandings* (2nd ed.). New York, NY: Oxford University Press.

Wendell, S. (1996). *The rejected body: Feminist philosophical reflections on disability.* New York, NY: Routledge.

CHAPTER 2

The "Critical Turn"

Alternative Approaches to Thinking About Ethics

LIMITATIONS OF CONVENTIONAL VIEWS
OF AUTONOMY

In Chapter 1 we touched on the growing concern about the ways in which autonomy is conceptualized and enacted, both generally and within the arena of aging. In this chapter we will explore how new ways of thinking about this protean concept can significantly expand our understanding of ethics and aging. As noted in Chapter 1, in its common understanding autonomy continues to mean self-directing action, encapsulated in informed consent procedures. This view, however, is far "thinner" than what a robust approach to aging requires. Autonomy is, for example, often reduced to making choices in the absence of attention to the conditions that make real choice possible (availability of options; ability to pay for them; choices that are meaningful for one's life), or it is narrowly defined so that it does not oblige us to attend "to those things that are truly and significantly meaningful and important for elders" (Agich, 2003, p. 123). It thus means more than removing barriers to and honoring choice: personal autonomy is more than uncoerced choice. We adopt those standards that make some decisions more desirable than others because they preserve our integrity, tell the world who we are, or reflect motivations that we find honorable (Meyers, 1989; Taylor, 1985). A vegetarian, who chooses not to eat meat because she is opposed to killing living things for food, would find no meaning in the choice between a hamburger and a pork chop. Furthermore, the simple fact of choice often obscures the institutional and other conditions that make choice so limited for so many. The autonomy of a 94-year-old woman severely incapacitated by heart disease and memory loss, living in subsidized housing, with mice clamoring in the walls, and drug dealing in the hallways is a rather reduced version of the Kantian man who consults his own reason and decides which, among all options, he would wish to make into a universal rule. To make it a bit more contemporary, her auton-omy is a pale imitation of the young, white, bourgeois male who stands before endless possibilities. Honoring self-interested choices (as dictated by conceptions of negative rights and autonomy) is of limited value in a world of intimates or of people rendered unequal by various dimensions of their lives.

At the end of life, perhaps especially in situations that involve dementia and extreme old age, people seek multiple goods and most often they must trade off one for the other while never achieving one good that satisfies all their values. But what do we know about those other values if we focus almost single-mindedly on choice? Without knowing what values buttress any person's wishes, longings, desires and what hinders their realization, the possibility for an authentic choice is constrained. What may be available is a pale reflection of what one really desires. In many home-care situations keeping a client home cannot withstand the scrutiny of reflective thinking, yet the available alternatives are undesirable from everyone's perspective. We can probably imagine many other situations where the choices available are all more or less bad, and that is setting aside situations where the badness comes from irreversible illness or other tragic occurrences. The problem may have its origins in public policy, cultural norms, insti-tutional structures, or other remedial situations that tend to become obscured when we think primarily in terms of individual autonomy. People want continuity, something as close as possible to what they had prior to becoming dependent upon others for assistance with the day-to-day activities like bathing, toileting, or eating. They want to preserve, to the extent possible, the habits, the situated ways of doing things that make them feel that they continue to be themselves. Philosopher and clinical ethi-cist George Agich (1995) describes this form of autonomy as interstitial rather than nodal autonomy. Yet it is the latter—the "moment of decision" or episodic kind of autonomy—that has gained prominence.

GETTING BEYOND INDIVIDUAL AUTONOMY

Feminist philosophers and ethicists often begin reflections about auto-nomy with a rethinking of the self. How we think about the self informs our understanding of the nature of autonomy. If, for example, we are entangled in webs of relationships that have helped form us and continue to motivate our actions, we must find a way to think morally about our inter-personal relationships (see, e.g., Mackenzie & Stoljar, 2000; Walker, 2007). The detached characteristic of Kantian ethics has no place in this understanding of the self. Further, if our lives are filled with unchosen obligations—to elderly parents, to our in-laws, to other frail relatives— then ignoring these obligations imperils our self-respect. We may rightly wonder about the person who does not feel the tug of these responsibilities. While one might call it a choice to respond to these expectations, the social penalties are high if we refuse, especially if we are women (see Holstein, 1999). Yet the received view of autonomy certainly gives us the freedom to refuse to care for others. Even our chosen obligations—to our spouse, to the children we choose to bear, to our friends, to our colleagues—often demand that we do things that, given total freedom, we might not elect to do. While our perceived need to meet these obligations differs from person to person and is likely a product of our socialization, it is not thereby inherently suspect. We could not survive as a human community unless someone took such obligations seriously. As Alasdair MacIntyre claims,

> The networks of giving and receiving in which we participate can be sustained only by a shared recognition of each other's needs and a shared allegiance to a standard of care. And what standard of care measures is not only the quality and quantity of the care afforded ... but also the success or failure in the exercise of the virtues by the members of the society [in question]
> —MacIntyre, 2000, p. 85

While supporting self-determination is a necessary corrective to professional paternalism, it cannot alone motivate moral action or affirm a morally generous society.

Our goal is not to eliminate autonomy from ethics and aging, but to alter the understanding of autonomy that is typically invoked in connection to the elderly. Respect for the choices and values of older persons are important, especially in the face of a culture that has largely denigrated the elderly and reduced them to the status of children. The way in which autonomy is defined and understood, however, affects our treatment of these citizens. If a concept of autonomy is to serve such persons, then it must be couched in a moral language that finds some "fit" with their actual experiences and capacities. For this reason, we advocate a relational conception of autonomy that is rooted in feminist ethics. When understood as "relational," autonomy is divested of both the voluntaristic model of human exchange conducted among equals, and the concept of self as detached and self-interested. Instead, human beings are viewed as beings-in-relationship— as being *necessarily* and not only contingently ensconced in relationships of care—and human relationships are understood according to vulnerability rather than a voluntaristic model. This "vulnerability" model treats human relationships as often unchosen, where

> ... the moral basis of special relationships between individuals arises from the vulnerability of one party to the actions of another. The needs of another call forth a moral obligation on our part when we are in a special position vis-à-vis that other to meet those needs ... all special relations, business relations, relations between a professional and a client or patient, family relations, friendships, benefactor–beneficiary relations, even promises and contractual relations are better described on the Vulnerability Model .... What is striking about this model is that the moral claim arises not by virtue of the properties of an individual—construed as rights, needs, or interests—but out of a *relationship* between one in need and one who is situated to meet the need.
>
> —Kittay, 1999, p. 55

So, to revisit the 94-year-old woman severely incapacitated by heart disease and memory loss who is living in difficult social circumstances, we would petition for an understanding of her autonomy in this relational sense, where her choices and our choices have mutual impact, and where we examine the relationship between her needs and those who are situated to meet them. A voluntaristic model of human relationships, and a conception of the self as detached and self-interested, could hardly motivate the meaningful identification and fulfillment of her needs. A voluntaristic model cannot easily identify the kind of care she requires, nor her dependencies. And understanding selves as detached and self-interested, this model fails to address the connectedness between her needs and desires and those of her neighbors. In very basic ways, the interests at stake in this situation are relational ones, since appealing to this woman's autonomy does not address issues concerning her impact on others. If she is leaving burners on in her apartment because she gets confused, for example, then appeals to traditional autonomy are of minimal utility in determining what to do. This is why we think a feminist conception of relational autonomy is so important to aging: it understands the complex relationship between individuals and addresses real conditions of frailty, dementia, fear, poverty, and vulnerability.

The understanding of feminist ethics we are invoking challenges the received view of autonomy as independent self-governance. It also takes nonvoluntary relationships of care as foundational to human relationships. Not only, as the saying goes, is one not able to choose one's family, but one is often unable to choose other relationships in which one becomes involved. As teachers, for example, we may not choose to form relationships with particular students: they may come to us in need, and we may be in the sole position to meet that need. Or as citizens we may be approached, in ways that may even be unwanted, by fellow citizens in need, and be placed involuntarily in relationships with them. So of primary importance is the nonvoluntary nature of many (or most) human relationships.

In addition, the feminist ethics to which we are appealing takes a particular ontological approach, understanding the self as largely (though not entirely) socially constituted. For example, feminist moral theorist Diana Meyers rejects traditional accounts that "the self" is constituted by an atomistic, independent agent, and argues instead that it is a socially embedded, relational subject. She focuses on the development of the self, and how we are to determine when (and whether) an agent's choices are autonomous and authentic. For Meyers, the main concern is how to balance an agent account that understands the self as autonomous, free from external impediments, and authentic with a social account that posits the self as thoroughly socialized, the product of social institutions and practices that mold and limit self-development. As Meyers claims,

> Autonomous people are in control of their own lives inasmuch as they do what they really want to do. But, if people are products of their environments, it seems fatuous to maintain that the agency of individuals has any real importance, for personal choice dissolves into social influence .... The chief task of a theory of autonomy, then, is to reclaim the distinction between real and apparent desires.
>
> —Meyers, 1989, p. 26

Meyers reclaims this distinction between real and apparent desires by positing a procedural or process view of the self: that is, she understands the "authentic" self to be one that is capable of directing, defining, and discovering one's self. The degree to which one is capable of engaging in these activities is a function of the extent to which one's autonomy competency is developed. Consider, for example, an older person's pre-reflective refusal to entertain the idea of moving to a nursing home. In a culture that eschews dependency and need, and that strongly associates freedom and autonomy with being in one's own home, the very notion of moving to a long-term care facility may appear abhorrent. Whether the desire to remain in one's own home is "authentic," then, is difficult to determine under such conditions of strong social influence. Upon further reflection, however, an older individual may be able to determine that much of her aversion to nursing homes is culturally given and that certain long-term care settings could actually be preferable to remaining alone and isolated in her own home. This highlights the distinction Meyers makes between one's real and "apparent" desires.

Meyers describes autonomy competency as "neither purely natural nor purely social" (1989, p. 57). Like innate musical talent or a natural sense of rhythm, autonomy has a natural component. But one's innate or natural capacity for autonomy is always affected by social environments: Meyers criticizes gender role socialization, for example, given the extent to which it limits the development of girls' and women's autonomy competency. Thus, Meyers' feminist account of autonomy development is neither the agent nor the social model of the self: instead, she suggests that one's autonomy competency is a combination of the two.

There is a final element to the feminist ethic we are applying to aging: a conception of self in relation to the body. That we enter and exit the world in particular *kinds* of bodies carries serious import concerning both how we view ourselves (personal conceptions of embodiment) and how our culture views us (cultural conceptions of embodiment). As moral theorists are increasingly aware, theories of autonomy, the self and normative claims concerning how we ought to behave cannot be posited sans an awareness of the body. While the Kantian man to which we previously referred has no particular kind of body—is body-less, so to speak—actual persons in their lived conditions are privileged or subordinated by their body's appearance in terms of gender, race, ability status, age, beauty, and so on. Rather than attempting to set aside these embodiment concerns as peripheral to our moral understandings of persons, however, feminist ethicists place embodiment at the core of them (Kukla, 2005; Roberts, 1997; Schott, 2002; Wendell, 1996). For example, in her account of "pregnant embodiment," Iris Marion Young identifies a phenomenology of the pregnant body: "Pregnancy challenges the integration of my body experience by rendering fluid—the boundary between what is within, myself, and what is outside, separate. I experience my insides as the space of another, yet my own body" (1990, p. 163). And on the association between women and the aged/aging body, Simone de Beauvoir says,

> Whereas man grows old gradually, woman is suddenly deprived of her femininity: she is still relatively young when she loses the erotic attractiveness and the fertility which, in the view of society and in her own, provide the justification of her existence and her opportunity for happiness. With no future, she still has about one half of her adult life to live.
> —*de Beauvoir, 1974, p. 640*

We argue that a feminist ethic of aging should incorporate a concern for embodiment, and the ways in which the often aged, frail bodies of long-term care residents inform our theorizing. For by including embodiment, we can develop a more robust understanding of ethics. In Chapter 3, we will develop this issue concerning the aging and aged body; let us now apply our conception of feminist ethics to understand how it encourages a different moral understanding of the issues in aging.

BUILDING TRUST: ATTENTIVENESS TO RELATIONSHIPS

As we have indicated, a feminist ethic is attentive to relationships and the mutual vulnerabilities created by them. By extension, we see this ethic as most conducive to building trust between parties who find themselves in relationship with one another. This is particularly important in such care situations as nursing homes, where residents, staff, and residents' families must come together in the spirit of mutual trust and goodwill in order to ensure that everyone's needs are met and that each party is cared for (and about). For example, while long-term care residents have unique needs and vulnerabilities to which others must attend, so, too, do facility staff require attendance to their needs and vulnerabilities. Indeed, the staffs' vulnerabilities may derive from the actions of the residents such that residents are not the only parties that require care: a resident may demand inordinate amounts of a staff member's time such that she feels pressure to stay with residents beyond her paid hours (this is also true in the home care setting). Family members may require care by others to ensure that their own caretaking does not leave them feeling isolated or "burnt out."

As we have argued, the received view of autonomy, while offering some measures to protect individual autonomy, ultimately fails to address the conditions necessary for its identification and expression. This is because the received view of the self does not go deep enough in presenting the particular contexts within which individuals do their decision-making. What we need is a relational approach to autonomy that takes into account the effect that external factors have upon the individual. As we have indicated, a relational approach to autonomy takes the individual as understandable in terms of her relationships with others, in terms of the social structures and institutions that shape her, and in terms of her economic, age, racial, ethnic, sexual orientation, and gender status. In contrast to the received view, we argue for an approach that recognizes structural conditions that interfere with individual autonomy. This view is echoed by other feminist ethicists that we have touched upon, who recognize the importance of understanding autonomy as a capacity developed or limited by social circumstances. On their accounts, autonomy is played out within social structures and relationships that shape the individual and determine others' responses to her attempts at autonomy. On this feminist conception, autonomy is only and always practiced in relation to other persons and to social institutions that shape the individual. Such a relational understanding of autonomy takes the self-in-relationships as the root of autonomous choice and action: individuals are, first and foremost, socially constructed beings, whose identities, values, concepts and perceptions are products of their environment to a significant degree.

FEMINIST AND NARRATIVE FRAMEWORKS: A CRITICAL TURN IN ETHICS

Feminist theorists are largely dissatisfied with the predominant moral theories and their prescribed approach to moral deliberation. They point out the inadequacies of such theories, which derive from the failure to address the realities of women's lives and the multiple responsibilities that many women have to care for their children, spouses, and elderly parents. The received, liberal view of autonomy that we have outlined thus far—an autonomous adult who is independently able to make self-regarding reasoned choices—does not resonate with the lives of many women, or with persons who at birth were not the winners of the natural or social lottery. As Margaret Urban Walker claims, feminist ethics grows out of a larger project that addresses the gender inequality embedded in traditional Western European philosophical ethics. As she indicates, with few exceptions every "canonized philosopher up to the twentieth century has contended (explicitly) that women are 'lesser or incompetent moral agents'" (2007, p. 20). Like the other feminist theorists we have highlighted thus far, Walker exposes the limitations inherent in the values and pre-commitments of traditional moral theories. These theories may represent some experiences and some citizens, but they are mostly the experiences of persons with power and privilege; they fail to reflect the realities of marginalized persons.

Feminists reject the received view of autonomy as put forth by dominant moral theories because it showcases a moral world that has little in common with the real-life situations that most women (and some men) experience. The vision put forth by such theories is skewed and thus deficient in its failure to recognize women and other marginalized groups that do not fit the mainstream discourse concerning rights, justice, and obligations. Feminist ethicists, by contrast, account for these marginalized groups by emphasizing how different social experiences can lead them to differently understand the relationship between self and other.

For example, in 1982 Carol Gilligan first published *In a Different Voice: Psychological Theory and Women's Development*. This book was the first to identify an ethic of care as foundational to women's lives, to identify a care voice that differs from the justice voice in which men speak, and to posit a feminine moral identity that differs from the masculine norm. Furthermore, Gilligan's work allowed women to embrace the ethic of care, since it was found to be no less justified than (and thus, not inferior to) the "justice" perspective—or focus on principles, objectivity, and impartiality that mark the traditional moral approach into which men are socialized. The ethic of care was liberatory for women in that it embraces women's particular ways of "doing" moral reasoning and it allows for the inclusion of personal moral considerations in moral theory. Rather than working from the level of abstract moral theories to determine what should be done in specific circumstances, Gilligan's ethic of care begins with the particular features of women's own personal relationships with others.

A care ethic has been discussed by a variety of feminist moral theorists, and while some have been critical of it, most embrace its underlying premise that human beings are interdependent beings in relationships of care. As Gilligan states,

> As a framework for moral decision, care is grounded in the assumption reflected in a view of action as responsive and, therefore, as arising in relationship rather than the view of action as emanating from within the self and, therefore, "self governed." Seen as responsive, the self is by definition connected to others, responding to perceptions, interpreting events, and governed by the organizing tendencies of human interaction and human language.
>
> —*Gilligan, 1987, p. 24*

Gilligan's research led her to appreciate how differently women perceive moral problems. As she relates, the women in her three studies did not see moral problems as the result of conflicting rights, and they did not find the answer to their dilemmas in a simple ranking of values. Instead of the hierarchical ordering of values characterized by the justice approach, Gilligan's female subjects described "a network of connection, a web of relationships that is sustained by a process of communication" (1983, p. 33). For these women, moral problems were embedded in context such that abstract, deductive reasoning could not solve them. Moral decision-making, for many of the women who participated in the studies, required a strategy that preserved ties where possible without sacrificing their own integrity.

In her 1989 essay entitled, "Women and Caring: What Can Feminists Learn about Morality from Caring?" Joan Tronto acknowledges that our conceptions of caring highlight some of the deepest gender norms in our culture. While Tronto challenges the traditional scripts surrounding men's and women's caring roles, she also cautions feminists to be mindful of the direction that their gender analyses take.

In her work, Tronto distinguishes between the activities of "caring for" and "caring about," basing her distinction on the object of the caring. "Caring about" suggests a general form of commitment that is not fixed on a particular subject or object, as in "I care about the state of the environment." But "caring for" implies a specific, particular individual or object toward whom the care is directed. The boundaries between these two forms of caring are not always clear but nevertheless, as Tronto claims, they "fit with the engendered category of caring in our society" (1989, p. 102).

"Caring for" involves responding to the concrete, particular needs of others, however, they may manifest themselves. Care needs that are physical, spiritual, intellectual, or emotional in nature are unified by the fact that other human beings are necessary to meet them. As Tronto suggests, traditional female occupations such as nursing, teaching, and social work—and the disproportionate amount of caretaking that women do in their homes—signify the degree to which "caring for" is a woman's responsibility. She claims that in our society, traditional gender roles generally mean that "men care about but women care for" (p. 103).

Furthermore, knowledge is required where one is attempting to discern one's obligations of care. Yet within the philosophical tradition, the accepted mode of ethical reflection involves introspection, an approach that Tronto claims is highly inappropriate as a starting point for arriving at caring judgments. In caring, one needs knowledge about the other's needs, a knowledge which can only come from others. While Tronto acknowledges that contemporary moral theory *does* address the needs of others, she claims that those needs tend to be addressed in relation to the self doing the moral discernment. Caring, by contrast "rests on knowledge completely peculiar to the particular person being cared for ... there is no simple way one can generalize from one's own experience to what another needs" (1989, p. 105).

A commitment to perceiving—without distortion—the genuine needs of the other can sometimes be very difficult. If a caretaker does not have self-knowledge regarding her own needs, it is highly likely that she will confuse her own needs with those for whom she is caring. As Eva Kittay puts it,

"The demands of dependency work favor a self accommodating to the wants of another; that is, a self that defers or brackets its own needs in order to provide for another's" (1999, p. 51). If one fails to do this bracketing, it becomes too easy to project one's own unmet needs onto those for whom she/he is responsible.

Providing attentive care to another requires the ability to balance one's own needs with the needs of the cared-for. Questions concerning how much to disregard one's own needs in order to be sufficiently attentive to the cared-for are ubiquitous for caregivers. For example, elderly parents can often create great stress for caregivers who struggle to determine how to meet their parents' real needs without totally disregarding their own. As Jean Grimshaw has queried,

> Is it a failure of care to insist on a holiday alone away from one's elderly parents? .... Women in particular are often prone to feelings of guilt if they try to seize a bit of space, time or privacy for themselves, away from other people. They are especially vulnerable to charges of not-caring, since they are so often seen as defined by their caring roles and capacities.
> —*Grimshaw, 1986, p. 217*

If one is solely responsive to the needs of others, how can one determine whether the needs are genuine, or as serious as one might believe? Oftentimes even the most attentive caregiver, who has a clear sense of her own needs in connection to those of the cared-for, is at risk of blurring boundaries, because caring always puts boundaries at risk. Tronto recognizes that because a connection between the caregiver and cared-for is necessary for one to care, the nature of this connection has the potential to be problematic for an ethic of care.

Tronto claims that more attention must be paid to understanding the moral characteristics of caring and responsibility. Her work, however, goes a long way toward addressing many of the relevant concerns that feminists claim traditional ethics has ignored; it also points out the degree to which a moral perspective based on caring and responsibility has enlarged or enhanced our moral thinking.

Likewise, Margaret Urban Walker has indicated the many limitations and deficits of traditional moral theories, putting forth her own approach as an alternative for addressing moral thinking. Walker aims to "remedy the exclusion or distortion of women's lives by representing understandings of value, agency, and responsibility embedded in practices that have been and still are 'women's work'" (2007, p. 23).

Feminist theorists have criticized the degree to which traditional moral theories contain gender bias. In this regard, Walker claims that the "preoccupation with equality and autonomy, uniformity and impartiality, rules and reciprocity fits voluntary bargaining relations of nonintimate equals, or contractual and institutional relations among peers in contexts of impersonal or public interactions" (p. 51). She argues that the moral lens through which the dominant justice theories view morality ignores the responsibilities of those who care for dependent others in the intimacy of private familial contexts. It also ignores the obligations that arise from these interdependent relationships that are central to so many women's lives. The traditional theoretical emphasis on universality, impartiality, and the unencumbered self obscures the degree to which relationship and particularities inform the choices and actions of moral subjects.

These dominant theories are encompassed by what Walker calls a "theoretical-juridical model," a model that offers code-like formulas that can be universally applied. Dominant theories are framed by "a highly selective view appropriate to certain kinds of relationships and interactions in certain public, competitive, or institutional venues" (2007, p. 53). This theoretical-juridical model, according to Walker, is the template that organizes moral inquiry according to a set of law-like propositions. The moral agent associated with this model is one that is impartial, objective, unencumbered by particular obligations to others, and that reasons from a universal perspective. As Walker points out, this view is associated with privileged white men and tends to exclude women and men of other races and classes. Here, we would add, it also tends to exclude old persons who lack the characteristics usually associated with the ideal moral agent. The theoretical-juridical model offers tools for determining the morally right action, without any concern for the agent in question—disregarding the life she might be living, her station in life, or the form of social life she may inhabit.

Walker tempers this model by recommending an approach that she claims is more representative of how *actual* persons live their lives and make moral decisions. She refers to her approach as an "expressive-collaborative model," one that directs us to consider the context of the individuals involved and that asks questions that differ from the theoretical-juridical model. It takes into account the ways that people understand themselves as "bearers of particular identities and actors in various relationships that are defined by certain values" (p. 68). Walker claims that morality is grounded in individuals' efforts to make their moral behavior understandable to others and to "... negotiate [the] inevitable differences and disagreements as we try among ourselves to determine where our moral responsibilities lie" (p. 68). According to Walker, narrative approaches are foundational to doing ethics within the expressive-collaborative model.

This alternative feminist view of morality treats moral life as a synthetic mutual acknowledgment, where we use narrative structure and a natural give-and-take to achieve moral understanding. Moral thinking is narrative both in its way of choosing morally relevant information within a particular deliberative moment and in that storytelling is a basic method for framing moral problems. As Walker points out, resolutions to moral problems will also often take narrative forms. On her expressive-collaborative model, a narrative takes on particular meanings based on the history that preceded the situation at hand. Moreover, the prior events may look quite different when interpreted within the context of present events. Determining one's concrete responsibilities, she claims, involves consideration of "... histories of trust, expectation, and agreement that make particular relationships morally demanding in particular ways" (p. 69). To know what general norms or values mean in a given situation requires one to have an appreciation of how they have been applied and interpreted in the past, within both individual and social histories. A narrative framework presents the opportunity to think backward in these ways and then forward in order to consider the costs and consequences of moral choices both within and between individuals.

Walker refers to three types of narratives—narratives of relationship, narratives of identity, and narratives of value. The narrative of relationship is the history we share with a particular other or others. It is a story that builds over time that includes expectations of and obligations to the others that are part of our narratives. In some cases, we may be obligated to others because of prior histories that allow them to make a moral claim upon us. As Walker states, "It is morally important for us to acknowledge the past character, present state, and future possibilities of [that] relationship" (p. 111). Her second form of narrative, moral identity, conveys the agent's own values by identifying what a person cares about, responds to, and who she takes care of. The patterns of value expressed in our narratives shape and control our responses to others such that we can be held accountable to them. Our value systems expressed by the stories we tell (and that are told about us) reflect and refine our moral self-identities and convey to others where we stand and what we stand for. Third, our narratives of moral value both include and support narratives of relationship and identity. It is constituted by our shared understandings of what kinds of things, relationships, and commitments really matter, and what their relative importance is. A narrative of moral value, "... involves a history of moral concepts acquired, refined, revised, displaced, and replaced, both by individuals and within some communities of shared moral understanding" (p. 111). Such a shared moral understanding means that I never understand values within a social vacuum; I am always partially dependent on how my society and culture understand those values as well. Walker claims that the intersection of these three narratives is essential in order to keep coherent our moral justifications. It is the coherence of each of the narratives, and their interconnections, that make for a distinctive and integrated moral life. This collocation of narratives enables moral agency and integrity because they allow the agent to understand herself while at the same time allowing others to depend on her in ways they can reliably anticipate.

Hilde Lindemann Nelson (2001) echoes Walker's claims, but goes further to argue that our very *identities* are narratively constructed. They are constructed by the stories about people, ideas, and things that matter to us, but also by the "stock plots" and "character types" that we take from those familiar stories that are the embodiment of our culture's socially shared understandings. Nelson focuses on marginalized groups in particular, claiming that they are defined by master narratives that society has created and that act as controlling images of them. Oftentimes, these master narratives deny individuals the opportunity to be themselves and instead force them into stereotypical roles that marginalize and reinforce prejudice against them. For example, whether old persons are characterized by master narratives of decline, or master narratives of successful aging, those narratives may delimit, control, and define how they fit in society and what roles are viewed as being appropriate for them. As Nelson phrases it, master narratives "... identify specific groups of people in ways that mark them as morally undesirable or in need of policing. At the same time, these narratives elicit responses, whether on the part of those others or the groups members themselves which unjustly constrict the group members' freedom of agency" (2001, p. 8). Nelson herself acknowledges that elderly women are the sufferers of double prejudice, based on their age and gender. As a result, they are marginalized and often ignored by society in general; this theme will be taken up in the chapters that follow.

We affirm Nelson's challenge to master narratives and her call to create "counter stories" to root out the master narratives that create oppressive identities. She offers a framework for recognizing the injustice that is generally unseen, and a way to empower old persons such that their voices can be heard and respected. In *Stories of My Old Age* (2004), Nelson (1999) gives an account of the challenges faced in particular by elderly women. She frames her account such that it focuses on how group and individual narratives are constructed, and how a person might challenge the stereotype or master narrative by which she has been marginalized.

Nelson argues that others have a significant impact on our "self-constituting" narratives. These influences can be powerful enough that they oppress and cause harm to both individuals and groups. For old women, the narrative that others tell about them may not accurately portray who they are; but nonetheless, it can have a significant impact on their ability to interact in the wider community. Nelson claims that much discrimination faced by older women is influenced by such master narratives. As a "stock character," the elderly woman is subject to society's decline narrative, which carries with it expectations for how she is expected to interact and behave.

Narratives of loss may in some cases accurately reflect changes in a person's functioning or personality. A debilitating stroke, loss of vision or hearing, or advancing dementia makes it very challenging or impossible for her to continue on with the projects and goals that may have been central to her self-identity. A woman who once took pleasure in babysitting her 2-year-old grandchild once a week may no longer be able physically or cognitively to reliably perform this activity. However, such narratives can become oppressive when they "... exaggerate the importance of a loss, use a decline in one aspect of a person's life to paper over strengths and abilities the person might still be developing, or insist that a particular loss now identifies the person as a whole" (1999, p. 85). It is particularly egregious when the narrative of loss is used to restrict an individual's access to relationships or roles that have been values and are still within her ability to continue even if other aspects of her life have changed.

According to Nelson, the elderly person trapped in a narrative of loss requires a counter story to reclaim or sustain her identity against the master narrative being told about her. A community must have within it a moral space that allows its members to come together to discern, to build, to refine, and to celebrate the community's story. One such example of this is found in Frida Furman's work on older woman and beauty shop culture. As Furman points out,

> I had occasion to observe a number of collective efforts of resistance during my involvement in participant observation at Julie's [beauty shop]. These are often expressed through seemingly self-deprecating humor, as when women laugh together at their double chins—*turkey necks*, as they often call them—or at their seemingly advanced stages of pregnancy, judging by the size of their bellies. In my view these moments of collective mirth contest the social unacceptability of women's aging, the loss of beautiful bodies and feminine attractiveness, by bonding women around the inevitability of aging.
>
> —*Furman, 1999, p. 17*

The community in question must provide a safe environment that is nonauthoritarian and nonarbitrary, allowing the community to define itself in moral terms. The stories that community members construct provide the community with integrity, coherence, and bonding. Nelson argues that this is especially true when they construct a story that allows the group members to take different positions from one another without fear of domination or rejection by the community. A group that is able to do this narrative work in an accepting way has provided its members with an opportunity to have a voice, to be listened to, and to be appropriately considered. And such narrative construction can also act as a counter story that challenges the stock characters and plots that are assigned to groups by the master narratives held within their culture.

DISCOURSE ETHICS AND AGING

A narrative account of ethics involves, at heart, the sharing of stories in such a way that the listener and teller are both transformed. By telling her story, the narrator expresses who she is and what she values and the listener becomes witness to the nonfungibility and singular value of the narrator. Conversely, in hearing the narrative, the listener must come face-to-face with the narrator as a subject with distinct values and perspectives. The listener may interject, respond or object at any point during the story, and as such she offers a differing perspective, and sometimes a corrective, to the storyteller.

This dialectical aspect of narrative theory is also reflected within a discourse ethical framework. Discourse (or communicative) ethics is narrative or conversation-based; it is concerned with ensuring the democratic participation of all members of a community, safeguarding each individual's opportunity to agree to and accept the conditions under which rational discourse takes place. A discourse "community" according to this ethic can be understood as localized (i.e., a relatively small group of people living in a certain district) or any group of persons whose interests affect one another (which could include an entire state or country). Discourses at the smaller, grassroots level—for example, neighborhood watch organizations—are particularly important in that "it is hoped that such discourses will generate an autonomous and critical public opinion aimed at radicalizing discussion regarding generalizable interests at the party-politics level" (Ingram, 1990, p. 145). In essence, then, communicative ethics aims at vocalizing the real interests of individuals that are identified through fair and impartial discussion and that result in rational agreement on issues of common interest. On this account ethics is social activity, where decision-making is done by the community and where the *process* by which the community comes to a consensus is as important as the moral consensus itself.

The discourse or communicative ethics approach was initially voiced by critical theorist Jurgen Habermas, but has since been adopted by scholars on aging such as Harry Moody. We will discuss Moody shortly, but first provide an account of Habermasian communicative ethics. Habermas' discourse ethics shares the deontologist's commitments to universalizability and reason. Like Immanuel Kant (mentioned in Chapter 1), Habermas claims that "under the moral point of view, one must be able to test whether a norm or mode of action could be generally accepted by those affected by it, such that their acceptance would be rationally motivated and hence uncoerced" (1989, p. 36). Autonomy and universalizability are of central importance for Habermas in that we cannot abandon autonomous agents to societal norms or "modes of action" and in that we must test the general acceptability of (i.e., we must be able to universalize) the norm in question.

But Habermas differs from Kant in many important respects. According to Kant, the process of autonomy development is private and independent; individuals do not need others for autonomous thought and decision-making, since we can rely on reason and universalizability to guide us. Indeed, on Kant's model, we must rather "block out" the others with whom we are in relationship in order to come to a rational, autonomous, impartial, reflective decision. Habermas, by contrast, asserts that the development of autonomy is social and occurs only within community; it is not a private undertaking. Autonomy develops through community, not in spite of it. Furthermore, Kant claims that the only moral actions are those that are universalizable (i.e., actions whose maxims can be willed consistently as a universal law). According to him we are never to be influenced by our mere inclinations when judging morally appropriate action. On the contrary, we must fight those inclinations by applying the constraints of reason and duty. Our preferences, desires, and needs must not enter into the critical evaluation of our maxims because they are biased and partial. Habermas, by contrast, views our preferences as a necessary part of our moral discourse because they reflect, and are reflected by, our community. In other words, we must include preferences and needs within the communicative ethic because our needs are part of our ethical lives. How we interpret our needs is determined by our ethical life and, like our principles and maxims should be subjected to rational moral deliberation. And when we deliberate about our needs, we may accept or reject them based on the potential benefits or harms to our community, as determined by the community through the process of discussion and communication.

Notice that, like Kant, Habermas gives us a procedural account of ethics. What matters is the procedure or process by which we identify needs and norms. But this is not to say that Habermas's communicative ethic lacks any concern for or interest in consequences.

Habermas's claim that we must subject our needs to rational moral deliberation, and that we will accept or reject those needs based on harms or benefits to our community, resembles a traditional consequentialist approach. According to Habermas, in evaluating needs and norms we are trying to reach consensus. The reason we agree to norms is because we evaluate our lifestyles and revise them to create the best form of life, a form of life which emerges through community discourse. As David Ingram expresses it,

> The ultimate aim of a communication ethic, then, is to bring about conditions of rational participatory democracy, in which existing needs can be critically assessed and transformed. For only by publicly discussing our needs can we begin to assess their impact on the lives of others. And, only by assessing their impact on the lives of others, can we determine their rationality, or compatibility with the general interest of all concerned.
> —Ingram, 1990, p. 147

There is a noticeable concern for consequences in Habermas's demand that we assess our needs and their "impact on the lives of others." The reasonableness and rationality of our needs is at least partially dependent on whether, as Ingram puts it, they are compatible with the general interest of all concerned. So although communicative ethics is largely concerned with the process by which consensus about our norms and needs is achieved (a deontological concern), there is also consideration of the impact that the fulfillment of our needs has on the lives of others, and a focus on maximizing community values as determined through rational community discourse (consequentialist considerations).

The needs and norms that regulate a community's life are not highly abstract, then, but are the actual norms and needs as identified by individuals within the community. While some of the principles we appeal to may remain abstract—such as "respect for individual rights"—communicative ethics, like feminist ethics, is concerned with real members of the community in their lived conditions. And although Habermas does appeal to the notion of an ideal community that is made up of individuals who are participating in a dialogue with all necessary knowledge, he does not suggest that this is how we *actually* are. This idealized conception is rather to make individuals involved in dialogue with others consider the conditions under which others find themselves and to "assume reflexive role-distance and the ability and willingness to take the standpoint of others involved in a controversy into account and reason from their point of view" (Benhabib, 1996, p. 76). Thus, communicative ethics is also like feminist and narrative ethics in that it accounts for oppression by differentiating fair, rational democratic discourse from ideological, oppressive discourse. Like feminist ethicists, Habermas also refuses to view our emotional lives as private, but treats them as important to, and indeed part of, our public dialogue and laws. Unlike deontology and consequentialism, then, communicative ethics sees the emotional aspect of our lives as integral and necessary to our public dialogue. On Habermas's view, the public/private distinction that has separated our "private" lives (including our emotions and all aspects of domestic life) from our "public" lives (work and politics) must be continually revised in discourse. What is "private" and "public" is not given but changes through dialogue. As philosopher Alasdair MacIntyre has pointed out,

> It is only insofar as we are disposed to give others a just hearing, to be generous in our interpretation of what they say, to be temperate in the expression of our own views, to take risks in exposing such views to refutation, and to be imaginatively sympathetic in our appreciation of opposing standpoints that we are able to participate constructively in such conversations and such practices. The corresponding vices of an adversarial attitude, the vices of insisting on an unjustly large share of the conversation, of advancing ungenerous interpretations of opposing contentions, of intemperateness in our rhetorical and argumentative modes, and generally a lack of openness to alien standpoints preclude such conversations and such practice. So, in general, it is only insofar as we are willing that others should identify and achieve their own good, what is best for them, that we are likely to be able to identify and to achieve what is best for us.
>
> —MacIntyre, 2000, p. 84

Here, MacIntyre eloquently expresses what a discourse or communicative ethics framework aims at: a shared conversation in which we seek common ends and work toward the good of all in the discourse community. The interlocutors in these discourse communities identify with the other individuals with whom they are in conversation, and understand that in seeking the good of others, they can at the same time achieve their own ends.

It is our contention that these feminist, narrative, and discourse models are best suited to addressing ethical issues in aging. To take just one example, good home care practice is dependent on the quality of communicative practices between parties in the home care enterprise. Many of the serious moral problems one encounters in home care practice arise because there tends to be no forum for parties involved in caregiving (families, clients, home care aides, supervisors, etc.) to communicate perspectives, worries, and needs. A communicative ethics approach is particularly useful in this setting, for example, because it calls for inclusive and democratic conversation, from the most empowered members of the group (representatives from the home care agency) to the most marginalized ones (home care aides and clients).

In his work, Harry Moody has also adopted a communicative approach to ethics and aging. Whether addressing hospital discharge planning for the elderly (2004), nursing home placement, or age-based rationing (1992), Moody's approach reflects the kind of Habermasian discourse ethic that we outlined above. Moody's communicative approach does not demand universal answers to the recurring ethical problems associated with aging, and he does not suggest that inclusive and open dialogues come easily. Indeed, he recognizes that "Free and open communication does not suppress conflict or differences." Yet he points out that the conceptual alternative of communicative ethics "achieves a compromise or negotiated settlement rather than a solution based on absolute rules and principles" (1992, p. 10). In summing up his book, *Ethics in an Aging Society*, Moody claims the following:

> ... this book ... is a call for *communicative ethics* as an approach to the ethical dilemmas of an aging society. But here, too, some virtues are important. If we want things to be different, the most important virtue we need is the virtue of prudence or practical wisdom. The principles of practical wisdom are familiar: deliberation, consultation, self-questioning, openness, respect for others. What Habermas calls an *ideal speech act* can flourish with nothing less. But conspicuously lacking in our society are institutions for nurturing practical wisdom and developing the skills of communication over the lifespan.
>
> —Moody, 1992, p. 246

Similarly, Tanya F. Johnson (1999) indicates how communicative ethics would organize and ground the conversations that take place within the arena of aging. Communicative ethics presupposes that one takes as starting points conditions such as the lack of hierarchy (all parties have equal status in the conversation); that all parties enter into a relationship in which they are open to one another, and are sharing, trusting, honest, fair, and earnest; that there is no such thing as a "disinterested" party in the conversation; and that the communication is necessarily social, and can only operate within the context of a group (1999, p. 336). To ensure inclusion and fairness, competent patients or clients must be part of the decision-making team for the resolution of issues and dilemmas; if they are not competent, then primary caregivers become their representatives and thus part of the decision-making process.

Like Moody and Johnson, we take a communicative ethic to be most instructive and well-suited to the domain of aging. Whether in nursing homes or home care settings; whether applied to culture and aging or questions of intergenerational justice, we believe that a communicative ethic serves best. However, we look to *micro-communities* (such as our friendships, peer groups, families, and other "grassroots," noninstitutionalized communities) as the venues for communication about our beliefs, values, preferences, narratives, and so on. As we will argue in this book, how we understand ourselves, our place in society, our needs, our identities, and our relationships with others is not primarily determined through communications at the cultural or political level (though these communications do affect us); rather, it is developed through our daily, mundane interactions—in our conversations at the beauty salon, with friends, around the dinner table with family, and so on. The stories we tell about ourselves and how we see ourselves are largely informed by our personal relationships and communities in which we are enmeshed, and for this reason we take a relational conception of autonomy, with a narrative, communicative ethic at its root, to be the grounding for our recommendations throughout this text.

REFERENCES

Agich, G. (1995). Actual autonomy and long-term care decision making. In S. K. Toombs, D. Barnard, & R. A. Carson (Eds.), *Chronic illness: From experience to policy* (pp. 129–153). Indianapolis, IN: Indiana University Press.

Agich, G. (2003). *Dependence and autonomy in old age: An ethical framework for long-term care.* Cambridge, MA: Cambridge University Press.

de Beauvoir, S. (1974). *The second sex.* (H. M. Parshley, Trans.). New York, NY: Vintage. (Original work published in 1949.)

Benhabib, S. (1996). Autonomy, modernity and community: Communitarianism and critical social theory in dialogue. In R. Manning & R. Trujillo (Eds.), *Social justice in a diverse society* (pp. 75–83). Mountain View, CA: Mayfield Press.

Furman, F. K. (1999). There are no old Venuses: Older women's responses to their aging bodies. In M. U. Walker (Ed.), *Mother time: Women, aging, and ethics* (pp. 7–22). New York, NY: Rowman & Littlefield.

Gilligan, C. (1982). *In a different voice: Psychological theory and women's development.* Cambridge, MA: Harvard University Press.

Gilligan, C. (1987). Moral orientation and moral development. In E. Kittay & D. Meyers (Eds.), *Women and moral theory* (pp. 19–33). New York, NY: Rowman & Littlefield.

Grimshaw, J. (1986). *Philosophy and feminist thinking.* Minneapolis, MN: University of Minnesota Press.

Habermas, J. (1989). Justice and solidarity: On the discussion concerning 'Stage 6.' *Philosophical Forum, 21,* 32–52.

Holstein, M. (1999). Home care, women, and aging: A case study of injustice. In M. U. Walker (Ed.), *Mother time: Women, aging, and ethics* (pp. 227–244). New York, NY: Rowman & Littlefield.

Ingram, D. (1990). *Critical theory and philosophy.* New York, NY: Paragon House.

Johnson, T. (1999). *Handbook on ethical issues in aging.* Westport, CT: Greenwood Press.

Kittay, E. F. (1999). *Love's labor: Essays on women, equality, and dependency.* New York, NY: Routledge.

Kukla, R. (2005). *Mass hysteria: Medicine, culture, and mothers' bodies.* New York, NY: Rowman & Littlefield.

MacIntyre, A. (2000). The need for a standard of care. In L. P. Francis & A. Silvers (Eds.), *Americans with disabilities: Exploring the implications of the law for individuals and institutions* (pp. 81–86). New York, NY: Routledge.

Mackenzie, C., & Stoljar, N. (Eds.) (2000). *Relational autonomy: Feminist perspectives on autonomy, agency, and the social self.* New York, NY: Oxford University Press.

Meyers, D. (1989). *Self, society, and personal choice.* New York, NY: Columbia University Press.

Moody, H. (1992). *Ethics in an aging society.* Baltimore, MD: Johns Hopkins University Press.

Moody, H. (2004). Hospital discharge planning: Carrying out orders? *Journal of Gerontological Social Work, 41*(1), 107–118.

Nelson, H. L. (1999). Stories of my old age. In M. Walker (Ed.), *Mother time: Women, aging, and ethics* (pp. 75–96). New York, NY: Rowman & Littlefield.

Nelson, H. L. (2001). *Damaged identities, narrative repair.* New York, NY: Cornell University Press.

Roberts, D. (1997). *Killing the black body: Race, reproduction, and the meaning of liberty.* New York, NY: Vintage.

Schott, R. M. (2002). Resurrecting embodiment: Toward a feminist materialism. In L. Anthony & C. Witt (Eds.), *A mind of one's own: Feminist essays on reason and objectivity* (pp. 319–334). Boulder, CO: Westview Press.

Taylor, C. (1985). *Human agency and language.* New York, NY: Cambridge University Press.

Tronto, J. (1989). Women and caring: What can feminists learn about morality from caring? In A. M. Jaggar & S. M. Bordo (Eds.), *Gender/body/knowledge: Feminist reconstructions of being and knowing.* Brunswick, NJ: Rutgers University Press.

Walker, M. (2007). *Moral understandings* (2nd ed.). New York, NY: Oxford University Press.

Wendell, S. (1996). *The rejected body: Feminist philosophical reflections on disability.* New York, NY: Routledge.

Young, I. M. (1990). *Throwing like a girl and other essays in feminist theory and social philosophy.* Bloomington, IN: Indiana University Press.

SECTION II

Ethics and Context

CHAPTER 3

Aging and the Aged Body

In our heart, we never feel old . . . . No matter how old you are, you still feel you are
young. You feel that you are attractive . . . . You cannot see your image like old.
When you look at the mirror, I'm {an} old lady, but I still don't feel old
——Elderly female interviewee (Clarke & Griffin, 2008)

INTRODUCTION

No book on aging and ethics would be complete without a chapter on the body. Within the past 25–30 years, feminist, disability, and queer theorists have addressed the impact that embodiment has on our self-identities, our autonomy, and our sexualities (Bartky, 1990; Breckenridge & Vogler, 2001; Conboy, Medina, & Stanbury, 1997; Vares, 2009; Weiss, 1998; Young, 1990). We live in the world in particular *kinds* of bodies that mark us in various ways—as being male or female, black or white, able-bodied or disabled, and young or old, to name a few. This chapter is specifically concerned with how one's aging or aged body is culturally "read" such that understandings are externally imposed but also internalized. Contemporarily, the aging and aged body has largely been devalued and feared because of its associations with frailty, loss of control, and death. In a youth-obsessed culture that hyper-values vigor, good looks, youthfulness, and freedom, reminders of youth's fleeting nature are not welcomed. Until very recently, those of us with obviously aging or aged bodies have been left with few options, including the use of cosmetic and anti-aging technologies to prevent the appearance of old age (see Chapter 5), the reclamation of the "hag" or "crone" identities (Thomason, 2006; Walker, 1988), or accepting the stereotype of old age as involving a certain asexuality and irrelevance.

Yet recently there has been a cultural-scientific shift in representations of aging and sexuality. This has been especially notable in the popular media, where, as Tina Vares claims, the predominant portrayal of asexual old age is increasingly accompanied by newer images of the 'sexy oldie' (2009).

While this shift counters conventional stereotypes of the asexual and disengaged elderly, the implications for seniors of such a change have only been recently researched. As Thomas Walz (2002) indicates, these more positive representations of embodiment and sexuality in older persons may open up the possibility for new self-understandings and identities.

In this chapter we explore old women's embodiment through cultural, moral, and biological lenses. We recognize that men, too, increasingly experience social pressure to emulate the ideal male appearance. The marketing of treatments for hair loss and age-related erectile dysfunction are but two examples of how men are pressured to live up to youth-oriented societal standards. Still, there is some truth to Sontag's assertion that older men's bodies are still likely to be perceived as being "distinguished" or "full of character," while women's bodies tend to be negatively perceived as unattractive and even revolting (Sontag, 1972). The double standard of aging persists, despite decades of feminist writing on this topic. Our goal is to integrate "materialist" and "social constructionist" views of the body while holding with Twigg that "not all discourses are equally possible" (2004, p. 63). Constrained by our biological bodies and the culture in which we live, we suggest that while we are not "cultural dupes," a subtle process of internalization makes resistance, particularly on the individual level, very difficult. And, as a further complication, the will to resist may be further impeded by the social necessity of conforming to certain norms regarding appearance to achieve socially desired ends, such as jobs.

Our intent is also to show why embodiment and body image *matter* in our social practices and in the moral life more generally. We take clues from disability studies, where the conditions of and limitations on individual bodies are unavoidable, as they are in old age, but the experience of handicaps are not. Handicaps are created by a society that erects visible and invisible barriers that threaten dignity and the chance to live robustly, despite disabling conditions. Old women, who are also often robbed of their dignity, face two critical tasks that must be engaged simultaneously—to refuse to deny age and to engage in self-exploration and resistance. We have few ways otherwise to respond to pervasive, and most often damaging, cultural norms that challenge our self-esteem. Such denial is ultimately self-defeating and threatening to our integrity.

From an early age, women experience subtle forms of discrimination that are only exacerbated as they grow older. Feminist literature that focuses on elderly women points out the multiple negative stereotypes older women face within our culture (Copper, 1988). Society imposes other limitations on women long before they are old: girls learn at a young age that society prizes and rewards physically attractive girls and young women. Society expects them to desire marriage and motherhood, and assumes that they will be good mothers, even at the expense of their own life projects. As women reach their forties and fifties, they are expected to be attractive and fit if they have any hope of being valued by the workplace, by men, and by society in general. Because women are so vulnerable to society's expectation of their physical appearance, they work harder and harder at maintaining their appearance, not only to achieve a full range of life options, but in order to have a sense of self-worth (Bartky, 1999). Elderly women have for years experienced the undoing that happens as they get older and have completed child-rearing tasks; with menopause, many women experience the diminished sense of being attractive, sexual persons. The change in their status is not a sudden event, but a continuous process that begins as many as 40 years earlier. Yet the pressure to stay attractive continues into old age for most women.

Disability studies and feminism share an important goal—to render visible issues and problems that are too often hidden because culturally dominant groups do not notice them or because they consider them unimportant or otherwise irrelevant. For older women, meanings attached to living and functioning with and through bodies that are not culturally esteemed receive almost no public attention. Because old women inhabit and live in and through culturally stigmatized bodies, they are usually acutely aware of their bodies as both material and constructed, even if they don't use these words. And they are aware of how others judge their bodies, including their age peers. How sad that old women fear losing status as the "not old," when serious health problems threaten their "youthfulness" (Hurd, 1999). How we experience our aging bodies is thus complex, influenced by structural, institutional, and cultural forces and the myriad interactions that occur in the overlapping and discrete contexts in which we live. Our embodied selves shape and are shaped by these forces and interactions. Yet the resulting personal, political, and moral ramifications are subjects still awaiting sustained study.

OUR BODIES, OUR SELVES

Simply understood, how we see our bodies and how others interpret them inform our relationships with individuals and with institutions. My body is "what I *am* in relation to objects and others" (Diprose, 1995, p. 209). My body so understood affects me on a daily basis; it challenges or affirms my self-worth and my moral standing in the diverse communities of which I am a part. The body is the "source of meaning and meaning construction . . . the perspective we bring to bear on the world" (Komesaroff, 1995, p. 14). We relate differently to it, for example, after a heart attack than before. Acutely aware of our vulnerability, we approach social interactions and movement differently. And these interactions and movements render our body a "social text"—though not an open-ended one as a conventional literary text might be, it is one that is formed and given meaning in culture (Twigg, 2004). It is the site for "judgments about age" (Oberg, 1996).

Jennifer Church argues that we can be said to have "ownership" over our bodies to the extent that we integrate "the psychological states of a body into the psychological states of a person or self" (1997, p. 91). As Church notes,

> A body belongs to a person when and if the psychological states of that body are integrated through reflection in such a way as to constitute a person or a self. When and if the mental states of a body are not so integrated, no ownership (of this fundamental kind) is possible because there is simply no person or self to be the owner; nothing can be *your* body if there is no *you*. Thus, coming to be a person or a self and coming to own one's body are not two different processes (first the creation of a will and then its application) but, rather, two faces of the same process— a process whereby the psychological states of a body are simultaneously integrated *by* and integrated *into* an overall conception of the self.
>
> —*Church, 1997, p. 92*

By combining Diana Meyers' (1989) account of the self (see Chapter 2) with Church's conception of ownership of the body, we can see how autonomy competency and the development of self are tied to our bodies. For our purposes it is important to connect the development of self with the body, for only then can one offer a robust account of how older person's experiences of embodiment relate to their autonomy competency, sense of sexuality, and self-identification.

If the development of one's self or identity is tied to the body, and one gains a sense of ownership over the body through the development of autonomy competency, then the significance of embodied experience becomes clear. Our *external* experiences of our bodies (through cultural taboos, the media, medicine, the law) inform our *internal* development of autonomy competency, and vice versa. We are not simply selves, then, but embodied selves; and the ways in which we are embodied affect the development of our autonomy and the ownership of our bodies.

Bodily deterioration poses threats to our identity and integrity as we witness others reading the "texts" we call our bodies. It may happen when we grapple for that discount coupon at the drugstore counter and the line behind us grows inpatient (read—what a tiresome old person), when we seek assistance at the makeup counter in tacit competition with the 22-year-old who gets service even though we were there first (read—older women are no longer sexually competitive and so hardly worth the invest-ment of time), or when we are at the checkout line at Bloomingdale's and the cashier helps the man with the briefcase before giving us her attention (read—we can't have anything as important to do as he has). Because the body cannot be divorced from discursive practices, encounters at the cos-metic counter or the employment office or the doctor's office are mediated by the cultural norms, expectations, and attitudes that are part of the generally pre-conscious, taken-for-granted lifeworld that infuses U.S. and probably most, if not all, Western cultures. In this "discursive grid" (Tulle-Winton, 2000, p. 79) the outward signs of aging discount the person display-ing those signs.

Bodies are also politicized. If older women fail to care for their bodies so that they can meet normative expectations to age "successfully," they may be viewed askance—at the simplest level for "letting themselves go" when "control" is putatively within their grasp—and, more problematically, as moral failures for being complicit in their own aging. Aging and aged women lose cultural relevance. This belief in the possibility for, and moral obligation to, control can also contribute to delegitimating old age as the foundation for policy responses. If old age can be just like middle age—if only we had behaved differently—why should public policy single out the old for political attention (see Hudson, 2005)? Blamed personally for the condition of their bodies and used as a tool politically, these new oppressions overlap and intersect with the familiar and interlocking oppres-sions of gender, race, and class. Ironically, those particular causes of inequal-ity, so effectively analyzed by political economists of aging, help to explain why some are more able than others to exercise control over their bodies. This form of oppression—the expectation of control and power over the body—escalates as individuals become more disabled; then the goal is often reduced to keeping them out of a nursing home (Minkler, 1990). Rather than "rehabilitating" old age no matter the condition of our bodies, older persons are relegated to the margins of society (Tulle-Winton, 2000).

THE STRONG VIEW: AGING AS PURE SOCIAL CONSTRUCT

Some commentators on the aging body take what we consider to be a strong social constructionist view: that the process of aging and the experiences of an aging or aged body are socially constructed and not biologically given. While we appreciate the spirit within which this strong view is offered—understanding the degree to which the aging body is culturally constituted may be liberating and may require us to rethink our categories—we reject the strong view that experiences of aging boil down to culture. Certainly, cultural expectations that one remain youthful, vigorous, attractive, sexy, and physically fit affect how individuals understand themselves; these cultural ideals inform our very identities. But as we argue, there are certain commonly shared experiences of having an aging body that cannot simply be written off as cultural norm: that one's body may begin to hurt, that it may no longer be able to do what we expect, and that its appearance may change over time cannot be eliminated by any cultural change, no matter how significant.

In *An Aging Un-American*, Kate Scannell relates an experience she had with a 76-year-old patient who was seeking help for her medical troubles. As Scannell recalls, the patient laid a yoga mat on the floor and then "[W]ithin seconds her nimble body twisted into implausible forms—a human pretzel, a sailor's knot, a fleshy corkscrew" (2006, p. 1415). The patient's concern? She couldn't do the downward dog or the cobra positions as easily as she used to; "I just want to know if there's something wrong with me," was her complaint to Scannell (2006, p. 1415). Scannell replied to her patient's concern by pointing out that she was healthy, and that losing elasticity and flexibility with aging is a perfectly natural phenomenon. This patient replied "Well .... just because that happens doesn't mean that it's healthy or inevitable, right? It's a physical process, so there must be a supplement or hormone or something physical I can take to counteract it" (2006, p. 1415). We take such a conversation to highlight what is dangerous and problematic with the strong constructivist view of the aging body: if bodily change over time is simply viewed as "variation," of no real biological import, then there is little ground left on which to understand and experience those changes over time as at least in part a natural, inevitable part of human life.

In *Declining to Decline*, Margaret Morganroth Gullette plainly states that, "The basic idea we need to absorb is that whatever happens in the body, human beings are aged by culture first of all" (1997, p. 3). And in a similar vein, Christine Overall claims that "Old age, like impairment, is not a biological given but is socially constructed, both conceptually and materially. That disability and aging both rest upon a biological given is a fiction that functions to excuse and enable the very social mechanisms that perpetuate ableist and ageist oppression" (2006, p. 134). While we, too, reject ableist and ageist oppression, we deny the claim that experiences of the aging body are solely or even primarily cultural. Much could be done to reduce or eliminate ageist beliefs and practices; but even with such important changes in place, Scannell's patient is going to experience bodily treachery when trying to do her yoga poses. And the women who frequent the beauty shop in which Frida Furman (1999) did her ethnographic study will continue to find common ground in their experiences of their aging and aged bodies.

BACK TO THE BIOLOGICAL BODY

Cultural constructions of aging aside, over time our bodies will gradually age; that is, they will become less resilient to environmental and other assaults. We will lose functional cells and tissues, our organs will become less efficient, and our reserve capacities will decline (Hillyer, 1998). We will heal less quickly and lose muscle mass and lung capacity. Biologist Leonard Hayflick (1994) has argued that the body's ability to repair cellular damage becomes more difficult as we age, whether the reason is the shortening of telomerase at the ends of our genes or other factors. These changes are not a sign of disease, but they contribute to such reactions as fear of falling because joints stiffen, or they lead to modifying behaviors, such as no longer carrying baggage that must be tossed into the overhead bins on planes. What we have long taken for granted becomes problematic; without estrogen, for example, older women often find sexual intercourse painful. This new "fact" of life is not life threatening, but it requires a reassessment of one's interactions with partners and decisions about possible medical interventions. Instead of a habitual body that we might ignore, we gain an attention-demanding body. Some changes like osteoporosis are more severe and may limit the most common tasks we perform, such as cooking and shopping. These physical limitations are associated with aging and will be chronic and recurrent; the longer a woman lives, the more likely that she will live in a narrowing physical space. These changes are authentically connected to or caused by aging (Hillyer, 1998) and will happen to us despite diet regimens, lots of green tea, and exercise. As Scannell writes,

> Certainly, we are all on a learning curve about aging, as the life span continues to increase ... requiring continual repositioning and reinvention of developmental markers. The relatively short span that was characteristic of the Average American born a century ago more easily abided the dichotomous division of life into *young* versus *old*. But as life expectancy has expanded incrementally, midlife and old age have had to be remapped constantly, while we simultaneously attempt to assess our unfolding human experience of aging.
>
> —*Scannell, 2006, p. 1415*

Aging will also change our physical appearance. When basal metabolism slows down, lean body tissue decreases and fat increases. Our shape changes (Chrisler & Ghiz, 1993). The skin on our faces and necks becomes drier and flakier, and it wrinkles and loosens. We get brown spots whether or not we want them. The passage of time leaves its mark. "Each of us is engaged in a losing battle with the ravages of time" (Blaikie, 1999, p. 86). We may be able to retard the process, and we certainly can affect its outward manifestations through simple procedures like hair dye to the more complex surgical and chemical overhauls. But, as Florida Scott-Maxwell (1968) reminds us about aging, "nothing in us works well, our bodies have become unreliable" (p. 35). Other older women writers like Doris Grumbach (1991) and Carolyn Heilbrun (1997) candidly describe aging bodies that no longer perform as before.

For biologists like Leonard Hayflick (1994), proponents of antiaging medicine are chasing the myth of the eternal fountain—that we can reverse or stop the aging process. Hayflick reminds us that even if we manage to chip away one by one at the diseases that devastate our bodies, we still will get old and die. In fairness, however, we note that other molecular biologists hold views that differ substantially from Hayflick's; but that debate is beyond the scope of this chapter (see Chapter 5). However this debate is resolved, we suggest that biology forces us to face the limits of social constructionism and self-creation, the treasured values of aging and postmodernism.

A recent study by Laura Hurd Clarke and Meredith Griffin (2008) indicates that older persons, but especially older women, maintain a concern about their weight and appearance even after they begin to experience chronic and debilitating health problems. This ongoing concern with weight and appearance is noteworthy in light of previous research that suggested that health issues supplant concerns for one's body size and appearance (Hurd Clarke, 2002). As Clarke and Griffin point out from their study,

> Our findings reveal that many older adults, particularly women, continue to be concerned about their appearances, specifically their weight, even following the onset of numerous and debilitating health issues ... None of the women we interviewed asserted that appearance was not important despite their often harrowing stories of pain and incapacitation. In this way, our data highlight the pervasive entrenchment and internalization of norms of female appearance as a gauge for women's social currency and illustrate another *meaning as significance* (Bury, 1988) outcome of having chronically ill bodies that deviate from extant cultural gender ideals.
> —*Clarke and Griffin, 2008, p. 1092*

These findings suggest the close connection between the way we experience our physical bodies and the cultural overlays that inform our *interpretation* of those experiences. We do not want to suggest there is no significant social aspect to how we experience and understand our bodies; but we do want to temper the strong view by pointing out that any account of the aging body must grapple with the fact of the body as biological phenomenon, which is intractable and inevitable.

CULTURE AND THE OLDER WOMAN

Ironically, after years of women's struggles to achieve a sense of agency that is stronger than ever before, they face an escalating set of expectations about their bodies. These expectations now infuse old age as consumer culture markets a certain aesthetic to the new gray market (Minkler, 1991). If healthy living allows us to age "successfully," then products abound to transform our appearance so that it synchronizes with our triumphal health status. The costly products and procedures they involve, whether bought at Neiman Marcus or Walgreen's, do not make us less old. They do, however, perpetrate the myth and the expectation that we can fix our brokenness with a growing range of often costly consumer products. Without their help we fail at beauty; with their help our image comports with what may be our self-understanding—the inner self that is always younger than the outer self, a peculiar but visceral reinforcement of the old Cartesian dualism.

This divorce of inner self and outer self, labeled the "mask of aging" (Featherstone & Hepworth, 1991), impedes seeing the ways in which the body and the self are "formed and reformed in a dialectical relationship" (Kontos, 1999). Rather it demands that we use whatever is available to publicly confirm our inner image of ourselves, a struggle that is ultimately self-defeating and demoralizing. "Constant fabrication of disguises can lead to denial of selfhood in that 'our true identity never acted out, can lose its substance, its meaning, even for ourselves'" (Macdonald & Rich, 1983).

Empirical research on older women and the ways in which they experience their bodies suggests that they do not ignore cultural expectations. They, like all others, are hardly immune from concern with body image. Rodin, Silberstein, and Striegel-Moore (1984) argue that women's chronic dissatisfaction with their bodies is a "normative discontent." Indeed, "older women exhibit body image dissatisfaction and distortion to the same degree and, in many cases, more profoundly than their younger cohort, suggesting that preoccupation with body shape and size persists and may actually become more pronounced over a lifetime" (Fey-Yensin, McCormick, & English, 2002, p. 69). Even women who define themselves as "not old" by virtue of their abilities and capacities are defeated by their changing physical appearances and judgment of their peers, as they may no longer be able to hide their generally overweight, and thus culturally unappealing, bodies.

Frida Furman (1999) suggests that these women—without hair because of cancer treatment or with deeply lined faces and large bodies—fail the test of "ordinariness," an experience that leads to stigmatization not because of the changes but because social constructions "read the older body in negative ways" (p. 10). She claims that "The aging female body comes into deep conflict with cultural representations of feminine beauty." This old body is "construed and experienced within the context of multiple power relationships" (Furman, 1997, p. 5) within which the older woman lacks power. One result is shame for failure to meet the "disciplinary practices of femininity" (Bartky, 1988). Shame, which is antithetical to the central value of human dignity (the heart of our ethical vision in this book) is nonetheless a familiar experience for many aging women. Older women notice their imperfections perhaps more dramatically than younger women because they are defined as outsiders, as the "other" by the dominant culture. But as Gullette (1997) points out, such depreciation begins far earlier—in our thirties—so these women have had lots of practice. And, as she also observes, women must be silent about the vagaries of their aging bodies lest they collaborate in their own devaluation. Because everything old women appear to be contradicts what culture values, it would seem unwise for them to bring attention to their deficits by talking about them.

Feminists have struggled with the combination of pleasure that many women get from makeup and other accoutrements of appearance and the potential repressive results of never feeling that we quite measure up. The shared pleasure in shopping and testing new makeup or hairstyles is marked by shared pain—we judge and evaluate our hair, our skin, our bodies (Bordo, 1993). While not automatons, we have a strong incentive to want to identify with those cultural representations of our identities that offer the greatest social recognition (Mackenzie, 2000). Living up to norms may make sense because it allows us to achieve other goals— jobs, for example. "One who takes seriously the strength and extent of appearance-related pressures on women should recognize the possible rationality of women's efforts to live up to norms of appearance" (Saul, 2003, p. 163).

There is, however, a hint that the situation may be better than we think. One of the few qualitative studies we have of how older women experience their bodies and their size shows that in the course of the interviews, some women began to express an increased defiance about responding to social expectations—and spousal criticisms—about their bodies (Tunaley, Walsh, & Nicolson, 1999). When cultural norms defined women as frail and fragile, middle-, and upper-class women were effectively denied higher education or we were negatively labeled "blue stockings," doomed never to marry or have children. Poor women, however, worked without professional comment or undue concern about their bodies. Today, many of these accepted understandings about women are gone, and we continue to negotiate norms about our bodies. Also more affirmatively, we are not wholly subject, in Foucault's terms, to the disciplinary practices that society tries to impose on us (Bartky, 1999). Despite everything, we are also agents; we can and do make choices about how we will regard our bodies. Our new and aged body thus gives us another chance to rethink our self-understandings and commitments (Meyers, 2003).

CULTURE MATTERS

As "situated" selves (Benhabib, 1992) or "second persons" (Baier, 1987), one's own body is not only (or perhaps even primarily) an individual affair. Even women who proudly insist that they are "not old" recognize the "power of the younger generations to define and constrain the realities of the 'old' and 'not old'" (Hurd, 1999, p. 8). In a subtle form of self-rejection and ageism, old women may simultaneously deny that negative images apply to them but so stereotype other people as old (Tunaley et al., 1999). And indeed, why would anyone want to be old? The word *old* connotes all that American society does not value—slowness, dullness, unattractiveness, inactivity—rather than suggesting someone mellow, glowing with a soft patina, confident, accepting but also filled with ambiguity and the "black dreads" and the indomitable passion in which Florida Scott-Maxwell rejoices.

While interest in the body has been growing in the past 10 to 15 years among scholars from many disciplines (Rosser, 2001), "the aging body has been relatively neglected" (Harper, 1997, p. 161; Tunaley et al., 1999; Twigg, 2004). We have little help from either feminists or gerontologists in this endeavor, and we are not helped by other disciplines that have "all but ignored body image issues of mid-life and older women" (Chrisler & Ghiz, 1993, p. 68). In an effort to avoid biological determinism and focus on the social construction of gender, feminists until recently have downplayed the body or, more specifically, the way women experience their bodies as opposed to what they do with them; for example, reproductive issues. Exclusion of older women from feminist work is symbolic of the "gerontophobia" of the larger culture (Arber & Ginn, 1991). And even now, when embodiment has become a keen interest of feminists, they have rarely been interested in older women. Only one philosophical volume, *Mother Time: Women, Ethics, and Aging* edited by Margaret Urban Walker (1999), has several chapters that address women and their aging bodies. And Frida Kerner Furman's (1997) groundbreaking *Facing the Mirror: Older Women and Beauty Shop Culture* is the one book-length ethnographic investigation of old women and their bodies, but it is limited to a small segment of that population—old Jewish women who patronize Julie's International Salon in a Chicago neighborhood.

Yet by ignoring the phenomenology of embodied experience, feminists elide their commitment to rendering visible the unexplored, the ignored. They participate in the cultural exclusion of old women and so fail to work toward remedying that exclusion. While contributing to social change, for example, by exposing the limitations of generalizations based on male subjects, feminists have made a difference in the lives of younger women by analyzing women's unique experiences, such as childbirth and menopause, and by politicizing the seemingly nonpolitical, calling attention to gender relations and to issues such as domestic violence and income inequality. They have not done the same for issues that predominantly affect older women. If feminism is about the liberation of all women, then feminists need to move beyond menopause and take a look at the 80-year-old woman who fears speaking out loud about her angina in apprehension that she will be denied the label "not old" (Hurd, 1999). If we accept the commitment to changing what is unacceptable to women as one hallmark of feminism (Calasanti & Slevin, 2001; Collins, 2000; Gottfried, 1996; Hooyman, 1999; Ray, 1996; Saul, 2003), then it has failed older women.

Critical gerontologists, in consciously counteracting the biomedicalization of aging, have focused on humanistic and social concerns. Similarly, political economists of aging address structural rather than physiological factors in explaining the experience of old age. From this perspective, attempting to emphasize the bodily can seem a retrogressive step that takes us back into the territory of biological determinism and the narrative of decline (Twigg, 2004, p. 6). In their recent and almost single-minded emphasis on the positive aspects of aging, gerontologists may judge a focus on the body as demeaning and therefore best avoided. Yet as Simon Biggs (2004) points out, critical gerontology, in partnership with feminism, can contribute, in important ways, to understanding the "tension between personal and structural identity and the strategies people use to continue to live and develop in circumstances not of their own choosing" (p. 46). Both, for example, are concerned with the embodied self and the power of appearance.

The time seems ripe for both feminists and gerontologists to affirm the materiality of the body at the same time that they take into account the ways in which biological limits can be stretched and cultural representations modified. These understandings can guide policy and practice, especially as women will more often age "in place" or in other community settings.

THE POWER TO RESIST

Knowing how norms about our aging bodies may affect us is the opening wedge in an effort to change ourselves and the culture. Because bodies are both biologically and culturally inscribed (Bordo, 1993), we are both agents and bearers of culture. This dual role, not surprisingly, necessitates dialectical thinking—to change the social environment simultaneously we must change our attitudes and responses to norms, which will, if done by many women, affect those social norms. Acts of resistance are the path, and cultural changes are the long-range goal. Hence, women must struggle to wear their bodies proudly and to affirm their unique qualities while accepting their nearly universal age markings, as they confront the rhetoric of agelessness and eternal youth. Here again, we may take lessons from the disability movement. Not content to adapt to the environment in which they lived, disability activists set about changing the environment while giving one another the strength to assert the dignity that others would deny to them.

Our intention in this chapter is not to argue that aging and aged women ought to be entirely free from cultural judgments concerning their bodies: for, as we recognize, as social being, the body is partly physical phenomenon and partly social construct. In the context of aging, then, our argument is not for old women's absolute freedom from appraisal and objectification, since this may arguably be a natural element in our human relationships. We *need* norms to function, and they serve an important social purpose; a life without social norms is unthinkable. Our argument is rather against the ubiquitous negative understanding of the aging body, an understanding that denies the very possibility of an authentic experience of it. When aging women are told that their self-understandings are illegitimate, then they are wrongly discriminated against in the denial of their bodily experiences and meanings.

Furthermore, since our bodies are not merely social constructs, there remains the possibility that older women can identify an authentic biological phenomenon of aging. While these experiences may be overlain with cultural meanings that go beyond, say, a woman's experience of her menopause (Callahan, 1993), it is still possible for her to authentically identify them. That the biological phenomenon of aging has an attendant cultural meaning does not mean that women will always experience it inauthentically: they are robbed of their bodily self-understandings when the dominant cultural meaning has a stranglehold on our minds and bodies. Though all meanings may be socially constructed to some degree, including our understanding of our physical experiences, some meanings are more open to voluntary appropriation than others. This is why we need to open up meanings of aging that contribute to older women's sense of self-worth and personal identity: and this is why aging and aged women need their communities to affirm and reflect their bodily experiences.

Within our communities we can be "authentic" and not evade age and its manifestations, where our lived bodies, of which we are ever conscious, are not marginal and devalued. Like the consciousness-raising groups of the late 1960s and early 1970s, change is easiest in the micro-worlds we all occupy; in these micro-worlds, women, especially older women, find their identities affirmed and their sorrows and joys shared. These are communities of resistance, "oppositional communities" (Ferguson, 1995, p. 372). They are

> embodied in the way that older women treat one another—with respect, affection, and attentiveness; in conversations and gestures that affirm and hence make visible older women's pride in and attention to their bodies, and that acknowledges the pain, suffering, and loss that accompanies embodiment; in discussions of caring as work that is valuable, necessary, and demanding.
>
> —*Furman, 1997, p. 168*

In these micro-worlds—secret spaces occupied by age peers—we can most often expose our fears and troubles. Florida Scott-Maxwell reports, "With one friend of my own age we cheerfully exchange the worst symptoms, and our black dreads ... but it is only to those of one's own age that one can speak frankly" (1968, p. 31). Similarly, the women who patronize Julie's International Salon support one another in hard times, delight in each other's company, and laugh at their double chins and wispy hair. In the absence of the dominant male gaze that would find them wanting, these women live affirmatively with their bodies and their evolving selves. Julie's liberated its patrons to speak openly because the mutually supportive relationships they experienced there freed them from the "prohibitions of the public square" (Furman, 1997, p. 5). Affirming our diverse experiences in alternative communities of meaning, Sandra Bartky (1999) both skewers U.S. culture's "disciplinary practices" vis-à-vis older women and reports that among themselves older women are often effusive and enthusiastic in their affirmations of one another's clothing and appearances.

Older women must find ways to develop and maintain positive bodily attitudes—outside the micro-communities where they may be appreciated and valued—"while living in a culture that objectifies female bodies and links women's social and economic power to their appearance" (Rubin, Nemeroff, & Russo, 2004, p. 28). The goal should be to transform social reality in order to "negotiate, redefine and reconceptualize women's position in society" (Reischer & Koo, 2004).

With other acts of resistance, we enlarge the chance for positive freedom. In trying to contest dominant representations of women, we reiterate bell hooks's (1992) "oppositional gaze." By demanding the right to stare, hooks counts on changing reality. "Even in the worst circumstances of domination, the ability to manipulate one's gaze in the face of structures of domination that would contain it, opens the possibility of agency" (hooks, 1992, as quoted in Furman, 1997: 177). So, one task is to develop transgressive strategies that will undermine the dominant culture's simultaneous devaluing of the aging woman's body while rendering it invisible. To not be seen is the ultimate devaluation. To stare is to demand visibility. To transgress is to change norms that devalue that which is now visible.

Ray (2004) suggests a new possibility for transgressive actions: the crone image, she suggests, allows us to come to and accept full maturity. And, we add, that such an image reflects an awareness of the biological reality of women's aging. In matriarchal societies, the crone has achieved queenly status that signifies authority, a status gained through time and experience only. Because we do not live in a matriarchal society, the struggle to affirm the crone status will not come easily, but we have tools at our disposal: wise anger (Woodward, 2003) and heterodox emotions such as bitterness and resentment (Meyers, 1997).

CONCLUSION

Negotiating a new status in old age will probably take place "at an intermediate level between that of the broad cultural scale and that of the individual personality" (Blaikie, 1999), thus calling attention once again to the micro-communities that give us strength and support. If our sense of self and our values are the "products of social relations with each other in particular primary communities" (Ferguson, 1995, p. 371), then such communities should try to bring younger and older women together so we can gradually transform generational differences and expectations. At last—and with one of the privileges of old age—we may actually have the time to work toward building such communities. In these communities, we will tell stories and build on memories and, when possible, in Gullette's (1997) words, write our "age autobiographies." Narrative repair (Nelson, 2001) through counter stories is another way of vigorously telling our own story and trying to take ownership of our identities.

In these circumstances, we propose a kind of principled relativism. It calls on us to build a case for how we will be old so that it makes moral and practical sense to ourselves and to others. It is not a defense of "anything goes" or an affirmation that pretense and creation is what old age is about. It is rather a belief that because outside guides about how we ought to age are not serving us well, we must take charge. How will we take the materiality of our bodies with all their ambiguities and create a story of our lives that makes them meaningful? And how will we tell these stories in such a way that they contribute to social regard for our non-ideal bodies that we no longer seek to deny? Masquerade is a temporary and finally a nonworkable solution. We should all do whatever we can to stay maximally healthy, while continuing to speak freely and often about the physicality of aging. Within this conversation, we can identify the opportunities to live well and fully, although (as Kate Scannell's yoga-practicing patient reminds us) not without occasional longing for what can be no more.

REFERENCES

Arber, S., & Ginn, J. (1991). *Gender and later life: A sociological analysis of resources and constraints.* London, UK: Sage Press.

Baier, A. (1987). Hume, the women's moral theorist? In E. F. Kittay & D. Meyers (Eds.), *Women and moral theory.* Lanham, MD: Rowman & Littlefield.

Bartky, S. L. (1988). Foucault, femininity, and the modernization of patriarchal power. In I. Diamond & L. Quinby (Eds.), *Feminism and Foucault: Reflections on resistance* (pp. 61–86). Boston, MA: Northeastern University Press.

Bartky, S. L. (1999). Unplanned obsolescence: Some reflections on aging. In M. U. Walker (Ed.), *Mother time: Women, aging, and ethics* (pp. 61–74). New York, NY: Rowman & Littlefield.

Benhabib, S. (1992). *Situating the self.* New York, NY: Routledge.

Biggs, S. (2004). Age, gender, narratives, and masquerades. *Journal of Aging Studies*, *18*, 45–58.

Blaikie, A. (1999). *Ageing and popular culture*. Cambridge, UK: Cambridge University Press.

Bordo, S. (1993). *Unbearable weight: Feminism, western culture, and the body*. Berkeley, CA: University of California Press.

Breckenridge, C. A., & Vogler, C. (2001). The critical limits of embodiment: Disability's criticism. *Public Culture*, *13*(3), 349–357.

Bury, M. (1988). Meanings at risk: The experience of arthritis. In R. Anderson & M. Bury (Eds.), *Living the chronic illness: The experiences of patients and their families*. London: Unwin Hyman.

Calasanti, T. M., & Slevin, K. F. (2001). *Gender, social inequalities, and aging*. Walnut Creek, CA: AltaMira Press.

Callahan, J. (1993). *Menopause: A midlife crisis*. Indianapolis, IN: Indiana University Press.

Chrisler, J., & Ghiz, L. (1993). Body image issues of older women. In N. Davis, E. Cole, & E. Rothblum (Eds.), *Faces of women and aging* (pp. 67–76). New York, NY: Haworth Press.

Church, J. (1997). Ownership and the body. In D. T. Meyers (Ed.), *Feminists rethink the self* (pp. 85–103). Boulder, CO: Westview Press.

Clarke, L. H. (2002). Beauty in later life: Older women's perceptions of physical attractiveness. *Canadian Journal on Aging*, *21*(3), 429–442.

Clarke, L. H., Griffin, M., & The PACC Research Team. (2008). Failing bodies: Body image and multiple chronic conditions in later life. *Qualitative Health Research*, *18*(8), 1084–1095.

Collins, P. H. (2000). *Black feminist thought* (2nd ed.). New York, NY: Routledge.

Conboy, K., Medina, N., & Stanbury, S. (Eds.) (1997). *Writing on the body: Female embodiment and feminist theory*. New York, NY: Columbia University Press.

Copper, B. (1988). *Over the hill: Reflections on ageism between women*. Trumansburg, NY: Crossing Press.

Diprose, R. (1995). The body biomedical ethics forgets. In P. Komesaroff (Ed.), *Troubled bodies: Critical perspectives on postmodernism, medical ethics, and the body* (pp. 202–221). Durham, NC: Duke University Press.

Featherstone, M., & Hepworth, M. (1991). The mask of aging and the postmodern life course. In M. Featherstone, M. Hepworth, & B. Turner (Eds.), *The body: Social processes and cultural theory* (pp. 371–389). London: Sage Press.

Ferguson, A. (1995). Feminist communities and moral revolution. In P. Weiss & M. Friedman (Eds.), *Feminism and community* (pp. 367–397). Philadelphia: Temple University Press.

Fey-Yensin, N., McCormick, L., & English, C. (2002, September/October). Body image and weight preoccupation in older women: A review. *Healthy Weight Journal*, *16*, 68–71.

Furman, F. (1997). *Facing the mirror: Older women and beauty shop culture*. New York, NY: Routledge.

Furman, F. (1999). There are no older Venuses: Older women's responses to their aging bodies. In M. U. Walker (Ed.), *Mother time, women, aging, and ethics* (pp. 7–22). Lanham, MD: Rowman & Littlefield.

Gottfried, H. (Ed.) (1996). *Feminism and social change*. Urbana, IL: University of Illinois Press.

Grumbach, D. (1991). *Coming into the end zone: A memoir*. New York, NY: W. W. Norton.

Gullette, M. M. (1997). *Declining to decline: Cultural combat and the midlife*. Charlottesville, VA: University Press of Virginia.

Harper, S. (1997). Constructing later life/constructing the body: Some thoughts from feminist theory. In A. Jamieson, S. Harper, & C. Victor (Eds.), *Critical approaches to ageing and later life* (pp. 160–174). Philadelphia: Open University Press.

Hayflick, L. (1994). *How and why we age*. New York, NY: Ballantine Books.

Heilbrun, C. (1997). *The last gift of time: Life beyond sixty*. New York, NY: Ballantine Books.

Hillyer, B. (1998). The embodiment of old women. *Silences*. *Frontiers: A Journal of Women's Studies, 19*(1), 48–60.

Hooks, B. (1992). *Black looks: Race and representation*. Boston, MA: South End Press.

Hooyman, N. (1999). Research on older women: Where is feminism? *The Gerontologist, 39*(1), 115–118.

Hudson, R. (Ed.) (2005). *The new politics of old age*. Baltimore, MD: Johns Hopkins University Press.

Hurd, L. (1999). We're not old! Older women's negotiations of aging and oldness. *Journal of Aging Studies, 13*(4), 19–39.

Komesaroff, P. (Ed.) (1995). *Troubled bodies: Critical perspectives on postmodernism, medical ethics, and the body*. Durham, NC: Duke University Press.

Kontos, P. (1999). Local biology: Bodies of difference in ageing studies. *Ageing and Society, 19*, 677–689.

Macdonald, B., & Rich, C. (1983). *Look me in the eye: Old women, aging, and ageism*. San Francisco, CA: Spinsters Ink.

Mackenzie, C. (2000). Imagining oneself otherwise. In C. Mackenzie & N. Stoljar (Eds.), *Relational autonomy: Feminist perspectives on autonomy, agency, and the social self* (pp. 124–150). New York, NY: Oxford University Press.

Meyers, D. (1989). *Self, society, and personal choice*. New York, NY: Columbia University Press.

Meyers, D. (1997). Emotion and heterodox moral perceptions: An essay in moral social psychology. In D. Meyers (Ed.), *Feminists rethink the self* (pp. 197–218). Boulder, CO: Westview Press.

Meyers, D. (2003). Frontiers of individuality: Embodiment and relationships in cultural context. *History and Theory, 42*(2), 271–285.

Minkler, M. (1990). Aging and disability: Behind and beyond the stereotypes. *Journal of Aging Studies, 4*(3), 245–260.

Minkler, M. (1991). Gold in gray: Reflections on business' discovery of the elderly market. In M. Minkler & C. Estes (Eds.), *Critical perspectives on aging.* Amityville, NY: Baywood Press.

Nelson, H. L. (2001). *Damaged identities, narrative repair.* New York, NY: Cornell University Press.

Oberg, P. (1996). The absent body—A social gerontological paradox. *Ageing and Society, 16*(7), 10–19.

Overall, C. (2006). Old age, ageism, impairment, and ableism: Exploring the conceptual and material connections. *NWSA Journal, 18*(1), 126–139.

Ray, R. (1996). A postmodern perspective on feminist gerontology. *The Gerontologist, 36*(5), 674–680.

Ray, R. (2004). Toward the croning of feminist gerontology. *Journal of Aging Studies, 18*(1), 109–121.

Reischer, E., & Koo, K. (2004). The body beautiful: Symbolism and agency in the social world. *Annual Review of Anthropology, 33,* 297–317.

Rodin, J., Silberstein, L., & Striegel-Moore, R. (1984). Women and weight: A normative discontent. Psychology and gender. *Nebraska Symposium on Motivation, 32,* 267–307.

Rosser, S. (2001). Now the body is everywhere. *NWSA Journal, 13*(2), 142–148.

Rubin, L., Nemeroff, C., & Russo, N. (2004). Exploring feminist women's body consciousness. *Psychology of Women Quarterly, 28,* 27–37.

Saul, J. (2003). *Feminism: Issues and arguments.* New York, NY: Oxford University Press.

Scannell, K. (2006). An aging un-American. *New England Journal of Medicine, 355*(14), 1415–1417.

Scott-Maxwell, F. (1968). *The measure of my days.* New York, NY: Penguin.

Sontag, S. (1972). The double standard of aging. *Saturday Review, 55,* 29–38.

Thomason, S. P. (2006). *The living spirit of the crone: Turning aging inside out.* Minneapolis, MN: Fortress Press.

Tulle-Winton, E. (2000). Old bodies. In P. Hancock, B. Hughes, E. Jagger, K. Paterson, R. Russell, E. Tulle-Winton, & M. Tyler (Eds.), *The body, culture, and society: An introduction.* Buckingham, UK: Open University Press.

Tunaley, J., Walsh, S., & Nicolson, P. (1999). I'm not bad for my age: The meaning of body size and eating in the lives of older women. *Ageing and Society, 19,* 741–759.

Twigg, J. (2004). The body, gender, and age: Feminist insights in social gerontology. *Journal of Aging Studies, 18,* 59–73.

Vares, T. (2009). Reading the "sexy oldie": Gender age(ing) and embodiment. *Sexualities, 12*(4), 503–524.

Walker, B. G. (1988). *The crone: Woman of age, wisdom, and power.* San Francisco, CA: Harper & Row.

Walz, T. (2002). Crones, dirty old men, sexy seniors: Representations of the sexuality of older persons. *Journal of Aging and Identity, 7*(2), 99–112.

Weiss, G. (1998). *Body images: Embodiment as intercorporeality.* New York, NY: Routledge.

Woodward, K. (2003). Against wisdom: The social politics of anger and aging. *Journal of Aging Studies, 17*(1), 55–67.

Young, I. M. (1990). *Throwing like a girl and other essays in feminist theory and social philosophy.* Bloomington, IN: Indiana University Press.

CHAPTER 4

The "Third Age"

Cultural Ideals, Ethics, and the Myth of Agelessness

INTRODUCTION

To have resonance and relevance, any answer to the ancient question, what does it mean to live a good life must "take into consideration and respect the particular circumstances of a human life" (Rentsch, 1997, p. 264). Age, we suggest, is one of these particular features. Once the basics of human existence are met (not always something to be assumed), our sense of self-worth in large measure depends on a belief that we are leading a good and decent life and that people we respect, also respect us. Yet, the task of defining a worthy self, especially in old age, is made more difficult by the conditions of modernity, if not postmodernity, which has detached the self from communal meanings and roles that once governed every part of human life (Cole, 1992). While not anticipating (or even wishing for) a return to communal meanings (which ones would we choose and how would we choose them?) the need for what Charles Taylor (1984) calls "horizons of meaning" goes on. This horizon offers some strong notion that certain ways of life are infinitely better than others. Culture, which reflects the values, beliefs, orientations, and underlying assumptions prevalent among people in a society" (Huntington, 2000, p. xv), provides many of the resources we need for developing meaning and a self-worthy of respect. At the same time, we need to be watchful about how cultural figurations, tropes, and narratives can lead to the internalization of values and expectations that may conflict with important elements of our biographical selves, elements that include our socioeconomic status, gender, race, as well as our important self-conceptions. The potential conflicts posed by these cultural messages are the subject of this chapter.

While we leave open for now the question of whether or not broad, culturally shared meanings are essential or even important for older people, the dearth of such meanings, even limited ones, is particularly apparent in old age (Cole, 1992, p. xx). The once popular belief that old age can be seen as a spiritual journey has little force even in this country where many people identify religion as a powerful source of identification and meaning. In the popular press and in many academic circles, discourses about older ages— the period before major disabilities set in, now often referred to as the "third age"—are premised on continued good health and relative affluence. These discourses move in two major directions: one emphasizing continued productivity and the other postmodern consumerism where status derives from consumption rather than production (Blaikie, 1999). With the further assumption that the demands of paid work and family responsibilities have been mitigated, these discourses suggest that as "age" itself loses its place as a meaningful category, ageism, lacking an anchor, will disappear.

These emerging discourses, built upon several disparate parts— successful aging, productive aging, civic engagement, and post-traditional or postmodern aging—assume that one *can* and *should* maintain good health into advanced old age. These norms are meant to replace the stereotypical "decline and loss" paradigm that once served as the dominant motif in talking about old age. They share several recognizable components: they are, at once, both descriptive and normative, establishing one way of life as the norm against which all are measured; they see the world of old age from a privileged perspective; they aim to demonstrate that the old are not burdens on society but rather contributors as producers or consumers; they strive to open opportunities and change images of aging but do not consider the structural inequalities that shape what is possible and probable for individuals. In these ways the "productive" stream is deeply traditional— it affirms voluntarism and the creation of certain forms of social capital, and is built on the American ideals of productivity and "success." In its postmodern form, it glorifies the voice of freedom and self-fulfillment, certainly another voice in this country's cultural repertoire.

While not explicitly answering the question of what old age ought to be about—what should give it meaning—the implicit answer to that question is that one should be active and engaged, perpetuate midlife norms for as long as possible, or, in the postmodern view, use newly found time to creatively refashion yourself to be whatever you wish to be. In these optimistic scenarios, good health and relative affluence, assumed to be broadly available, would allow individuals to use their good health and relative affluence to grow in new ways (Sadler, 2006).

While we will not enter the discussion about the reality/value of a "third age" as a new period in human development, we note that these diverse discourses, while quite different in their specifics, share the assumption that something new is afoot, that the old negative view of old age must be replaced or, at least postponed. As such, they can perhaps be subsumed under the "third age" rubric. Introduced by social historian Peter Laslett (1991) to account for expanding time between the end of traditional paid work and family responsibilities and the onset of debilitating illnesses, the third age, for Laslett, in his aptly titled book, *A Fresh Map of Life: The Emergence of the Third Age*, ought to be a time for personal fulfillment on an individual and collective level since older people are "trustees for the future" of society (p. 196). In the years since the publication of his book, the protean concept of the "third age" has evolved and has been, at least in the US, filled in with more explicit ideas of how the time ought to be used. As shall become clear, what we are questioning are both these explicit ideas and the sharp demarcation of the "third" from the "fourth" age of decline and death.

In this chapter, we will describe, in greater detail, what we see as the now-dominant expressions of what one ought to do and be as one gets older. We will then explore what we are calling the "particular circumstances" that mark older ages. While understandings of "age" might be socially constructed, they rest on material and existential foundations that are not eliminable. These circumstances are keys to one's ability to realize the aims these discourses promote but they also suggest the possibilities that open up if we consider old age (both the third and the fourth ages) as a unique time in human lifespan development to be honored for itself, neither split into two ages nor erased in favor of "agelessness" (Andrews, 1999).

With these background conditions clarified we will critique these new "oughts" on multiple grounds with two assumptions in mind—that we all care about how our lives go over the long term and that it is particularly important at a time toward the end that we are able to see ourselves as living moral lives. We will thus ask if images, ideals, or norms that are upheld as worthy or good and desirable are oppressive, possible for individuals to do, and reflect a view of the moral life that is fitting for most, if not all, of the people at whom it is directed. We will argue, on these grounds, that the prevalent normative images of a "good" old age do a disservice to large numbers of older people today, especially non-affluent women and people of color.

We will conclude with tentative proposals for how older people can claim their voices in the context of these emergent cultural messages. Because we maintain that systems of meaning are social in nature and that personal identity requires social recognition (Lindemann Nelson, 2001), we turn to a communicative process that can occur in the many or few micro-communities of which we are a part. In these micro-communities, sometimes communities of resistance, one can challenge identities that others impose on us and redefine what it means to live a good and worthy life—for us and others like us. A morally significant life is built on bricolage, not on a master narrative.

Conceptually, this work builds upon the view that "norms matter because we [individuals] are situated selves, embedded in society and culture . . . [we] resonate with what is valued in the environment" (Holstein & Minkler, 2003, p. 791). Hence, we gain our identities, self-respect, effective agency, and even contentment from participation in complex social systems (Flanagan, 1991). While these social systems often impose constraints on what is possible, as does our health status, income and so on, they contain the images and ideals that help us to make sense of our lives, to decide how to live, and to gain (or not) self-respect. This view of the relational self (see Mackenzie & Stoljar, 2000) reminds us that our environments give us the materials that help us determine what we value; without those environments, autonomy would be impossible.

DOMINANT NORMATIVE IDEALS
FOR THE "NEW" OLD AGE

Over the past 20 or so years, four different ways of changing how we think about old age have emerged: "postmodern or post-traditional aging," "productive aging," "successful aging," and "civic engagement." In a direct challenge to the view that old age burdens society, these views promote the reverse—older individuals ease the demands on social resources by engaging in socially valued activities. They work; they volunteer; they respond to communal needs; they are productive; they consume—all culturally resonant attributes. These discourses serve as counterweights to long-held views that old age is primarily about individual decrements or losses to which elders and societies needed to adapt (Phillipson, 1998). In a culture that venerates youth and devalues old age, calling attention to relative good health, continued contributions, and freedom challenges prevailing imagery.

In a bid for total freedom, postmodern (or post-traditional) gerontology upholds an image of older individuals, free to reinvent themselves in whatever way they choose. Essentially playful, this image has a certain seductiveness—sexy grandma (perhaps with purple hair), running on the beach or returning to school at 85—as if we do not have to age at all. These views attest to the power of agency as individuals negotiate their "multiple selves in an ongoing, open-ended, and meaningful fashion" (Chapman, 2004, p. 13). For postmodernists, self-creation, self-invention, consumerism, and change are the new hallmarks of aging well (see Gergen & Gergen, 2000; Gilleard & Higgs, 2000).

These oddly contradictory views—productivity and civic engagement do not fit well with playful post-modernism—nonetheless share the underlying idea that "old" applies only to those in the 4th age, the time when physical and cognitive decrements assume a central place in our lives. The message is that we are only as old as we feel, that 60 is the new 40, and that one-by-one, biomedicine and the new genetics will chip away at the diseases that we cannot prevent by good and healthful living (see Chapter 5, Friedan, 1993; Post & Binstock, 2004). The young body is projected on the old body as a norm (Harper, 1997, p. 167). Underscored by research into successful aging (Rowe & Kahn, 1987) what has emerged as a vision for the "new" third age (no longer old age) seems to be the contemporary evocation of the "golden years."

We take a closer look at these ideas. Introduced in the late 1980s, productive aging or, as some prefer, a "productive aging society" emerged, in part, as a response to the "greedy geezer" image of older people propounded by Americans for Generational Equity (AGE). These older individuals are conceived by AGE as busily and happily spending their children's inheritance and impoverishing society along the way. To counteract AGE's campaign against entitlement programs and the burden of the old, gerontologists demonstrated that older people contribute in significant ways to their families and their communities (Bass, Caro, & Chen, 1993). The generally unexamined implication of this attack and response is that human value is only associated with those who do not burden society. While not silencing AGE's attack on entitlement programs, an attack that periodically resurfaces, the notion of productive aging helped to launch what has become a major theme in gerontology—that of "positive aging."

While the concept of productive aging has not disappeared, civic engagement has largely supplanted it. Government, foundations, and private organizations have committed significant resources and attention toward promoting significant voluntarism among older people to fulfill community needs. Not surprisingly, civic engagement caught on. It captures this country's self-image—individual initiative, private action as opposed to government intervention, neighbors helping neighbors, transforming into a national priority what we have seen happen in times of disaster. It also challenges the "bowling alone" phenomenon that Putnam (1995) describes by seeing voluntarism as a renewed commitment to creating social capital. It does not, however, include political organizing among its valued (and therefore funded) activities. Encouraging such political action would importantly broaden the reach of civic engagement and make it less a symbol of privilege than a symbol of the ongoing struggle for justice (Martinson & Minkler, 2006). Instead, essentially conservative, it emphasizes, as noted above, the "career self" in which life plans, built upon a solid economic foundation and internalized self-control, unfold with a certain continuity (Walker, 1999). Oddly Victorian in its emphasis on control, it universalizes a way of life that lacks universal resonance.

What, however, is particularly troubling is a subtle sub-text in both "productive aging" and "civic engagement": there is an implied belief here that *could* implies *should*. If it is possible, then it is obligatory to continue contributing. In direct contrast to the playful postmodern self, the self that the "movement" for civic engagement praises is the responsible self who must pay civic "rent" for the space he or she occupies. Comparing it to the civil rights movement, its advocates describe it as "the creation of a national vision for aging that fosters productive engagement *as an expectation* of later life ..." (Reilly, 2006, emphasis added). By fulfilling this obligation, older people can serve their communities while relieving the pressure on public dollars.

THE "PARTICULAR CIRCUMSTANCES" OF BEING OLD

When Betty Friedan (1993) set out to write *The Fountain of Age* she didn't know that she was "deeply embedded in an ageist ideology." She soon came to realize that "the fountain of age didn't mean, *can't* mean, the absence of physiological, emotional, or situational change" (Friedan, 1993, p. xxviii cited in Andrews, 1999, p. 309). As 79-year-old Connie Goldman, a writer and producer, notes (personal communication, March 16, 2010), we come to recognize that what we are now is not what we once were; thus, we should not try to hold on to whom we used to be. If we deny age, we deny the importance of what has happened to us over our lifetime. With Sara Ruddick (1999), we see that "people in their seventies *typically* and *predictably* have a different relation than people in midlife to illness, death, and decline" (p. 49).

We start with one of the most fundamental differences that begins in early life and deepens in later life: the effects of social and economic location. To be born with the proverbial silver spoon in one's mouth, unless one has been a profligate spender, leads to quite a different range of opportunities in old age than being born in a low income housing project or even into a working class family that is marginally making ends meet. Race, class, and gender matter. Who hears rats in the walls at night and who travels to Sun City, Arizona? Who takes care of whom? Who faces a rich array of choices and who does not? Income insecurity is a particularly serious problem for many older people, especially women (see Wider Opportunities for Women Elder Economic Security Initiative, www.wowonline.org). Our health status also varies with our economic status (Minkler, Fuller-Thomson, & Guralnik, 2006). Advantages and disadvantages accumulate (Dannefer, 2003).

But there are also some important commonalties, each of which raises additional questions about norms that elevate a particular vision of the good life in old age. First, by 65, all individuals have lived far longer than they will live. So, too, have their friends and relations. "Facts and fears of decline and loss are central to the lives of the elderly" (Ruddick, 1999, p. 49), yet what should be a truism becomes something to resist acknowledging. Perhaps this resistance occurs because it is too hard to associate this fact with the possibilities for continued joy and growth. Second, no matter how well older people have cared for themselves, with rare exceptions, one's physical capacities change as the years go by. Bodies do not perform as well as they once did even if one remains able to manage one's day-to-day life with relative ease. Older people are more vulnerable—to the icy streets, steep bus steps, and long climbs into subway stations. There may be a fear of falling as balance becomes less reliable. Third, family relationships change. For women, widowhood is likely since women live longer than men and tend to marry men who are older than they are. Relationships with children may change, as they are forming their own nuclear families and are busy with career building. For less traditional families, the ending of long relationships because of death or illness or the absence of such a relationship paired with possible social discrimination (although many states are moving to ease this problem) can make isolation problematic. Fourth, older people often experience a cultural disjuncture. They grew up in a very different time and so can easily feel disconnected from contemporary culture. Individuals need an authentic voice that can guide them in making decisions about how to live when many of their former anchors are no longer available to them.

Jumping ahead 20 years or so, individuals are apt to have left the "third age" of relative well-being and entered the "fourth age" when the possibilities for "agelessness" are no longer possible; the major goal becomes staying out of an institution (Cohen, 1988; Minkler, 1990). The fact of embodiment becomes ever more important. Physical changes alter relationships with the world. These changes inform the choices that are possible. So 80-year-olds might stop doing certain things. Perhaps there will be some memory loss or other cognitive difficulties even in the absence of dementia. Perhaps getting on and off airplanes will be harder and so travel will not seem as enticing as it once did. More friends may die or become ill; and if not already widowed, widowhood becomes more likely. These changes require individuals to reinterpret their lives as some identities disappear and others appear. It becomes, as Furman (1999) astutely observed, "a struggle of the soul to affirm what is possible, to let go what is not" (p. 102). Often one's inner voice will sound very different from one's public voice. One's self-conception may not be what the mirror reflects.

In sum, heightened awareness that our bodies are no longer reliable, a sense that life is foreshortened and that the end is nearer than the beginning and a belief that others cannot see us as we see ourselves are important markers as we age. From the "third" to the "fourth" age these changes evolve most often without a radical departure although at times it is one event, a fall and a broken hip, cognitive changes, or serious illness that catapults us into the "fourth age." And these changes are all occurring during a time of deep global shifts that have weakened the social safety net and strengthened the individualistic strain in this country.

THE CRITIQUE: AN OVERVIEW

Against this sketch about the particular features of old age—like the rest of life, neither all negative nor all positive—we outline our concerns. We start from a concern about norms that value a certain kind of subjectivity. First, because the new or emerging discourses about the "third age" emanates from a position of relative privilege, they can marginalize alternative ways of life, threaten the well-being of the less well-off or less healthy, and they can flatten the vast differences among people who are old. When older people may need a rich array of cultural ideals and norms, they are greeted with mutually reinforcing ideals that seem to deny the fact of age. Denying age seems to be a peculiar way of respecting it. These norms may then be experienced as oppressive, irrelevant, or frustrating. While all may benefit from narratives that see older people as full and competent adults, they may be morally problematic if such recognition depends on one meeting already powerful cultural expectations such as productivity, control, and mastery, a form of life most often associated with masculine ideals (Walker, 1999). Second, by not acknowledging contingency and ambiguity, these narratives deny the developmental possibilities that can emerge from these seemingly negative features of old age. To integrate change with continuity as we age means acknowledging what has been and what one is becoming—both the good and the problematic (Atchley, 1987; Baltes & Baltes, 1990). We are not what we once were. Third, in the effort to eliminate negative stereotypes about old age, these narratives birth a new form of ageism now directed at the less vigorous and less healthy. Fourth, the emphasis on good health and relative affluence can serve to undercut public policies that are essential for the late life well-being of many older people, especially women and people of color. These narratives are peculiarly apolitical—while urging the creation of opportunities they are silent about the structural origins of inequalities that only worsen in old age.

Finally, because we cannot be expected to do what we are unable to do, we challenge the presuppositions that each of these related ideals set forth— that people will have the health, and the material, emotional, and social supports necessary to live up to the expectations these norms create. Yet, empirical evidence makes it stunningly clear that even this basic expectation cannot be assumed. Recent research (McLaughlin, Connell, Heerings, Li, & Roberts, 2009), for example, demonstrates that few older people (11.9%) aged "successfully" by the "successful aging" (Rowe & Kahn, 1987) standards. Not surprisingly, advanced age, female gender, and lower socioeconomic status were keys in predicting who would not be able to meet these standards. Aging well is thus heavily dependent on socio-structural factors.

We find these problematic elements of the "third age" discourse to be morally significant because they are the backdrop against which older people define themselves and test their identities as changes take place. As Lindemann Nelson (2001) observes, "personal identity, understood as a complicated interaction of one's own sense of self and others' understandings of who one is, functions as a lever that expands or contracts one's ability to exercise moral agency" (p. xi).

THE VIEW OF PRIVILEGE

Our first concern is the individualistic and privileged standpoint from which these new ideals originate. It is unable to account, for example, for the woman who cannot afford her day-to-day expenses. While the postmodern and the productive self are diametrically opposed in what they see as new ways to age, they are both totalizing narratives that speak from and to the center and not the margins. Successful aging shares this problem. To age "successfully" demands much of us throughout our lives, much of which is beyond our control. We can stop smoking but we cannot easily escape poverty. Proponents who see aging through a lens of privilege thus falsely assume that living these versions of a good old age is available to all by dint of our private efforts.

What we see through a lens of privilege is quite different than what we see through a lens of gender and class. A lens of privilege means "not having to notice or think about people who aren't like you" (Lindemann, 2006). Simply then, to be civically engaged or productive is a choice primarily for the privileged. There is a vast difference between starting a new housing service in one's community using one's life experiences and contacts or returning to work as a white collar part-time consultant and having to work at a minimum wage job just to make ends meet. Further, for the privileged, work and civic activities have been and may continue to be sources of respect and often substantial earnings that also leave time for self-care and nurture. For those who are privileged, continuation of such activities may be ongoing sources of self-esteem.

For women and people lower down on the income scale, work is often arduous and not the source of respect. For these workers, time or resources for self-care and nurturance are limited. A lifetime of "women's work" like caring for older people at home or a nursing home or flipping burgers at McDonalds will most likely make her a failure rather than a successful aged person. This blindness to the interlocking system of inequalities marginalizes those who, through no fault of their own cannot, or will not, meet expectations.

Looking at civic engagement and productivity through the eyes of a woman who has struggled to make ends meet all her life might make it seem more like a burden than a privilege, one more expectation or necessity no different than what she experienced during her earlier years. Young (1990) suggests that "cultural imperialism" renders many people both invisible and marked out and stereotyped (p. 123). This observation is not to suggest that many people, who have worked very hard for a living and have little in the way of income or assets, do not want to keep on giving. Many do, especially in the role of caregivers to other family members. Our point, however, is that this singular vision can place them in a position of being negatively judged if they want to rest—even if they still have the good health to continue. That's the difference between opening opportunities and creating new expectations. So a major problem that we see in these prevailing ideas for the "third age" is its appropriateness for only a small percent of the American population. This means that "blaming the victim" for not fulfilling the new requirements for a good old age will further devalue an already devalued group. Banishing negative fears about old age from public discourse does not eliminate them.

Elevating the positive elements of aging, like continued vigor and productivity, perpetuates dominant cultural ideals by extending them to old age. It underscores valuing people for their market and volunteer sector contributions (Biggs, 2001) and rewards a unique kind of subjectivity—the independent public 'man' who embodies traditional ideas about autonomy (Holstein, 2006). If life is pictured as something like a step-by-step progression, what is left in old age when retirement arrives means "surrendering ... eligibility for a centrally valued moral and social identity" (Walker, 1999, p. 104). Since retirement signals exit from culturally valued norms of productivity and mastery, we can save ourselves from the threats to our identity that result if we turn our post-work years into a time of continued productivity and engagement, what Ekherdt (1996) has described as the "busy ethic." To be busy demotes "private acts of sustenance and nurture, including self-nurture, without which life could not continue" (Minkler & Holstein, 2008, p. 197). To be productive and engaged—even for people who do so—can also devalue and make invisible other aspects of those people's lives and being.[1]

PERSISTENCE OF AGEISM

Advocates for productive aging and civic engagement hold that once the public becomes aware of all the contributions that older people make, ageism will disappear and we will become an "ageless" society. Neither approach has eliminated ageism; they have either pushed it to the new fourth age, forced it inward, or created the setting for insidious comparisons of one 70-year-old with another. The underlying assumption was that as long as one conformed to midlife norms, ageism might be contained if not eliminated. This elevation of the third age transferred age-related prejudices to people in the fourth age or even more broadly, to anyone who fails to live up to expectations regarding social contributions and vigorous good health (Holstein & Minkler, 2003), that is, anyone who is not "young."

To claim that the now dominant images of aging reinforce rather than challenge ageism may, at first glance, seem counter-intuitive. Isn't it better, one might ask, to see images of busy, apparently happy, fit-looking, even sexy, older people in film and TV, in magazine ads, and foundation reports than seeing the caricatures that now are marketed as humorous birthday cards or in ads for walkers or wheelchairs? Isn't it better that our image of an older woman is Academy award-winning actress Helen Mirren rather than the 70ish woman on the bus wearing unfashionable clothing and 40 extra pounds? Admittedly, this is a dilemma. The dilemma is, in part, created by this country's inability to overcome its historical patterns of dichotomous thinking in which there is a "good" and "bad" old age joined to the belief

---

[1]We thank Marty Martinson for this important observation.

that looking like Helen Mirren or a woman as elegant as she is or the woman on the bus is largely under our control (Cole, 1992). "Elevating the third [age] ... is only done by treading down the fourth. The labeling problem is wished on to even older and more defenseless older people" (Blaikie, 1999, citing Young & Schuller, 1991, p. 181). Affirming that one is not old or assuming the mask of aging by divorcing the inner from the outer self is self-defeating, for then one is "participating in one's own erasure" (Healey, 1994, p. 83).

To the extent that we are socially constituted, the unintentional de-valuing of people who no longer meet the norms of midlife can result in behaviors that are self-defeating—not asking for the loving arm, as Maggie Kuhn, the founder of the advocacy movement, the Gray Panthers, so comfortably did (also explored by Agich, 2003). The societal goal for fourth-agers, often internalized by these elders (Cohen, 1988) compared to the active engagement expected from third-agers, is rarely about a full life, albeit constrained by physical or cognitive changes, but more about preserving independence, which seems to mean little more than staying in the community (Cohen, 1988; Minkler, 1990). Choice continues to be a central commitment but it is too limited—choice itself is what is important even if that choice has little or no meaning to them (Agich, 1990, 1995). Deep old age thus becomes ever more frightening.

As people negotiate the changes that mark later life, the need for identity-preservation or re-creation and the maintenance of integrity are often urgent. Those goals cannot be met by the limited social goals just noted. As a result individuals may experience a sense of abandonment and isolation. We are not suggesting these problems were nonexistent prior to the advent of positive aging or the creation of the "third age" but rather that the inability to measure up to the emergent norms reinforces an already existing problem and deepens the possibilities for critical appraisal of one's life situation. The risk of reduced self-regard can further affect one's ability to make choices that reflect individual and social integrity, a challenge to the autonomy paradigm that so dominates thinking (see Chapter 10).

A FURTHER CONCERN: THE NON-POLITICAL AGENDA

As we have argued throughout this book, we see ethics as a means to expose hidden values and call attention to their differential impact on people based on the particular features of their lives. We are interested in the background conditions and messages that shape public attitudes and public policy and influence the contextually based choices that we make. Feminist work calls for analysis and social action. It calls for, in the words of Diana Meyers (1997) "heterodox moral perceptions" that "challenge established cultural values and norms" allowing one to see "suffering or harm that others do not notice ..." (p. 198). Hence, we add one more area of concern: that none of the manifestations of third age fillers has a substantive political agenda.

Not only do organizing efforts in the pursuit of social justice remain side-lined in these discourses, but they are strangely unconcerned with how their agendas build upon a lifetime of relative advantage. If one thinks, as we do, that autonomy is relational, as described in Chapter 2, then social institutions, public policies, and other features outside of the individual are critical to the choices we make and how we make them, and how we actually live. Personal dilemmas and choices are structured by public factors; hence altering the contexts affects our self-understanding and also establishes the conditions of possibility for us. Further, as Setterstein (2007) astutely observes, "amidst all this agelessness ... we do ourselves and old people a great disservice in the process. These emphases threaten to obscure ... the real underbellies of aging, and old age that must be acknowledged if they are to be dealt with effectively" (p. 25). In a clear synergy between social science and moral philosophy, Meyers (1997) notes that "unless some people see injustice and oppression that others deny, there will be no impetus for change" (p. 198). To see from the perspective of the marginalized is a critical political task.

Given the contrasts with the civil rights movement and the recognition that many older people are unable to be engaged in civic projects, we would expect that advocates of civic engagement, for example, would be committed to supporting projects that build a movement for improved social conditions not only for the old, but for families and younger people in different parts of their lives. This would not be easy to do but it would be desirable. Instead, it seems quite possible that the result of these efforts will be the erosion of popular support for key policies. It is hard to make a case for strengthening social security, for example, if health and relative affluence become the core identifiers of people in old age. As noted above, the "greedy geezer" is back in the news. Without organized effort, the drive to portray positive images of aging, can fuel efforts to change programs so essential for the well-being of far too many older people (see Chapter 6).

Thus, we find it peculiarly ironic that the senior employment program that develops low wage work opportunities for low income older people is often considered a form of civic engagement. For people so engaged, work is a necessity rather than an opportunity for joining self-fulfillment to social good. We wonder what choices these men and women would make if asked to consider what self-fulfillment would mean for their lives.

A TENTATIVE PROPOSAL: THE MEANING OF OLD AGE FOR INDIVIDUALS AND SOCIETIES

While we have probed and challenged emerging discourses about a "good" old age, we know that the cultural environment, whether explicitly normative or not, will influence us as we try to make sense of our own lives. So it is in our interest that this environment is not limited to images that are both unrecognizable and unrealizable by large numbers of people. In this last phase of our lives, we might want and need the greatest freedom possible to flourish in whatever way makes the most sense to us. While some 72-year-olds can still wear a bikini or a Speedo, most can't and probably have no wish to.

How then might older people find ways to differentiate their values and what they want and need from the dominant discourses? How might they create images that permit them to "construct their own self-portraits and self-narratives" that will enable them to lead lives of their own choosing (Meyers, 2002, p. 5). Meyers (2002) asks: How can we get in touch with ourselves and speak in our own voices when culture bombards us with its messages? While it is good that 25-year-olds see the 64-year-old Helen Mirren, looking glamorous and sexy, when they go to the movies, it is not good if her image reflects a dominant idea of what we all can or should be at age 60 or beyond. That the normative impact of civic engagement, productive aging, or postmodern aging is unintentional does not lessen its harm. What then would it take to create social conditions that "permit and encourage us to critically assess and influence the social ideals that in turn shape our lives?" (Clement, 1996, p. 25).

Since social groups are identity confirming (Nelson, 2001) and since we are encumbered selves that are influenced by culture, we can use dialogue or conversation with others, as a way to sort through what is valuable for us and what is not. The affirmation that we are leading valuable lives will gain strength in these micro-communities where we can consider and talk about the different elements of our identities. We can read about ways in which older individuals wrestle with what affirms that their lives are still worthy in biography, autobiography, fiction, poetry. Phillip Roth's recent novels (2007, 2006) capture, in his unique way, the struggles of a man increasingly shaped by his aging body. May Sarton's (1988, 1984, 1996) journals do not permit erasure of the effects of a stroke or the loss of intimate relationships or the joy of discovering a new one. Building on the communicative-dialogic model we support for "doing" ethical work (see Chapter 2), we propose a similar approach to telling stories of our old age. We look to these various sources—written and participatory—as ways to develop what Hilde Lindemann Nelson (2001) calls counter stories that repair damaged identities or lead us to our own voice so that we can re-tell our own story in the company of others. Such stories are flexible and adaptable to changes we experience. They do not demand a universal theme or a master story, especially one that demands we be "healthy, sexually active, engaged, productive, and self-reliant" (Cole, 1992). Nor do they demand that we be slim, graceful, and energetic. What if one is fearful and not so spry?

If communities of meaning—formal and informal—are critical elements in helping us to explore and grapple with what we fear, hope for, or find meaningful as we age, there is a further way that living well in old age takes more than individual effort. This means assuring that the foundation for a decent life is in place for all, not by relying on the efforts of elder volunteers but by public guarantees of a social safety net and by further developing opportunities for the possibilities for paid work or for voluntarism for those who may need or want to work or to volunteer. Opportunities are different than expectations. We support recent commitments to focus on changing the environment to meet the evolving needs of individuals as they age rather than focusing on the individual's need to adapt as his or her physical or cognitive capacities change. People around the United States today are developing elder friendly communities or expanding the village concept so that environments work for older people in wheelchairs or walkers or for those who simply must adopt a slower pace in general.

As people turn to communities of meaning, created or already existing, often hidden resources can be brought out to facilitate the claiming of one's own voice. Sara Ruddick's (1999) defense of virtues for old age, for example, tells us that older people want to be accountable and want to confirm their sense of agency but do so in non-oppressive ways. This means that virtue is never something we achieve but rather we work toward *ongoing efforts of virtue* (p. 52, italics in the original) in relation to other people. Ruddick thus, offers a relational definition of virtue—something that people make together as long as they have the network of "social relations and policies" that allow them to "watch thunderstorms, purchase sweaters, control some of the conditions of their death, and demand analgesics" (p. 54). They reflect a "slow journey to moments of insight and kindness" (Minkler & Holstein, 2008, p. 200). We may try to be kind, to not wear our pains too heavily, to help out where we can. Compared to other accounts of the virtues, Ruddick's view does not expect achievement, but only effort toward realizing virtues, knowing that we will have certain good days and certain bad ones.

The writings of older people, their art, and their ways of life, offer alternatives to the univocal vision of the active life. Consider how writers talk about their old age. Through their words they speak to us about triumphs, defeats, and everything in between. Petrarch, a humanist in the early years of the Italian Renaissance, gracefully acknowledges old age and does not regret the changes it has brought. Poet Stanley Kunitz (2000) ends his poem *Touch Me* with these words:

> So let the battered old willow
> thrash against the windowpanes
> and the house timbers creak.
> Darling do you remember
> the man you married? Touch me,
> remind me who I am.
>
> —*Kunitz, 2000, p. 266*

Jungian analyst Florida Scott-Maxwell (1979) seethes with a wild energy that she cannot express and then delights in sharing talk about her infirmities with her age peers. Writer Doris Grumbach (1991), in her 70s, still traveling, still writing nonetheless sees the time ahead as if she's in a closed room, with the door shut in front of her and the wall behind her moving closer. As Rentsch (1997) affirmed, from a distance, finitude does matter. We regret that these views from literature lack the attention in print or in the media that, for example, civic engagement has achieved. Late writings can tell us much about old age from the inside, yet, they are marginal to the conversation about the "third age."

We can learn about the varied ways people have made sense of aging and old age without first denying that it actually exists. We take succor from others around us who help to sustain our identity and values even as the facts of our material bodies and our socioeconomic location may challenge us. We've explored the risks associated with overarching narratives of what it is good to be in old age. While we are sympathetic to the intent of these narratives, we are wary of their seeming certainty. Old age is a bundle of contradictions but not an unhappy time if basic needs are met. Hence, we reaffirm the heterogeneity of the category "old" and argue for the "bottom-up" development of stories about "my old age." The stories grow naturally in micro-communities like the beauty shop studied by Frida Furman (1997) where women could support one another in their resistance to the dominant ideal of the world outside the beauty shop that derogated their thinning hair and "turkey neck." Their concern about how they are perceived in that world, however, is an indication of how powerful those images are. We can hear these stories any place where people gather to talk about aging and old age from the inside much like the consciousness raising groups that ushered in second wave feminism in the early 1970s.

This many pronged approach to seeing, hearing, and reading about how people actually make sense of old age avoids the relentlessly positive view that does a disservice to the many people who are hurting both physically and psychologically. Bodies are real and our identities are inevitably influenced by our experiences as embodied selves. Denial is not a good strategy but, as Florida Scott-Maxwell (1979) so effectively points out, complaint is only for our age peers; younger people don't want to hear of our aches and pains but with others like us, we can complain, but also laugh, about them.

Thus, in our view, we cannot evade the dark side of aging. Instead, we need a model of resistance that allows older people to integrate the changes that are happening despite their best efforts at control. The "third age" is "lived against a background of realization of what comes next." The meaning of any activity ... is colored by awareness of a powerfully ambiguous future (Rubenstein, 2002, p. 39). Yet, by emphasizing the "dark side" we further separate the old from everyone else and reassociate aging with illness and death. There must be another way to regain a balance that existed prior to the 19th century between the positive and negative poles of aging so that we do not marginalize people whose physical or cognitive capacities make them dependent upon others, or elevate those who are fortunate enough to retain vigor and good health into their 80s or 90s. It is here as well that the humanities, where nuance is central, can help us.

CONCLUSION

Throughout this chapter, we have noted the critical importance of context in making later life a place of reasonable contentment and acceptance. We have also called for a political agenda since, in its absence, too many older people will have little of that leisure to do anything with their lives but work and fear falling off the edge. If later life is to be truly a time of freedom (for women especially, given that this may be the only time they are free to pursue their own dreams and goals) they need the resources to enjoy this freedom. A mere right to choose, to be left alone, does not offer many older persons the opportunity to experience the freedom they might otherwise enjoy.

From small groups, whether in living rooms or public places, conferences or virtual communities, much like the consciousness raising groups of the 1970s, older people can work to claim their own voices. From there, ideas may travel "upwards" so that they can begin to transform cultural attitudes and reflect the facts of aging and the multiple voices of people from the margins as well as from the center. The starting place for a denser, more democratic sense of the potential for both the third and the fourth ages is "the embodied, socially situated, and divided self" who is able to develop a "rich understanding of what one is like" and is also able to make adjustments as one's capacities change (Meyers, 2002, p. 22). What is seen as a valued life in old age must be open to more than the relatively few.

Yet, culture remains important and thus the now-dominant norms for the "third age" require continued scrutiny and challenge. This task will not be easy. While gerontologists might not have social power, the media and other cultural vehicles that pick up the new discourses do. That's why media giants like Helen Mirren or Meryl Streep are so important. While most older people recognize that these images are not them, the norms that this chapter has discussed encode meanings of aging that we have argued are not reflective of or suitable for many, if not most, older people in this country. They create social and personal expectations that can damage a self already trying to make sense of changes that are not culturally favored. Acts of resistance are difficult, in part because these "third age" ideals are so attractive, but they are necessary lest these emergent norms become even further entrenched. We have proposed micro-communities as places of support and meaning-making that can confront figurations that don't fit one's self-conception. In such communities, one can tell the truth about oneself, and the communities can correct one's story or redirect one's thinking in ways that are helpful and enlightening. We have also suggested that for such communities to flourish, basic security is critical. One is apt to worry less about meaning and identity than getting food on the table.

In closing, we suggest that challenges to these norms must also occur in the professional circles in which they have taken hold. The excitement that these new norms generate is palpable. Using ethics as a source of critical consciousness, we can raise questions about the unexamined commitment to norms that are potentially damaging to so many. We must take advantage of every opportunity (and create opportunities) to offer more emancipatory imagery. This chapter is one such opportunity.

REFERENCES

Agich, G. (1990). Reassessing autonomy in long-term care. *Hastings Center Report*, 20(6), 12–17.

Agich, G. (1995). Actual autonomy and long-term care decision making. In L. B. McCullough & N. L. Wilson (Eds.), *Ethical and conceptual dimensions of long-term care decision making*. Baltimore, MD: Johns Hopkins Press.

Agich, G. (2003). *Dependency and autonomy in old age: An ethical framework for long-term care*. New York, NY: Cambridge University Press.

Andrews, M. (1999). The seductiveness of agelessness. *Ageing and Society, 19*, 301–318.

Atchley, R. (1987). *Aging: Continuity and change*. Belmont, CA: Wadsworth.

Baltes, P., & Baltes, M. (1990). *Successful aging: Perspectives from the behavioral sciences*. Cambridge, UK: Cambridge University Press.

Bass, S., Caro, F., & Chen, Y.-P. (Eds.) (1993). *Achieving a productive aging society*. Westport, CT: Auburn Press.

Biggs, S. (2001). Toward a critical narrativity: Stories of aging in contemporary social policy. *Journal of Aging Studies, 15*, 303–316.

Blaikie, A. (1999). *Aging and popular culture*. Cambridge, UK: Cambridge University Press.

Chapman, A. (2004). Ethical implications of prolonged lives. *Theology Today, 60*(4), 479–496.

Clement, G. (1996). *Care, autonomy, and justice: Feminism and the ethic of care*. Boulder, CO: Westview Press.

Cohen, E. (1988). The elderly mystique: Constraints on the autonomy on the elderly with disabilities. *The Gerontologist, 28*(Suppl.), 24–31.

Cole, T. (1992). *The journey of life: A cultural history of aging in America*. New York, NY: Cambridge University Press.

Dannefer, D. (2003). Cumulative advantage/disadvantage and the life course: Cross fertilizing age and social science theory. *Journal of Gerontology: Social Sciences, 58B*(6), S327–S337.

Ekherdt, D. J. (1996). "The busy ethic": Moral continuity between work and retirement. *The Gerontologist, 26*(3), 239–244.

Flanagan, O. (1991). *Varieties of moral personality: Ethics and psychological realism*. Cambridge, MA: Harvard University Press.

Friedan, B. (1993). *The fountain of age*. New York, NY: Simon & Schuster.

Furman, F. (1997). *Facing the mirror: Old women and beauty shop culture*. New York, NY: Routledge.

Furman, F. (1999). There are no older Venuses: Women's responses to their aging bodies. In M. U. Walker (Ed.), *Mother time: Women, aging, and ethics*. Lanham, MD: Rowman & Littlefield.

Gergen, K., & Gergen, M. (2000). The new aging: Self construction and social values. In K. W. Schaie & J. Hendricks (Eds.), *The evolution of the aging self: The social impact on the aging process* (pp. 281–306). New York, NY: Springer.

Gilleard, C., & Higgs, P. (2000). *Cultures of aging: Self, aging and the body*. New York, NY: Prentice-Hall.

Grumbach, D. (1991). *Coming into the end zone: A memoir*. New York, NY: W. W. Norton & Co.

Harper, S. (1997). Constructing later life/constructing the body: Some reflections from feminist theory. In A. Jamieson, S. Harper, & S. Victor (Eds.), *Critical approaches to aging and later life* (pp. 160–172). Buckingham, UK: Open University Press.

Healey, S. (1994). Growing to be an old woman: Aging and ageism. In E. Stoller & R. Gibson (Eds.) (1999), *Worlds of difference: Inequality in the aging experience* (1st ed.). Thousand Oaks, CA: Pine Forge Press.

Holstein, M. (2006). A critical reflection on civic engagement. *Public Policy and Agency Report, 16*(4), 1, 21–26.

Holstein, M., & Minkler, M. (2003). Self, society and the 'new gerontology.' *The Gerontologist, 43*(6), 787–796.

Huntington, S. (2000). Foreword. In L. Harrison & S. Huntington (Eds.), *Culture matters: How values shape human progress*. New York, NY: Basic Books.

Kunitz, S. (2000). *The collected poems*. New York, NY: W. W. Norton & Co.

Laslett, P. (1991). *A fresh map of life: The emergence of the third age*. Cambridge: Harvard University Press.

Lindemann, H. (2006). *An invitation to feminist ethics*. New York, NY: McGraw-Hill.

Lindemann Nelson, H. (2001). *Damaged identities, narrative repair.* Ithaca, NY: Cornell University Press.

Mackenzie, C., & Stoljar, N. (Eds.) (2000). *Relational autonomy: Feminist perspectives on autonomy, agency and the social order.* New York, NY: Oxford University Press.

Martinson, M., & Minkler, M. (2006). Civic engagement and older adults: A critical perspective. *The Gerontologist, 46*(3), 318–324.

McLaughlin, S., Connell, C., Heerings, S., Li, L., & Roberts, J. S. (2009). Successful aging in the United States: Prevalence estimates from a national sample of older adults. *Journal of Gerontology: Social Sciences, 65B*(2), 216–226.

Meyers, D. (1997). Emotion and heterodox moral perception: An essay in moral social psychology. In D. Meyers (Ed.), *Feminists re-think the self* (pp. 197–218). Boulder, CO: Westview Press.

Meyers, D. (2002). *Gender in the mirror. Cultural imagery and women's agency.* New York, NY: Oxford University Press.

Minkler, M. (1990). Aging and disability: Behind and beyond the stereotypes. *Journal of Aging Studies, 4*(3), 245–260.

Minkler, M., Fuller-Thomson, E., & Guralnik, J. (2006). *New England Journal of Medicine, 355*(7), 695–703.

Minkler, M., & Holstein, M. (2008). From civil rights to … civic engagement? Concerns of two older critical gerontologists about a "new social movement" and what it portends. *Journal of Aging Studies, 22*, 196–204.

Morrow-Howell, N. (2000). *Productive engagement of older adults: Effects on well-being.* Center for Social Development St. Louis, MO: Washington University.

Phillipson, C. (1998). *Reconstructing old age: New agendas in social theory and practice.* London: Sage.

Post, S., & Binstock, R. (2004). *The fountain of youth: Cultural, scientific, and ethical perspectives on a biomedical goal.* New York, NY: Oxford University Press.

Putnam, R. (1995). Bowling alone: America's declining social capital. *Journal of Democracy, 6*(1), 65–78.

Reilly, S. (2006). Transforming aging: The civic engagement of adults 55+. *Public Policy and Aging Report, 16*(4), 1, 3–7.

Rentsch, T. (1997). Aging as becoming oneself: A philosophical ethics of late life. *Journal of Aging Studies, 11*, 263–271.

Roth, P. (2006). *Everyman.* Boston: Houghton Mifflin.

Roth, P. (2007). *Exit ghost.* Boston: Houghton Mifflin.

Rowe, J. W., & Kahn, R. L. (1987). Human aging: Usual and successful. *Science, 237*, 263–271.

Rubenstein, R. (2002). The third age. In S. Weiss & S. Bass (Eds.), *Challenges of the third age: Meaning and purpose in late life* (pp. 41–54). New York, NY: Oxford University Press.

Ruddick, S. (1999). Virtues and age. In M. W. Walker (Ed.), *Mother time: Women, aging, and ethics* (pp. 45–60). Lanham, MD: Rowman & Littlefield.

Sadler, W. (Fall 2006). Changing life options: Uncovering the riches of the third age. In *The LLI Review, 1*, 11–20.

Sarton, M. (1984). *At seventy.* New York, NY: W. W. Norton & Co.

Sarton, M. (1988). *After the stroke.* New York, NY: W. W. Norton & Co.

Sarton, M. (1996). *At eighty-two: A journal.* New York, NY: W. W. Norton & Co.

Scott-Maxwell, F. (1979). *Measure of my days.* New York, NY: Penguin Books.

Setterstein, R. (2007). 10 reasons why shake-ups in the life course should change approaches to old-age policies. *Aging and Public Policy Report, 17*(3), 1, 21–27.

Taylor, C. (1984). *Sources of the self.* Cambridge, MA: Harvard University Press.

Walker, M. (1999). Introduction. In M. Walker (Ed.), *Mother time: Women, aging, and ethics* (pp. 1–6). Lanham, MD: Rowman & Littlefield.

Wider Opportunities for Women. *The elder economic security initiative.* www.wowonline.org.

Young, I. M. (1990). *Justice and the politics of difference.* Princeton, NJ: Princeton University Press.

Young, M., & Schuller, T. (1991). *Life after work: The arrival of the ageless society.* London: HarperCollins. Cited in A. Blaikie 1999.

CHAPTER 5

Anti-aging Medicine

INTRODUCTION

In 1999, futurist and transhumanist Max More wrote "A Letter to Mother Nature," in which he lays out his transhumanist position. In his letter he states:

> Mother Nature, truly we are grateful for what you have made us. No doubt you did the best you could. However, with all due respect, we must say that you have in many ways done a poor job with the human constitution. You have made us vulnerable to disease and damage. You compel us to age and die—just as we're beginning to attain wisdom ... You made us functional only under narrow environmental conditions ... . And, you forgot to give us the operating manual for ourselves!
>
> What you have made us is glorious, yet deeply flawed. You seem to have lost interest in our further evolution some 100,000 years ago. Or perhaps you have been biding your time, waiting for us to take the next step ourselves. Either way, we have reached our childhood's end.
>
> We have decided that it is time to amend the human constitution.
> —More, 1999 (http://www.maxmore.com/mother.htm)

More's transhumanist mission statement exemplifies an increasingly common view that human biology is malleable and that in the near future we will be capable of overcoming much of our current biological "programming." Like other such futurists—most notably, Ray Kurzweil (2005), Marvin Minsky (2006), Judy Campisi (2000), and Roy Walford (2000), More holds that aging is a genetic "mistake" that nanotechnologies will be capable of fixing at the genetic, microlevel.

Most famously, inventor, scientist and scholar Ray Kurzweil has argued that, within the next 30–40 years, we will achieve "the Singularity," a predictable, theoretical future point in time where technological progress surpasses anything we have ever seen before. As Kurzweil claims,

> The key idea underlying the impending Singularity is that the pace of change of our human-created technology is accelerating and its powers are expanding at an exponential pace .... The Singularity will allow us to transcend ... our biological bodies and brains. We will gain power over our fates. Our mortality will be in our own hands. We will be able to live for as long as we want ...
>
> —*Kurzweil, 2005, pp. 7–9*

That human beings are journeying toward this "posthumanist" future where technology allows us to overcome our human nature may be difficult for many critics to take seriously; but the commitment to developing and using cutting-edge technology to overcome biology does not run against prevailing social attitudes. As Carole Haber (2001, 2004) indicates, in some regards this desire for longevity has persisted over the ages. As far back as the ancient Egyptians, people, especially those with discretionary resources, sought ways to stall or reverse the effects of aging (Mori & Sasakura, 2009). The majority of such products or efforts have been purely cosmetic, resulting in various makeup products, ointments, and emollients (see, e.g., Angerhofer, Maes, & Giacomoni, 2008). We have through the millennia also consumed various dietary supplements touted as relieving the ravages of aging, not just cosmetically, but also internally. Furthermore, the medical profession has played its own role in anti-aging endeavors, offering face-lifts, breast-lifts, and the like in order to forestall or temporarily reverse the appearance of aging. Certain medical interventions—from arthritis medications to hip or knee replacements to treatment for osteoporosis—may help alleviate some of the unwanted bodily changes for which advancing age is a risk factor. Interventions of these sorts, however, do not actually stop or alter the aging process itself; they merely camouflage or treat some of its unwanted effects. More radical thinkers or adventurers have thus attacked the very root of the "problem," by attempting to cure old age itself: take, for example, Ponce de Leon's search for the proverbial "fountain of youth" (Olshansky, Hayflick, & Carnes, 2002).

Our present age, then, is no exception to this long-standing human wish to somehow control the seemingly undesirable effects of advancing age. If anything, our youth-oriented culture (Westerhof & Barrett, 2005) would seem to exacerbate this inclination amongst human beings. And unlike the snake-oil salesmen of previous eras, the biomedical enterprise, with its remarkable rate of technological and scientific advancement in recent years, would appear to have treatments that are indeed far more effective than anything previously seen. Nevertheless, this contemporary anti-aging movement leaves many persons quite unsettled. We may very well wonder what kind of changes we are talking about, whether they would they really work, and whether we are sensible, or morally wise, to pursue such innovations. While transhumanists like Kurzweil and others are focused on the ultimate goal of achieving human longevity, in this chapter we are more concerned with the ethical, social, and political implications of doing so. Thus, our focus will be on the promise of anti-aging medicine and its implications in an ageist, economically stratified, and autonomy-obsessed society.

WHAT IS ANTI-AGING MEDICINE?

It is widely understood that biomedicine is attacking aging in two different ways: by researching compressed morbidity (Buckley, 2001; Fries, 2003), and by attempting to slow or even reverse the aging process itself (De Gray et al., 2002; Juengst et al., 2003). With regard to compressed morbidity, most people are well aware that advanced aging is associated with a variety of undesirable medical effects or events. The list might include osteoporosis, arthritis, weakening immune system, loss of muscle tone, increased risk of cardiovascular disease and various cancers, and, of course, dementia of various types, especially Alzheimer's disease (Juengst et al., 2003). The goal in compressed morbidity is to identify these undesired conditions that are associated with aging and to find effective treatments for them. The aim is neither to defeat age itself nor to extend the human life span; rather it is to treat the bad effects associated with aging (Fries, 2003). The ideal is a long, full life, relieved of the painful and debilitating chronic conditions that so often plague old age. Under compressed morbidity, when death does come, it does not follow a long, slow, downward decline, but instead comes as a rather (pleasantly) abrupt ending to a full, active, rewarding life; a lifestyle that one is able to maintain until the very end (Fries, 2000).

Whether a distinction can be sustained between such morbidity-reduction aims versus life extension aims, remains open to debate. As Eric Juengst aptly points out, in many instances, effective treatment of particular diseases may often also contribute towards longer life (Juengst, 2004, pp. 321–339). In that sense, there is a certain "creep" in biomedical technology application: research and implementation couched with one goal in mind will often wind up contributing to other aims as well. Thus, while there might be some conceptual distinction that can be made between the intent to decrease morbidity and the intent to extend the human life span, in practice there is likely to be considerable overlap.

Between successful public health measures and biomedical innovation, western developed nations have been relatively successful in their efforts to extend average life expectancy. Average life expectancy has risen substantially over the last century in these nations (Oeppen & Vaupel, 2002), and while advanced years continue to be associated with undesirable chronic conditions, quite a few of them now have meaningful biomedical interventions. On the public health side, improving water and food quality, general nutrition, and a reduction in smoking (Mann, 1997; Overall, 2003; Taylor et al., 2002) have all contributed to longer average life and decreased morbidity. On the biomedical side, anti-inflammatory medications and, in extreme cases, joint replacements have done much to relieve the symptoms of connective tissue diseases and disorders. The treatment of infectious diseases has vastly improved. Interventions with at least some limited success now exist for osteoporosis, urinary incontinence, and erectile dysfunction, while statins hold the promise of significantly reducing cardiovascular disease.

Still, it must be acknowledged that there are some resistant, stubborn afflictions for which advancing age is a significant risk factor. There has been no silver bullet found for cancer, despite decades of work and promise, and, similarly, dementia continues to prove remarkably resistant to treatment. Decreased sensory sensitivity—taste, touch, smell, vision—remain challenges to the aging population, though there has been some progress.

Nevertheless, in principle, who could possibly object to such ambitions? There may, perhaps, be some social justice issues such as those posed by Callahan (1987) and Daniels (1988) who raised the question some years ago: Is it morally right to devote such resources to curing afflictions late in life when so many persons of younger generations are quite lacking in adequate health care or even decent educational opportunities? These are issues to which we will return later in this chapter.

The ambition to compress morbidity at least on the surface accepts that there is a natural, preordained human life span. What it supposedly tries to do is to maximize the average life expectancy within that life span and minimize morbidity during those life years. Successfully curing or effectively managing the various diseases associated with old age may indeed add some years to average life expectancy, but doing so is not thought of as adding significantly to a given upper limit of human aging, an upper limit that many biologists suggest hovers between 100 and 120 years (Olshansky et al., 1990; Wilmoth, 2000). But, aggressive anti-aging theorists and researchers argue that such an upper limit need not be seen as an absolute given (Campisi, 2000; Caplan, 2004; Kurzweil, 2005). Instead, their efforts are explicitly geared towards changing that seemingly given upper limit. Anti-aging medicine thus aims to change our human nature, our human biology, such that we not only live healthier but substantially longer.

As noted above, extended life has, for centuries now, been the wish of many humans. Over time, various pseudo-doctors have enticed customers with elixirs and exotic treatments that promise to extend life. All of these interventions have so far proven to be false promises (Olshansky et al., 2002; Wick, 2002). However, the past two decades have seen considerable interest, investment, and enthusiasm for finally achieving this long-sought-after goal. Indeed, in no small way, the field of gerontology has been divided between those who see both promise in anti-aging medicine and the need to aggressively pursue it (de Grey et al., 2002; Miller, 2002) against those who see such promises as nothing more than false, deceptive, and harmful propaganda (Hayflick, 2002; Holden, 2002). The schism represents not only differing visions, but more concretely, an intense competition over limited research funds and the prospect of immense commercial revenues (Binstock, 2004).

THE PROPONENTS OF ANTI-AGING TECHNOLOGY

Proponents of anti-aging medicine have gained substantial media attention in the recent decade. They can now boast several journals such as *The International Journal of Anti-Aging Medicine*, the *Journal of Longevity*, and the *Journal of Anti-Aging Medicine*. One of the most prominent organizations in the cause is the American Academy of Anti-Aging Medicine, now colloquially known as the "A4M." The A4M, under the leadership of its president, Ronald Klatz, and its chairman, Robert Goldman, argues that the dramatic increase in life expectancy over the last century in particular is a direct result of the exponential increase in biomedical technology (Klatz, 2006; Klatz & Goldman, 1996, 1997). Extrapolating from the growth curve describing life expectancy over the last several centuries, they project a future where the human life span will be indefinitely extensible.

The means by which we are to achieve this age revolution remain somewhat vague. The more recent entrants into this contest of biomedical technology have included hormone therapy, calorie restriction, and human stem cells. Hormone therapy focuses its promise on the use of human growth hormone, estrogen, progesterone, and testosterone. The theory is that if these hormones are abundant in the body in youth, but decline in quantity precipitously as we progress through adulthood, then pumping the body up with replacement human growth hormone would help us recover the bloom of youth (Bartke et al., 2000; Harman & Blackman, 2004). While billions of dollars were spent by eager consumers in this endeavor, the accumulating clinical evidence has revealed no improvement in quality of life or in length of life. In contrast, the tactic of calorie restriction has been clinically effective in certain mammals, adding as much as 30–40% to the usual maximum life span. But, by many measures, the quality of life of these calorie-restricted mice may seem to leave something to be desired: they are physically diminutive, physically and psychologically aggressive, and apparently hungry all the time (Heilbronn & Ravussin, 2003). Not surprisingly, few humans have shown sufficient enthusiasm to stick with such severe calorie restriction.

Stem cell research has also been suggested as holding some promise in this regard. As particular organs begin to fail through aging, a rejuvenating dose of youthful stem cells would be used to revitalize the organ in need. Such trials have had, thus far, very limited success, marginally improving pancreatic function or speeding the process of the heart growing new vessels for cardiovascular circulation. But, results in treating the brain—Parkinson's disease being an experimental candidate—have not been very encouraging thus far.

The newest promise and current star, however, in this quest for seeming immortality has been the idea of genetic therapy. The premise here is that as our cells divide during our lives, they gradually experience wear and tear in our genetic material. The ends of these long chains of telomeres, in particular, become broken, losing bits and pieces. For some unknown causal reason, such aged cells gradually lose certain self-maintenance skills, apparently giving rise to many of those age-related diseases or conditions. The energy of this research, therefore, is into methods of repairing those telomeres, thus restoring those cells to a kind of youthful state, not just cosmetically, but at a basic biological cellular level (Caplan, 2004).

While it may be tempting to focus on the technologies at issue, there is also a moral question that drives the anti-aging movement. Whether or not one chooses to regard advanced age as a disease in and of itself is not really the crux of the issue. Instead, a major concern is that aging tends to be expensive to society and causes vast human suffering. As Tom Mackey (2003) claims, the anti-aging movement seeks to fulfill a duty to maintain health and prevent disease, a duty to efficiently reduce morbidity and mortality, a respect for autonomy (those who want should be allowed to purchase anti-aging products and services, so long as they are not harmful), and the promotion of a better quality of life.

THE CRITICS OF ANTI-AGING TECHNOLOGY

The critics of anti-aging medicine remain convinced that the effort will be a failure, and suggest that, even worse, it could prove harmful.

As already acknowledged, the compression of morbidity has seen real progress. Still, some of the worst scourges of older age, such as Alzheimer's disease, remain resistant to such interventions. There remains the worry in some quarters, therefore, that while we may have been fairly successful at reducing early death, some of the worst, chronic conditions associated with advanced age are still with us (Fukuyama, 2002). We may have bought some more time, but it is not always necessarily a great bargain if the price of that extended time means chronic pain, debility, and/or dementia.

Yet ardent proponents of cellular rejuvenation, particularly through genetic therapy, still hold out the promise that this time, with this technology, we will finally succeed. We confess to being somewhat skeptical of this claim. Wishing is one thing; and seducing investors or customers is yet another. But real success may be something else. The history of medicine, including biomedicine, is littered with golden promises that fail to deliver. Many of us may still recall the earnest pleas of the American Cancer Society, starting in the 1960s, that "the cure" for cancer was just around the corner. Yet more than 40 years later, while there have admittedly been significant improvements in particular types of cancer care, there is no silver bullet cure. And no matter how many presidential mandates there are to find such a cure, it proves elusive. Part of the problem, as scientists have learned, is that cancer is a variegated and complex disease. Even breast cancer, though it may have a single umbrella term, seems not to be one single, universal disease.

Likewise, researchers are learning that aging is not controlled by one single gene. It is not triggered by one single environmental factor. Furthermore, genetic therapy, which has been held out by some as having the most promise in terms of cellular rejuvenation, does not have an encouraging track record. As research scientists worked enthusiastically in the decade of the 1990s at "decoding" the human genome, biomedical researchers touted the coming golden age of genetic therapy. But thus far, the hundreds of human protocols attempting genetic therapy have had precious few good outcomes. In the vast majority of protocols, researchers simply could not find an effective vector for introducing and distributing the desired genetic material into the millions upon millions of existing cells in the human body. In the most regrettable of cases, there was actually injury to the research subjects, including in at least one publicly notable protocol (the

"Gelsinger" case at University of Pennsylvania), in which a research subject died as a direct result of the attempted genetic modification. In a different protocol, human subjects subjected to attempted genetic therapy developed leukemia type cancers.

In *The Quest for Immortality: Science at the Frontiers of Aging* (2001), Olshansky and Carnes offer a critical and sobering assessment of the anti-aging movement (see also, Olshansky, Hayflick, & Carnes, 2002; Olshansky et al., 2004). Hormone therapies have been clinically proven to be not only useless, but harmful. Estrogen supplements, in particular, are now tied to an increased risk of breast cancer in women. Major successes in stem cell therapies are seemingly lacking. And attempts at genetic therapies have been mostly useless, and on occasions, deadly.

Admittedly, it may well be true that responsible research may wind up adding a few years on to average human life expectancy; but that is not the same thing as actually making any meaningful increase in human life span. For a variety of reasons, therefore, we remain skeptical of the rather grand claims on behalf of anti-aging medicine that are geared toward real, significant extension of normal human life span. Nevertheless, this is not a question that can be settled, *a priori*, by armchair philosophers. It remains a question of biomedical science.

Let us first suppose that the technology will eventually work. If so, we feel we must ask some important questions. First, would it be wise, that is, morally wise, to adopt and use such technology? Second, and relatedly, would it be morally just to offer such a technology? After exploring those questions, we shall revert to the possibility that the technology simply will not work, at least not in any grand and meaningful way, and we shall then ask if there is a hidden moral cost—in human suffering—that seems to result simply from our enthusiastic pursuit of this ambition, even if it never truly works.

IS AN ANTI-AGING AGENDA MORALLY WISE?

As noted above, proponents of anti-aging medicine argue that not only is their quest morally permissible, but there are compelling moral obligations to work in this direction. The potential to relieve pain and suffering, to promote health, to serve economic efficiency, and to uphold individual choice all seem like worthwhile ends. Nevertheless, the desirability, moral or otherwise, of life extension is a point that has been debated for centuries. The durability of Pone de Leon's quest is a testament to our continuing interest, as a species, in this possibility.

One very vocal criticism of such anti-aging endeavors is grounded upon the notion that there is something about altering human nature that is fundamentally morally wrong. Proponents of this critique include Leon Kass (2003), Francis Fukuyama (2002), and Daniel Callahan (1987). In their own ways, each of these authors seems to invest "nature" or the natural order" with a kind of moral status, a version of the naturalistic fallacy: the way things are, is the way things are supposed to be. According to Kass,

> Conquering death is not something that we can try for a while and then decide whether the results are better or worse—according to, God only knows what standard. On the contrary, this is a question in which our very humanity is at stake, not only in the consequences but also in the very meaning of the choice. For to argue that human life would be better without death is, I submit, to argue that human life would be better being something other than human.
> —Kass, 2003, p. 330

If we attempt to dramatically alter human nature by tinkering in such a way as to significantly increase the current maximum life span, then we are hubristically engaged in trying to eliminate human nature itself.

Such natural law or traditionalist arguments founder, as we can see, on some common sorts of worries. Just what do we mean by "natural"? Consider that, contrary to Kass' concerns, Arthur Caplan has understood aging as *unnatural* and thus, like any other medical problem, something to be prevented. Caplan states that "Aging has all of the relevant markings of a disease process. It has none of the attributes of a functional process. The explanation of why aging occurs has many of the attributes ... [of a] chance phenomenon. And this makes aging unnatural and in no way an intrinsic part of human nature" (2004, p. 283). Thus, who decides what counts as "natural"? If we are wary of the argument that would make anti-aging efforts morally wrong on the basis of their "unnatural" intent, we may look to likely outcomes as the kind of information that might help us to see such interventions as morally right or wrong.

Would successful anti-aging technology be desirable? Would we really, in the end, find it beneficial? Philosophers seem to be of a mixed mind about this question. Bernard Williams, in discussing "The Makropoulos Case," (1973) paints a philosophical picture of the agony of living indefinitely. Thomas Nagel (1979), on the other hand, sees no reason why a life of 200 or 300 years might not still be full of varied and interesting experience. Indeed, he suggests that Williams simply suffers from a lack of imagination.

How might one decide these types of questions? These do not appear to be problems of logic; they are empirical questions. And good answers to empirical questions are grounded, we believe, on good empirical data. But in these questions, we need to be clear about what kind of empirical data we need.

When we come to the case of dramatic extension of human life span, where shall we look for our empirical evidence from which to make our moral arguments? It is important here that we are not discussing relatively small, incremental change; we are speaking of a dramatic extension of human life span (Kurzweil, 2005). Since the evolutionary emergence of homo sapiens, we have faced a seemingly absolute upper limit of about 100 years, with 122 being the oldest well-documented human life (Whitney, 1997). Human families, communities, economic relations, and life rituals are all structured around what has been seen as a "given." Marital relations and obligations, social power structures, inheritance (not just economic, but more importantly political and environmental), are all built around the understanding of the rise and passing of generational cohorts.

We believe that what we see as moral virtues, and what we perceive as ethical obligations, are to some extent the result of our lived environment. The virtues we might have admired in a stone-age hunter–gatherer society are likely to be different from those we admire most in a developed, consumer–capitalist society. But, in at least this sense, the "naturalists" are right in arguing that dramatically resetting the human biological clock would fundamentally alter our human nature. With such a different human nature, can we really imagine in any reliable sense what life would be like? If death is not around the corner, then why hurry? As Kass points out, "To know and to feel that one goes around only once, and that the deadline is not out of sight, is for many people the necessary spur to the pursuit of something worthwhile" (2002, p. 324). If death is not relentlessly approaching, why strive at certain kinds of tasks? For many philosophers and theologians, the unavoidable approach of death is what drives and frames our efforts at creating meaning (Callahan, 1988; Heidegger, 1962; Kass, 2002). The indefinite postponement of death may significantly alter one's pursuit of a meaningful life.

FEMINIST AND SOCIAL JUSTICE CONCERNS

Absent from much of the debate surrounding anti-aging medicine is a serious focus on the feminist and social justice concerns that we believe are core to an adequate ethical and social/political analysis of it. We take from feminist theologian and social ethicist Karen Lebacq (1995) some basic criteria for practices that are acceptable from a feminist viewpoint: they must be life giving and just ice inducing, as defined by women, and they must positively address the poor and oppressed.

A robust ethical examination of anti-aging medicine also addresses the visions or ideals for later life that it upholds. It is our view that, short of a major cultural upheaval, older women will experience the negative effects of anti-aging medicine more forcefully than will men. Our concerns are connected to Karen Lebacq's criteria of practices acceptable to feminists: (1) women are more disadvantaged socially and economically than men (especially in the global context), a cause of women's relative powerlessness and marginalization; (2) perceptions of women's bodies are central to their experiences in the world, with ethical and practical consequences that are often negative (see Chapter 3); and (3) women's bodies have historically been "medicalized," that is, treated as if normal conditions were pathological, requiring medical intervention, and placed under the control of men. Furthermore, because anti-aging medicine will be a commodity, invidious class, race, economic, and ethnic distinctions related to who receives what will also arise, leading to the further marginalization of women already defined as "other" and made invisible as subjects (Young, 1990). These implications of anti-aging medicine are morally and practically significant because they can influence in negative ways the perceptions women have of themselves, their identity, and their sense of moral worthiness, while at the same time exacerbating class distinctions.

As we argue in Chapter 2, to study an issue through the lens of gender is to expose what a more "neutral" analysis often fails to notice. A gender-based analysis identifies unacknowledged problems or alternative definitions of problems. To take just one example, when Nora Kizer Bell (1997) criticized Daniel Callahan's (1991) call to limit life-extending care to the elderly, she did so from a perspective that was absent from his argument: the impact such limiting of care would have on women, who survive to be the "oldest old" members of society. Thus, feminist analysis has the power to redefine problems, to elevate new problems, and to include previously excluded forms of knowing.

Feminism is a particularistic lens; women see differently not because of their sex, but because material and historical conditions have given them a particular vantage point from which to view the world. A different perspective can lead to perception of a problem and, thus, action to remedy it. A different perspective can also redefine needs and hence the manner in which society addresses them. That very act of defining needs—often ignored but highly political—establishes the concerns that public policy addresses.

The questions are several. Will anti-aging medicine improve or worsen the position of women within society? Will it support or undermine the prevailing social order and accompanying social arrangements? Will anti-aging medicine affect, in any way, the constraints imposed by poverty, social position, and primary responsibilities for caring tasks? Does anti-aging medicine reflect and reinforce conventional gender images in the U.S. consumer culture—in particular cultural attitudes that demean a woman's aging body? What are the implications of anti-aging medicine when we take the facts of privilege and disadvantage seriously? We must consider how anti-aging medicine may influence a woman's self-development as she encounters changes associated with aging, when the social message is that these changes are preventable.

These questions are not answered in the same way by all feminists. For example, Martha Holstein (2001) anticipates some potentially negative implications of anti-aging medicine, while Christine Overall (2003) regards it in a more positive light. For example, Holstein claims that

> Anti-aging medicine does not address causes of ill health that have their roots throughout the life course like poverty, hard physical labor, environmental degradation, or consistent stress that affect great numbers of women. By so focusing on the end of the lifespan, anti-aging medicine supports the political tendency to ignore the causes of much ill health.
> —Holstein, 2001, p. 41

Overall, by adopting a feminist virtue ethics approach to the prolongation of human life sees positive potential in anti-aging medicine. As she states,

> ... the extension of human life is of significant value because it provides human beings with opportunities for engaging in activities and seeking experiences that they would not otherwise have enjoyed if their lives had ended sooner .... A longer life provides a greater chance for human flourishing, for learning virtues, and for living a good life.
> —Overall, 2003, p. 302

Overall's claim is that, if we are to significantly extend human longevity, then we will be pressed to develop virtues and ways of being that positively impact our future moral lives: a feminist virtue ethics framework offers us a way of thinking differently about what will be a vastly different kind of human existence. But, as Holstein worries, extended human life may actually threaten the possibility for being virtuous since many individuals (women especially) may spend more years "living at the economic margins." As she concludes, "I would prefer cultural norms that valued what I am becoming as I try to come to terms with a face and a body in process" (2001, p. 42).

As we know all too well, our current society is already a youth- or middle-aged oriented culture. The widely shared premise behind the anti-aging movement is that aging is a place that we do not and should not want to go. To wind up old becomes a kind of failure—though it is a failure that few of us can possibly hope to avoid. Once we arrive there, we become a painful reminder, an embarrassment, a sort of obscenity that the rest of society would prefer not to see lest we be reminded of our own journey toward old age. When one has been identified as a failure, an obscenity, and perhaps been so thoroughly acculturated as to share that self-assessment, what room could possibly be left for maintaining some semblance of a positive self-image or self-respect? The anti-aging movement feeds upon and reinforces harmful prejudices and conceptions of being aged. And we fear that this is a harsh price to pay for an enterprise that has little real chance of meaningful success in the foreseeable future.

CONCLUSION

What are we to do? Realistically, our abilities to change the momentum behind the anti-aging movement are limited. Using somewhat similar arguments—social justice, the harmful perpetuation of social prejudices, and concerns for sexist understandings of women—some feminists have argued that purely cosmetic plastic surgeries, such as face lifts, breast enhancements or liposuction, are socially unjust and perpetuate a harm to women (Bordo, 1995; Morgan, 1991; Rosen, 2004). Yet the prospects of banning such cosmetic surgical procedures are quite remote. They thrive under the rubric of respect for self-determination, and they are a hugely lucrative source of revenue. Much the same would seem to be true of the anti-aging movement.

Some of the money for this research does come from the U.S. government through the National Institute of Health, though this tends to be the research that emphasizes the compression of morbidity. Research that explicitly addresses the extension of the human life span is funded by private enterprise; these are investors who see an enormously profitable market if and when the technology is developed. And our society has placed very few social controls on such basic science research. Indeed, in a society without any clear consensus against such research, and where the research is being conducted with private funding, how could government possibly be expected to intervene and forbid such research? Freedom of individual choice and the prospect of a thriving, economically lucrative industry are likely to rule the day.

Rather than simply yield, we would prefer to argue against such negative stereotyping of the elderly, even if it means swimming against the tide. The anti-aging movement gains what momentum it has by means of denigrating the lives of our elderly as they in fact live. This, we think, rather than senescence and eventual death, is the real tragedy. We prefer to think that there can be, and indeed are, virtues that are possible in and appropriate to being elderly. If we lose sight of those virtues, we will all be less well off.

REFERENCES

Angerhofer, C., Maes, D., & Giacomoni, P. (2008). The use of natural compounds and botanicals in the development of anti-aging skin care products. In N. Dayan (Ed.), *Skin aging handbook: An integrated approach to biochemistry and product development*. Norwich, NY: William Andrew.

Bartke, A., Brown-Borg, H., Kinney, B., Mattison, J., Wright, C., Hauck, S., Coschigano, K., & Kopchick, J. (2000). Growth hormone and aging. *Age, 23*(4), 219–225.

Bell, N. (1997). What setting limits may mean: A feminist critique of Daniel Callahan's *Setting Limits*. In M. Peaarsall (Ed.), *The other within us: Feminist explorations of women and aging* (pp. 151–159). Boulder, CO: Westview Press.

Binstock, R. (2004). Anti-aging medicine and research. *Journal of Gerontology, 99A*(6), 523–533.

Bordo, S. (1995). *Unbearable weight: Feminism, western culture, and the body*. Berkeley, CA: University of California Press.

Buckley, B. M. (2001). Healthy ageing: Ageing safely. *European Heart Journal Supplements, 3*(Suppl. N), N6–N10.

Callahan, D. (1987). *Setting limits*. New York, NY: Simon & Schuster.

Callahan, D. (1991). Limiting health care for the old. In N. Jecker (Ed.), *Aging and Ethics* (pp. 219–226). Clifton, NJ: Humana Press.

Campisi, J. (2000). Aging chromatin and caloric restriction: Connecting the dots. *Science, 289*, 2062–2063.

Caplan, A. (2004). An unnatural process: Why it is not inherently wrong to seek a cure for aging. In S. G. Post & R. H. Binstock (Eds.), *The fountain of youth: Cultural, scientific, and ethical perspectives on a biomedical good* (pp. 271–285). New York, NY: Oxford University Press.

Daniels, N. (1988). *Am I my parents' keeper?* New York, NY: Oxford University Press.

de Gray, A. D. N. J., Ames, B., Andersen, J., Bartke, A., Campisi, J., Heward, C., McCarter, R., & Stock, G. (2002). Time to talk SENS: Critiquing the immutability of aging. *Annals of the New York Academic Sciences, 959*, 452–462.

Fries, J. F. (2000). Compression of morbidity in the elderly. *Vaccine, 18*(16), 1584–1589.

Fries, J. F. (2003). Measuring and monitoring success in compressing comorbidity. *Annals of Internal Medicine, 139*(5), 455–459.

Fukuyama, F. (2002). *Our post human future: Consequences of the biotechnology revolution.* New York, NY: Picador.

Haber, C. (2001). Anti-aging: Why now? *Generations, 25*(4), 9–14.

Haber, C. (2004). Anti-aging medicine: The history. *Journal of Gerontology, 59A*(6), B515–B522.

Harman, S. M., & Blackman, M. R. (2004). Hormones and supplements: Do they work? Use of growth hormone for prevention or treatment of effects of aging. *The Journals of Gerontology Series A: Biological Sciences and Medical Sciences, 59*(7), B652–B658.

Hayflick, L. (2002). Anti-aging medicine: Hype, hope, and reality. *Generations, 25,* 20–26.

Heidegger, M. (1962). *Being and time* (J. Macquarrie & E. Robinson, Trans.). New York, NY: Harper & Row.

Heilbronn, L. K., & Ravussin, E. (2003). Calorie restriction and aging: Review of the literature and implications for studies in humans. *American Society for Clinical Nutrition, 78*(3), 361–389.

Holden, C. (2002). The quest to reverse time's toll. *Science, 295,* 1032–1033.

Holstein, M. H. (Winter, 2001–2). A feminist perspective on anti-aging medicine: Ethical and practical implications. *Generations,* 38–43.

Juengst, E. (2004). Anti-aging research and the limits of medicine. In S. Post & R. Binstock (Eds.), *The fountain of youth* (pp. 321–339). New York, NY: Oxford University Press.

Juengst, E. T., Binstock, R. H., Mehlman, M., Post, S., & Whitehouse, P. (2003). Biogerontology, "anti-aging medicine," and the challenges of human enhancement. *Hastings Center Report, 33,* 21–30.

Kass, L. (2002). Why not immortality? In W. Kristol & E. Cohen (Eds.), *The future is now: America confronts the new genetics* (pp. 321–332). New York, NY: Rowman & Littlefield.

Kass, L. (2003). *Beyond therapy: Biotechnology and the pursuit of happiness.* New York, NY: Harper Collins.

Klatz, R. (2006). New horizons for the clinical specialty of anti-aging medicine: The future with biomedical technologies. *Annals of the New York Academy of Sciences, 1057,* 536–544.

Klatz, R., & Goldman, R. (1996). *Stopping the clock: Why many of us will live past 100—and enjoy every minute!* New York, NY: Bantam Books.

Klatz, R., & Goldman, R. (1997). *Stopping the clock: Dramatic breakthroughs in anti-aging and age reversal techniques.* New York, NY: Bantam Books.

Kurzweil, R. (2005). *The singularity is near, when humans transcend biology.* New York: Penguin Books.

Lebacq, K. (1995). Feminism. In W. T. Reich (Ed.), *The encyclopedia of bioethics.* New York, NY: Simon & Schuster.

Mackey, T. (2003). An ethical assessment of anti-aging medicine. *Journal of Anti-Aging Medicine, 6*(3), 187–204.

Mann, J. M. (1997). Medicine and public health, ethics and human rights. *Hastings Center Report, 27*(3), 6–13.

Miller, R. (2002). Extending life: Scientific prospects and political obstacles. *Millbank Quarterly, 80*(2002), 155–174.

Minsky, M. (2006). *The emotion machine: Commonsense thinking, artificial intelligence, and the future of the human mind.* New York, NY: Simon & Schuster.

Morgan, K. P. (1991). Women and the knife: Cosmetic surgery and the colonization of women's bodies. *Hypatia, 6*(3), 25–53.

Mori, I., & Sasakura, H. (2009). Aging: Shall we take the high road? *Current Biology, 19*(9), R363–R364.

Nagel, T. (1979). *Mortal questions.* Cambridge: Cambridge University Press.

Oeppen, J., & Vaupel, J. W. (2002). Broken limits to life expectancy. *Science, 296*(5570), 1029–1031.

Olshansky, S. J., & Carnes, B. (2001). *The quest for immortality.* New York, NY: Norton.

Olshansky, S. J., Carnes, B., & Cassel, C. (1990). In search of Methuselah: Estimating the upper limits to human longevity. *Science, 250*(4981), 634–640.

Olshansky, S. J., Hayflick, L., & Carnes, B. (2002). No truth to the fountain of youth. *Scientific American, 286*(6), 92–95.

Olshansky, S., Hayflick, L., & Perls, T. (2004). Anti-aging medicine: The hype and the reality—Part I. *The Journals of Gerontology, Series A: Biological Sciences and Medical Sciences, 59*(6), B513–B514.

Overall, C. (2003). *Aging, death, and human longevity.* Berkeley, CA: University of California Press.

Rosen, C. (2004). The democratization of beauty. *The New Atlantis, 5,* 19–35.

Taylor, D. H., Hasselblad, V., Henley, S. J., Thun, M. J., & Sloan, F. A. (2002). Benefits of smoking cessation for longevity. *American Journal of Public Health, 92*(6), 990–996.

Walford, R. L. (2000). *Beyond the 120-year diet.* New York, NY: Four Walls Eight Windows.

Westerhof, J. G., & Barrett, A. E. (2005). Age identity and subjective well-being: A comparison of the United States and Germany. *The Journals of Gerontology Series B: Psychological Sciences and Social Sciences, 60*(3), S129–S136.

Whitney, C. R. (1997). Jeanne Calment, world's elder, dies at 122. *New York Times.* Accessed May 5, 2010, from http://www.nytimes.com/1997/08/05/world/jeanne-calment-world-s-elder-dies-at-122.html.

Wick, G. (2002). "Anti-aging" medicine: Does it exist? A critical discussion of 'anti-aging health products.' *Experimental Gerontology, 37*(8–9), 1137–1140.

Williams, B. (1973). *Problems of the self.* Cambridge: Cambridge University Press.

Wilmoth, J. R. (2000). Demography of longevity: Past, present, and future trends. *Experimental Gerontology, 35*(9–10), 1111–1129.

Young, I. M. (1990). *Throwing like a girl and other essays in feminist philosophy and social theory.* Indianapolis: Indiana University Press.

CHAPTER 6

Aging and Public Policy

A Normative Foundation

*Everyone is fragile at some point in time. We need each other. We live our lives in the
here and now, together with others caught up in the midst of change. We will all be
richer if all of us are allowed to participate and nobody is left out. We will be stronger if there is security for everybody and not only for a few*

—Bauman, 2008, p. 142

ETHICS, AGING, AND PUBLIC POLICY:
STRANGE BEDFELLOWS?

Policy and ethics share a central commitment—to make evaluative
judgments of what is good or right in human conduct. Both are concerned
with what values we ought to embrace (Churchill, 2002), albeit one explicitly and the other most often tacitly. Aristotle saw what may seem arcane
now—that "ethics and politics are two aspects of one path leading to the
same good for man [sic]" (Tong, 1986, p. 43). Policies are about how governments allocate resources, encourage or discourage certain behaviors, and
help assure security. In these endeavors, policy choices express some
common consensus about values. But they also tell a story—about people,
the nation, and what is important—a story that is expressed in terms of metaphors (Lakoff, 1996). Having watched politics over time, one may notice
how this narrative framing—the story—has changed. This reframing is
visible in policies directed at older people. In the past 50 years, we have
witnessed a move from a sympathetic framing of older people as needy
that Binstock (1983) labeled "compassionate ageism" to a very different
narrative. Supported by the neoliberal assumption that individuals, families
and the market are the vehicles to a secure old age, this narrative rejects the
old "decline and loss" paradigm with a new story about relative affluence and
good health as what marks the "new old age" (see Chapter 4). This optimistic

scenario, unfortunately not universally applicable, threatens to undermine support for public policies such as social security and Medicare (Holstein & Minkler, 2003).

In this chapter, we will argue that policies based on commitments on a faulty idea of the self that is the independent, autonomous, "Kantian man" will be unable to respond appropriately to the needs of the vast majority of the population. In contrast to this image of a person, we have argued that it is more accurate to see us as irreducibly social and involved throughout our lives in situations of mutual dependency. As that kind of person, background social conditions that give us "the resources for a thick, well-integrated, and well-understood identities which are also the worthy subjects of self and social respect" (Flanagan, 1991, p. 133) are critical. Public policy is one important element in making those social conditions possible. To that end, we will construct what Lindemann-Nelson (2001) calls counter stories that will account for shifting conceptual ideas about human nature and the realities of being old in America today. These counter stories can serve as conceptual texts for policymaking.

Before we do this, however, we will consider the ways in which ethics can importantly contribute to policymaking while being mindful of the serious impediments to constructing effective bridges between the two. To lay the foundations for our counter story, we will challenge the ideology known as neoliberalism, which threatens the well-being of both old and young, indeed of anyone not well served by the market. To that end, it will also examine briefly the generational equity framing of policy choices. We will bring the chapter to a close by arguing for a value foundation for policy that supports both families and elders so that individuality and interconnectedness can thrive (Harrington, 1999; Minow & Shanley, 1996) without the gender and class exploitations now so prominent (Calasanti & Sleven, 2006; Holstein, 1999; Hooyman & Gonyea, 1995). It will call for social, economic and institutional supports that permit freedom commensurate with physical and cognitive abilities. This alternative value foundation rests on a relational ontology and commitments to personal and social interdependence and solidarity, dignity, and gender justice. This chapter is one step in an act of resistance to those politics, ideologies, and individualistic moral values that disregard context and the conditions of possibility for people of different kinds.

POLICY AND ETHICS

Consider the numerous policy debates of our time, including access to health care, embryonic stem call research, research on vulnerable populations, and entitlement programs. What seems to be valued (or devalued) in our society becomes apparent when we attend to the issues that policy-makers choose to recognize and address. When policymakers determine whom to serve, for what reasons, and with what boundaries between the compelling and legitimate claims of individuals, families, and communities they are making choices that are just as ethical in nature as the more visceral debates about abortion or gay marriage. Even the popular cost-benefit analy-sis assumes the priority of one value—efficiency—and requires a determi-nation of what goods will count as benefits. Policies try to solve problems (e.g., how to provide health care coverage to more people) or support core beliefs (e.g., people should be able to choose [or not] the time and place of their own death). These questions are, in part, technical ones but they are also value questions that raise legitimate and likely disagreements. Understood this way, every policy has a value dimension. Martin Rein (1983) states what should be obvious to every policymaker and citizen—behind every answer lays a question. Questions are never neutral. We would, for example, address the soaring costs of Medicare differently depending on how we defined the causes of the cost explosion. Further, the way the problem is defined leads to the "facts" that policymakers seek as they pursue answers. Thus, a different definition of the problem leads to the seeking of different facts. Many policymakers, for example, have been advocating for a more privatized system of health insurance for Medi-care beneficiaries since, in their view, cost containment can be achieved from more vigorous competition. Hence, they will seek facts that support compe-tition as the answer to the cost problem. If managed care, as reflected in Medicare Advantage Plans, is the answer to costs, health policy experts can probably design a cost effective managed care system. What they can't do is determine if unfettered access is more important than depth of coverage.

More generally, before deciding how to expand access to health care, legislators have to accept that access itself is a socially and ethically desirable end. Once the value of access is accepted, and facts pursued, ethical analysis can analyze how different value commitments support different approaches to expanding access. In terms of long-term care, one might ask how to reduce or even eliminate the fundamental injustices that now prevail in home care (see Chapter 7; Holstein, 1999). For these legislators, the problem would be defined as the basic human right to have needs met without exploiting anyone, such as women family members. That problem definition would lead to a very different approach than we have now (as described in Chapter 7). Further, legislators might ask questions about the different ways this country treats long-term care and acute care. Why is acute care funded through a public age-based entitlement program like Medicare and long-term care through the means-tested Medicaid program with primary responsibilities vested in the private arena of families? They might then look to many Western European countries to see how the argument for an entitlement to publicly funded long-term care services was developed and how this policy is working in practice. Comparing the United States to Western Europe would reveal very different value commitments (*New York Times*, March 10, 2010).

The language of ethics—rights, norms, values—offers a way to frame our narrative about what outcomes we seek. We might, for example, affirm that older people should be able to live as fully integrated into their communities as their physical and cognitive capacities allow—but not so that it requires "informal" caregivers to be responsible for this integration. Affirming this value leads us in pursuit of facts that will suggest how it might be achieved. We may also use values as a way to look at existing policies to see how well they respond to those identified values. The United States, for example, seems to uphold a commitment to family values but an examination of policy choices and outcomes might suggest that this value is poorly reflected in the policies now in place. A value-based analysis thus gives us a strategy to evaluate as well as design public policies. It can expose the fissures and fractures in contemporary social policy for the aged and offer a reframing that might heal these fissures. Medicare, for example, by its emphasis on acute care, meets the needs of men better than it meets to needs of women who tend to suffer from more chronic conditions. An examination of social security based on a value commitment to evening out benefits between men and women would help to explain why women are poorer than men in old age. When social security was passed in 1935, it responded to family arrangements that no longer are operative today but the social security system has not responded. Women still do not get credit for drop-out years and for their historic patterns of lower earnings than men (Rogne et al., 2009).

Values remind us that we ignore framing language at our peril. A "customer" of home care services is very different than a "client" or a "patient." For those following the health care debate in the summer of 2009, the importance of language and framing was obvious—talk of "death panels," "killing granny," and "government takeover" came very close to derailing an effort that included no such aims. Yet, these catch phrases, based on erroneous information, served to galvanize action. If "killing granny" can succeed as a way of framing a debate, why not language such as, "save 62 people who die each day for lack of health care"? Of course, this framing is not nearly as catchy as "killing granny" even if it is more accurate.

Consider some other examples. An ethical analysis can ask if health care and/or economic security are civil rights issues or individual problems;

whether they should be solved by a commitment to equal opportunity or by individual merit and action. It can render visible the ideological presuppositions that support managed care or social security privatization and systematically inquire about who benefits and who loses as new policies are developed. As Chapter 4 showed, this country is writing a new story about being old in the United States that is value-based and has potentially important policy implications. Our analysis shows how asking who benefits and who loses exposes another way to assess this situation.

Ethics can encourage listening to others without assuming that one already knows the answer in advance of discussion and analysis. It can identify the possibilities for making integrity-preserving compromises because the commitment to getting the work done recognizes that we might not get everything that we want (Churchill, 2002; Goodstein, 2000). It can critique ideological presuppositions on both fact and value dimensions. It can expand normative possibilities to support alternative policies. If, for example, we adopted a norm that demands that we do not humiliate and subjugate recipients of public benefits in this country, then we would develop eligibility requirements that were as simple and straightforward as possible and we would defend basic age-based entitlements. If we acknowledge that the United States' commitment to individualism, independence, and choice is not realizable by people without the social and material foundations necessary to make that a reality, then we would seek a more inclusive value set that recognizes the universal need for care and the necessity of a structural response to inequities and inequalities. For example, keeping people out of nursing homes is an important aim but not if it fails to account for the possible transfer of responsibilities to "informal" caregivers if the community is unprepared to care for them. Ethicists can question how we understand the nature of human beings, a seemingly abstract topic that nonetheless has practical implications. As the feminist dependency critique (Dodds, 2007; Kittay, 1999; Tronto, 1993) argues, for example, we, as a society would act very differently if we started from the assumption that dependency rather than independence is the central fact of the human condition. This idea supports the universal need for care and leads us to build policies around essential relationships of care. Taking the relational self as our focus and a commitment to family justice as a corollary, we would challenge policymakers to develop a new family policy that centers on the ability to care well and that recognizes and responds to the changes in work, family, and gender relations that have occurred in the past few decades.

Lastly, ethics can help to reduce morally egregious behavior by exposing how respected moral principles can be used in perverted and faulty ways thus giving otherwise bad behavior moral justification (Buchanan, 2009). While the most devastating examples of this perversion involve such atrocities as the Nazis using the concept of "honor" to induce its members to exterminate Jews, it can also be seen in what we consider the condemnation of living wills by the President's Council on Bioethics. It based its criticism on the faulty belief that the use of Living Wills gives families an option to abandon the old once their care becomes too burdensome. This assumption simply ignores the commitment of family members to care at a significant personal cost, as discussed in Chapter 7. To take another example, the honorable value of eliminating poverty among children has been perverted to assume an intergenerational divide between old and young. Pitted against children in poverty are the "greedy old people" who supposedly squander their grandchildren's inheritance. This view omits the fact that social security is the key reason why poverty among elders is reduced. It also overlooks the fact that close to 50% of older persons still hover in the zone of economic hardship (Russell, Bruce, & Conahan, 2006).

In our view, ethics can shape the cultural and intellectual backdrop against which policy issues emerge (Buchanan, 2009), by challenging hegemonic understandings of such fundamental concepts as equality or autonomy. It can inform the discussion about a pivotal although rarely asked question: Ought social policy rest on emancipatory aims, which call for mitigating actual and persistent inequalities, or should it target creating opportunities that support individual achievement? Whatever end policymakers choose, they must also consider the narrower but equally significant ethical question—what are the "relative distribution of rights and responsibilities between state and citizen" in achieving whatever aims it chooses? (Lewis, 2000, p. 3). We will defend an approach to policy grounded in ethical norms that upholds a strong commitment to collective responsibility and emancipatory ends. By returning to our framework of feminist and communicative ethics, we will argue for a transformative approach that rejects the liberal individualism at the heart of much current public policy.

While we have suggested that ethicists can contribute by parsing elements of important policy areas like access to health care and by developing well-honed arguments to justify certain actions, we defend a stronger role. Ethicists can be "passionate scholars" (Holstein & Minkler, 2007) dedicated to exposing the impact of value assumptions, tracing the origin of those values in powerful institutions articulated by authoritative spokespeople, and putting forward strong arguments for alternative framings of public issues, and, at times, insisting that what were once defined as private issues be redefined as public ones.

IMPEDIMENTS TO BRIDGING ETHICS AND PUBLIC POLICY

While we have just outlined some important roles that ethicists can play in policy development and evaluation, we must offer the other side of the situation and identify the impediments to this collaborative role. Most obviously, policy experts work in different settings and rely on different intellectual habits than ethicists. The policy-making environment is hardly conducive to the kind of rational discourse upon which ethical analysis relies. Reinforcing what any attentive news watcher noticed in the summer and fall of 2009, as Congress debated health care reform, "public policy making is extraordinarily messy" (Kingdon, 2002, p. 97). Further, as Lindblom (1959) pointed out so many years ago, policymaking is best done incrementally— an observation that is both descriptive and evaluative. Clarifying goals in advance may actually doom the policy (Kingdon, 2002; Lindblom, 1959). Yet, as ethicists, we may have the nagging feeling that clarifying goals and the underlying values that support them serves an important purpose in helping to screen out actions that divert us from achieving those goals and values. The tension between what may be a pragmatic necessity and an ethical ideal may simply be a function of living in a highly politicized environment where pragmatic ends trump "purer" ethical analysis. We do, however, need to understand the nature of the compromises we are making and why we are making them.

Interestingly, however, this incremental approach may serve to bring ethics and policy into a more intimate conversation. Doing ethics is, as Larry Churchill (2002) points out, humanizing. We need to listen, to be attentive to the views others express, and to start from a position of "moral agnosticism" meaning that we do not have the final truth in advance of discussion (Churchill, 2002, p. 55). So often, in ethical deliberation, we hear the expression that we must do the best we can, "all things considered." Thus, "Respectful accommodation is thus almost always necessary" (Churchill, 2002, p. 56).

Presidential Bioethics Commissions or Councils exemplify deliberate efforts to bring ethics and policy into conversation. Yet, not surprisingly the results reflect the political and ethical orientations of the chair and council members. Members are political appointees and thus are no different from the rest of us—rather than reflecting a "view from nowhere," they start from very particular places. Reports they issue reflect those starting places. A recent publication particularly relevant for aging policy demonstrates this. *Taking Care: Ethical Caregiving in Our Aging Society* (2005), issued by the President's Council on Bioethics, chaired by the University of Chicago's

Leon Kass, is one such example. Addressing the care of older people who are chronically ill and impaired, especially those with Alzheimer's disease (AD), it importantly acknowledges that aging cannot be "solved" and that independence and autonomy are too limited to serve as core values in an aging society. Yet, its overwhelmingly negative portrayal of AD leads it to warn against family abandonment. But perhaps most disturbing is that its acknowledgment that families have major caregiving responsibilities for frail or sick loved ones is not taken as an occasion for asking what can be done, especially for female family members; but rather the Council calls on families not to abandon the old when the going gets tough. As Kane (2007) points out, "the Council's account of care systems lacks precision and, at times, accuracy" as it both recognizes and criticizes family members who privilege career advancement, for example, over caregiving (p. 562). Instead of addressing why older people in need of long-term care might not want to be a burden and then making recommendations to address that problem, the Council ignores empirical evidence about care and fails to notice recent work, particularly among feminist scholars (Dodds, 2007; Kittay, 1999; Parks, 2003; Tronto, 1993) about the relational aspects of care. The Council thus overlooked the fact that care is central to all human life and, as such, cannot sustain itself without strong collective responsibility. The Council thus places caregivers and care receivers in opposition to one another, engaged in clashes of rights, with the danger of betrayal hovering in the background, rather than seeing them in relational terms. It made no move to heal the care-equality divide either for family caregivers or for paid workers. We argue, as we did in Chapter 4 that faulty perception is almost inevitable when one sees through a lens of privilege and, in this case, the limited perception that its subject matter is, in essence, about justice and not about getting family members to do more. The report explicitly rejects any reworking of the health care system so as to expand benefits for long-term care.

An additional barrier is that much work, especially in bioethics, has addressed ethical issues that focus on the individual. Analyzing the dynamics of the individual physician-patient relationship garners more attention than the broader social/structural reasons that explain why some people can access care and experience a trusting, attentive relationship with a physician, while others never make it through the door, except the doors at the emergency room. An individual entitlement to health care as the foundation for equal opportunity has been the focus of discussion more often than recognizing that care is a human need, a "species activity" that should ground all policy choices (Churchill, 2002; Holstein, 2005; Tronto, 1993).

THE IDEOLOGY OF NEO-LIBERALISM

Neo-liberalism, with its many tentacles, represents the most overarching and serious threat to the well-being of the old. While so far it has not realized its fullest aims, it is committed to transferring "more and more of the risks associated with aging—the threat of poverty, the need for long-term care, and the likelihood of severe illness—to individuals and families" (Putney, Bengston, & Wakeman, 2007, p. 123). In response to the glaring differences in wealth and social position among people and groups, neo-liberalism places responsibility on each individual to make decisions about his or her own life. This ideology meets the practical end of reducing government spending but does so in the name of avoiding dependency. Thus, it serves a dual purpose—responding to calls for deficit reduction not through taxation or other means of bringing more resources to government but through cuts in social spending while elevating the traditional American value of independence. Its belief in market and technocratic solutions to human problems and its erasure of inequality as a matter for public concern (since individuals should have done a better job of preparing for old age) threatens the tenuous security of many older people, especially women, and, most particularly, women of color. It also allows policymakers to sidestep resource allocation questions and the value-laden issue of what government owes to whom and why. When old age insecurity becomes primarily a private and not a public problem, it moves off the public agenda.

Neo-liberalism shrouds the difficulties faced in old age by those who are unable to "compete effectively during the relatively few years in which capital must be earned and partially invested for the future" (Baars, 2006, p. 31). The so-called equal opportunities mean little in a nonequal labor market. Nor can opportunities be equal if institutions, like education that are foundational to later market success, are unequal. As we come to understand the consequences of neo-liberal ideals such as opportunity, we need to accept either the near permanence of lifelong inequality or to offer a strong reframing of the socio-political "ought." Equal opportunity cannot exist without addressing fundamental inequalities attributable to race, class and gender (Calasanti & Slevin, 2001; Minkler & Estes, 1999; Phillipson, 1998). We have learned from second wave, liberal feminism, which stressed equal opportunities for jobs or education, that this goal is only one step in a transformational process (Holstein, 2007). For people who are now old, it is rather late to rely on equal opportunity. Equal opportunity is inevitably tainted by social location. Another indicator of this problem—as families assume more responsibilities for older relatives, they are less likely to have the capacity to save for their own old age. "Thus, an ever-renewable cycle of family responsibility begins that will have consequences for each generation and each person within the family" (Holstein, www.wowonline.org).

Neo-liberalism is, therefore, an ideology that best suits the privileged. Much as emerging cultural norms for the "third age" described in Chapter 4 rely on health and relative affluence that do not have broad resonance, neo-liberalism supports values that harm the already least advantaged. This ideology and its practical ramifications (no improvement in public benefits, possible reductions in social security, increased reliance on the family for care-giving) can mean that more and more people will no longer have enough income to retire. This possibility will further exacerbate inequality, an additional moral harm. The pension elite and other affluent individuals will be able to retire; lower wage workers will have no choice but to continue working in whatever jobs they can find. For these people, financial necessity—not a commitment to civic engagement—will be the reason for continued work, a direct challenge to the "third age" scenario of freedom to experiment. For many, it is a sad and undesirable end to a long working life (Phillipson, 2007). Since globalization has also witnessed increased migrations of people, this gap will be played out in communities where diversity combined with racial and other prejudices can provoke social unease and dissension. But it will be done in the name of powerful American values such as independence, limited government, and individuals rather than communal assessments of the good.

Richard Sennett (1999) notes that, "the system radiates indifference . . ." and "brutally diminishes the sense of mattering as a person, being necessary to others" (as quoted in Phillipson, 2007, p. 5). This dehumanizing effect directly contradicts the relational self and broader ideas in feminist ethics discussed in Chapter 2. If opportunity is primary and one is blind to the fact that opportunity is never equal, then it is defensible to blame the person who has not taken sufficient advantage of his or her opportunities. If one is blamed for the condition in which one finds oneself, flourishing in old age is further impeded. This ideology thus undermines any sense that we have a common stake in the good of our communities.

Policies which rest on a neo-liberal ideology cannot meet a minimalist criteria of what people need for a decent old age—a chance to make meaningful choices and a sense of self-respect that derives from social regard (Agich, 1990, 2003; Holstein & Minkler, 2003). It also threatens the security of future generations as families are expected to assume responsibilities for both the young and the old. Thus, neo-liberalism can easily undercut generational solidarity and reawaken the socially constructed generational "wars" of the 1980s. If each person is supposed to have equal opportunities to provide for his/her own future then it becomes very difficult to defend cross-generational support. Further, by not making explicit the values that support certain public policies, the argument that programs for older people are harming the young can morph into the regularly recurring "greedy geezer" language, introduced by a cover story in the New Republic in the 1980s and repeated as late as 2010 by David Brooks, an op-ed columnist for the *New York Times*.

Ideological support for individualism and self-interested behavior also threaten a persistent, albeit secondary value—a commitment to the common good (Achenbaum, 1978; Bellah et al., 1985)—that has been an important foundation for aging programs such as social security. How this reiteration of the "greedy geezer" and related themes affect commitments to pensions and retiree health benefits, which were in part designed to encourage loyalty, "a virtue that once had a strong place in American business" (Holstein, 2008) remains to be seen.

GENERATIONAL CONFLICT OR GENERATIONAL SOLIDARITY

The question of generational justice is a recurrent political and ethical theme. Philosophers may ask: what are critical dimensions of the life world that ought to be protected at different ages? In contrast, the framers of the generational equity argument created an oppositional strategy. In their zero-sum approach, benefits for the elderly diverted resources that ought to go to the young, identified as the poorest demographic, according to the Federal Poverty Guidelines (Preston, 1984). Rather than viewing the reduced poverty rate of older people as a policy triumph and what may be possible for all age groups, this approach triggered a bitter campaign to blame the old for the condition of the young, as they putatively and thus selfishly sought government benefits that crowded out everything else.

While the extensive sociological research on these questions is beyond this chapter's scope, one role for the ethicist, as noted above, is to deconstruct an edifice built on erroneous facts. We touch upon these here. In the first place, there is "little evidence to suggest that current policies toward the elderly are directly or indirectly harmful to the welfare of children and young adults" (Williamson, McNamara, & Howling, 2003, p. 5). Nor do the downward trends in elder poverty change the fact that poverty rates among America's older population are still the highest among the rich nations (Smeeding & Sullivan, 1998, cited in Myles & Quadagno, 1999). Moreover, families demonstrate support for one another, a commitment that carries over to "supportive attitudes about societal-level policies benefiting the old."

While much more can be said about arguments related to generational equity (Minkler, 1991; Schulz & Binstock, 2006; Williamson, McNamara, & Howling, 2003), for now, we highlight the ethically problematic elements of neo-liberalism and the generational equity debate. Neo-liberalism, as discussed above, exposes many people who have been poorly served by the market to considerable risk—that is, the social safety net is increasingly tattered. This means that while negative rights may be protected from state interference, they have little or no ability to rely on the state when they face threats to their health and well-being through no particular fault of their own but because they are women, or people of color, or disadvantaged because of ill health or other events basically out of their control. This is problematic because they are fundamentally denied the full rights of citizenship—to participate actively in government, to have the liberty to choose among options about where and how to live, to exercise the so-called freedom of the "third age." Economic insecurity not only makes it difficult to live in valued ways but it damages self-respect. Visible dependencies in a society of presumed independent equals, further harms one's sense of being a person of worth. Yet, a simple look at the market reveals that it is a poor guarantee of economic security. The average income of today's 30-year-old male is lower than his father's income a generation ago. The market is a mechanism that is wildly unequal (Herbert, 2007). Both advantages and disadvantages accumulate (Crystal & Shea, 1990; Dannefer, 2003; O'Rand, 2006). This includes visible dependencies—needing help with bathing or eating and not with ironing shirts. We rarely, if ever, can catch up. Choice in later life, as it was in earlier life, is thus a myth.

Moreover, the demands on income are rising precipitously, reinforcing the already existing threat of income insecurity. The increasing costs of private health care and housing contribute to this devastating situation. This cost escalation means that after-tax income for people in the middle of the wage distribution will be 22% less in 2030 than it was in 1998 (Baker, 1997 as quoted in Polivka & Longino, 2006, p. 196). With Larry Polivka and Charles Longino, we maintain that the "true threat to the economic well-being of families arises from neo-liberal policies of tax cuts for the wealthy, reductions in spending for education, childcare, and other social programs, privatization and deregulation, anti-union measures and other policy initiatives that fuel rising inequality and healthcare costs" (pp. 196–197).

While we do not pretend that it will be easy to challenge this prevailing ideology with a normative vision that honors what connects, rather than what isolates, us, we want to propose a very different grounding for public policy. Perhaps we can take a lesson from the European Union where there is little conflict among generations, (Bengston & Putney, 2006, p. 27). Conflict is avoided because whatever problems exist are embedded in a commitment to social welfare programs that benefit the entire population. Thus, a synoptic vision is one way to see the common stake among generations, who, on the micro-level, maintain strong ties of love and assistance. We make this argument in the belief that without a vision, we have no direction in which to move; that going beyond critique is minimally a way to instigate conversation and to affirm the kind of society in which care is at least equal to competitiveness and individualism. We further argue that social context significantly influences the possibility that older people have to exercise the value that seems to dominate over all others, that is, autonomy. Opportunities to exercise autonomy are contextual. To this end, we turn to the broadest role for ethics: to consider what might constitute a normative vision for aging policies and, in our mind, a more just society.

THE FEMINIST ETHICS OF CARE

In direct opposition to the neo-liberal ideology, which reduces the role of government and hence policy initiatives as remedies, we propose that the feminist ethics of care serve as the framework for policy. Tronto (1993) observes that care is crucial to making societies more moral, which is, contributing to human flourishing. A feminist ethics of care elevates the connectedness among people rather than their separateness. It situates elders in families and communities, where dependency and vulnerability are understood as universal and care is an organizing principle. We see it this way: the privileged have their dependency needs met almost invisibly—meals appear, beds are made, bills paid, suits pressed—and in socially acceptable ways that honor norms of independence. They are "normalized" and do not face threats to their adult status. The 84-year old woman in a wheelchair is visibly dependent and is out of the mainstream, an anomaly. Making care central would see these individuals as alike—both have dependency needs that others meet. Such a shift in vision also revives a submerged voice about communal values in U.S. society that has few means of expression in our highly individualistic culture.

On a micro-level, it would mean that despite the deeper vulnerability of older people, especially those needing long-term care, our societal obligations would extend to "shaping policies and service strategies that help preserve a disabled person's sense of self and extends the boundaries of his or her own volitional capacities" (Polivka, 1998, p. 24). It would support a richer array of options and provide support for developing and maintaining essential nurturing relationships. It would move us beyond cost effectiveness criteria in supporting programs and environments that foster a person's ability to remake his or her life despite serious physical or cognitive impairments. This shift would also make honoring an expanded view of autonomy integral to our social commitments to others.

NEXT STEPS

In Chapter 7, we examine home and community-based care and seek to expose the fractures in that system that originates in the separation of public and private and the assumption that families, primarily women, are both able and willing to assume caring responsibilities for older family members. We observe that women placed in this situation, without exit options, are rendered fundamentally unequal. They are also devaluated because they are not engaged in productive labor; nor are they independent (Dodds, 2007; Kittay, 1999). The assumed voluntariness of caring work further reinforces care as a private rather than a public activity. An ethic of care would take these issues as serious moral concerns since they involve matters of justice, respect, and dishonor. While it would not discard the liberal idea that people should live as freely as possible, it would take as equally important that sustaining the connections that help make people who they are and that give them strength, no matter how frail they become is also essential. It would strive toward balancing freedom, individual rights, and connections (Harrington, 1999; Minow & Shanley, 1996). If we want to support individuals, we need to support families; not by leaving them alone but by assuring that they have the ability to engage in caring and supportive roles while meeting the obligations that living in families creates (Harrington, 1999). Thus, interest would turn to family policy with special attention to vulnerable populations of all ages (Schulz & Binstock, 2006). It would defend the obligations of the more affluent to provide for the more vulnerable since that benefits society as a whole, enriches communities, keeps everyone healthier, creates a more productive work force, and even reduces crime. Recalling that every answer has a question behind it, we are suggesting that the question move from how to support individual older people in the community to how we can strengthen the relationships that sustain people without penalizing women, especially lower income women, who give much of the care.

To argue for a care framework is not new. Many feminist scholars have articulated arguments for care as a national goal (Harrington, 1999; Held, 2006; Kittay, 1999; Shanley, 2001; Tronto, 1993) but these arguments have not become part of the moral and social backdrop for policy formulation. By presenting these arguments in whatever way they can, ethicists can make an important contribution to public policy in direct contradiction to the core values of neo-liberalism and the pitting of young against old. Since the need for care is universal, policies must reflect this fact. But political action is essential. As Tronto (1993) argues, morality can prescribe correct action but it cannot make it happen. Change requires a political solution.

BROADENING NORMATIVE COMMITMENTS: DIGNITY, SOCIAL SOLIDARITY, AND GENDER EQUITY

An ethics of care is intertwined with other important normative values. It supports dignity, for example, as a relational achievement, not as an individual one. Dignity requires recognition—that someone we respect respects us. It reflects the social dimensions of regard, a normative achievement of great importance (Flanagan, 1991). By challenging the commonly held insistence that independence and self-governance are normative values sufficiently rich and satisfactory to ground sustainable policies, it demands that the polity search for ways to elevate social solidarity and collective responsibility. As Alan Walker (2006) observes, "risk pooling and collective support should enable people to make choices and limit the structural constraints on them. Thus social welfare policy should promote "choice and flexibility and empower people to negotiate their way through the changing life course" (Walker, 2006, p. 77). Policies should "redistribute resources through universal programs that constrain rather than escalate gender, race, and class inequality, and spread the costs and risks of old age dependency across families rather than concentrating them within families" (Harrington-Meyer, 2005, pp. 85–86).

These aims will have the best opportunity to unify generations and different social and economic strata (Holstein, 2009). Social solidarity, another way of describing the relational ontology we favor, is a "necessary condition for the flourishing of the subjective life;" a human being understood holistically is more socially committed, socially shaped, and socially nourished than much recent ethical thinking would have us believe (Anjos, 1994, p. 139). Without visible expressions of community, we lack the social glue that binds individuals into a society. Yet, we rarely acknowledge such social goals and so do not stimulate informed discussion about the losses that might occur if those goals withered. While relations of social obligation and reciprocity are not always freely chosen, they are required for the continuity of a just society (Baier, 1994). Such bonds are not merely incidental; they are morally honorable and necessary. In contrast, the neo-liberal state affirms that people can be whomever they want to be but lacking the economic security that makes real choices possible hollows out this apparent right and exacerbates inequalities. If we cannot claim our rights, Margalit (1996) points out, the price is humiliation.

As a further value, all public policy must be assessed in terms of what it does or does not do to support gender equity (and race equity). This value can serve as a criterion for assessing all public policy. Social security, Medicare, and long-term care policy, for example, all are gender biased. Further, for women to benefit from the liberating potential that so many see in posttraditional life styles, policies must democratize these possibilities.

Policies ought to be designed with three ends in mind. The first end is to account for the intricate ways in which public support for older and younger individuals and families interact. In the absence of support for older people, who would bear the burden of responsibility for their well-being? In the absence of support for younger people, who would work to keep the economy rolling, and who would care for younger people with disabilities or for those without jobs if there were no adequate policy responses? Each generation will further deplete their resources. The second end is to improve the economic security of younger people both because it is good in itself and because it is one way to alleviate later life hardship. The third end is to respond to the contemporary condition of people now old, who are unable to make ends meet. These three aims are good for older people and for families. Policies should represent a commitment to intergenerational solidarity and a rejection of the view that individuals, families, and the market, if left alone, can address profound economic, social and existential difficulties. This commitment can facilitate the enlarged ideas about autonomy threaded throughout this book. Like dignity, actual autonomy is not an individual achievement but one that relies on a supportive social context that takes a commitment to care as obligatory, that recognizes the universality of human dependency and sees the generations as mutually reliant on and responsible to one another. This view will not eliminate distributional issues or other difficult policy choices but it will reflect concerns that exist at the margins where the market is punitive and dependencies devalue the person.

CONCLUSION

We have argued that, whether articulated or not, ethics and values matter in public policy development. It is essential, we believe, to find ways to include many different people, especially the marginalized, in the articulation of problems, values, and approaches that address this particular definition of the problem and the values. Technocrats can supply the facts necessary to design policies. They cannot provide the values. We have further called for policies that take care as a central fact of human life and dependency rather than independence as the heart of the human condition. We need to tell stories of what it would mean for policy formation to start from these premises rather than from narrow understandings of autonomy and independence (see Chapter 2). As currently understood, these values assume that all people have equal opportunity to be both independent and autonomous. Because equal opportunity does not exist, this assumption can exacerbate inequality. Because we think that people care deeply about moral values—and not only those that fuel such debates as abortion or gay marriage—they need to have a chance to write the story of what dignity-respecting, non-humiliating policies would be like. What we are thus recommending is both procedural and substantive so that this country is better prepared for what lies ahead.

REFERENCES

Achenbaum, A. (1978). *Old age in a new land: The American experience since 1790*. Baltimore, MD: Johns Hopkins University Press.

Agich, G. (1990). Reassessing autonomy in long-term care. *Hastings Center Report*, 20(6), 12–17.

Agich, G. (2003). *Dependence and autonomy in old age: An ethical framework for long-term care*. Cambridge, UK: Cambridge University Press.

Anjos, M. (1994). Bioethics in a liberationist key. In E. Dubose, R. Hamel, & L. O'Connell (Eds.), *A matter of principles: Ferment in U.S. bioethics*. Valley Forge, PA: Trinity Press International.

Baars, J. (2006). Beyond neomodernism, antimodernism, and postmodernism: Basic categories for contemporary critical gerontology. In J. Baars, D. Dannefer, C. Phillipson, & A. Walker (Eds.), *Aging, globalization, and inequality: The new critical gerontology* (pp. 17–42). Amityville, NY: Bayview Publishing Co.

Baier, A. (1994). *Moral prejudices: Essays on ethics*. Cambridge, MA: Harvard University Press.

Baker, D. (1997). The privateers' free lunch. *American Prospect*, 81–84.

Baker, D. (1997). Cited in Polivka, L., & Longino, C. (2006). The emerging postmodern culture of aging and retirement security. In J. Baars, D. Dannefer,

C. Phillipson, & A. Walker (Eds.), *Aging, globalization, and inequality: The new critical gerontology*. Amityville, NY: Baywood Publishing Company.

Bauman, Z. (2008). *Does ethics have a chance in a world of consumers?* Cambridge, MA: Harvard University Press.

Bellah, R., Madsen, R., Sullivan, W., & Tipton, S. (1985). *Habits of the heart: Individualism and commitment in American life*. Berkeley, CA: University of California Press.

Bengston, V., & Putney, N. (2006). Future 'conflicts' across generations and cohorts? In J. Vincent, C. Phillipson, & M. Downs (Eds.), *The futures of old age* (pp. 20–29). London: Sage Publications.

Binstock, R. (1983). Interest-group liberalism and the politics of aging. *Gerontologist, 12*, 265–280.

Buchanan, A. (2009). Philosophy and public policy: A role for social moral epistemology. *Journal of Applied Philosophy, 26*(3), 276–290.

Calasanti, T., & Slevin, K. (2001). *Gender, social inequalities and aging*. Walnut Creek, CA: AltaMira Press.

Calasanti, T., & Slevin, K. (2006). *Age matters: Realigning feminist thought*. New York, NY: Routledge.

Churchill, L. (2002). What ethics can contribute to health policy? In M. Danis, C. Clancy, & L. Churchill (Eds.), *Ethical dimensions of health policy* (pp. 51–64). New York: Oxford University Press.

Crystal, S., & Shea, D. (1990). Cumulative advantage, cumulative disadvantage, and inequality among elderly people. *The Gerontologist, 30*(4), 437–443.

Dannefer, D. (2003). Cumulative advantage/disadvantage and the life course: Cross-fertilizing age and social science theory. *Journal of Gerontology: Social Sciences, 58B*(6), S327–S337.

Dodds, S. (2007). Depending on care: Recognition of vulnerability and the social contribution of care provision. *Bioethics, 21*(9), 500–510.

Flanagan, O. (1991). *Varieties of moral personality: Ethics and psychological realism*. Cambridge: Harvard University Press.

Goodstein, J. (2000). Moral compromise and personal integrity: Exploring the ethical issues of deciding together in organizations. *Business Ethics Quarterly, 10*(4), 805–819.

Harrington, M. (1999). *Care and equality*. New York, NY: Routledge.

Harrington-Meyer, M. (2005). Decreasing welfare, increasing old age inequality: Whose responsibility is it? In R. Hudson (Ed.), *The new politics of old age* (pp. 65–89). Baltimore: The Johns Hopkins University Press.

Held, V. (2006). *The ethics of care: Personal, political, and global*. New York, NY: Oxford University Press.

Herbert, B. (Oct. 6, 2007). Send in the clowns. *New York Times*, Section A, p. 27.

Holstein, M. (1999). Home care, women, and aging: A case study in injustice. In M. U. Walker (Ed.), *Mother time: Women, aging, and ethics*. Lanham, CO: Rowman & Littlefield.

Holstein, M. (2005). A normative defense of universal age-based policies. In R. B. Hudson (Ed.), *The new politics of old age* (pp. 23–41). Baltimore: Johns Hopkins University Press.

Holstein, M. (2007). Long-term care, feminism, and an ethics of solidarity. In R. Pruchno & M. Smyer (Eds.), *Challenges of an aging society* (pp. 156–174). Baltimore, MD: Johns Hopkins University Press.

Holstein, M. (2008). *Economic secrutiy across the generations: Background analysis and policy recommendations.* A white paper. Washington, DC: Wider Opportunities for Women.

Holstein, M. (2009). A normative approach to social security: What dignity requires. In L. Rogne, L. C. Estes, B. Grossman, B. Hollister, & E. Solway (Eds.), *Social insurance and social justice: Social security, and the campaign against entitlements* (pp. 233–250). New York, NY: Springer.

Holstein, M., & Minkler, M. (2003). Self, society and the 'new gerontology.' *The Gerontologist, 43*(6), 787–796.

Holstein, M., & Minkler, M. (2007). Critical gerontology: Reflections for the 21st century. In M. Bernard & T. Scharf (Eds.), *Critical perspectives on ageing societies* (pp. 13–26). Bristol, UK: Policy Press.

Hooyman, N., & Gonyea, J. (1995). *Feminist perspectives on family care.* Thousand Oaks, CA: Sage.

Kane, R. A. (2007). Do not cast me away when I am old: Life and death in old age. *The Gerontologist, 47*(4), 559–565.

Kingdon, J. (2002). The reality of public policy making. In M. Danis, C. Clancy, & L. Churchill (Eds.), *Ethical dimensions of health policy* (pp. 97–116). New York, NY: Oxford University Press.

Kittay, E. F. (1999). *Love's labor: Essays on women, equality, and dependency.* New York, NY: Routledge.

Lakoff, G. (1996). *Moral politics: What conservatives know that liberals don't.* Chicago: University of Chicago Press.

Lindblom, C. (1959). The science of muddling through. *Public Administration Review, 14*, 79–88.

Lindemann-Nelson, H. (2001). *Damaged identities, narrative repair.* Ithaca, NY: Cornell University Press.

Margalit, A. (1996). *The decent society.* Cambridge: Harvard University Press.

Minkler, M. (1991). 'Generational equity' and the new politics of victim blaming. In M. Minkler & C. Estes (Eds.), *Critical perspectives in aging.* Amityville, NY: Baywood Pub; Co.

Minkler, M., & Estes, C. (1999). *Critical gerontology: Perspectives from political and moral economy.* Amityville, NY: Baywood Publishing Company.

Minow, M., & Shanley, M. L. (1996). Relational rights and responsibilities: The family in liberal political theory and law. *Hypatia, 11*(1), 4–29.

Myles, J., & Quadagno, J. (1999). Envisioning a third way: The welfare state in the twenty-first century. *Contemporary Sociology, 29*(1), 156–167.

O'Rand, A. (1996). The precious and the precocious: Understanding cumulative disadvantage and cumulative advantage over the life course. *The Gerontologist*, 36(2), 230–238.

Parks, J. (2003). *No place like home: Feminist ethics and home health care.* Bloomington, IN: University of Indiana Press.

Phillipson, C. (1998). *Reconstructing old age: New agenda in social theory and practice.* London: Sage Publications.

Phillipson, C. (Nov. 2007). *Redefining work and retirement: Globalization and the culture of capitalism.* Paper presented at the Annual Conference, Gerontological Society of America, San Francisco, CA.

Polivka, L. (1998). The science and politics of long-term care. *Generations*, 22(3), 21–25.

Polivka, L., & Longino, C. (2006). The emerging postmodern culture of aging and retirement security. In J. Baars, D. Dannefer, C. Phillipson, & A. Walker (Eds.), *Aging, globalization, and inequality: The new critical gerontology* (pp. 183–204). Amityville, NY: Baywood Publishing Company.

President's Council on Bioethics (2005). *Taking care: Ethical caregiving in our aging society.* Washington, DC: President's Council on Bioethics.

Preston, S. (Nov. 1984). Children and the elderly: Divergent paths for America's dependents. *Demography, 21,* 435–457.

Putney, N., Bengston, V., & Wakeman, M. (2007). The family and the future: Challenges, prospects, and resilience. In R. Pruchno & M. Smyer (Eds.), *Challenges of an aging society: Ethical dilemmas, political issues* (pp. 117–155). Baltimore: Johns Hopkins University Press.

Rawls, J. (1971). *A Theory of Justice.* Cambridge, MA: Harvard University Press.

Rein, M. (1983). Value-critical policy analysis. In D. Callahan & B. Jennings (Eds.), *Ethics, the social sciences, and policy analysis* (pp. 83–111). New York, NY: Plenum Press.

Rogne, L., Estes, C., Grossman, B., Hollister, B., & Solway, E. (Eds.). (2009). *Social insurance and social justice.* New York, NY: Springer Pub. co.

Russell, L., Bruce, E., Conahan, J., & Wider Opportunities for Women (2006). *The WOW-GI national economic security standard: A methodology to determine economic security for elders.* Washington, DC: Wider Opportunities for Women.

Schulz, J., & Binstock, R. (2006). *Aging nation: The economics and politics of growing older in America.* Westport, CT: Praeger Press.

Sennett, R. (1999). *The corrosion of character.* New York, NY: W. W. Norton, cited in Phillipson, C. 2007.

Shanley, M. L. (2001). Public policy and the ethics of care. *Hypatia, 16(3),* 157–160.

Smeeding, T., & Sullivan, D. (1998). Generations and the distribution of economic well-being: A cross-national view. Luxembourg Income Study, working Paper series, No. 173. Cited in Myles, J. & Quadagno, J. *Envisioning a third way.*

Tong, R. (1986). *Ethics in policy analysis.* Englewood Cliffs, NJ: Prentice-Hall.

Tronto, J. (1993). *Moral Boundaries: A political argument for an ethics of care.* New York, NY: Routledge.

Walker, A. (2006). Reexamining the political economy of aging. In J. Baars, D. Dannefer, C. Phillipson, & A. Walker (Eds.), *Aging, globalization, and inequality: The new critical gerontology* (pp. 59–80). Amityville, NY: Baywood Publishing Company.

Wider Opportunities for Women. *The elder economic security initiative.* www.wow online.org.

Williamson, J., McNamara, T., & Howling, S. (2003). Generational equity, generational interdependence, and the framing of the debate over social security reform. *Journal of Sociology and Social Welfare, 30*(3), 3–14.

CHAPTER 7

Care and Justice

Older People at Home

Any real society is a care-giving and a care receiving society and we must therefore discover ways of coping with these facts of human neediness and dependency that are compatible with the self-respect of the recipients and do not exploit the caregiver
—NUSSBAUM, 2002

INTRODUCTION

Caring for older people at home has become a central theme in policy and practice in this country and elsewhere. The reason is obvious: home is where most of us want to be, especially when we face loss of any kind. At home, we can experience delight in familiar objects, photographs, and memories, all sources of self-recognition; at home, we know who we are and what matters to us. Home is where we are most able to be ourselves, however we define that self. It is where we feel psychologically and emotionally safe (Collopy, 1995). The more difficult it becomes to do what we had formerly taken for granted (like cooking, bathing, or dressing), the more important familiar surroundings become.

Home also offers a sense of continuity and connection. It is where we can gradually adapt to what we can no longer easily do. As we becomes less "at home" in our changing bodies, we more than ever need to be "at home" in a familiar physical space (see Shenk, Kuwahara, & Zablotsky, 2004). Being home means that the "sick identity" need not be central (Miller, unpublished data). Instead, we may live in ways that affirm identity, that permit the continuity of familiar habits that are part of the enriched notion of autonomy that George Agich (1990) proposed two decades ago. These identity-preserving features of home are comforting and meaningful, and therefore morally important. The key question is how one can support the sacred value of home without trumping other important values (Holstein, 1999).

These values focus on the other side of home care. Older people who need assistance to remain at home can do so only by relying on others to compensate for what they can no longer do for themselves. Public policy, cultural norms, and the structure of the labor market dictate that these helpers are most often family members, and, more specifically, female family members. Although publicly-funded support is available to older people who have very low incomes, such care is rarely sufficient to meet needs; hence, families must retain their involvement in their loved-one's care. Yet, our culture's reverence for independence and autonomy transform both caregiving and care receiving into anomalies rather than accepting them for what they are: essential features of human life. As a result, dependency and the resulting inability to meet the normative demands of productivity, mastery, and responsibility for oneself (Herskovits & Mitteness, 1994; Luborsky, 1994) threaten one's self-regard and hence one's moral agency. Dependency thus taints both caregiver and care receiver (Dodds, 2007; Parks, 2003) and compounds the already difficult realities they experience. They simply fail to fit into a society in which "personal autonomy and independence are valued and interdependence is not recognized" (Barry, 1995, p. 366).

Home care "provides a lens through which to view the complex relationships [among] cultural assumptions, public policy, and private lives ... It focuses attention on context and on gender and class injustices that are historically endemic to American social welfare policy" (Holstein, 1999, p. 227). Thus, we open this chapter by looking at care as an essential fact of human life and by situating it within the values and structures that now govern home care in this county. These parameters limit the goals or ends that home care can meet and expose the underlying moral concerns that are problematic for both caregiver and care receiver, issues that we explore in the next section. In concluding this chapter, we will bring these perspectives together into a single vision, what we are calling an "ethics of solidarity," which supports the essential relational elements of caring practices. We will further argue for continued narrative framing of the caring experience, so the voices of both care receiver and caregiver can be heard and re-told. This counter narrative Lindemann Nelson (2001) can ground the development of polices and practices responsive to this narrative. Above all, it can redefine our moral language, commitments, and cultural ideals so that they are inclusive of the realities of needing and giving care.

For our arguments, we find support in the work of feminist gerontologists, moral philosophers, and political and legal theorists (Calasanti & Slevin, 2006; Dodds, 2007; Harrington-Meyers, 2000; Holstein, 1999,

2010; Hooyman & Gonyea, 1999; Kittay, 1999; Parks, 2003; Sevenhuijsen, 2000; Tronto, 1993) who have been developing philosophical and political arguments that support a rich view of care, and a commitment to equality for women caregivers, while also re-conceptualizing the hegemonic commitments to independence and autonomy. Theorists on home and long-term care raise political questions about how societies should equitably allocate public resources and, perhaps as importantly, they focus attention on who makes those allocation decisions. As Young (1990) suggests, justice is not only about allocation: it is also about who sits at the table when those decisions are made. Our commitment to discourse, and to hearing voices from the margins, makes this conception of justice particularly relevant.

Care at home raises other important moral questions. It challenges many standard perceptions about the voluntariness of obligations and conventional social roles. What would happen to those among us who cannot care for themselves if no one actively *chose* to give care (Scheman, 1983)? It reminds us that caring work is rarely a free and unimpeded choice. The burden falls the heaviest on low-income women whose choices are already constrained; how their lives "go" is not solely within their control. The practice of home care presses the adequacy of a moral vision that is individualistic rather than relational, and further exemplifies this book's central stance on privilege and care: that individuals with privilege can afford to (and oftentimes do) overlook the invisible care work that makes such privilege possible (Holstein, 1999).

Commonly held ideas about the nature and scope of moral problems fit poorly with the situation of home care. People who need care are clearly "fourth agers" who cannot maintain the myth of agelessness and norms associated with youth and midlife that we challenged in Chapter 4. They certainly cannot meet expectations that their lives will reflect "independence and full reciprocity in human relationships" (Walker, 2003, p. xvi). Moreover, an ethics that focuses on choice, as it evolved in the acute care setting, does not notice the most complex problems in home care. The primary issues in home care are not what Agich (1990) has called "nodal autonomy," that is, a single decision about a critically important issue. While there are discrete and urgent decisions that must be made in chronic care situations, decision-making within this arena involves much more. It involves living with loss in an ageist society that privatizes and devalues dependency needs; it is about the gendered nature of care and the euphemistic language of "family care" that obscures this fundamental fact. Home care is also about the conflicting demands that care providers face, and the tacit assumption that care is a private activity. Care at home is about very human situations that are not easily fixable: it addresses existential angst about meaning and purpose, loss and death, and families and relationships. These issues become especially pertinent when they are situated within a political setting like the Unites States, where the government treats individuals, families, and the market as the parties responsible for elder care. The neo-liberal ideology discussed in Chapter 6 has little regard for people poorly served by the market. Care at home cannot be governed by a single, universal value, and it cannot be reduced to a set of instrumental tasks. We must take seriously that older people, who need help to make it though the day, deserve help that sustains their identity and self-respect. Yet such help must be possible without exploiting others, whether wives, daughters or home care aides. Therefore, we must design a very different system of home care that achieves good for the elder care recipient without doing harm to her caregivers.

CARE: AN ESSENTIAL HUMAN NEED

That we are all dependent and vulnerable at different times in our lives is an essential fact of being human. As we age, that likelihood increases. Our bodies will wear down no matter how well we have tried to care for ourselves. Hence, we will need to be cared for. Older people who need such care are "part of the ongoing relations of care" (Tronto, 1995, p. 41) that permits society to function. None of us would be alive today if someone had not cared for us; and many more older people would be in institutions if there were no one to do for them what they cannot do for themselves. Yet, bombarded by messages about independence, many older people will often go to great lengths to deny their needs, thereby imperiling their health and well-being (Agich, 2003). In so doing, they sacrifice what caregivers can offer—relief of suffering and pain "so that they can carry on with their lives as well as possible" (Engster, 2005, p. 53). This is not a luxury. Yet, we also recognize how hard it must be to accept help.

Authentic caring, we stress, differs from meeting needs and providing services. Care is created in and through relationships, and is something that happens between two or more people. It is not done for someone; it is done *with* someone. Care is better characterized by the interactions between mother and child than the interactions between a mechanic and a client. Care "requires understanding that people are bound together with hopes and fears, opportunities and challenges" (Caputo, 2002, p. 4) and is, therefore, not a casual activity to be entered into lightly. It must be competent, attentive, respectful, adequate to meet needs, and cautious about the potential for abusing power as a result of one person's vulnerability.

Understanding care in this way suggests why the commitment to a thin and individualistic conception of autonomy that governs public sector provision of care is so limited. Hoffmaster (April 14, 2008) noted that autonomy "represents the moral easy road. When respecting autonomy is the way one *cares for* a person, *caring about* that person can be lost." As such, the ideals of "autonomous individuality" clash with the "concrete realities of aging" and caregiving (Walker, 1998, p. 99).

DEPENDENCY, VULNERABILITY, AND FRAILTY

Over the past two decades, feminist philosophers (see, e.g., Hekman, 1995; Mackenzie & Stoljar, 2000; Meyers, 1989) have been critiquing commonly held ideas about the nature of the self and proposing alternative conceptions. While their work goes beyond the scope of this chapter, one thread is relevant—the proposal that the self is essentially dependent and vulnerable (see Dodds, 2007; Kittay, 1999). To accept this kind of self would go a long way toward mitigating the anomalous place that people who need and give care occupy in our society. Certainly, people who need care are unavoidably dependent on others; but, as Kittay (1999) observes, those who give care experience a derivative dependency, since to care adequately for others they need care themselves. Recognizing and accepting these dependency needs might ease the stigma associated with dependency and, importantly, might sever the tie between self-determination and self-esteem. That tie, as Kittay (2006) observes, makes self-esteem "terribly precarious" and the "state of independence much in need of defending. Because we want to deny our dependency when we need it the most we make those, who provide that care, invisible" (p. 35).

Home care programs, with their almost singular emphasis on independence, thus deny the most important reason elders rely on these programs for services. People who are vulnerable lose much control over their lives because they lack the energy or even the interest to make decisions, even if someone else can implement them (Hoffmaster, 2006). Without understanding and appreciating frailty, vulnerability, and the relationships these necessitate, community care programs can easily miss morally important elements of care. Independence, for example, has little room for the relational elements that the feminist ethics of care sees as central to caregiving. To morally respond to vulnerability and frailty calls for values other than independence and choice (Hoffmaster, 2006), which are the articulated goals of public programs. At a minimum, the feminist care ethics calls upon us to see caregiver and care receiver as intimately bound together in a necessarily unequal relationship. By acknowledging this inequality and solidarity, we can rethink the state's responsibility for care, ensuring that the inequality between caregiver and care recipient does not become exploitative.

GIVING AND RECEIVING CARE: BASIC FACTS

"Caregiving by women has ... become the unarticulated cornerstone of American long-term care policy" (Holstein, 1999, p. 234). It is what women are expected to do and what they, themselves, expect to do. The issue of caregiver "burden," especially the "informal" caregiving of family members, has been subject to considerable research. In contrast, the experience of receiving care has been largely under-researched. With the exception of a few studies (Aronson, 1990; Barry, 1995), we know little about how older people, mostly women, assess the meaning of needing care. What we do know is painful. Because the formal system of care is tacitly rationed, older women learn to do without, accepting that their important goals will not be met. Aronson (1990) notes that "motivated to reduce feelings of guilt and shame, women implicitly suppress assertion of their own needs, so that the broad pattern of care of old people goes unchallenged—rather it is sustained and reproduced" (p. 77). Further, because care receivers perceive care as instrumental and minimalist, they gradually stop expecting that things can change. When care is provided by their family members, they want "caring about" rather than "caring for," preferring that more instrumental tasks be tended to by formal caregivers (Barry, 1995). Practically, however, most older people who have long-term care needs (about 65%) rely solely on family members for care; another 30% supplement this care with paid caregivers. This reliance makes many care receivers uneasy; few wish to burden their loved ones, although the fear of being a burden may itself be gendered.

Research on caregivers, which has been more extensive, shows that the responsibilities are substantial and the costs are real. The unspoken assumption is that family caregivers not only *should* but *will* be available to provide care services. This tacit assumption prevailed when, in 1965, Congress passed Medicare and decided not to cover long-term care services. The exclusion of such services was supported by the fear that if a public benefit was available for family caregivers, they would come "out of the woodwork" to claim it. Instead, research has shown that caregivers do not ask for replacement care but for a "supplement and respite from what they continually provide" (Hooyman & Gonyea, 1999, p. 163). The unsubstantiated "woodwork" concern, then, is rooted in an anti-welfarist bias that persists to this day.

"Informal" caregivers, primarily women, have substantial out-of-pocket costs, lose wages, and experience other practical difficulties that cannot be easily resolved. Even if they receive assistance from publicly supported programs, they burn out or wear out, making continued care at home difficult if not impossible. The experiences of caregiving translate into a generalized and "fairly constant anxiety, relentless tiredness, and an urgent need to protect the parent's dignity and maintain his or her sense of self" (Holstein, 1999, p. 238). Caregivers are sensitive to the problem of role reversal and so strive to preserve the essence of former relationships. They are proud of what they do—especially their commitments to support identity and continuity (Caron & Bowers, 2003)—and often express responsibility for protecting their parents' autonomy, independence, and choice, which can create contradictory pressures between their sense of responsibility and their commitment to respecting autonomy (Funk, 2010).

As Kittay (1999) and Goodin (1985) have pointed out, the obligation to give care is grounded in a response to vulnerability. Women, as a result of ideology, cultural expectations, power relationships within families, the gendered division of labor, and their social experiences, seem to act on, and perhaps experience, this obligation differently than men (Brewer, 2001; Bubeck, 2002). Thus, while many men assume great responsibilities in caring for their wives and elderly parents, women provide 60–75% of "informal" care and spend 50% more time on caregiving activities than men (Family Caregiver Alliance, 2001). Further, men are more likely to do the instrumental tasks that can be scheduled—paying bills or mowing the lawn—and not the personal care services like bathing or dressing. It is unlikely that this situation will change anytime soon (Holstein, 1999; Hooyman & Gonyea, 1999). Even when an older person receives help from the public sector, if a family member is available, public benefits are reduced. As a result, the value of family caregiving, when translated into dollars, amounts to more than $195 billion a year (Arno, Levine, & Memmot, 1999). Family care is a significant factor in keeping older people out of the nursing homes they dread. Lacking family caregivers, 50% of older people with long-term care needs are in nursing homes; only 7% who have a family member to care for them are placed in long-term care institutions (Administration on Aging, 2000).

Caregiving is also directly costly: for example, buying medical equipment, installing assistive devices, purchasing drugs, and hiring help can sometimes mean financial hardship (Family Caregiving Alliance, 2001). These consequences are set against a background of collapsing pensions, climbing medical costs, and the erosion of job security. They further exacerbate the already existing inequality in late life when women are more likely than men to be poor. There are also personal costs. Depression and anxiety are familiar accompaniments of caregiving (Family Caregiver Alliance, 2001). Other health effects, such as not filling one's own prescriptions or failing to take advantage of preventive care, are also common.

Many of these consequences flow from the atypical situation of caregivers in a society that presumes most people can take care of themselves and that views choice as the essential feature of moral agency. Caregivers are not autonomous agents; caring responsibilities may "impose themselves" in ways that may render the caregiver's "life plans unrealizeable" (Bubeck, 2002). But as long as it is assumed that caregiving activities are freely chosen, even among those who give care, the problems of justice and the disregard of other moral values will be effaced. Walker (1998) reminds us that "some prejudices are so culturally normative" (i.e., that women make better caregivers) "that they are hardly experienced as problematic, which means that even those who are at the losing end of the prejudices do not deliberate about them" (p. 181). In particular, "the voices of middle- and lower-income groups, who are the most likely to face serious caregiver-related problems, are absent from the public conversation" (Verba, Schlozman, & Brady, 1995, cited by Harrington, 2000, p. 179). Thus, the ability to perceive the problems created by the current system is further limited. This limitation is important because the first step in moral responsiveness is to perceive that a problem exists. To distribute the caregiving responsibilities more equitably is partly an individual problem, but it is also a social one. Until large campaign contributors or legislators change the diapers of the old or prepare a meal or take them on slow walks around the block, they will have difficulty empathizing with either the people who are unable to do such tasks or those who assume responsibility for them. Until decision makers either are (or hear from) the people who need such care and those who provide the care, it is unlikely that they will address the relevant instrumental and personal costs.

Public sector care provision, while often intimately connected to family care, raises concerns of another sort. Medicaid, the most important source of public funds for home care, while vitally needed, is no panacea. Recipients often perceive this means-tested program as "welfare" and hence stigmatizing. To qualify, they must have almost no assets (except their home and a car) and a very low income, often well below the poverty line. As a result, they often resist applying for and choose to do without the help it might make available. The need to reveal personal details of their lives to qualify, and fear for the well-being of a spouse, makes it even more unattractive. State Medicaid recovery policies, which ask that states recover costs to Medicaid from whatever assets are left at a client's death, adds to their reluctance to apply.

Resources are inadequate to meet care needs. Home care workers may often not speak the same language as the person for whom they have the most basic and often intimate responsibilities. They are poorly paid, rarely topping the poverty line in terms of annual pay, and get few, if any, benefits. The organizational imperatives their employers face to serve a certain number of clients in the least amount of time and the accountabilities that workers are expected to meet, often clash with what the workers and their clients perceive as being most important (Parks, 2003; Stone, 2000). These aides, again mostly women, face the corrosive effects of feeling unrecognized for the work they do. They often are placed in dangerous situations, such as bad neighborhoods, sexually intimidating clients, or abusive family members, and thus may experience low morale as a result. The annual turnover of home care workers in some parts of the country exceeds 100%. These facts affect the quality of care and contribute to the inadequate supply of well-trained caregivers. The consequences are important because competence and sustained, trusting relationships are essential moral qualities in any good caregiving relationship (Tronto, 1993).

This "formal" system of care constrains the central value of "home" in important ways. The primary function of the community care system is to assure that the older person's basic physical needs are met so that they can stay out of a nursing home. "Consumers" of such services are subject to the technocratic expertise of a system that determines eligibility and identifies the help that is available. Because of limited resources, this help tends to be pragmatic and instrumental, albeit essential. In this environment, care is reduced to services that are "unbundled" so that one can purchase a little of this and a little of that. As a result, the system, however, well-intended, offers what Baars (2006) describes as a "pitstop" model of care. Low wage workers, also predominantly women, are assigned a limited amount of time to achieve certain tasks. This expectation leaves them little opportunity to engage in the relationship-building, identity-affirming activities that they, much like "informal" caregivers, find so important. Often, they resist the rules and so endanger their jobs (Parks, 2003; Stone, 2000).

In some states, consumers can hire their own home care aide, including family members, to implement care plans. Known as consumer-directed care, states vary in how freely clients may use the money they are allocated. Evaluations (Doty, Benjamin, Matthias, & Franke, 2009; Polivka & Salmon, 2001) of consumer-directed care have generally been favorable especially when the older person can choose between consumer-directed care and agency-organized care. Consumers particularly appreciate the greater flexibility about who provides the care and in what way. Critics, however, are concerned about the need to assure that caregivers receive adequate training and that professionals monitor the care that is provided. Since the line between paid and unpaid care is hard to draw, especially if the caregiver is a family member, the potential increased burden on family caregivers must also be monitored.

The consequences of this situation—that long-term care resides primarily in the private or family realm and that its financing is treated differently than that of acute care—raises ethically important questions that touch upon the lives of elderly care recipients and their caregivers. Both parties are fundamentally unequal those who seem to neither need nor give care.

The following case study highlights some common problems that arise in the home care setting. We include it here in order to provide a narrative that speaks to the caregiver/care recipient relationship, and the context within which it takes place.

EVERYONE WANTS THE BEST, BUT . . .

Frances Olds just celebrated her 82nd birthday. She is forgetful but has not been diagnosed with Alzheimer's disease. The major problem is her lack of mobility because of severe arthritis and congestive heart failure. She lives in her own home and has been very insistent that she wants to stay there. Her daughter, Jodie Green stops by every day and makes her mother breakfast, gets her up and dressed, and leaves her food for later in the day. She also calls several times a day. Jodie worries about her all the time especially since Mrs. Olds has fallen twice and has, on occasion, been incontinent because she cannot get to the bathroom fast enough. When Jodie broached the idea of Depends, her mother became very upset and refused to talk about it. Mrs. Olds is not a difficult woman but her care needs are significant and chronic. Jodie is a social worker. She has started to work part time but is very concerned about money since one of the Green children is in college and the other two will be in a few years. Jodie's husband, Max, is an attorney with a non-profit advocacy organization. Money has always been a little tight but the Greens are committed to living according to their core values and so have not sought jobs that would pay more. Their two teen-age children, who are still at home, love their grandmother but are pretty busy with their own lives. They help out on weekends but not on school days. Jodie's two brothers live about 50 miles away. They visit and send money as often as they can but they don't have much to spare given that they each have four children, and wives who do not earn very much. They visit as often as they can taking care of household chores and mowing the lawn. They would like to help out more but at the moment, they can't see doing more than they are already doing. Jodie admits that she is exhausted. Her own blood pressure has started to climb and she is not sleeping well. She takes advantage of the support group that a local social services agency convenes whenever she can find the time. She finds it very helpful and values the help of the caregiver specialist who answers many of her questions.

Another year goes by. During this period, Mrs. Olds was placed in the hospital a few times, which for Jodie meant periods of respite, even though she visited every day. When her mother returns home, her needs seem to have expanded since she requires a special diet and needs monitoring to be sure that she takes her medications regularly. Jodie now visits her mother two times a day and calls at other times. She is still working but finds that she is distracted and often unable to focus. She wonders if it would be easier for her mother to move in with her or perhaps to an assisted living facility. Her family is not comfortable with the idea of Mrs. Olds moving in with them. The house is small and there are stairs so the family room would need to become Mrs. Olds' bedroom thus dislocating the family gathering place. Jodie decides to talk to her mother about moving to assisted living, hoping that her condition will not necessitate a nursing home since she knows that her mother has been very insistent that going to a nursing home would devastate her. Mrs. Olds is unwilling to discuss moving. "This is where I have lived for 40 years. I intend to die here. If that happens sooner rather than later, I'm okay with that. I love my home where I can relive so much of my past. It's where my memories are and where I happily lived with your father for almost our entire marriage. Take me away from here and you take away much of what I am." Jodie understands what her mother is saying but that doesn't solve her problem of feeling that she cannot continue as she has been doing for the past 2 years. She has had no real break, has had to give up almost all the activities that she loves, and often feels that she is neglecting her husband and children. She is at her wits end. Her mother's very legitimate wishes and her needs can't both be achieved without some change and she is not sure what that will be. She knows that she can hire someone to come in for a few hours each day but she worries about the costs, even with help from her brother, and is also concerned that nobody can care for her mother like she can. Her mother's income just about covers her basic costs but is too high to qualify for any publicly funded services. She has very limited assets but is still over the eligibility line for Medicaid. And she hasn't even broached the subject with her mother of some stranger coming to help out.

This case reflects the delicate balance that must be achieved between what Mrs Olds and Jodie most want, what Mrs Olds needs, and what is possible given Jodie's situation. The situation they now face is part of an ongoing story of their long and loving relationship with one another. Practically speaking, Mrs Olds is too "rich" for publicly funded services and too "poor" to purchase adequate help at home; she is intensely resistant to leaving home for reasons that are fully understandable. The practical advantage of moving is that her house can then be sold, providing some resources for care. But then Mrs Olds loses her home, which is her source of meaning and identity. Jodie is "right" for saying she can do no more and Mrs Olds is "right" for her passionate wish to stay home, even if it shortens her life. Jodie thinks that her mother can be persuaded to have someone come in to help. Mrs Olds won't like it, but she does care about her daughter's health and well-being. The problem is that limited resources mean that Jodie will still have to be deeply involved in the instrumental aspects of her mother's care, unless her brothers can contribute more money to cover the costs of hiring an assistant.

Jodie wants to protect and affirm her mother's personhood. She also has obligations to herself and to her family. Suppose that she and her mother start to talk about what is at stake, what is needed and what is practical. As a result Mrs Olds agrees to a regular visit from a paid home care aide, to meet basic needs like getting up in the morning, having her bath, getting dressed and having breakfast. This home care aide, however, will not take over all the care that Jodie has provided.

Within a short time, Mrs Olds "spends down" and becomes eligible for Medicaid-supported home care. At their request, she and Jodie meet with the care coordinator; a care plan is developed and a list of home care agencies offered. Without a great deal of information, Jodie and her mother select the ABC Agency. Margie, the home health aide, comes to the house to assist Mrs Olds. She is very efficient, friendly and does her assigned tasks, leaving within her scheduled two hours. Mrs Olds is appreciative but feels as if she is an object and not a person with a history, preferences and ideas. Over time, she comes to know Margie better and one day asks if she can just sit and talk for a little while. Margie replies that she has a job to do and that she may be fired if she fails to complete all the assigned tasks. Jodie continues to be involved in her mother's care but she is back to work full-time and has less time than she would like to have to be with her mother.

Gradually, Mrs Olds gives up trying to engage Margie or to have things as she likes them. She is in that period of being a recipient of care in which she no longer asks for much because she knows she won't get it, not because Margie or Jodie don't care, but because of the implicit rationing of care and the conflicting pressures that Margie and Jodie are experiencing (Aronson, 1990). Mrs Olds is lucky: she still has Jodie to remind her that she is loved and valued for who she is. As we see in this case, frailty abuts a publicly rationed system of care and the multiple pressures that the best-intentioned family caregivers face.

Yet, Mrs Olds has managed to avoid a nursing home; and she has partici-pated in choosing the agency that provides her home care. Together she and Jodie helped to develop her plan of care. Margie is competent although hurried. In most ways, the goals of publicly funded community care have been met. Despite these positive aspects to her situation, Mrs Olds has basically given up. She doesn't try to engage Margie and while she continues to eagerly anticipate Jodie's visits, her daughter is also rushed. Jodie gets little help from her siblings, who have reduced the frequency of their visits; and she still worries about her mother all the time, especially as Mrs Olds' memory seems to be worsening. She is beginning to wonder if her mother might not be better off in an assisted living facility: then she would have other people around, and help available as needed. Additionally, the sale of her house would free up some money for extra care.

At this point, one might wonder if there are any good ways to respond to the panoply of problems that arise in this case: a worn out daughter, a competent but task-oriented paid caregiver, Mrs Olds' escalating frailty, and the problem of maintaining her meaningful and self-expressive choices within these complex relationships of care.

A RESPONSE

Supporting Kittay's argument that those who give care ought to be entitled to "a socially supported situation in which one can give care without the care giving becoming a liability to one's own well-being" (1999, p. 66), we start with a defense of a collective responsibility for giving care. Given that there are no morally relevant differences between those who do and do not provide care, caregivers have justice-based claims on society to support their caregiving activities. Any rich conception of justice would hold that a response to the threats to equality posed by an inequitable distribution of caregiving responsibilities must be remedied. It is not women's work. Care is as much a collective responsibility of society as is military defense or keeping our cities clean. It is a "public responsibility to guarantee a minimal level of services to all citizens as a public good in which all citizens should participate without undue burden" (Hooyman & Gonyea, 1999, p. 165). Practically, this can be accomplished by a small increase in Medicare taxes. It has been done in Western Europe without severely burdening the system. We thus begin with recommendations that support this end.

We ground our argument for collective responsibility for caregiving by noting first that caregivers have legitimate interests that cannot be set aside indefinitely (Arras, 1995). We contend that old cliché that one mother can take care of several children but one child cannot take care of an older parent is a faulty and unjust analogy. A daughter caring for her 84-year-old mother is different than a mother caring for her children. The daughter is literally the person in the middle with expectations from others and from herself to meet multiple and often conflicting needs. A mother to young children also faces conflicting demands but her parenting role is generally a central one. A daughter taking responsibility for her mother is assuming a physically and emotionally demanding role for which she gets little support, little recognition, for which she often pays a high price, and which will become increasingly more difficult. To assume that she can do this without help is once again to see through the lens of privilege. One can affirm that it is the daughter's responsibility if one has never been in the position to assume that role whether one wants to or not. Among family members we look for a fair distribution of responsibilities. This redistribution means redefining care as a family's, not a woman's, responsibility. Women are better at caregiving, it is claimed; but if that is so, it is only because they have had more practice.

The recent economic crisis has made it increasingly clear that the neoliberal solution to human need is unable to respond to the caring needs of many older people (see Chapter 6). Neither the market nor families, nor individuals can replace a strong social safety net. Further, the crises have reinforced the recognition that states, with their need to have balanced budgets, will never have adequate resources to assure good care at home (Fahey, 2007). These facts point to the need for stronger federal commitments. Any society that purports to be just needs to take the need for care as a central fact of human life deserving of a response.

Yet, the continued focus on individualistic notions of autonomy cannot support this view of justice since it elides the relational elements of care that moral philosophers have defended and family caregivers enact. It is relatively easy to give a person choice of one home care agency over another. That does not demand structural or policy changes. It is relatively simple, and not unimportant, to offer support groups or some respite to caregivers. It is much more difficult, however, to support the view of care that we have been defending in this chapter. Because the older person rarely recovers lost functions and therefore does not cease needing care, the intensity of the caring experience can tax the most committed family members. While much in today's society challenges these familiar bonds, they are demonstrated repeatedly in the community. The existence of these bonds and the ways in which different people enact the responsibilities that these bonds evoke, in a microcosm, say much about our particular moral identities—who we believe we are and what we count as morally important. Societal recognition of these bonds, what they lead people to do, and then to provide support for them would be a visible affirmation of the politically correct, but so far, impoverished, notion of "family values." Caregiver support programs that exist in most communities are important but they do not alter the structural inequalities and gender inequities that make the current caregiving situation so problematic.

VALUES TO SUPPORT CARE AT HOME

We are not convinced that autonomy, as now defined in community care, deserves the weight assigned to it. When relationships resulting from dependency constitute the difference between making it and not making it for many older people like Mrs Olds, autonomy cannot be only about Mrs Olds' wishes. While her deepening frailty calls for a response, the response must be an inclusive one that recognizes and finds ways to support Jodie's commitments to her mother, to her nuclear family, and to herself. By obscuring the family, ethical individualism isolates the elder and negates the interdependencies that exist. Autonomous choice so understood can easily efface concerns about justice. The goal for long-term care, in Margaret Walker's (2003), words is to achieve a moral world where individuals, families, and others can live and flourish as well as possible. The dominant voices of independence, individualism, and even self-interested choices fail to adequately account for what matters most to people—the connections that tell them they continue to be persons of worth. Neither independence nor autonomy can capture the importance of subjectivity and the striving for identity preservation or reconstitution that accompany the expected losses of old age. As a socially situated person, the individual receiving care needs love and compassion as much or more than autonomy and choice. The language of relationships becomes hijacked by the language and usually the myth of independence. An ethics of solidarity for care at home that we uphold would place the relational elements of caregiving and care receiving as central. It would acknowledge that these relationships cannot survive and thrive in the absence of the background conditions that make them possible.

Appropriate aims may not be about decision-making but rather about "being present to one another ... and responding to need—which might entail comforting, celebration, or companionship ... ." (Furman, 1997, p. 29). This holistic view supports integrity not only as an individual's commitment to him or herself but that incorporates our accountability to others, Mrs Olds to Jodie as well as Jodie to Mrs. Olds. We highlight the goals that we see as being essential for care at home. On the individual level we ought to sustain and nurture relationships; enhance dignity irrespective of an individual's physical or cognitive condition; create meaningful opportunities and choices; make it possible for people to live as free from pain and suffering as possible; and to feel both safe and secure. We must honor privacy, give people the chance to make *informed and meaningful choices*, provide them with competent, adequate, and respectful care, and assure basic economic security. While care at home cannot guarantee a good quality of life, it should not foreclose imaginative consideration of how a different vision of care at home can improve quality of life (Kane, 2001). We need to (1) take care seriously, (2) embrace the changing family as a liberal ideal and find ways to support mutual caring activities, (3) make the possibility of equality real for those who give care, whether as a family member or as a paid caregiver, (4) challenge the cultural assumptions that take women for granted, and (5) introduce new normative ideals that focus on solidarity and obligations to others as necessary for human survival and thriving.

NEXT STEPS

To start, we want to counter the frequently spoken belief that no society can afford the burgeoning population of its sickest and oldest members. While there are certainly elements of truth to this claim, we argue that this should not be a reason to abandon the ideal however; far away it might seem at this time. Without it, we will never know what might be possible. In concluding, we will suggest some ways to try to edge us closer to the ideal. Immediately, however, we need to infuse the system with more money through such possibilities as state income tax increases, an income tax check-off for long-term care, or a tax on retirement income for people with higher incomes. Bringing more dedicated money into the system would help, but even that cannot remedy the diversion of Medicaid resources from women and children to elderly people. A few simple changes would also help a little. Family leave policies—especially if they can be modified to include some pay—would help to address this problem. Using Medicaid waivers or other housing resources to create different housing options with services is another option. While congregate living might be less desirable than staying in one's own home, it is more efficient and is clearly not an institution. Older people can bring much of "home" with them. Increasing the asset and income level for community-based and institutional services is also useful. We must make it easier for older people to accept Medicaid benefits by streamlining application procedure, making it less invasive of privacy, and finding ways to protect some reasonable legacy for the working middle class even if they spend down to Medicaid limits. Reductions in the estate tax serve that end for the more affluent. Poorer people have at least an equal need to leave a legacy as richer people do. Our ability to accumulate resources is not equal; but the wish to leave something behind is a common human wish.

We might also look at models that are in use in other parts of the world. For example, in 1994 Germany introduced a landmark national social insurance program for long-term care (Cuellar & Wiener, 2000). Family members can receive payment for care, but, significantly, they earn pension credits and a four-week vacation each year, with the state paying the costs of replacement care. They also receive special training. This system achieves certain important ends. The informal caregiver is not taken for granted; nor is a care plan built around her or his availability. Family care is rewarded by cash payments, if that option is chosen, and by vacation time and pension benefits. These elements go a long way toward reducing exploitation. It is beyond the scope of this chapter to consider the actual workings of the system, which are not without concerns (Cuellar & Wiener, 2000), but its broad philosophical underpinnings, based on beliefs that the operating value is solidarity rather than individualism, are worth some attention in this country. And contrary to what some might have expected, the system costs less than what was projected, perhaps because more people than expected chose the cash option, which is only 60% of the service option.

Further steps, which we believe are necessary and defensible, are less concrete. Earlier in this chapter, we introduced feminist reconsiderations about the nature of the self, including the view that dependency and vulnerability are essential conditions of all human life. We return to that idea now. As we argued in Chapters 3 and 4, we are concerned about the effects on self-worth and moral agency that normative ideas about beauty or culture create. Privileged in origin and ill-suited for large numbers of older women and men, these ideals continue, albeit in a reduced fashion, for people who need help at home. While the central goal might be staying out of an institution, the moral language supporting that goal is independence and autonomy. We rejected that language in favor of solidarity and the need to see care receiver and caregiver through a single lens. What might it mean to push the envelope further and openly speak the language of vulnerability and dependency as a universal human condition? The notion of interdependency is now increasingly entering the public conversation. The aims of changing—and internalizing—a new language are to reaffirm the value of people who need and give care as having no less self-worth than any other citizen. It would permit severing the ties between self-determination and self-worth and make it less difficult to ask for and accept help when needed.

We do not know, for sure, if the language of dependency and vulnerability would result in the changes that we and others suggest are possible. There is also the language of virtue that can transform the values associated with care at home. Hence, we turn, as we do in other chapters, to communities of meaning where people young and old, healthy and ill, in need of care or giving care, can discuss how the acceptance of care and the rendering of it can be fully integrated into what it means to be a worthy person. They can also consider other questions that address ways to "modify cultural conditions that serve as mechanisms of social control" (Holstein, 1999, p. 241) while engaging in imaginative exercises that situate healthy persons in circumstances that resemble that of persons who are frail. They can develop a different language of need that is based on different questions about what care ought to be about. They can "generate a new language that can situate notions like dignity, self-respect, and cultural inclusion within the context of relationships of dependency" (Holstein, 1999, p. 242).

CONCLUSION

An ethically based long-term care system will situate older people in the context of home, family, community, and the larger society without exploiting others. It will aim for cultural recognition that the measure of a good society is how well it commits itself to the idea that "everyone is entitled to receive adequate care throughout their lives" (White & Tronto, 2004, p. 445). Support for family caregivers would make it easier for them to engage in the quotidian activities that support memory, identity, and dignity. It will recognize that the market is an inadequate vehicle for the provision of care and will involve both recipients and providers of care in a public process that determines how society ought to respond to the universal need for care. We also argued for better wages and benefits for paid home care aides and giving them greater freedom to respond to the particularities of each client's situation. These policy and pragmatic changes are morally defensible on basic grounds of equal treatment but also on the grounds of morally responsive care. They will allow more examples of exemplary care to develop and reduce frayed nerves and exhaustion—and even though caregiver stress is not the primary case of elder abuse and neglect, these changes might also reduce the incidence of those tragic events (see Chapter 10 for a full discussion on this topic). Until the background conditions that "mediate life's possibilities and reinforce the conditions of inequality" (Holstein, 1999, p. 242) change, both equality and authentic care will remain elusive.

An ethical long-term care system will also make information about access and quality easily available. Such access supports our commitment in this book to democratic processes of knowledge production and deliberation: we should involve as many people as possible in deciding if what we are proposing moves us in the direction of enhancing well-being of both the receiver and giver of care. We ask that both recipients and providers of care engage in a public process that determines how society ought to respond to the universal need for care.

In our synoptic view of caregiving and care receiving, a collective response to the human need for care can make it possible for family members to continue doing what they can do better than anyone else: to protect and maintain the care recipient's sense of self and continuity (Caron & Bowers, 2003). While, based on concerns for justice, we do not believe that family members are required to provide care (Jecker, 2002), we believe that *they* have claims in justice to get whatever assistance they need to continue their caring work. Furthermore, in the publicly-funded system of care, home care aides deserve both a participatory role in deciding how they will do their work and improved wages and benefits. These front line workers should also receive what many of them claim is most important of all: respect from supervisors and others, and recognition that their work has value.

The language of community care needs to be rethought so that it can account for more than a narrow understanding of autonomy and choice. It must conceptualize the elder and his or her caregiver as partners in making care at home supportive of identity and value. As we argued in Chapter 6, ethics can offer a morally sustainable background analysis that can provide a setting for policy development. By even suggesting that the norms of independence may be a faulty description of what and who we are, we can pose different questions about what we owe to people.

We close where we began, but with a slight caveat. Care at home is important for all the reasons identified in our introduction, but there may come a point when it cannot be continued. In those cases, there is a related obligation to ensure that nursing homes or other sites of care put an emphasis on *home*. While they cannot exactly replicate one's private home due to regulations, design features, and lack of privacy, there are nevertheless ways to make such places more welcoming and home-like. We look to a new generation of alternative living arrangements to accommodate those for whom it is no longer possible to stay at home.

REFERENCES

Administration on Aging. (2000). *America's families care: A report on the needs of America's family caregivers.* Retrieved from www.aoa.gov/carenetwork/report.html

Agich, G. (1990). Reassessing autonomy in long-term care. *Hastings Center Report*, *20*(6), 12–17.

Agich, G. (2003). *Dependence and autonomy in old age*. New York, NY: Cambridge University Press.

Arno, P., Levine, C., & Memmot, M. (1999). The economic value of informal caregiving. *Health Affairs*, *18*(2), 182–188.

Aronson, J. (1990). Women's perspectives on informal care of the elderly: Public ideology and personal experience of giving and receiving care. *Ageing and Society*, *10*, 61–84.

Arras, J. (1995). Conflicting interests in long-term care decision making: Acknowledging, dissolving, and resolving conflicts. In L. McCullough & N. Wilson (Eds.), *Long-term care decisions: Ethical and conceptual dimensions* (pp. 197–217). Baltimore, MD: Johns Hopkins University Press.

Baars, J. (2006). Beyond neomodernism, antimodernism, and postmodernism: Basic categories for contemporary critical gerontology. In J. Baars, D. Dannefer, C. Phillipson, & A. Walker (Eds.), *Aging, globilization, and inequality: The new critical gerontology* (pp. 17–42). Amityville, NY: Baywood Publishing Company.

Barry, J. (1995). Care-need and care-receivers: View from the margin. *Womens's International Forum*, *18*(3), 361–374.

Brewer, L. (2001). Gender socialization and the cultural construction of elder caregivers. *Journal of Aging Studies*, *15*(3), 217–235.

Bubeck, D. G. (2002). Justice and the labor of care. In E. F. Kittay & E. K. Feder (Eds.), *The subject of care: Feminist perspectives on dependency* (pp. 160–85). Lanham, MD: Rowman & Littlefield.

Calasanti, T., & Slevin, K. (2006). *Age matters: Realigning feminist thought*. New York, NY: Routledge.

Caputo, R. (2002). Social justice, the ethics of care, and market economies. *Families in Society*, *83*(4), 355–364.

Caron, C., & Bowers, B. (2003). Deciding whether to continue, share, or relinquish caregiving: Caregiver views. *Qualitative Health Research*, *13*(9), 1251–1271.

Collopy, B. (1995). In L. McCullough & N. Wilson (Eds.), *Long-term care decisions: Ethical and conceptual dimensions*. Baltimore, MD: Johns Hopkins University Press.

Cuellar, A. E., & Wiener, J. (2000). Can social insurance for long-term care work? The experience of Germany. *Health Affairs*, *19*(3), 8–25.

Dodds, S. (2007). Depending on care: Recognition of vulnerability and the social contribution of care provision. *Bioethics*, *21*(9), 500–510.

Doty, P., Benjamin, A. E., Matthias, R., & Franke, T. (2009). In-home supportive services for the elderly and the disabled: A comparison of client-directed and professional models of service delivery. *U.S. Department of Health and Human Services*. Retrieved from Aspe.hhs.gove/daltcp/.../ihss.htm

Engster, D. (2005). Rethinking care theory: The practice of caring and the obligation to care. *Hypatia*, *20*(3), 50–74.

Fahey, C. J. (2007). The ethics of long-term care: Recasting the policy discourse. In R. A. Pruchno & A. M. Smyer (Eds.), *Challenges of an aging society: Ethical dilemmas, political issues.* Baltimore, MD: Johns Hopkins Press.

Family Caregiver Alliance. (2001). *Selected caregiver statistics.* San Francisco. Accessed at http://www.caregiver.org/jsp/content_node.jsp?nodeid=439

Funk, L. (2010). Prioritizing parental autonomy: Adult children's accounts of feeling responsible and supporting aging parents. *Journal of Aging Studies, 24,* 57–64.

Furman, F. (1997). *Facing the mirror: Old women and beauty shop culture.* New York, NY: Routledge.

Goodin, R. (1985). *Protecting the vulnerable: A reanalysis of our social responsibility.* Chicago, IL: University of Chicago Press.

Harrington, M. (2000). *Care and equality.* New York, NY: Routledge.

Harrington Meyer, M. (2000). *Care work: Gender, class and the welfare state.* New York, NY: Routledge.

Hekman, S. (1995). *Moral voices, moral selves.* University Park, PA: The Pennsylvania State University Press.

Herskovits, E., & Mitteness, L. (1994). Transgressions and sickness in old age. *Journal of Aging Studies, 8*(3), 327–340.

Hoffmaster, B. (2006). What does vulnerability mean? *Hastings Center Report, 36*(2), 38–45.

Hoffmaster, B. (April 2008). Presentation on autonomy and long-term care at a conference sponsored by the Health and Medicine Policy Research Group, Chicago, IL.

Holstein, M. (1999). Home care: A case study in injustice. In M. U. Walker (Ed.), *Mother time: Women, ethics, and aging.* Lanham, MD: Rowman & Littlefield.

Holstein, M. (2010). Ethics and aging: Retrospectively and prospectively. In T. Cole, R. Ray, & R. Kastenbaum (Eds.), *A guide to humanistic studies in aging* (pp. 244–268). Baltimore, MD: Johns Hopkins University Press.

Hooyman, N., & Gonyea, J. (1999). A feminist model of family care: Practice and policy directions. *Journal of Women and Aging, 11*(2–3), 149–169.

Jecker, N. (2002). Taking care of one's own: Justice and family caregiving. *Theoretical Medicine and Philosophy, 23*(3), 117–133.

Kane, R. A. (2001). Long-term care and a good quality of life: Bringing them closer together. *The Gerontologist, 41*(3), 293–305.

Kittay, E. F. (1999). *Love's labor: Essays on women, equality, and dependency.* New York, NY: Routledge.

Kittay, E. F. (2006). Beyond autonomy and paternalism: The caring transparent self. In T. Neys, Y. Denier, & T. Vandervelde (Eds.), *Autonomy and paternalism: Beyond Individualism and good intentions* (pp. 1–29). Leuven: Peeters.

Lindemann Nelson, H. (2001). *Damaged identities, narrative repair.* New York, NY: Cornell University Press.

Luborsky, M. (1994). The cultural adversity of physical disability: Erosion of full personhood. *The Journal of Aging Studies, 8*(3), 239–253.

Mackenzie, C., & Stoljar, N. (Eds.). (2000). *Relational autonomy: Feminist perspectives on autonomy, agency, and the social self*. New York, NY: Oxford University Press.

Meyers, D. (1989). *Self, society, and personal choice*. New York, NY: Columbia University Press.

Nussbaum, M. (2002). The future of feminist liberalism. In E. F. Kittay & E. Feder (Eds.), *The subject of care: Feminist perspectives on dependency* (pp. 186–214). Lanham, MD: Rowman & Littlefield.

Parks, J. (2003). *No place like home? Feminist ethics and home health care*. Bloomington, IN: University of Indiana Press.

Polivka, L., & Salmon, J. (2001). Consumer-directed are: An ethical, empirical, and practical guide for state policymakers. *Florida Policy Exchange Center on Aging*, Tampa, FL.

Scheman, N. (1983). Individualism and psychology. In S. Harding & M. Hintikka (Eds.), *Discovering reality: Feminist perspectives on epistemology, metaphysics, methodology, and philosophy of science*. Dordrecht, Netherlands: Reidel.

Sevenhuijsen, S. (2000). Caring in the third way: The relation between obligation, responsibility and care in Third Way discourse. *Critical Social Policy, 20*(1), 5–37.

Shenk, D., Kuwahara, K., & Zablotsky, D. (2004). Older women's attachments to their home and possessions. *Journal of Aging Studies, 18*, 157–169.

Stone, D. (2000). Caring by the book. In M. Harrington Meyers (Ed.), *Care work: Gender, class and the welfare state* (pp. 89–111). New York, NY: Routledge.

Tronto, J. (1993). *Moral boundaries: A political argument for an ethics of care*. New York, NY: Routledge.

Tronto, J. (1995). Care as a basis for radical political judgments. *Hypatia, 405*(2), 141–149.

Verba, S., Schlozman, K. L., & Brady, H. E. (1995). *Voice and equality: Civic voluntarism in American politics*. Cambridge, MA: Harvard University Press.

Walker, M. U. (1998). *Moral understandings: A feminist study in ethics*. New York, NY: Routledge.

Walker, M. U. (2003). *Moral contexts*. Lanham, MD: Rowman & Littlefield.

White, J., & Tronto, J. (2004). Political practices of care: Needs and Rights. *Ratio Juris, 17*(4), 425–453.

CHAPTER 8

The Nursing Home

Beyond Medicalization

Adele sat in her wheelchair, along with ten others in the lobby area. Her hips ached, but what was new? After all, that was one of the reasons she as here. It was five o'clock, and they were lined up to be wheeled in for dinner as soon as the early seating was done. Why they had to eat at five thirty, like children, rather than at an adult dining hour, was beyond her comprehension. But worse than time of day was sitting like baggage in the hallway with the others waiting to be trundled in her wheelchair across the hall and rolled up to the table. She had complained at the beginning, but had quickly learned her survival mantra: "Resistance is useless."

In *Thoughts on Meaning in Frailty,* Wendy Lustbader (1999) writes:

> The end of my soul's dominion will surely arrive on the day that I find myself lined up in a hallway in a row of wheelchairs waiting to be loaded into an elevator, then transported to a dining room and positioned into a row of waiting mouths. I may overhear one staff member say to another, *I've got to cut this one's meat, then I'll feed that one.* At this juncture, I will have become an object rather than a subject. I will have become *that one* who must be acted upon, rather than a person engaged in her own life. I will have become someone's task. I will have become my needs.
>
> —*pp. 21–22*

Despite its recognized problems, the nursing home, in one form or another will not disappear from the long-term care continuum. While home and community-based care has reduced the number of elders inappropriately placed in nursing homes, when a person reaches 65, there is a 50% chance that she/he will spend some time in a nursing home before dying; only 10% of those stays will be short term stays (Gillick, 2006). The nursing home serves a function that no other site of care can match.

While some facilities now primarily provide sub-acute care, in this chapter, we focus on the traditional nursing home patient—individuals who need 24-hour care, many of who have Alzheimer's disease or other dementias, and for whom the nursing home is truly their last "home." These levels of incapacity, combined with the structural and financial problems endemic to nursing home life, place substantial barriers in the way of creating a more home-like and person enhancing environment. Yet, "culture change" movements, which focus on the structural/institutional features that largely determine what is possible in a resident's daily life, give us much hope. Ultimately, we argue, a nursing home committed to being an ethical institution must do much more than guarantee certain individual rights. Change must happen at the organizational level. Placing organizational change as primary does not imply that change at the individual level is unimportant. Rather it suggests that without an organizational commitment to genuine caring and the changes that this commitment requires, residents will continue to experience life as excessively diminished. Many core ethical problems, which are visible in day-to-day life, are rooted in scheduling, inadequate staffing, hierarchical structures, unequal power relationships, and regulatory mandates, reinforced by the limited social policy commitment to care (Tronto, 1993; see Chapters 6 and 7). What happens to the patient on the floor of the nursing home is thus embedded in institutional culture and structure, in public policy, and in overarching cultural norms that devalue both people who are old and frail and those who care for them (Gubrium, 1975; Abel, 1991; Dodds, 2007).

In this chapter, we will argue that nursing homes should adopt as core ethical commitments the following: to help residents maintain and/or reconstruct identity and personhood; to assure the availability of meaningful choices that permit residents to exercise in George Agich's (1990) words, "actual" or "interstitial" autonomy, to facilitate the possibilities for companionship and even friendship; to create opportunities for reciprocity and responsibility toward others, key features of living in a moral community; to honor the dignity and knowledge of all who live and work in the institution, and to ease the dying process by effectively utilizing hospice and palliative care and by memorializing patients who die. In addition to these commitments, we argue that nursing homes must avoid shaming and humiliating residents, however, unintentional such actions might be. Women like Adele, lined up waiting to go into the dining room, vividly display what it means to be shamed. This, we contend, assaults one's self worth and self-concept in ways that no guarantee of rights can restore.

Most modern nursing homes post a Patient's Bill of Rights. They encourage patient participation in care planning as an expression of autonomy and they offer opportunities for advance care planning. These ethical commitments are important but they mean little if the necessary background conditions are lacking. The right to privacy is useless if a

knock on a closed door constitutes permission to enter (Ray, 2008). Participation in care planning has little value if choices are constrained by the menu
of options that are actually available. The right to refuse treatment matters
little if there is no opportunity to have—at least at times—one's favorite
food or a quiet conversation with an aide or another patient to whom one
is deeply known.

To explore these issues, we start by briefly tracing the evolution of the
contemporary nursing home. This social history helps to explain the
seeming intractability of many problems that we now face. From there,
we will identify what we see as the root causes at play in our abiding disaf-
fection with nursing homes and identify the barriers to change. These barriers are importantly rooted in attitudes toward deservingness, cultural
norms about family and gender, and, despite the substantial public dollars
dedicated to long-term care, the continued belief that it is primarily a
private responsibility. Deeper and perhaps more difficult to pin down are
barriers that are vested in ideals of the "autonomous man" and in the
unasked question of how much society ought to be expending on very
old, disabled individuals, who are long-term occupants of nursing homes.
With contending claims for Medicaid resources on both the state and
federal levels, what is a fair expenditure of resources for nursing home
care? While every problem does not come down to resource allocation,
it is an unavoidable concern but one that might be eased if the government
adopted an ethics of care as a core commitment for people of all ages
(see Chapter 6). We will draw this chapter to a close by offering some
suggestions about various strategies we might take to ameliorate the
negatives, to implement the ethical commitments we defend, and to boost
the too-often-overlooked potential positives of the nursing home as an
institution.

SOCIAL HISTORY OF THE NURSING HOME

While the nursing home, in its contemporary iteration is relatively new, it has
deep societal roots. Tracing its origins to the much dreaded 19th century
almshouses, the nursing home has never been able to fully escape its problematic association with abandonment, poverty, illness, and the warehousing
of the old (Holstein & Cole, 1995). Victorian ideas of individual responsibility and healthy living, not unlike today's "successful aging mantra"
reinforced the negative imagery by insisting that those who become poor
or even disabled were somehow morally responsible for their plight (Cole,
1992). Accompanied by a mood of great pessimism regarding the

possibilities for ameliorating the pathological conditions that seemed to dominate in old age, little was done to change conditions. By the time of the Great Depression, the elderly came to represent about two thirds of all poor house residents at a time when conditions deteriorated significantly (Cole, 1992).

The Great Depression then offers two key steps in the story: first, the economic dislocation of the Depression swelled the rolls of those, predominantly elders, who ended their lives in the poor house. The overwhelming numbers threatened to crush a public system already stretched thin and poorly funded. Second, the passage of Social Security in 1935 meant that, while not by any means generous, many older people had some income. This income reduced the demand for custodial care as the result of pauperism. Yet, the dismal record of the almshouses and the social stigma associated with them meant that until 1950 social security regulations forbade payments to older people who were in public institutions (Holstein & Cole, 1995). As a result, private facilities, which could receive social security dollars, sprang up as group homes for the poor elderly. That policy decision also helped to assure that institutional care would become primarily a for-profit enterprise. While profit itself may not be necessarily problematic, it diverted limited resources from care to profit and paved the way for increasing institutional segregation based on race and class, a feature of nursing home life that persists today (Holstein & Cole, 1995).

The next dramatic chapter in this story comes with the 1960s. First, a major effort to de-institutionalize the mentally ill, many of whom were elderly, meant that many elders with dementia were transferred from mental institutions to private nursing homes (Talbott, 2004). Second, federal funds were also dispersed generously to promote the construction of hospitals, which evolved into today's model of high-technology, acute care. The nursing home, by default, became the location for low-technology chronic care. And third, the creation of Medicare and Medicaid in 1965 helped fund these enterprises. Medicare, an age-entitlement program, covered "medical" interventions, largely in physician offices or in hospitals, or for skilled but temporary care in nursing homes. In contrast, Medicaid, a means-tested program, helped to support the low technology, "custodial" care that characterized the nursing home. With it came the historic stigma associated with "welfare." Targeted at the very poor, Medicaid now covers the costs of formerly middle class elders who have "spent down" to Medicaid eligibility levels. Having long-term care needs thus often led to impoverishment. Medicaid now covers approximately 45% of all nursing home revenues. Without the federal government, the nursing home industry would not and could not exist as we know it.

With government money came increasing government regulation, and with government paying a large portion of the bills, nursing homes also increasingly tailored their activities to respond to regulatory requirements. These developments served to steer nursing homes toward a medical model, parroting analogous developments in the acute care setting. Thus, nursing homes increasingly assumed a medical, institutional feel, rather than that of a dwelling. This made them well-suited for their more recent role as sub-acute facilities but less suited for long time residents. With earlier discharges from hospitals, many patients are transferred to nursing homes for short-term, Medicare-reimbursed rehabilitation services or for an extended period of recovery. Intended to be short-term patients, these individuals often become long-term residents because regular re-assessments do not occur. A recent federal effort, managed by the states, called Money Follows the Person (MFP), has targeted this problem. Its immediate goal, which we support, is to re-integrate back into the community individuals who do not need 24-hour care. We do have one caveat— such re-integration must not increase the responsibilities of "informal" family caregivers (see Chapter 7).

HISTORY OF BIOETHICS IN THE NURSING HOME SETTING

The dramatic emergence of a "bioethics" discipline began in earnest in the 1970s. Its development was largely provoked and nurtured by high profile and high technology life-or-death cases. Not surprisingly, the setting for such a bioethics was almost exclusively the high tech, acute care hospital. Cases that captured the imagination revolved around such drama as transplants, intensive care and life support, and brain death. At the core of these ethical debates was the preeminent devotion to the principle of respect for autonomy, that is, individual self-determination in choosing the direction of medical interventions. In a watershed publication, Beauchamp and Childress (1978) gave us what would become the common currency of biomedical ethics: the four principles (see Chapter 2 for an extended critique of this approach). Topping the list was the principle of respect for autonomy, instantiated through informed consent procedures. And while there were three other principles—beneficence, nonmaleficence, and justice—there was no mistaking the primary place of autonomy in how this approach was implemented in practice.

In retrospect it is not surprising, though it went quite unnoticed and unremarked for several years, that the first foray of bioethics into long-term care carried much of the acute-care framework and mode of thinking with it.

It also brought what may be described as masculinist values—independence and self-sufficiency—that suited neither women nor older people, especially people who needed 24-hour care. Yet, questions were not initially raised about how the unique features of nursing home life mattered for bioethics. After all, if bioethics is universal, why should the principles or concerns really change from one setting to another or for one group of people to another? Yet, as we will show below, and as other chapters have argued, context matters greatly in the type of problems that arise and in the approaches we use to address them. If one neglects the particular features of the people who are cared for in nursing homes compared to hospitals, one can lose sight of issues that simply do not occur in acute care settings. What is not perceived as morally problematic does not receive attention. If one does not consider the ethical implications of the long-term stay of most residents or the limits on action that policy and regulations impose, or the fact that women are both the primary residents and employees in nursing homes, one may fail to notice what is important and what might need to change to create a more hospitable context suited to these features of nursing home life.

It is clear today, as witnessed by the culture change movement, context establishes the terms of life in the nursing home. Context determines the quality of life that most residents place above health and safety (Gillick, 2006). "Until these contextual features—for example, minimal staffing and wages, regulatory expectations, unequal power because of hierarchical structures, irregular physician and ancillary medical personnel presence—are addressed improvements can only be modest" (Holstein, 2010, p. 251).

Thus, despite the very important work undertaken in the 1980s, spurred on by the Retirement Research Foundation's initiative on "Autonomy and Long-Term Care," nursing homes have continued to be ethically problematic institutions, As Collopy, Jennings, and Boyle (1991) note, the 1960s–1980s had, in some ways, been an ugly period for nursing homes. They write,

> Through the next two decades, however, there were constant revelations of scandal—substandard and negligent care, outright abuse of residents, and a wide range of fiscal malfeasance, from embezzlement of residents' assets and extortion of money from families, to vendor kickbacks and reimbursement and capital finance fraud.
>
> —*Collopy et al., 1991, p. 4*

These scandals led to further government regulations, regulations that were designed to protect the residents but unintentionally contributed to regimenting their lives. Quality of care (health and safety) took priority over quality of life (Gillick, 2006). Stringent regulations also helped to push the smaller "mom" and "pop" homes out of business since they could not afford the adaptations that the new regulations required (Holstein & Cole, 1995). Yet, the taint had a positive effect—it stimulated interest in ethics and nursing home care. Though the long-term care setting never garnered the kind of enthusiastic bioethics activity generated by the acute care setting, a number of ethicists did turn attention in that direction (Agich, 1990, 1993; Collopy et al., 1991; Kane & Caplan, 1990; Lidz, Fischer, & Arnold, 1992; McCullough & Wilson, 1995).

The Nursing Home Reform Act of 1987 (Omnibus Budget Reconciliation Act of 1987), pressured the industry to articulate and enforce ethics policies. Borrowing from the acute care model, ethicists and others at the frontlines, placed autonomy, or, at least, respect for patient autonomy at the forefront of the ethical agenda. They did not try to modify the basic structures of the nursing home nor its medicalized environment, although, ironically, nursing homes actually provided little in the way of medical care. This medical model permeated both the nursing home and bioethics discourse. Medical care choices might be assured but there was no similar commitment to facilitating autonomous expressions of selfhood (Lidz, Fischer, & Arnold, 1992) nor have there been significant efforts, except in the varied experiments related to culture change, to transform nursing homes into communities that support communal needs while also protecting individual identities (Mitty, 2005). For reasons noted above, this situation is unsurprising. Giving the person some control over treatment choices—not a central feature of life at "home"—is far easier than enacting the virtues of attentiveness and responsiveness on a regular basis.

Hence, mimicking acute care hospitals, many nursing homes created Ethics Committees. Not surprisingly, these ethics committees imitated hospital committees in both structure and agendas. Policies were crafted for Do Not Resuscitate (DNR) orders, for the withholding and withdrawal of artificial nutrition and hydration, the filing of Advance Directives, and other issues relating to long-term care. These ethics committees also intervened and facilitated decision-making in cases of conflict among residents, family members, physicians, nurses, and social workers.

These first steps were important but the long-term care environment is simply not an ideal place to play out such acute care concerns, either in a medical model sense or in an ethical sense. As Zweibel and Cassel (1988), observed, a thoughtless adoption of the acute-care model for use in nursing homes fails to recognize that the central issues in nursing home care are not about medical care choices. In the acute care setting, championing patient autonomy makes sense. The typical acute care patient is someone who has been living an independent life outside of the hospital. An event—trauma, a new illness, a disease that needs treatment and cure—happens and the patient is admitted to the hospital. For most of us, the fact of the illness itself combined with the unfamiliar high technology of the hospital puts us at a decisional disadvantage in relation to the physician. It becomes all too easy for the medical team to simply assert its will while the patient is neglected, ignored, and sometimes even browbeaten into agreement. An ethics that reasserts patient autonomy to counter-balance physician power makes a great deal of sense. Patients regain some control over their medical treatment and thus, to some extent, over their own lives. With any luck, the agreed-upon treatment works, the patients are cured, and they return to their former lifestyles. The acute event is time-limited, a temporary hiatus in the person's everyday life.

The nursing home patient's circumstances are generally very different. Most nursing home residents are not facing pivotal *medical* choices. Their choices, such as they might be, are more about everyday living. As Kane and Caplan (1990) learned, nursing home residents worry far less about DNR orders then mundane questions like who gets the bed by the window? Who gets the one stuffed arm chair in the day room? Who chooses the television stations and volume? Who chooses the menu? Who chooses dinner time? These sorts of questions are driven by a fundamental difference between acute care patients and nursing home residents: nursing home residents *live* in the facility, and it becomes their *home*, while for acute care patients, the hospital is but a brief interruption in a life lived outside of the hospital. No one *lives* in the hospital. Nursing home residents, by contrast, *live* in a home that is not their home; and they live with a large number of other residents in close quarters who are not their family. To simply import acute care bioethics into the nursing home is thus to bring a set of issues/questions to bear that do not deeply resonate.

Unfortunately, the medicalization of the nursing home, the modes of financial reimbursement, unequal power structures, staff turn-over, and constraints on fiscal resources (and thus also on personnel time and energy), all conspire to limit or undermine what we might call residents' everyday autonomy (Agich, 1990, 2003). Residents may be denied choice and control over when and what they eat, whether they stay up late and watch television, whether they share a room, and when they take a bath. To provide these kinds of choices demands a much thicker view of autonomy than the one that currently prevails. Once again, we note that as long as choice is limited to what is laid before the person, whether or not those choices are meaningful or not, actual autonomy, in Agich's terms (1990) cannot exist. Nursing home's aims and even the physical layout, is not directed, for example, at actively cooperating with an older person's efforts "to reorient themselves" as they seek to "remake their world" (Agich, 1995, p. 124).

Regulations further reinforce medicalization. While both necessary and unavoidable given the vulnerability of nursing home residents and the past history of abuse, they also inform facilities of what federal regulators value. Beyond their protective function, regulations can, for example, seek a balance between standards of care and professional discretion to "respond to their [the professionals] own particular problems of care as they make creative use of the dependency that is an essential fact of nursing home life" (Collopy et al., 1991, p. 13). Regulations can be designed to leave sufficient flexibility so that staff, who are generally motivated to do the right thing, can respond ethically to vulnerable residents (Holstein, 2010). Moral knowledge, we have argued throughout this volume, can come from many different places. While not a simple task, regulations can be developed so that staff are supported in their efforts to make the nursing home a home. Some do so but often face reprimands for doing so. Recall the situation of Adele and the ways in which her life in the nursing home life eroded her sense of being a person. Beginnings have been made as the Centers for Medicare and Medicaid Services has trained surveyors to recognize culture change practices that might make nursing home routines look different than standard practice (Mitty, 2005) but progress is slow.

In the face of such realities, a second wave of long-term care ethics tried to make more sense of autonomy in the nursing home setting. A highly engaging example of such work can be found in the writing of George Agich (1990, 1993, 1995, 2003). What characterizes this genre is the effort to reinterpret what "respect for autonomy" should mean in the nursing home care setting. Basing his analysis on a phenomenological account of life in the nursing home, Agich (1990) makes an important distinction between what he calls "nodal autonomy" and "interstitial autonomy," that is, the ability to live in habitual ways, arguing that it is the latter that is most important to residents in nursing homes. They rarely have to choose whether or not they want life-extending therapies such as ventilators but they would like to choose when to have a cup of tea or be acknowledged as a person with a past as well as a present. Agich (2003) observes that respecting the autonomy of persons in long-term care entails a commitment to identifying and establishing the concrete conditions that encourage individuals to face adversity and threats to self that inevitably result from the chronic illnesses and functional deteriorations that bring elders to long-term care in the first place. Respecting autonomy requires attention to those things that are truly and significantly meaningful and important to elders (p. 123). In a sense, we value our ability to exercise autonomy in and of itself. That implies that we find value in autonomy even when the choices are not of deep, existential magnitude (Whitler, 1996). Therefore, we can enhance personal self-esteem, moral satisfaction, and psychological well-being of nursing home residents by working with them not only to make personal choice a reality in their everyday lives but also to work with them as they integrate their current lives with what has been meaningful in the past. When it comes to choices, they will often be about relatively "mundane" matters, but that does not destroy the value of those self-affirming acts of decision-making to those residents. Through negotiation between resident and caregivers/ staff, the institutional routines of the nursing home can be made to work with rather than against resident choice.

RECONCEPTUALIZING THE NURSING HOME: AN ETHICAL AND PRACTICAL AGENDA

We suggest several thematic changes that will help in fashioning more "humane" and ethically committed nursing homes and in putting into place the ethical commitments we identified in the opening section of this chapter.

1. Design structures and rhythms in nursing homes so that they acknowledge that, for many residents, this is their home, not simply a temporary interruption of their "real" lives. This requires substantive organizational and structural reform so that emphasis is on the "home" while not neglecting the nursing aspect of nursing homes.
2. Design and carry out care of residents in ways that recognize them as persons and that respect their individuality and humanity. Such care would acknowledge the individual's physical and/or cognitive losses and compensate for them while drawing attention to the capacities that remain. It would emphasize the possibilities for growth and development despite loss.
3. Honor autonomy, not only as a minimalist ethical ideal, but rather as a commitment to making choices meaningful, to helping people live in familiar ways, and to supporting the relational potential in nursing home life.
4. Accept dependency as a part of the human condition rather than a shameful state to be denied at all costs (Dodds, 2007; Kittay, 1999). As we argued in Chapter 7, by recognizing dependency and vulnerability as endemic to

human life, the nursing home resident and those people who care for her are no longer anomalies to be viewed askance but rather a reflection of life more generally. It is only the privileged who need not see that they, too, are dependent on others for so much that happens in their lives.

5. Acknowledge and accept that death is often the final outcome of a stay in a nursing home and so foster end-of-life care planning and facilitate palliative care and hospice (see Chapter 12). Recognize the effect of resident death upon caregivers as well as other residents, and the need to respond to that grief.

6. Support the development of staff so that they are integral members of the care team and have opportunities to exercise independent judgment. Care and respect for the caregiver are central elements in an ethics of care.

ORGANIZATIONAL SUPPORT FOR ETHICAL ACTION

Except for that minority of residents who reside in nursing homes for a couple of months as a transition from the hospital to home, when individuals are placed (not usually "move to") in nursing homes their former residences cease to be their homes. They are generally sold or rented, with material goods dispersed. For many residents the transfer from "home" to nursing home is a *fait accompli*, done while they are hospitalized. With no rituals of leave-taking, an abrupt departure from what is familiar can be especially painful. Yet, they quite literally "move" into the nursing home. Moving to a different dwelling is psychologically stressful for all of us; but the nursing home resident must also confront the reality that her new residence is not really her own. It is a relatively crowded environment, where what little "private space" there may be merges indistinguishably with public space. As Collopy et al. (1991) describe it, "Living quarters sometimes amount to a shared bedroom with only a few feet around a bed to call one's own, and no ultimate say over who occupies the next bed. Privacy and space are at a minimum" (p. 9). To enter most nursing homes is to enter an alien and often sad place where the appearance of biding time may mask a rich internal life (Ray, 2008). Further, unlike the true home environment, the rhythms of life are governed not so much by personal choice as by institutional routines and scheduling, necessitated by regulation and economic efficiency. Is it any wonder that nursing home residents, whose sense of identity is already fragile, often feel a loss of self, both of self-identity and self-esteem? Thus, the concepts of "home" and identity are intricately connected.

In line with the movement toward culture change, this source of confusion and loss calls for systematic organizational change rather than a new set of rights. When we speak of elder residents being part of a moral community, we mean an environment that supports their individual goals and values, to the extent possible, while also expecting them, also to the extent possible, to live reciprocally with others, assuming whatever responsibilities they are capable of assuming. Nursing home residents suffer from a profound sense of uselessness (Gillick, 2006). In our own homes we are useful; we should have the chance to be useful, and not only be entertained, in the nursing home.

Thus, we view with enthusiasm the culture change movement. Culture change, as a generic idea, holds that "the nursing home should revolve around the needs and wishes of its residents, and that means attending to spiritual as well as mental and physical concerns" (Gillick, 2006, p. 133). We would add attending to existential concerns more broadly. The Pioneer network (see Lustbader, 2001), *The Eden Alternative* and the Green House approaches are examples. These movements toward culture change have the potential to radically change the context in which older people live and staff work. Such contextual changes are ethically as well as practically significant. If the environmental context impedes rather than supports expressions of individual personhood, such as imposing rigid meal or bathing times then identity is gradually eroded. Thus efforts to change environments can empower elders and staff and reduce the sterile and medicalized environment that now prevails in so many nursing home. They are thus to be watched and supported at the same time that they are evaluated against ethical ideals as well as practical ones.

In *The Eden Alternative*, for example, Thomas (1994) argued not only for changes in how care is delivered, but in the actual physical environment of care. By emphasizing spaces with plants and the presence of animals (especially birds), Thomas has argued for an environment that encourages positive interaction among residents and staff. If boredom, a sense of helplessness, and loneliness are leading complaints in the nursing home setting, then an environment that stimulates and encourages interaction becomes a crucial contribution to quality of life. Changes often are quite simple, such as having plant beds raised so that a person can appreciate them without having to bend over, yet reflect the actual needs of residents. Pathways through garden areas can be made to be wheelchair friendly: broad, never steep, no sharp turns. Music—of the sort that appeals to the residents—is another simple way to encourage stimulation and environmental interaction.

Similarly, the "Green House Program," a further development of Thomas's ideas, encourages a physical environment conducive to quality care: housing on a small scale, with private rooms in a small house where several older people live together with 24-hour care. A study by Kane and colleagues (Kane, Lum, Cutler, Degenholtz, & Yu, 2007) notes that while *The Eden Alternative* expresses laudable goals, the actual outcomes have not proven to be as effective as one might wish. Kane et al. then argue that to maximize improvements, not only ought one introduce the kinds of green spaces, birds, and so on that *The Eden Alternative* advocates, but one must also reconstruct the scale and configuration of the nursing home, so that it more closely resembles a traditional "home" environment. In the study, statistically significant differences between qualities of living in a Green House nursing home versus a more conventional arrangement were observed (Kane et al., 2007). In such a context, Adele would not be lined up waiting to be pushed into the dining room. Yet, the introduction of culture change has been slow and research still needs to be done to see if these forms of care make a difference in happiness, health, and alleviation of depression (Gillick, 2006).

To facilitate the formation of a moral community in these types of nursing homes but also in more conventional ones, we need to manage negotiated compromises, between resident and staff as well as between resident and resident (see Moody, 1992). One clear example of this need is the divergent views about safety that residents and the nursing home often have. Residents might be willing to take risks that support what they value—a walk when they want to do it rather than waiting for an aide to accompany them—while the nursing home is preoccupied with physical safety. Falls, after all, must be reported. Residents care most about quality of life while nursing homes may care the most about the quality of care since this is both more definable and responds to regulatory requirements. Unfortunately, they often do not overlap especially when definitions of quality of life may vary greatly. While residents will differ and the issues will differ, negotiation is one way to try to bridge differences. Powers (2003) reminds us that we can be attuned to what kind of negotiating strategy will be best for each individual. Ironically, the long-term fact of nursing home life opens opportunities. Unlike the acute care setting, staff actually do have the time to learn the unique ways in which each individual approaches choices and defines goals. By encouraging line staff to talk to residents and rewarding them for developing insights about residents to share with other staff during care planning meetings, much can be achieved without it taking a great deal of time. It also means that as socially embedded selves living in a communal environment, older residents will be expected to take others into account as they consider what it means to them to live in ways that support their personhood. This idea shifts our notions of autonomy in two ways. It suggests that autonomy for nursing home residents is expressed by having as much opportunity as possible to live in ways that support their identity while also taking others into account as they consider their options. Living so intimately with others, who are variously incapacitated, requires compromise. The goal in any negotiation is to try to achieve compromise while protecting individual integrity (Goodstein, 2000). Nursing home residents, perhaps with the exception of those with dementia, should not be permitted to abuse any more than others or behave solely in self-interested ways than residents of any other congregate setting.

THE FACT OF DEPENDENCY

Shame of dependency begins even before nursing home placement and all too often then continues to permeate the reality of institutional life. Older people are typically resistant to nursing home placement in large part because it is a confession of loss of independence and self-sufficiency. After a life in which they have striven to exemplify the values of industriousness, productivity, accomplishment, and self-sufficiency, the prospect of placement in a nursing home is a vivid judgment about incapacity and a threat to loss of adult status. Thus, in addition to the psychic blow occasioned by the prospect of leaving behind one's home, one is also confronted with the loss of esteem. To compound this particular problem even further, family members are very often involved in the placement process. Given the negative connotations that our society has for so long attached to lack of self-sufficiency, nursing home placement is an admission of the individual's incapacity but also an admission that the family can no longer care for their loved one. Nursing home placement thus, often occasions a rich stew of guilt, a sense of failure, and loss of esteem on the part of both the individual and the family (Ryan, 2002; Ryan & Scullion, 2000).

Dependency is, of course, an inescapable reality of nursing home life. If there were not some significant dependency, then the individual would not have been placed in the nursing home to begin with. Such dependency may be physical, cognitive, or both but it is a given. However, need it be cast as a failure? As we have argued in Chapter 7, dependency is a fact of human life. By acknowledging its universality, older people and those who care for them are no longer cast as anomalies. By acknowledging that dependency is universal, we also come to see why social welfare is a universal human good (Dodds, 2007). None of us would make it without the help and support of others, whether that help and support is a visible arm or lift or an invisible act of home maintenance. This condition may be exaggerated in nursing home life but it is not different than each of us turning to others or to the state or our employers for the support we need. No one is independent in the conventional understanding of that term except that the privileged status of some allows them to be blind to such dependencies. Thus, a major cultural task that transcends nursing home ethics is to integrate these understandings of human dependency into a more general vocabulary of human good.

Given the largeness of that task, we suggest more immediate ways of dealing with dependency that can be implemented immediately. One approach is to silently gloss over the individual's dependency in the course of caregiving. Whether it is bathing someone, cleaning up as a result of incontinence, spoonfeeding, or providing a word which the resident with dementia cannot, one simply does it without drawing attention to the act. We thus engage in a kind of silent collusion: the resident and the caregiver both know that there is a dependency, but neither speaks of it, and instead pretend to each other that nothing really happened. Perhaps in such a way, dignity can be preserved as much as is practical. While this strategy is appealing to many caregivers and perhaps to many residents as well, the regrettable side of the strategy is that it leaves intact and unchallenged the negative moral assessment of dependency. The psychological comfort drawn by not acknowledging it reflects an abiding acceptance of an element of shame and failure. Can we manage a fundamental change in attitude?

LOSS AND GAIN, SELF AND RECOGNITION

As we have noted elsewhere in this text, efforts to counter the decline and loss paradigm that once dominated ideas about old age have been focused on affirming the health and well-being of large numbers of "third-agers" (see Chapter 4). The model of "successful aging" specifically contrasts the man on the ski slope with the woman in the wheelchair, placing primary responsibility for these different positions on the individuals (Rowe & Kahn, 1987). This emphasis has sharply demarcated the third from the fourth age when the primary goal has been staying out of a nursing home. Thus, given these views, the nursing home resident is clearly a "failure." Her subjectivity becomes the least valued among the alternatives. Hence, it should be no surprise that the overwhelming sense of those who face placement in nursing homes or of those family members, who are considering the placement, is a sense of loss and even failure. While the losses are obviously real and damaging, when they are compounded by societal attitudes toward the "unhealthy" the threat to self is as damaging as physical and cognitive losses. Thus, the nursing home faces the powerful challenge of mitigating the impact of all these losses so its residents can find within nursing home life the opportunity for renewed social contact and interpersonal interaction, which has often eroded as their health kept them relatively isolated at home. This opportunity is often lost in professional talk about "socialization" that involves offering painfully limited activities when the real task is an existential one—to preserve, restore, or otherwise honor this changed self while facilitating intimacy (here we are not referring to sexual intimacy) in whatever ways that is possible.

Other goods can come with a move to a nursing home. With the day-to-day responsibilities for care addressed, families can play the role that they usually can do better than anyone else—the co-creators of identity and memory (Caron & Bowers, 2003). Thus, while it may seem obvious in principle to say that home is the best environment rather than an institutional one, in many cases that is not true (Kuhn, 2001). For many individuals, placement into a decent nursing home can markedly enhance their life quality, providing better trained caregivers, more caregivers, as well as greatly increased social interaction. We, of course, note the importance of the adjective—decent—an assumption that cannot be made for many nursing homes, particularly for patients that rely on Medicaid to cover costs.

In reflecting about how this morally important aim can be realized, we note what must now be obvious—good ethics is realized within our practices. It is not socially modular, occurring in a different realm than the everyday interactions we have with others (Walker, 1998). To facilitate the goal of supporting personhood, we turn once again to the critical importance of narrative. As our lives change, particularly in socially devalued ways, what Nelson (2001) calls "narrative repair," becomes essential. Through the use of counter-stories, people with damaged identities especially identities that oppressive social conditions have helped to forge, can re-story their lives, trying to discard the negative judgments imposed by culture and other norms. Particularly for nursing home residents, whose very presence in the home is a negative judgment, narrativity becomes a vehicle to claim what is left and learn to live with what is gone. Many nursing homes have introduced writing or other forms of biographical work (Ray, 2008) and have extended such opportunities to individuals with dementia through plays and other forms of dramatic activities (Basting, 1993).

Another common strategy for this is the construction of a visual story board that can be posted in the resident's room or outside their door, a story board with photographs and notable details from the resident's preplacement biography (Clark, Hanson, & Ross, 2003). Obviously, family members are a crucial asset in constructing any such story board. Yet, even the best of these efforts can produce only a truncated version of the resident's personal narrative. But these truncated versions are still a distinct improvement over the blank pre-placement biography that is so common. Mr. Smith *is* an attorney, not *was* an attorney, perhaps a small matter of tense but a large matter in terms of identity.

Of course, even the best narratival story board will be of limited value if caregivers do not take the time and effort to notice it, learn it, and use it in their day-to-day caregiving of the resident. Unlike charting the tasks of bathing, the dispensing of medication, and so forth, such engagement resists scheduling and resists reduction to certain rote mechanics. While a bath successfully given is easy to document; a meaningful conversation falls outside the highly regulatory framework. Engagement through the use of story boards and other narrative approaches takes time and a commitment to responsiveness and attentiveness but, above all, it takes the support of administrative staff. If biography is to be honored at the same time that it doesn't replace present realities, it needs the wholehearted endorsement of management, encoded in evaluations and pay. Regrettably, then, once again we must note that current fiscal and regulatory incentives do not encourage this truly "humane" work (Parks, 2010). But for residents in the nursing home, who are most likely to feel diminished, devalued, and rejected by society, the caring recognition of them as the persons they are (and were) can be the most fundamental and the most valued kind of caring. Even the person who is in the final stages of dementia can appreciate touch, music, and the attentiveness of and recognition from others. Remaining social graces are not *just* a relic from the past but a to-be acknowledged part of the present.

LIVING TOWARD DEATH

The nursing home presents an especially challenging environment in which to facilitate dying well. Inevitably, nursing homes witness death regularly; yet, the very *density* of such deaths, so to speak, can wear upon caregiving staff as well as the residents themselves. In past years, death has not been a welcome visitor in the nursing home. From a regulatory point of view, deaths in the nursing home can be interpreted as evidence of poor quality care. And, as just explained, its frequency can be a source of grief and depression for both residents and staff. Hence, in many nursing homes there is an unwritten, but well-understood, policy that the resident is not supposed to die there. As the individual's pneumonia begins to progress, as her gangrene begins to show signs of septicemia, the resident is transferred to the hospital. In this way, death takes place "off stage."

When asked, the overwhelming majority of citizens say that they would prefer to die at home rather than in the hospital (Holstein, 1999). We think the emotional reasons for this are common and familiar. Yet, this tendency to transfer dying nursing home residents to the hospital effectively robs them of the possibility of dying at home in the nursing home, with familiar faces and routines. Fortunately, the practice of transferring out residents is now far less common than it once was. That change is also part of a larger picture that has been gradually changing for the better: It is now, in many homes, not only acceptable to discuss the dying process ahead of time, but it may be actually encouraged. An effort can be made to identify the realistic goals of care when the dying process begins. With resident (when possible), family members, and staff all in joint deliberation and in common conclusion, the dying process can be a less stressful, more meaningful, and ultimately more gratifying experience than it might otherwise have been.

Reducing transfer from the nursing home to the hospital as death approaches is only one of the changes that nursing homes can support in their efforts to improve end-of-life care. As discussed in Chapter 12, both hospice and palliative care have become important elements in humanizing care. It is important that patients, staff and families find a way to acknowledge that the dying trajectory has begun so that palliative care or hospice can be initiated while the patient can still benefit from it. Appropriate care will "balance rehabilitation with that [of] palliation" (Hoffmann & Tarzian, 2005). Greater use of both hospice and palliative care services in the nursing home accepts the reality of dying and makes it possible for the person to die in what has, in effect, become her home.

NURSING HOME ETHICS PROGRAMS: MAKING CHANGE HAPPEN

The changes that we have been discussing in this chapter—change in culture, change in physical environment, change in organizational practice, change in everyday practices—do not happen by accident or without sustenance. Furthermore, while these changes are not fundamentally about regulations, they call for regulatory change that incorporates quality of life more fully into what regulators assess in nursing homes. Most important, however, are changes in attitude and daily lived practice, supported by organizational aims and purposes. To make such change real at the local level, it has to be nurtured by the leadership of the institution, nurtured sometimes in the face of countervailing forces. We believe that this calls for a conscious, thoughtful ethics program. As the above makes clear, the kind of ethics program we advocate will differ from the ethics programs developed in the late 1980s and into the 1990s.

First, the traditional "ethics committee" must be understood not as a quasi-judicial committee; rather it must see its responsibilities as a systematic reassessment of organizations impediments to fostering more humane values, values that will assure that Adele doesn't feel like a piece of baggage, essentially unknown to anyone. Instead of focusing upon medical treatment choices (though this facet of concern will not go away), the committee must recognize and emphasize creating a moral community that acknowledges dependency and loss, encourages reciprocal relationships among all people who live there, supports staff in their efforts to apply what they have learned from experience, and integrates families into efforts to nurture an elder's unique personhood. This may involve such mundane-seeming issues as control of the television or as worrisome as accusations of neglect, abuse, or coercion. The home that is not quite home may be rife with such challenges. A reimagined nursing home can generate conversations among staff, residents, and families so that all members of the community have a say in what happens within it. We have written elsewhere in this book about a "bottom-up" identification of values through communicative practices in micro-communities. The nursing home can become such a community.

Second, much that affects how residents are cared for, and feel cared for, will be a function of how the nursing home operates on a daily basis. This responsibility lies with management and the ways in which it organizes the facility and treats and trains frontline staff. To facilitate real cultural change, which we think is essential, the institution must attend to organizational ethics. Even the best-intentioned Certified Nurse's Assistant (CNA) cannot effectively offer quality care if the institution's policies make it impossible for her to do so (Bishop et al., 2008). Therefore, higher-level administrators must not only make the effort to have an ethics program that articulates humane goals of care as an institution; they must also foster policies and routines that support the relational aspects of care. Reviews and incentives must actually encourage the kind of support for identity, meaningful choice, and other elements of care that we have described. In other words, rather than leaving ethics to be something that must be done "against the flow," we should reengineer the organization so that all caregiving flows in the ethical and humane direction. We also feel that there is also a deeper, underlying problem that will continue to bedevil us, and that is our culture's fixation on autonomy, self-determination, and independence. In drawing this chapter to a close, we once again look at the issue of autonomy.

From the Enlightenment we have inherited the idea of the person as independent, rational, and self-determining. This foundational belief runs through a wide variety of moral and political philosophies, and found resonance in the emerging United States. As we discuss in Chapter 11, the identification of the individual's moral worth in terms of his/her rationality has devastating effects upon the perceived moral status and moral worth of individuals with dementia. But particularly as we consider the nursing home, we must acknowledge that popular thinking in this regard has extended the notion of individual autonomy beyond the simple idea of rationality, to include a broader sense of independence or self-sufficiency. In some details, the popularization of this creed has strayed from its more purely philosophical origins. Nevertheless, the popular notion has become a hallmark of American thought. Human excellence, and thus virtue and moral esteem become inextricably twined with independence. Those individuals who are unable to survive independently thus necessarily fail some sort of moral test. Their virtue, their worth, and to some extent their very moral status, are all deeply eroded.

As we saw, traces of this moral devaluation were evident even when we were considering the poor house of the 19th century. If anything, within a secular society that emphasizes productivity, consumption, and independence, to be placed into a nursing home might be an even deeper personal "failure" than to have been placed in the almshouse. Understood in this way, the nursing home is not simply a quasi-medical facility where patients receive treatment and remain personally untouched by their experience. Rather, it is a home that is not a home, admission into which necessarily denotes a kind of moral/personal failure. As noted in Chapter 4, recent emphasis on "successful" aging simply reinforces the moral failings of dependency. Unless and until social conceptions concerning age, frailty, and dependence can be revised, nursing homes will continue to carry a taint of loss and failure.

In reality, of course, none of us is truly self-sufficient. We are social-communal beings who all, to some extent, depend upon each other (Kittay, 1999; Mackenzie & Stoljar, 2000; Meyers, 1997). What we need, then, is an ethical culture, or a culture of ethics, that recognizes us as inherently social beings, not as inherently isolated, self-authenticating individuals. We are naturally and morally members of communities; the nursing home, by congregating many highly dependent individuals into one crowded space, uncomfortably shines a powerful light upon questions of negotiation, compromise, frailty, and communal obligation. However, while such a social transformation may at best be in the distant future, that does not mean that there are not measures that we can take today to at least ameliorate some of these negative aspects of nursing home life, and thus to help pave the road for an eventual broader social change.

Our opening story about Adele is not high drama; there is not a crisis, there is no neon-light ethical "dilemma." What we have been arguing is that some of Adele's most basic human needs are going unmet in a typical nursing home of today. What Adele needs is what we all so need: recognition and the human care that can come with it. She also needs to be free of shame and humiliation, feelings that she most likely will experience often throughout the day.

Nursing homes have improved in the past 30 years. But there is still ample room for improvement. Our aim in this chapter has been to sketch out some ideas of where the moral and humane values of the nursing home lie, and to show that in practical terms improvement not only has begun, but that much can still be accomplished. As a caring, social community, we will all be better off for such changes.

REFERENCES

Abel, E. (1991). *Who cares for the elderly?* Philadelphia: Temple University Press.

Agich, G. (1990). Reassessing autonomy in long-term care. *Hastings Center Report, 20*(6), 12–17.

Agich, G. (1993). *Autonomy in long term care.* New York, NY: Oxford University Press.

Agich, G. (1995). Actual autonomy and long-term care decision making. In L. McCullough & N. Wilson (Eds.), *Long-term care decisions: Ethical and conceptual dimensions* (pp. 113–136). Baltimore, MD: Johns Hopkins University Press.

Agich, G. (2003). *Dependency and autonomy in old age: An ethical framework for long-term care,* 2nd and revised addition. Cambridge, UK: Cambridge University Press.

Basting, A. (1993). Reading the story behind the story: Content and context in stories by people with dementia. *Generations, 27*(3), 25–29.

Beauchamp, T., & Childress, J. (1978). *Principles of biomedical ethics.* New York, NY: Oxford University Press.

Caron, C., & Bowers, B. (2003). Deciding whether to continue, share, or relinquish caregiving: Caregiver views. *Qualitative Health Research, 13*(9), 1251–1271.

Clark, A., Hanson, E. J., & Ross, H. (2003). Seeing the person behind the patient: Enhancing the care of older people using a biographical approach. *Journal of Clinical Nursing, 12*(5), 697–706.

Cole, T. (1992). *A journey of life.* New York, NY: Cambridge University Press.

Collopy, B., Boyle, P., & Jennings, B. (1991). New directions in nursing home ethics. *The Hastings Center Report, 21*(2), S1–S15.

Dodds, S. (2007). Depending on care: Recognition of vulnerability and the social contribution of care provision. *Bioethics, 21*(9), 500–510.

Gillick, M. (2006). *The denial of aging: Perpetual youth, eternal life, and other dangerous fantasies.* Cambridge, MA: Harvard University Press.

Goodstein, J. (2000). Moral compromise and personal integrity: Exploring the ethical issues of deciding together in organizations. *Business Ethics Quarterly, 19*(4), 805–819.

Gubrium, J. (1975). *Living and dying in Murray Manor.* New York, NY: St. Martin's Press.

Hoffmann, D., & Tarzian, A. (2005). Dying in America-An examination of policies that deter adequate end-of-life care in nursing homes. *Journal of law, medicine and ethics, 33*(2), 294–309.

Holstein, M. (1999). Home care, women, and aging: A case study of injustice. In M. U. Walker (Ed.), *Mother time: Women, aging, and ethics* (pp. 227–244). New York, NY: Rowman & Littlefield.

Holstein, M. (2010). Ethics and aging: Retrospectively and prospectively. In T. Cole, R. Ray, & R. Kastenbaum (Eds.), *A Guide to humanistic studies in aging: What does it mean to grow old?* (pp. 244–268). Baltimore: Johns Hopkins University Press.

Holstein, M., & Cole, T. (1995). Long-term care: A historical reflection. In L. McCullough, & N. Wilson (Eds.), *Long-term care: Ethical and conceptual dimensions* (pp. 15–34). Baltimore, MD: Johns Hopkins University Press.

Kane, R., & Caplan, A. (1990). *Everyday ethics.* New York, NY: Springer Publishing.

Kane, R., Lum, T., Cutler, L., Degenholtz, H., & Yu, T. (2007). Resident outcomes in small-house nursing homes: A longitudinal evaluation of the initial green house program. *Journal of the American Geriatrics Society, 55*(6), 832–839.

Kittay, E. F. (1999). *Love's labor: Essays on women, equality, and dependency.* New York, NY: Routledge.

Kuhn, D. (2001). In M. Holstein & P. Mitzen (Eds.), *Ethics and community-based elder care.* New York, NY: Springer Publishing Company.

Lidz, C., Fischer, L., & Arnold, R. (1992). *The erosion of autonomy in long-term care.* New York, NY: Oxford University Press.

Lustbader, W. (1999). Thoughts on the meaning of frailty. *Generations, 23*(4), 21–24.

Lustbader, W. (2001). The pioneer challenge: A radical change in the culture of nursing homes. In L. S. Noelker & Z. Harel (Eds.), *Linking quality of long-term care and quality of life* (pp. 185–203). New York, NY: Springer Publishing.

McCullough, L., & Wilson, N. (Eds.) (1995). *Long-term care decisions: Ethical and conceptual dimension.* Baltimore, MD: Johns Hopkins University Press.

Mackenzie, C., & Stoljar, N. (Eds.) (2000). *Relational autonomy: Feminist perspectives on autonomy, agency, and the social self.* New York, NY: Oxford University Press.

Meyers, D. T. (Ed.) (1997). *Feminists rethink the self.* Boulder, CO: Westview Press.

Mitty, E. (2005). Culture change in nursing homes: An ethical perspective. *Annals of Long-Term Care, 13*(3). Accessed June 1, 2010, downloaded from www.Annals of long-term care.com/article/3870. June 1, 2010.

Moody, H. R. (1992). *Ethics in an aging society.* Baltimore, MD: The Johns Hopkins University Press.

Nelson, H. L. (2001). *Damaged identities, narrative repair.* New York, NY: Cornell University Press.

Parks, J. (2010). "Lifting the burden of women's care work: Should robots replace the 'Human touch'?" *Hypatia, 25*(1), 100–120.

Powers, B. A. (2003). *Nursing home ethics.* New York, NY: Springer Publishing.

Ray, R. (2008). *Endnotes: An intimate look at the end of life.* New York, NY: Columbia University Press.

Rowe, J. W., & Kahn, R. L. (1987). Human aging: Usual and successful. *Science, 237,* 263–271.

Ryan, A. (2002). Transitions in care: Family carers' experiences of nursing home placement. *Nursing Times Research, 7*(5), 324–334.

Ryan, A. A., & Scullion, H. F. (2000). Nursing home placement: An exploration of the experience of family carers. *Journal of Advanced Nursing, 32*(5), 1187–1195.

Talbott, J. A. (2004). Deinstitutionalization: Avoiding the disasters of the past. *Psychiatric Services, 55,* 1112–1115.

Thomas, W. H. (1994). *The Eden alternative.* St. Louis, MO: University of Missouri Press.

Tronto, J. (1993). *Moral boundaries: A political argument for an ethics of care.* New York: Routledge.

Walker, M. U. (1998). *Moral understandings: A feminist study in ethics.* New York, NY: Routledge.

Whitler, J. (1996). Ethics of assisted autonomy in the nursing home. *Nursing Ethics, 3*(3), 224–235.

Zweibel, N., & Cassel, C. (1988). Ethics committees in nursing homes: Applying the hospital experience. *Hastings Center Report, 18,* 23–25.

SECTION III

Issues in Care

CHAPTER 9

Working With Clients and Patients

As we have argued throughout the chapters thus far, a conception of autonomy as relational best characterizes relationships within the long-term and home care settings. Nursing home and home care clients, families, caretakers, social workers, and other individuals involved in care giving relationships are not well described as the independent, rational, autonomous, and unencumbered selves of traditional philosophical theories (Holstein, 1999; Parks, 2003). Rather, as we have suggested, selves are interdependent, relying on others for support and confirmation that we are, indeed, unique and worthy individuals who are loved by others.

Such a relational conception of autonomy also impacts the moral judgments we make about the quality of the relationships involved, whether in people's homes or in long-term care facilities. If human beings are, as feminists claim, interdependent beings, and if our very identities come out of the relationships in which we are involved, then we ought to judge care giving by the quality of the relationships in question and the way in which the choices we make with, for, and about people affect their identities. So, for example, in attempting to make a moral judgment about whether to remove an elderly woman from her beloved home, we must consider such an action in terms of the effect on that woman's self-understandings and her relationships with others, as well as their relationship with her (Nelson & Nelson, 1995). A relational conception of autonomy leads us to consider not just practical questions about an elderly person's safety or concerns about efficient care giving, but also the impact of our actions on identities and relationships.

A relational approach provides a different lens from which to judge the morality of how we care for our elders. Rather than a universalistic, principled morality of human relationships, we advocate a contextualized, concrete one. What this means is that one cannot judge the quality of these long-term and intimate relationships based on a universal understanding of acceptable behaviors. Once real people are taken into consideration, moral judgments become rich and complex. It may not be so clear whether the right thing to do is to take an elderly woman out of her home (even though in a family's or home care supervisor's best judgment, that woman is not getting the best care) if the woman does not want to leave it. This chapter will deal with a variety of such relational considerations that arise in long-term and home care settings, and offer some direction as to what we should do about them.

The received view of autonomy and the autonomous self fail to adequately represent real selves in the real world. Conversely, the relational approach to autonomy taken by many feminist and narrative theorists (Agich, 2003; Held, 2006; Kittay, 1999; Lindemann, Verkirk, & Walker, 2008; Mackenzie & Stoljar, 2000) treats us as selves-in-relationships, where these relationships are largely constitutive of the selves that we become. This feminist conception of autonomy also takes seriously the extent to which social institutions, social values, and gender role socialization affect the choices and actions of the autonomous agent (Meyers, 1989; Wendell, 1996). As we argue in Chapter 4, the sense of self and life possibilities one develops is, to some degree, socially constructed. As Linda Barclay claims,

> Numerous moral and political theories promote a vision of the autonomous self as essentially independent and self-sufficient, a vision that denies the inescapable connectedness of selves and the fact that their immersion in networks of relationships forms their desires, aspirations, indeed their very identities. In other words, what is denied is that the self is essentially social.
> —Barclay, 2000, p. 52

As Barclay and other feminists argue, one's very identity is derived from socialization processes and the relationships into which one is born. As Annette Baier (1985) phrases it, we are all "second persons" skilled in the art of personhood through relationships of dependency that we share with others. She indicates that each individual's life history—and our collective human history—depends on each of us having a childhood where a cultural heritage is transmitted. Thus, we do not become autonomous persons *despite* our relationships with others but *because* of them. And as Eva Kittay (1999) has indicated, liberal theories that understand selves as primarily independent and self-sufficient do violence to the relational quality of our selves and our autonomy.

There are almost endless relational moral issues that arise in care giving for the elderly; this chapter could not possibly account for all of them. In what follows, however, we take a sampling of issues that routinely arise in this arena, including issues of confidentiality, power, boundaries, bias, and conflicts of interest. We will examine these issues as they emerge in different settings, both in the community and within institutions. In particular, we seek to incorporate the new approaches to doing ethics that have been discussed in previous chapters. We will consider a case study that highlights a commonly occurring relational dilemma in the nursing home setting—the development of romantic relationships between nursing home residents and the conflicts those relationships may cause.

Before we consider the issues that arise in working with elderly persons at home and in long-term care, however, we will address some of the attitudes and practices that often negatively impact the elderly care recipient. Some of the wrongs experienced by these individuals include: (1) ageist attitudes that minimize or supplant their agency and treat them as mere burdens; (2) alienation from communities that may occur due to physical and social isolation; (3) power relationships at work that make it easier to take over the lives of old people, even against their will (e.g., forcing an old person into a nursing home); and (4) degrees of dementia that make the elderly easy targets for exploitation and abuse. We will briefly consider each of these issues in turn to better understand the complexity of relationships within the long-term and home care settings.

FIGHTING AGEIST ATTITUDES

Since the 1980s, and the start of an increasingly "graying" U.S. population, articles and books have focused on ageist attitudes that pervade our culture (Arber & Ginn, 1991; Brickner, 1997; Pearsall, 1997; Post, 1995). These attitudes infiltrate all aspects of society and may even be applied by the elderly against themselves, by sometimes expressing through their own actions and attitudes a vilification of aging processes (Levy & Meyers, 2004; Ron, 2007). Ageism is expressed in different ways, some intentional and some accidental, and results from cultural ideologies and practices. For example, the U.S. medical focus on acute care emphasizes autonomy, independence, and self-sufficiency—all values to which many of the frail elderly cannot aspire. Since they fail to live up to the ideal of the "autonomous man," and since medicine cannot return them to the ideal independent self, these citizens in particular face a real paucity of care. Indeed, some elderly persons may refuse to ask for the help they need, out of fear that they will appear needy and weak, qualities that do not sit well with a society that is autonomy-obsessed. That autonomy is the guiding principle of health care—that dependency is to be eschewed and hidden because it is embarrassing and undignified—has ageist (not to mention ableist) implications.

The focus on autonomy and independence in health care is what we consider an unintentional form of ageism, that is, it does not necessarily involve or intend discrimination against older people, but has that net effect. Media images, popular writing, even professional writing on aging has been used to categorize, stereotype, and discipline the elderly; it serves to contain and objectify them. Such accounts hold old persons to standards that are impossible for them to achieve such that they are vilified for "letting themselves go." As George Agich claims,

> The negative attitudes toward old age, especially toward disabled elders, is a corollary of the stress on individualism in the literature on aging, a stress that seems, in part, to be a projection of the standards of middle-aged behavior onto old people, in which activity and independence function as tacit norms. There appears a latent assumption that successful aging consists in being as much like a middle-aged person as possible.
>
> —Agich, 2003, p. 53

The biological effects of aging are not what best or only explain the condition of elderly people; it is rather the socioeconomic structures that serve to deprive the elderly of control over their lives that may rob them of status and power. Furthermore, given the strong associations between women and the body (see Chapter 3 for more on this), elderly women in particular are held up for criticism as their bodies and faces age. Beyond a focus on appearance, ageism serves to limit available understandings of aging and old age.

Ageist attitudes toward the elderly also tend to minimize (or even discount) their agency and treat them as burdens. For example, depictions of care givers tend to assume that only younger women are caught in dilemmas of care for the elderly, yet elderly citizens (women especially) are increasingly carrying their own care giving burden. Beyond spousal care, older women are caring in increasing numbers for their grandchildren, sometimes maintaining full guardianship of them with only meager retirement incomes for support. According to the U.S. Census, nearly six million grandparents were living with their grandchildren in the year 2000, and more than 40% of those grandparents were the children's primary caregivers (http://www.census.gov/Press-Release/www/releases/archives/census_2000/001442.html). Once we get beyond our ageist assumption that older citizens are unable to reciprocate care, we can begin to actually see the amount of care work that is being done by the elderly, both women and men (Kramer & Thompson, 2005).

PHYSICAL AND EMOTIONAL ALIENATION

When considering the care issues particular to elderly persons, we should not overlook the isolation and alienation they may experience, whether they are living in communal situations (nursing homes or other long-term care facilities) or in their own homes. For a variety of reasons, including dementia, frailty, mobility problems, depression, and ageism, the elderly individual may be a stranger in her own neighborhood or facility, isolated and overlooked. In many cases elderly persons have no interactions with people in their communities or neighborhoods, so they spend a great deal of time alone and lonely. Elderly women are especially likely to find themselves isolated and alienated, given that they tend to outlive their spouses and end up spending years or decades alone. Their children often live in other cities, and visits may be rare. The impact of such isolation and alienation is grave, since it can lead to depression, loss of mental acuity, a loss of interest in their surroundings, or even death (Arehardt-Treichel, 2005; Stek et al., 2005).

Of course, this is not to suggest that alienation and isolation are inherent to the aging process. As we highlight in Chapter 4, many older individuals enjoy extraordinarily active and fulfilling social lives. The successful aging, productive aging, and civic engagement movements represent attempts to appreciate and emphasize the degree to which older citizens remain busy, active, and socially engaged (Gergen & Gergen, 2000; Gilleard & Higgs, 2000). Yet we argue that the realities of economic deprivation can make this ideal of social engagement difficult if not impossible for many older persons to achieve. Like so many other areas of life, poverty in old age—which is tragically widespread within our aging population—can lead to isolation and deprivation. It requires some money, if not a great deal of it, in order to engage in the activities that keep one socially, psychologically, and physically engaged; those who are economically deprived may suffer the added social and psychological side effects of being isolated and alienated from broader society.

Beyond emotional alienation, elderly individuals may experience physical isolation, by virtue of being shut away from the rest of their communities and by lack of physical touch. While elderly residents of nursing homes or home care clients must be touched in order to be bathed and to have their toiletries accomplished, this is not the kind of touching associated with caring about another. Certainly, being bathed and dressed can be pleasurable activities for individuals if done attentively by the care taker and not as just another task that must be accomplished. But often nurses and their aides, or even family members, are on a tight time schedule such that these ministrations become more mechanical than human. So in the midst of being cared for, elderly individuals may feel a sense that they are not cared about, and may yearn for a pat on the hand, a back or foot rub, or an embrace.

POWER RELATIONSHIPS

Relationships of power are closely linked to the ageism we highlight above. If ageist assumptions, stereotypes and ideologies support much of our thinking about the elderly—including stereotypes that suggest the elderly are mentally infirm—then it is not a large step from there to treating them in dismissive and authoritarian ways. The dynamics that are often at work when dealing with older adults are rooted in power relationships between themselves and their care givers. These relationships of power are fleshed out by appealing to the work of Michel Foucault, a historian and philosopher who has offered scathing critiques of our major social institutions.

Foucault's work forces us to question the obviousness and naturalness of our social structures, our ways of talking, and our social institutions—such as medicine (1973), prisons (1978a), insane asylums (1965), and human sexuality (1978b). He urges us to accept the way in which seemingly natural facts are social constructions or interpretations. But most importantly, perhaps, Foucault leads us to consider the ways in which subjects are managed, not just through restrictions and prohibitions, but, as Carlos Prado puts it

> through enabling conceptions, definitions, and descriptions that generate and support behavior-governing norms. What is also new, and intellectually jarring, is [his] description of this degree of management as requiring the complicity of those managed. Complicity is required because what needs to be achieved ... is the deep internalization of a carefully orchestrated value-laden understanding of the self.
>
> —*Prado, 2000, p. 55*

What this means in the context of home and long-term care relationships is that not only the institutions and their staff but also the elderly recipients of care participate in the construction and maintenance of behavior-governing norms that are foundational to these sites of care. For example, in the daily carrying out of their work, home health aides are complicit in the very norms that serve to marginalize and subordinate them. And perhaps this relates to the care fatigue and burnout that is part of their work, as they resist and reject while at the same time living out and reinforcing the norms surrounding the practice of home health care. How can this be?

First of all, according to Foucault, power is never totalizing or complete. This means it presupposes that those over whom power is exercised can resist; it exists only where there is potential resistance. Power is evident in its active application against resistance, and because to have power over someone means they are allowed some initiative, it can then become resist-ance. Prado claims that "Power constrains *actions*, not individuals. Power is a totality made up of individuals being dominated, coerced, or intimidated; and of individuals resisting domination, coercion, or intimidation" (2000, p. 37). Thus, the idea is not that elderly persons are simply dominated by others; they can also resist.

Power is not merely something that functions negatively to oppress indi-viduals; it is essential to the positive empowerment of resisting agents as well. Agents take advantage of existing techniques, strategies, and discourses to take initiative in reinvesting them with a power and meaning that is more affirming of their own sense of who they would like to be. Judith Butler (1990) has taken up this issue of power and indicated the multifarious ways in which we can parody or lampoon existing power structures in order to expose and "denaturalize" them.

Issues of power, abuse, and resistance arise in all areas of care for the aged, and in a variety of relationships, including the family, the supervisor–client–aide relationship within the home care setting, and the relationships between staff members and residents within the nursing home. For instance, the abuse by some home health aides of their clients, when understood from this Foucauldian perspective, is connected to relationships of power within the home care industry. Just as aides are used and abused by this system of care provision, so aides may use and abuse their clients. So the instances of theft, extortion, cheating in reporting hours, physical abuse of clients, and emotional abuse, while inexcusable, are the inevitable result of the power dynamic in home care (Parks, 2003). Power manifests itself in a variety of ways and on a variety of levels.

It is often easy to explicitly engage a power dynamic with persons who are elderly, especially if they are female, frail, demented, frightened, or depressed. Indeed, there may be appropriate times when a care giver may exert her power over an elderly person in order to achieve certain important ends, like getting her to bathe. One must take care in determining when the use of such power is justified and when it is not. We do not claim there is a formula for determining when authoritarian attitudes toward the elderly care recipient are justified; but some very general guidelines may help to determine how to proceed in particular circumstances.

For example, we argue that where elderly individuals refuse nursing home care and demand to stay in their own homes, the other parties involved have an obligation to cooperate because so much is at stake for that individ-ual. Choosing the place and manner in which one lives, and the kinds of relationships in which one wishes to engage, are some of the most important choices one can make, and they seriously impact one's life enjoyment.

However, this obligation is not absolute, since the elderly individual may be too confused, frail or ill to remain at home. Furthermore, such requests must be balanced against the interests of family members or neighbors, who may also be put at risk if she forgets to turn off the burners on her stove or to extinguish cigarettes. At the very least, we believe the elderly individual should be allowed to remain at home as long as possible, taking measures that will extend his or her ability to remain there. This is not because we believe that the principle of autonomy should reign supreme, but rather because such a decision speaks directly to an individual's identity and self-understandings.

We need, then, to accommodate the expressed wishes of elderly persons insofar as they are capable and competent to make self-regarding claims. But this is not a black or white issue: competency comes in degrees, and an individual may be competent in some areas of life, but not others (see Chapter 11).

RELATIONSHIPS IN INSTITUTIONS

The guidelines for care giving within formal institutions, such as hospitals and nursing homes, are encoded and universalized. Strict rules and regulations must be followed to prevent harm from occurring and to avoid litigation; for this reason one often finds a tension between the care needs of individual elderly patients or residents and the highly structured and sometimes regimented rules of the institutions. For example, a nursing home resident may prefer to sleep later in the mornings but nevertheless be forced up early in the morning in order to maintain the strict schedule of the nursing home; or an elderly hospital patient may wish to walk the hallway of the ward but, due to concerns for potential falls, be barred from doing so. In both cases institutional policies and regulations come into conflict with the wishes and needs of the individual. In the same vein, a nurse or social worker might wish to allow or even encourage patient/resident freedom but be tied to the institution's policies such that individualized treatment and interaction become difficult if not impossible.

Within the institutional setting, one finds a host of issues that arise with regard to confidentiality, conflicts of interest, and the setting of boundaries, to name a few. These issues are driven by the communal context in which nursing home residents and hospital patients live, the close living quarters, and the conflict between institutional rules and individual preferences or desires. A case study helps to characterize the kinds of relational problems that arise in these settings.

AN AFFAIR OF THE DEMENTED

Mrs. O'Brien, 75-years-old, is a widow of 10 years and is diagnosed as being mildly demented. Mr. Jackson, 73-years-old, is a widower of 12 years and is mild-to-moderately demented. Both are residents of a nursing home. Mr. Jackson has been in the facility for 5 years; Mrs. O'Brien moved in just five months ago.

Shortly after her arrival, Mrs. O'Brien struck up a friendship with Mr. Jackson. That friendship soon progressed into a sexual relationship. Mr. Jackson frequently accompanies Mrs. O'Brien around the facility—to meals, to the day room, etc.—and frequently wants to spend the night with her. They relate to one another the way they related to their marriage partners, with Mr. Jackson taking the lead, guiding Mrs. O'Brien around, and taking care of her in ways that are somewhat overbearing. Mrs. O'Brien, however, accepts and even welcomes the attention and care, especially since her marriage followed the same pattern.

He is under the impression that she is his deceased wife. Mrs. O'Brien, however, recognizes that he is not her husband, but she nevertheless welcomes the relationship and gets somewhat agitated when staff removes Mr. Jackson from her room.

Mr. Jackson's two children are accepting, even pleased, with their father's new found relationship. Mrs. O'Brien's two children, however, are appalled and are complaining to the nursing home about how their mother is being abused and that the nursing home is not providing proper care. They are also upset that the staff is letting their mother engage in a relationship with Mr. Jackson that, in their opinion, she would never normally consent to. As they put it, "Our mother was always faithful to our father, and would never be with another man." A couple of the staff members who provide care for Mrs. O'Brien are also opposed to the relationship. They complain that Mr. Jackson gets in their way, and that the mornings after he has spent the night, Mrs. O'Brien's dementia is exacerbated by the decreased sleep. On the other hand, some staff members find that the relationship has a positive effect on these residents, and that trying to keep them apart requires a Herculean effort that only results in agitation and upset for everyone involved.

As this case exemplifies, the needs and desires of particular individuals in long-term care settings can come into conflict, and indeed, the needs of the institution or the community may conflict with the individual good of the residents or patients. In the case of Mr. Jackson and Mrs. O'Brien, conflict arises between the couples' family members, the staff members, and the desires of the couple in connection to the smooth running of the nursing home.

This case also highlights the chronic, mundane sorts of ethical issues that arise in connection with older adults: care for older adults largely concerns chronic care issues, such as those that arise in nursing homes or skilled nursing facilities. The case of Mr. Jackson and Mrs. O'Brien is just one example. While it clearly does not represent a life or death issue, it certainly relates to issues of quality of life (for the couple, the other residents of the nursing home, the staff, and the adult children of Mr. Jackson and Mrs. O'Brien) and to patient autonomy.

Dementia is a very common problem in the long-term care setting. According to the Alzheimer's Association, there are currently 5 million people living with Alzheimer's disease in the United States; every 72 seconds someone develops the disease, and by the middle of the century one person will develop the disease every 33 seconds (http://www.alz. org/national/documents/report_alzfactsfigures2007.pdf). The situation in which we find Mr. Jackson and Mrs. O'Brien is not unusual, then, given the prevalence of dementia and/or Alzheimer's disease within long-term care. Persons with Alzheimer's disease tend to lose their inhibitions, especially concerning sexual matters; it is commonplace for nursing home residents to develop relationships, including sexual ones, with their peers (Archibald, 2002; Berger, 2000; Kuhn, 2002; Wright, 1998). Justice Sandra Day O'Connor found herself in a similar situation with her husband after he developed Alzheimer's disease and was moved to an Alzheimer's ward at a long-term care facility. In his dementia, he developed a relationship with another person with Alzheimer's disease who was living at the same institution. O'Connor went public with her husband's situation to raise awareness surrounding care of persons with Alzheimer's. Rather than being upset by this newfound relationship, and despite 55 years of marriage, she was relieved to see her husband so content. Similarly, the ethical issues surrounding Mr. Jackson and Mrs. O'Brien's relationship involve concerns for both their own health and well-being, and that of the staff, other residents, and their adult children.

"This affair raises questions concerning the interests of other nursing home residents. One might argue that the rules of a nursing home are in place to protect and serve *all* the residents, even if some individuals might be benefited by breaking them. Thus, from a rule-based moral perspective, even if this couple is not harmed by their relationship, allowing it to continue could very well violate the rights and interests of other residents of the home. For example, if the sleeping quarters are shared then the other women sharing Mrs. O'Brien's space may be disturbed by the nightly sleepovers. Mr. Jackson's possessiveness concerning Mrs. O'Brien could have a negative impact on relationships between the residents, creating relationships of inclusion and exclusion. So even barring any negative outcomes for the couple, the duty to follow the rules may prevail.

With regard to the staff of the nursing home, there is a division in their responses to the relationship between this couple. Some of the staff is disgruntled because they find the affair inconvenient and even problematic in accomplishing Mrs. O'Brien's care. When Mr. Jackson is in the bed with her they find it difficult to get access to do her care; and some of the staff find it difficult to deal with her when she is sleep deprived and mentally confused. Yet other staff members are happy that the couple have one another for companionship and support, and welcome the liaison. The problem, then, is which staff members' wishes should be adhered to: those who want an end to the relationship, or those who want to see it continue?

Perhaps an even greater conflict of interest arises in connection with the couples' adult children. Mr. Jackson's children are delighted with the match, and express their pleasure that their father has a new love interest; but Mrs. O'Brien's children are horrified, claiming that if their mother were in her "right mind" she would never consent to such a relationship. Though the children are certainly connected to and concerned about their mother, one might wonder how much their wishes should be taken into consideration, given the little time they actually spend at the home with their mother. One solution might be to separate Mr. Jackson and Mrs. O'Brien while her children are visiting her at the home, thus allowing them to visit their mother without the pain of seeing her with another man.

If, however, dementia is present, we might question the degree to which either party can truly consent to the relationship. Mr. Jackson has confused Mrs. O'Brien with his deceased wife, so he is not appreciating her as a unique individual. While Mrs. O'Brien may suffer dementia to a lesser degree, her children claim that she would never consent to such a relationship under normal circumstances. It may be the case that her prior values and wishes as a person without dementia should be protected over the newly developed desires and interests of the demented Mrs. O'Brien.

Thus, while the issues raised by this case are not life threatening or urgent, they do raise important questions about patients with compromised decisional capacity, the duty to adhere to institutional values and rules, and the rights of families to make decisions for their elderly and/or demented members. Such cases highlight the contextual nature of these dilemmas, and the difficulties of applying a standard principle of autonomy to situations where the individuals involved are not the ideal rational agents and where boundaries are not so easily drawn. How might one puzzle through such issues from a relational approach that understands moral agents as interdependent, embedded in situations that are often not of their own choosing?

We argue that the relationship between Mr. Jackson and Mrs. O'Brien should be accommodated, keeping in mind the needs of the staff that cares for them and the family members who visit them. So, for example, while Mrs. O'Brien's children may not have a moral right to demand that the staff completely separate her from Mr. Jackson (after all, the children do not live at the nursing home, are not a daily part of their mother's life, and may not even know their mother as well as the staff who interact with her every day), their wishes could be respected insofar as Mr. Jackson is not present when they come to the home to visit their mother. Such decisions and arrangements, however, can only be made in the context of the particular situation and with consideration for the individuals involved. If we start from a relational approach to autonomy, which we argue more closely character-izes the reality of long-term care relationships, then the focus moves away from rights and rules toward a context-based approach to boundary-setting. Such an approach takes into account the particulars of the individuals involved, the nature and quality of their relationship, and the needs and wishes of those individuals.

PROBLEMS IN SETTING BOUNDARIES

A relational conception of autonomy is well suited to long-term and home care for the elderly. Instead of understanding selves as "islands unto them-selves" and processes of individuation as setting us apart from one another, relational autonomy sees our selves as developing out of the relationships in which we are enmeshed. While a relational conception of autonomy does not deny that autonomy is possible—it resists situating the self as wholly social such that no authentic self-regarding choices are possible—it sees autonomy as developing out of relationship. This is certainly reflected in the home care setting, where clients' selves are intimately tied to the quality of relationships with their family care takers and home care workers (Agich, 2003; Moody, 1992; Nelson & Nelson, 1995). A relational approach to autonomy works best in long-term care situations because it can be applied to both familial care taking relationships and formal care relationships.

While nursing home or home care workers are not involved in the early formation of residents' or clients' selves, they are nevertheless an important part of the maintenance of selves. Like familial caretakers, their relationships can also be understood from a model of relational autonomy. As what can reasonably be termed "intimates" with their clients, nursing home and home health aides have the power through their words and actions to either support or destroy the selves of those for whom they are caring. Aides see and hear things that reveal much about the elderly persons for whom they are caring, and these bits of information are sometimes crucial to under-standing and accommodating them. Indeed, a familial ethic may apply in such cases, given the degree to which such care workers become viewed as part of the client's family.

That care workers may be treated as "fictive kin," and that they may feel deep connections to their care recipients, highlights the way in which virtues in long-term care also become vices. As many studies show, it is these kinds of connections that make care taking work fulfilling and satisfying for the workers. But such relationships also make workers vulnerable to unintended exploitation by those for whom they care, who may be lonely or frightened and as a result may demand care beyond the workers' paid hours. To take just one example, a study by Eileen Chichin (1992) indicates that a large pro-portion of home care workers put in extra hours without pay, usually for relational reasons. The altruism already associated with "women's work" coupled with the personal attachment formed through these relationships indicates how aides can become deeply committed to their clients. As Tracy Karner (1998) points out, with status as an honorary family member comes certain obligations: care workers may take on obligations that go well beyond a contractual model of human relationships.

Since care worker/cared-for relationships are neither simply contractual nor personal relationships, we need a more nuanced understanding of them. Workers and clients both must have exit options for getting out of uncom-fortable or destructive care relationships. Though it is difficult in the context of such strong relationships, some way must be found to set boundaries so that neither care workers nor their cared-for are exploited or over-burdened. This is not to revert to a contractual way of thinking in the long-term care setting; it is only to recognize the complexity of these relationships, where workers and cared-for are more than just contracting parties but less than families.

CONFIDENTIALITY AND PRIVACY IN LONG-TERM CARE

The Health Insurance Portability and Accountability Act (HIPAA) was enacted in 1996 by the U.S. Congress. Most individuals have had some experience with HIPAA, either when they seek care at a health clinic or undergo treatments or surgeries, since the law requires that patients be informed about limitations on their health care privacy. HIPAA's Privacy Rule was put into place in 2003: it regulates the use and disclosure of patients' health information held by "covered entities," including (among other health care entities) nursing homes (Terry, 2009).

In sharp contrast to the strict privacy rules that are (in theory) adhered to in clinical, acute care settings, there may be problems with maintaining confidentiality within institutional close quarters like nursing homes, as well as with home and community-based care. Questions arise such as: What information needs to be shared by care management teams in order to provide safe, effective care for nursing home residents and home care clients? Who should have access to this information? And how do we best ensure and protect the privacy of elderly persons in long-term care settings, who may have a variety of health care professionals and paraprofessionals coming in and out of their rooms and homes?

Factors such as old age, degrees of dementia, and close living quarters may make confidentiality and privacy seem like less pressing issues in long-term care. There may be a tendency to think that an individual of advanced age who suffers from Alzheimer's disease lacks the necessary reason and dignity to make his or her personal matters or health care records worthy of protection. Failure to adequately protect personal information in these settings is another sign of the ways in which ageism works against these elderly individuals: it may be thought that respect for privacy and confidentiality simply aren't highly valued by them.

Yet the very notion that medical records are kept confidential is a myth that might be driven by our culture's strong belief in patient autonomy. As Robert Gellman (1999) claims, in reality:

> If you are hospitalized, hundreds of hospital employees may see some or all of your records. Records may be shared with labs, x-ray facilities, nursing homes, physical therapists, pharmacists, and others involved in treatment. At each institution, computer operators, lawyers, and accountants can access records. If you have third party insurance, bills will be sent to claims processors and clearinghouses before the bills reach your insurer. If your employer pays for your health insurance, then the employer may be able to obtain your treatment records. Records are also routinely shared with or used by public health authorities, medical researchers, dozens of government agencies at the federal, state, and local levels, schools, courts, fraud and abuse investigators, cost containment managers, outcomes researchers, licensing and accreditation organizations, police, coroners, and others. Some records are routinely sent overseas for transcription (http://lists.essential.org/med-privacy/msg00449.html).

Medical records, then, are not confidential; on the contrary, they may be the most widely shared of all records that are kept by third party record keepers. The routine sharing of patient records is an essential feature of the culture of the medical establishment in the United States. Most disclosures occur without notice to patients and without any patient consent

(Francis, 2006). Most individuals are completely unaware of the routine sharing of health records, and even many health professionals still think that records are private.

This means that the status of confidentiality in long-term care may not be all that different from its status in situations of acute, clinical care. Confidentiality, as some critics have long claimed, is a decrepit concept (Siegler, 1982). Yet we believe there are reasons for being particularly concerned about confidentiality and privacy in long-term care: the kinds of ageist attitudes and power relationships we highlight at the beginning of this chapter make it far too easy to treat resident or client information as being "fair game" for those involved in the individual's care, even if only marginally so. That elderly persons may not be considered the moral equals of others whose information is worthy of protection is of serious concern: this is evidence again that our cultural conception of fully human persons deserving of dignity and respect is contingent upon that individual's ability to reason and govern his/her own life.

Being realistic, it may be very difficult to protect an elderly individual's medical records and information. Information may be widely shared amongst nursing home administrators and staff, social workers, physicians, and beyond. Even with HIPAA standards in place, information continues to be shared; there is no "sanctity" of medical records. This may be especially true in cases of elder care, where there may be many caregivers involved who may need access to an elderly individual's medical records. Yet, by sharp contrast, the treatment of simple inquiries by family and friends— "how is my friend Sally Smith doing?"—is one way in which HIPAA sacrifices ordinary virtues of concern for others in order to protect a legalistic bottom line (Gross, 2007).

The goal in such cases, we believe, should be to ensure that residents of nursing homes and home care clients are not subject to reduced concern for their privacy and confidentiality simply because of their age or mental status. It may be true that confidentiality of medical records is not of the status that the public may expect; but eroding protection simply because a patient is old and suffering some degree of dementia only shows a general lack of respect for the elderly population.

While the confidentiality of medical records is, indeed, an important consideration in elder care, we believe that more mundane privacy issues may be of greater significance. This is because respect for a nursing home resident or home care client has more to do with how we view and treat them on a daily basis, and the behaviors that signal our attitudes toward them. As the case study concerning Mr. Jackson and Mrs. O'Brien conveys, with shared rooms, busy corridors, and frequent visitors being commonplace in many nursing homes, couples can encounter difficulty when trying to find a time and place to be intimate. Or, conversations may take place between home care or nursing home aides within the corridors where private (and often, embarrassing) information may be shared during shift changes. Particularly where issues of sexuality and bodily function are concerned, respecting older persons' dignity and right to privacy is a significant sign of their worth as equal moral and sexual beings.

We return to issues of sexuality in this chapter because it is the arena in which privacy may be most disrespected, and where care takers may experience the most discomfort in dealing with clients or residents. Making jokes about behaviors, spreading rumors about clients or residents, or discussing an individual's private matters in corridors and other public areas are all signs of both discomfort with and lack of respect for that individual. This discomfort is unsurprising given that senior sexuality can be an uncomfortable subject for many. In a society that equates sexuality with youth, seniors are not expected to have sexual desires or to be sexually active (DeLamater & Sill, 2005). Yet cases like that of Mr. Jackson and Mrs. O'Brien abound; addressing that fact and making arrangements such that individuals' privacy and dignity is respected is of paramount importance.

Of course, maintaining privacy and "alone time" for people under close quarters (in many cases, where rooms are shared by two or more individuals) may be a challenge. Especially in nursing home settings, where space and opportunities to be alone are limited, careful arrangements may have to be made in order to ensure that residents have the opportunity to spend time alone or with their intimate partners. When such relationships do take place in long-term care facilities, it may be important for staff to be aware of it, but it may not be necessary to inform the residents' families about them; indeed, it should be left up to the individuals involved (where possible) to share that information with their family members. Even in cases, like Mr. Jackson and Mrs. O'Brien, where the partners may suffer degrees of cognitive impairment, families should not be *asked* if the resident may engage in the relationship, but should simply be *informed* about it. The distinction here may seem trivial, but it can have a significant impact on respect for residents and the quality of their everyday lives.

In negotiating privacy within these constrained living conditions, staff can take steps to maintain as much as possible the freedom and privacy of those who live there. If, for example, a staff member enters a room and finds a couple in a sexual situation who are known to have a relationship, the staff worker should make it a point to talk later, separately, with both residents to explore how each of them individually understands the relationship, and how, if appropriate, the institution might best accommodate the situation. Or, if the couple in question is not known to be in relationship, the staff member would need to ensure that both parties are consenting, but also inform the charge nurse and social worker so that other staff members can be notified. To protect resident privacy and confidentiality, information about their personal and sexual lives should only be shared insofar as it directly relates to their good care and proper treatment in the home: otherwise sharing information may erode the residents' dignity and create an institutional culture where privacy and confidentiality are simply not taken seriously or respected.

AN OVERVIEW: RESPECT FOR ELDERS, RESPECT FOR OURSELVES

How we address social relations within long-term care is important for both caretakers and residents. It is of significance that how society treats its elders is likely to reflect how younger generations in turn will be treated under the same conditions when their time comes. As Eva Kittay has indicated in her work on care taking, "what goes round, comes round" (1999, p. 107), thus making questions about working with clients and residents in long-term care even more relational in nature than one might initially think. How we treat our nursing home residents and home care clients relate directly to how we are likely to be treated ourselves some day.

Furthermore, it behooves us to remember that the long-term care spaces where caretakers spend their days working are *homes* to the residents or clients with whom they work. It is easy to forget that skilled nursing facilities, nursing homes, and assisted living facilities are home for the individuals who reside there; they are not temporary spaces where these individuals are visiting or spending a short period of time. The same can be true of home care practice, even though it might seem obvious that the site of care is the individual's place of residence. The issues that arise in these settings are not the sort of life-or-death concerns that one sees in the acute care setting: but they are issues that directly speak to the quality of life and relationships of senior citizens who are subject to long-term care situations.

As we have argued in this chapter, an appeal to traditional autonomy is not responsive to the rich and complex relational issues that arise between caretakers and the elderly in long-term care. If we take seriously the relational autonomy approach for which we are advocating, we can more effectively address the complex social relationship issues that arise in the long-term care setting. A feminist conception of relational autonomy best characterizes the relationships between care takers and care recipients and recognizes the unique features of each relationship. If human beings are, as this view claims, interdependent beings, and if our very identities come out of the relationships in which we are involved, then we ought to judge the ethical nature of long-term care by the quality of the relationships in question, not by the degree to which individual autonomy is respected.

REFERENCES

Agich, G. (2003). *Dependence and autonomy in old age: An ethical framework for long term care.* New York, NY: Cambridge University Press.

Arber, S., & Ginn, J. (1991). *Gender and later life.* London, UK: Sage Press.

Archibald, C. (2002). Sexuality and dementia in residential care-whose responsibility? *Sexual & Relationship Therapy, 17*(3), 301–309.

Arehardt-Treichel, J. (2005). Depression plus loneliness may hasten death in elderly. *Psychiatric News, 40*(2), 53.

Baier, A. (1985). *Postures of the mind: Essays on mind and morals.* Minneapolis, MN: University of Minnesota Press.

Barclay, L. (2000). Autonomy and the social self. In C. MacKenzie & N. Stoljar (Eds.), *Relational autonomy: Feminist perspectives on autonomy, agency, and the social self* (pp. 52–71). New York, NY: Oxford University Press.

Berger, J. T. (2000). Sexuality and intimacy in the nursing home: A romantic couple of mixed cognitive capacities. *Journal of Clinical Ethics, 11*(4), 309–313.

Brickner, P. W. (1997). Long-term home health care for the frail aged. In P. W. Brickner, F. R. Kellogg, A. J. Lechich, R. Lipsman, & L. K. Sharer (Eds.), *Geriatric home health care: The collaboration of physicians, nurses, and social workers.* New York, NY: Springer Publishers.

Butler, J. (1990). *Gender trouble: Feminism and the subversion of identity.* New York, NY: Routledge.

Chichin, E. R. (1992). Home care is where the health is: The role of interpersonal relationships in paraprofessional home care. *Home Health Care Services Quarterly, 13*(1–2), 161–177.

DeLamater, S. J., & Sill, M. (2005). Sexual desire in later life. *Journal of Sex Research, 42*(2), 138–149.

Francis, T. (2006). Spread of records stirs fears of privacy erosion. *The Wall Street Journal.* Retrieved December 28, from http://www.post-gazette.com/pg/06362/749444-114.stm.

Foucault, M. (1965). *Madness and civilization: A history of insanity in the age of reason* (R. Howard Trans.). New York, NY: Pantheon. (Original work published 1961.)

Foucault, M. (1973). *The birth of the clinic: An archaeology of medical perception* (A. M. Sheridan-Smith Trans.). New York, NY: Pantheon. (Original work published 1963.)

Foucault, M. (1978a). *Discipline and punish: The birth of the prison* (A. Sheridan Trans.). New York, NY: Pantheon. (Original work published 1975.)

Foucault, M. (1978b). *The history of sexuality, Vol. 1: An introduction* (R. Hurley Trans.). New York, NY: Pantheon. (Original work published 1976.)

Gellman, R. (1999). *The myth of patient confidentiality.* Retrieved from http://lists.essential.org/med-privacy/msg00449.html.

Gergen, K., & Gergen, M. (2000). The new aging: Self construction and social values. In K. W. Schaie & J. Hendricks (Eds.), *The evolution of the aging self: The social impact on the aging process.* New York, NY: Springer.

Gilleard, C., & Higgs, P. (2000). *Cultures of aging: Self, aging, and the body.* New York, NY: Prentice-Hall.

Gross, J. (2007). Keeping patients' details private, even from kin. *New York Times,* July 3. Retrieved from http://www.nytimes.com/2007/07/03/health/policy/03hipaa.html?ex=1341115200&en=19160c75b9633d68&ei=5090&partner=rssuserland&emc=rss.

Held, V. (2006). *The ethics of care: Personal, political, and global.* New York, NY: Oxford University Press.

Holstein, M. (1999). Home care, women, and aging: A case study of injustice. In M. U. Walker (Ed.), *Mother time: Women, aging, and ethics* (pp. 227–244). New York, NY: Rowman & Littlefield.

Karner, T. X. (1998). Professional caring: Homecare workers as fictive kin. *Journal of Aging Studies, 12,* 69–83.

Kittay, E. F. (1999). *Love's labor: Essays on women, equality, and dependency.* New York, NY: Routledge.

Kramer, B. J., & Thompson, H. E. (Eds.) (2005). *Men as caregivers.* New York, NY: Prometheus Books.

Kuhn, D. R. (2002). Intimacy, sexuality, and residents with dementia. *Alzheimer's Care Quarterly, 3*(2), 165–176.

Levy, B. R., & Myers, L. M. (2004). Preventive health behaviors influenced by self-perceptions of aging. *Preventive Health, 39*(3), 625–629.

Lindemann, H., Verkerk, M., & Walker, U. M. (Eds.) (2008). *Naturalized bioethics: Toward responsible knowing and practice.* New York, NY: Cambridge University Press.

Mackenzie, C., & Stoljar, N. (Eds.) (2000). *Relational autonomy: Feminist perspectives on autonomy, agency, and the social self.* New York, NY: Oxford University Press.

Meyers, D. T. (1989). *Self, society, and personal choice.* New York, NY: Columbia University Press.

Moody, H. R. (1992). *Ethics in an aging society.* Baltimore, MD: The Johns Hopkins University Press.

Nelson, J. L., & Nelson, H. L. (1995). *The patient in the family: An ethics of medicine and families.* New York, NY: Routledge.

Parks, J. A. (2003). *No place like home? Feminist ethics and home health care.* Indianapolis, IN: Indiana University Press.

Pearsall, M. (Ed.) (1997). *The other within us: Feminist explorations of women and aging.* Boulder, CO: Westview Press.

Post, S. (1995). *The moral challenge of Alzheimer disease*. Baltimore, MD: Johns Hopkins University Press.

Prado, C. (2000). *Starting with Foucault* (2nd ed.). Boulder, CO: Westview Press.

Ron, P. (2007). Elderly people's attitudes and perceptions of aging and old age: The role of cognitive dissonance? *International Journal of Geriatric Psychiatry, 22*(7), 656–662.

Siegler, M. (1982). Confidentiality in medicine: A decrepit concept. *New England Journal of Medicine, 307*(24), 1518–1521.

Stek, M. L., Vinkers, D. J., Gussekloo, J., Beekman, A., van der Mast, R. C., & Westendorp, R. G. (2005). Is depression in old age fatal only when people feel lonely? *American Journal of Psychiatry, 162*, 178–180.

Terry, K. (2009). Patient privacy: The new threats. *Physicians Practice Journal, 19*(3). Retrieved from http://www.physicianspractice.com/index/fuseaction/articles.details/articleID/1299/page/1.htm.

Wendell, S. (1996). *The rejected body: Feminist philosophical reflections on disability*. New York, NY: Routledge.

Wright, L. K. (1998). Affection and sexuality in the presence of Alzheimer's disease: A longitudinal study. *Sexuality and Disability, 16*(3), 167–179.

CHAPTER 10

What Do We Do Now?

Abuse, Neglect, and Self-Neglect

INTRODUCTION

The problem of abuse and neglect experienced by older community-dwelling citizens is both sad and familiar. Most states now have mandatory reporting laws so that such cases come to the attention of appropriate officials. What is less certain is what can be done. The elder is often reluctant to leave the place where the abuse or neglect occurred and, in truth, there are few good options to offer. That said, however, a number of different responses and interventions have been developed, broadly categorized as protection, empowerment, and advocacy (Anetzberger, 2000). Ironically, abuse always happens in the context of the very social interactions and relationships that otherwise are central to an elder's well-being. As we know from other forms of domestic violence, intimacy has its flip side.

In contrast to abuse and neglect, the problem of self-neglect does not directly involve another person. It is, however, the most commonly reported problem to Adult Protective Services or other monitoring agencies, thus overshadowing more familiar forms of abuse and neglect. It is also a risk factor for other types of mistreatment (Connolly, 2008). What "it" actually is, its causes, and its remedies, are gaining increased attention in the literature; but we are still far from fully understanding it. To some, it is a social construction, describing individuals who live outside the mainstream and are therefore considered deviant, while to others it is a medical condition rooted in physical or psychological problems. A recent study (Iris, Ridings, & Conrad, 2009) proposes a conceptual model of self-neglect that includes personal, environmental, and social risk factors as well as self-care deficits. All this suggests that researchers are still working out issues related to causes, which will then influence both the ethical responses to it and the practical interventions that are put in place.

The ethical problems that emerge from abuse, neglect and self-neglect often appear to be intractable. Like many problems that are not solved by a single decision in a limited time frame, they reflect life problems that are exacerbated by age, physical and mental problems, poverty, isolation, family dysfunction and/or stress. The "self-neglecter," for example, may be struggling to maintain a sense of individuality and identity in the face of multiple threats. The need to neglect oneself cannot be easily "cured"; and the fact that few good alternative living arrangements are available worsens efforts at resolution. Similarly, the long, and often complicated, history of mothers, daughters, grandchildren and others in a social environment that devalues both dependency and vulnerability make a satisfying solution all the more difficult. Context looms large.

For families or professionals encountering such situations, concerns about the autonomy of the older person inevitably abuts concerns for physical as well as psycho-social safety and general well-being. Additionally, recognition that self-neglect is "inextricably linked to other aspects of elder mistreatment that involve wrongdoing" (Connolly, 2008, p. S245) deepens the complexity of addressing self-neglect. When, for example, does the failure to give care slip from respecting autonomy to culpability? We emphasize this complexity, not to excuse what is abusive or seriously harmful behavior, but to suggest that it calls for an ethical response that is deeply dependent upon narrative. As we will argue, appropriate responses to abuse, neglect, and self-neglect are not founded on principles, but are more closely linked to the care perspective that arises from a feminist ethic of care. One important exception, however, is the need to remedy the injustices "informal" caregivers' experience, which contributes to abuse or neglect. The two cases presented below—one on apparent self-neglect and the other on abuse and/or neglect—represent the types of situations in which ethical concerns arise. They suggest why no single ethical approach to addressing ethical problems in practice can "reduce complexity, facilitate resolution, or overcome differences in fundamental values" (Holstein, 1995, p. 170).

Grace Jones

Grace Jones is 83 years old. She has lived in the same small house in a poor neighborhood for the past 30 years. Her husband died 15 years ago; her 3 children live in different parts of the country. While they care about their mother, her children can visit only occasionally because travel costs are not easy for them to meet. So, they call and visit as often as they can.

After a six month absence, Grace's daughter Margie visited and was very distressed by her mother's living conditions. It was a lot worse than the last time she was there. The piles of newspapers seemed to have grown significantly; there was a lingering odor in the house; the stove didn't seem to work; and Mrs. Jones seemed to have lost a great deal of weight. Margie pleaded with her mother to get someone in to give the house a thorough cleaning and to repair the stove. She also insisted that her mother see the doctor about her weight loss. She got nowhere. Her mother calmly listened to her and insisted that everything was just fine, that her appetite was decreasing since she wasn't very active. She ate cold food or stuff that could go into the microwave, which looked as if it was about ready to fall apart. She told Margie that she hated going to the doctor and that she already knew what was he going to tell her. When Margie asked her mother if she was taking her medications (for blood pressure and congestive heart failure), Mrs. Jones responded that she didn't like how they made her feel and so she had stopped taking them. Margie was at her wit's end. She didn't want to leave her mother that way but she couldn't stay much longer. She finally located a phone number for the Elder Services Center in the community and called them. They promised to send a social worker to her mother's house.

Toni Jacobsen visited when Margie was still there. She also saw the clutter and disarray and noticed the unpleasant smell. She offered to have someone come in to do a thorough cleaning and someone else to repair the stove and make sure that the other appliances worked. She requested permission to have a nurse practitioner come by to check Grace's vitals. Mrs. Jones refused all these options; she insisted that she needed no help and was perfectly fine. She had no explanation for the odor. Margie and Toni thought it was probably the result of too few showers and unwashed clothing. They could not convince Mrs. Jones to do anything.

Paula Chase

Perry Grimshaw lived in his grandmother's house. At 23, he was unemployed and not on good terms with his mother. In exchange for doing very light chores and some errands for his grandmother, he lived rent free. Paula Chase welcomed her grandson's presence even though he was sometimes rough with her and often asked her for money. She wished he would get a job, but he always was her favorite. Ten years ago Mrs. Chase, a 75 year old widower, bought her home, and retired with a small pension. That pension plus social security allowed her to live modestly but with relative security; that is, until Perry moved in. Her food budget skyrocketed and Perry's regular requests for money ate into her income. Because she had multiple health problems that limited her activity, she received services from the Down Home Care Agency. A home care aide, Polly Tallis, came three times a week for two hours. She made sure that Mrs. Chase had food to eat and that her house was reasonably neat. The two women liked one another and talked as Polly did her work.

It was different when Perry was around. He stormed through the house, demanding that Polly make his lunch and do his laundry. One day, Polly arrived and saw bruises on Mrs. Chase's arms. When she mentioned them, Mrs. Chase said that she got up in the night and walked right into the door frame. A week later, she had more bruises, which she also attributed to an accident. Polly became more and more concerned as Perry seemed to be angry whenever she was there. Mrs. Chase seemingly did not recognize any of the behaviors that so troubled Polly. "He's a good boy," she said, "he's just frustrated because he has no job. You'll see, he'll be fine once he starts earning some money. He's always been my pet. I guess I've spoiled him." Polly didn't know what to do.

While these situations are different in many important ways, both cases may evoke an emotional response, an important trigger that something morally important is occurring. Yet emotions do more than act as a trigger. Brody (1994; cited in Marshall, 2001, p. 147), for example, suggests that emotional empathy may yield important moral insights. It is thus important to ask not only what one might think about situations like these, but what one *feels* about them. What is troubling? What values might one emphasize? Might one wonder whether Mrs. Jones and/or Mrs. Chase can make decisions on their own behalf? How might one understand their actions? Should one be concerned about the content of their choices, or only about how they make those choices, that is, whether they are free and uncoerced?

Following some definitional and background information, we will develop an argument concerning how we might address these situations of abuse, neglect, and self-neglect. These problems are particularly complex because the background conditions loom so large: there may be a large gap between what is good to do and what is practically possible. Impediments to right action may involve resource constraints, the poor reputation of institutional life, the lack of good living alternatives, caregiver responsibilities, the intricacies of family life, and many of the basic difficulties of becoming old and progressively more disabled in an ageist society that devalues need and dependency. Whether or not there is a perpetrator, these problems are inevitably contextual and often beyond fully satisfactory resolution. Deepening the complexity are the prevailing practices in the provider community. Providers generally elevate autonomy (defined as self-determining choice) in sharp opposition to beneficence or paternalism. A de-contextualized, individualistic, and rationalistic account of decisional capacity is the final determining factor in deciding what can and cannot be done. These factors and the situations to which they are applied, bring into sharp relief the dual and often conflicting commitments providers and society have to vulnerable older people: to respect their choices and to keep them from serious harm.

These conflicting commitments create an almost irresolvable feeling of dissonance, an indicator of just how important each of the values are. Thus, it is morally important to see if there is a way to allay the unease that results when it seems impossible to both respect the person and to mitigate harm. Our approach, to be described in detail below, relies on the narrative and communicative approach to ethics that is a central theme in this volume. Its goal, in these situations with different etiologies and practice interventions, is to make it easier for the older person to speak in his or her "authentic voice" (Meyers, 2002). To further the chance that this aim will be realized, we argue that real world complexities need sustained attention and that solutions are often temporary, to be re-visited as often as necessary and, most importantly, they mean that we cannot "fix" all problems.

DESCRIBING ABUSE, NEGLECT, AND SELF-NEGLECT

Abuse and Neglect

Mrs. Jones and Mrs. Chase represent two painfully familiar examples of what has been called "self-neglect" and elder abuse or neglect. In the first case, the conditions under which Grace Jones is living, while acceptable to her, are a cause of serious concern to her daughter and the social worker. In the second case, the home care aide is deeply concerned about Perry's treatment of his grandmother, particularly when she notes the bruises on Mrs. Chase's arm. When he is not badgering his grandmother for money or meals, Perry seems to neglect her most of the time, and physically hurt her some of the time. In practice, this kind of situation usually leads to a call to the aide's supervisor, which then results in reporting it to Adult Protective Services (APS). Responsibility for addressing the situation is thus transferred to a person skilled in understanding the complexities of abuse and neglect cases.

Despite all the years of attention to this problem, debate continues over what actions count as abuse. For the purposes of this chapter, we use the following definition: abusers are those individuals who willfully bring harm to others. Lisa Nerenberg (2000) questions whether abuse has to be willful in order to count as abuse, since it is often not easy to distinguish between intentional and nonintentional behaviors. Is it abuse when a spouse ties down his wife in order to give her a bath after she consistently lashes out at him every time he touches her with water? Must there be a perpetrator for a situation to be considered "abusive"? What about "undue influence," when one person seems to engage in subtle and sustained manipulation of another? Does sexual activity between individuals in nursing homes when one or both are cognitively impaired constitute abuse? (Nerenberg, 1998; see Chapter 8 in this volume).

Holly Ramsey-Klawsnik (1998) identifies five types of offenders, that is, people who have abused older relatives or friends. These offenders are: (1) caregivers who are normal and capable of providing good care but who are chronically stressed and lash out through abuse and neglect; (2) people who are well-intentioned but who have significant impairments themselves which prevent them from providing adequate care; (3) narcissistic persons with "user mentalities" who get themselves into caregiving arrangements because of what they expect to get out of them; (4) persons with abusive personalities who are unhappy, frustrated, easily angered, and who feel entitled to lash out at others with less power; and (5) sadistic personalities who enjoy inflicting harm and terrifying others. The mistreatment of older people is thus multidimensional and heterogeneous. These factors compound difficulties in making decisions about appropriate and ethically justifiable interventions. Moreover, fully satisfactory resolution is often impossible. In an extensive review of closed cases, Killick and Taylor (2009) observe that "in a substantial number of cases, the victim refuses to cooperate with protective services. In others the complexity of case factors, including relationships and impairment, often hinder successful protections" (p. 223).

Self-Neglect

Self-neglect has emerged in recent years as an increasingly serious concern. It is the most common form of elder abuse reported to APS, accounting for more than 50% of the cases investigated by them (Dong & Gorbien, 2006); yet it remains inadequately conceptualized and understood (Ernst & Smith, 2008). In brief, self-neglecters are individuals who engage in behaviors that threaten their safety and well-being. These threats range from potential for harm to serious and imminent danger. Most of those who self-neglect are women. The National Association of Adult Protective Services (1991) describes this behavior as "an adult's inability, due to physical or mental impairments or diminished capacity, to perform essential self-care tasks." This definition would seem to presume that all self-neglecting adults have, by definition, compromised capacity, an issue to which we will return. Self-neglecters are often socially isolated and, in contrast to Mrs. Jones, tend not to have supportive family involvement (Longres, 1995). They may suffer from depression and dementia (Dyer & Goins, 2000). Many also have mobility-limiting physical illnesses. They may be experiencing cognitive decline; they may be abusing drugs or alcohol; and they may have serious family problems (Ramsey-Klawsnik, 2004). Such individuals sometimes hoard trash and rubbish, have little food in their homes and often have no working appliances or utility services. They do not "maintain a socially and culturally accepted standard of self-care with the potential for serious consequences to [their] health and well-being . . . and perhaps even to their community" (Gibbon et al., 2000, cited by Iris et al., 2009). Yet, self-neglecters show little embarrassment about their condition and generally refuse help of any kind (Byers & Zeller, 1994). In a recent study using the tool of concept mapping, Iris et al. (2009) identified core clusters of behaviors related to self-neglect.

In spite of living in conditions that outsiders find deeply problematic, individuals described as self-neglecters tend to maintain their dignity, honor independence with intensity, and appear to be satisfied with their living conditions (Rathbone-McCuan, 1996). The fact that the causes are so varied—declines in cognitive or physical capacity, loss of family and friends, loss of a sense of self-worth that often comes from living in an ageist society, economic stress, feelings of uselessness—highlights the need for interventions that respond to these particular causes and an ethical analysis that is more particularistic than universal.

Complicating our understanding of "self-neglect" (and motivating our use of quotation marks surrounding the term), is the debate as to whether there really is a set of actions that constitute self-neglect, or whether it is primarily a social construction. People who generally fit the category of self-neglect fail to live up to the commonly accepted standards of cleanliness and hygiene that exist in their communities. Does that mean something is wrong with them, or are the standards applied to judge them a mere cultural product? Is such neglectful behavior a coping mechanism for people who have been marginalized in turn by a neglectful society? Does society expect too much of people who must struggle to make ends meet, even in advanced old age and often in the absence of strong social and economic supports? These questions and uncertainties do not negate the fact that people who live in the kind of conditions often encountered in situations of "self-neglect" are at risk for serious harm.

BACKGROUND

Estimates are that there are probably just under 450,000 incidents of elder abuse each year. Of those, only 16% are reported (National Center on Elder Abuse, 2005). The reasons for such limited reporting include the isolation of so many older people, the lack of uniform reporting laws, and the reluctance of many professionals to report suspected cases (Tatara, 1993, cited in Bergeron & Gray, 2003, p. 97). Additionally, the older person may not report abuse since the abuser is usually a family member upon whom she is dependent. Often, too, family loyalty is a strongly held virtue, as indicated in the scenario involving Mrs. Chase. In some states, the alleged victim must give permission for an investigation to go forward.

In some circumstances, the elder's needs are such that he/she might be better off in a nursing home. Yet, resistance to such a move is often considerable whether the reasons derive from cultural differences, concerns about the quality nursing home care, or a promise made "never to put mom in a nursing home." In most communities, there are few other alternatives. At times, the elder's income from social security or pensions is viewed as family income so the loss of it, should she be placed in a nursing home, would be felt by everyone. While the dominant culture might view this situation as financial abuse, in other cultures it has been common for income to be shared.

ETHICAL THINKING ABOUT ABUSE, NEGLECT, AND SELF-NEGLECT

It is hard to escape the central ethical question in cases of abuse, neglect, and self-neglect: how can a society negotiate its fundamental commitment to protect people from harm while at the same time avoid trampling on those person's rights to make autonomous decisions? In a liberal society such as ours, the "right" to self-determination has generally trumped protection. Most state laws hold that an elder has the right to refuse services, even if abuse has been substantiated. Yet, APS workers are often placed in an ethical bind: they are charged with protecting their elder clients at the same time that these elders may uphold their right to remain in an abusive situation (Bergeron, 2006).

Prior to discussing the ethical issues involved in abuse, neglect or self-neglect, we offer a caveat. We recognize that the abuse and neglect committed by the hands of others often have very different and complex etiologies from the neglect an individual might visit upon him or herself. As a result, the interventions that health and social service providers propose also differ. There is a large and growing literature on these issues. Our intent, however, is not to examine specific etiologies or interventions, but rather to explore the ways in which recent ethical work, particularly that focusing on narrative, communicative approaches, and what Walker (1998) describes as an "expressive-collaborative" model for "doing" ethics, can help to resolve the seemingly sharp divide between autonomy and beneficence or paternalism. In cases of abuse, neglect, and self-neglect, decisional capacity (or lack of it) is the critical element in determining whether one opts for beneficence or autonomy. To overcome this divide, much hinges on the professional's ability to become what Eva Kittay (2006) calls a "transparent self." By inviting narrative and drawing out important features of the person's experiences, transparency allows one to discover what the other person most cares about. In so doing, one can then seek to reflect in action that individual's wishes and values. The aims of this kind of ethical work are to help the older person find and maximize her "authentic voice" (Meyers, 2002). Further, the transparent self understands the core principles that have dominated ethical thinking in this country for so many years as "starting points and reference points for moral deliberation," (Walker, 2003, p. 127), not end points.

Thus, we observe that standard, principle-based categories such as beneficence and autonomy are too absolute, and too starkly divided to adequately account for the individual, relational, and contextual complexities associated with abuse, neglect, and self-neglect. Yet, these categories are so dominant in medical and community-based practice that, for professionals, they function as taken-for-granted rules. However, as we have argued, these rule-based commitments don't work very well in the messy, complicated world of everyday life (see Chapter 1). As we have suggested, context is critical: in the painful, troubled situations that this chapter addresses, neither elder nor perpetrator (if there is a perpetrator) can be separated from the life they have lived or continue to live. Many years of forming identities, often in oppressive circumstances, of developing (and losing) relationships, and of confronting change and loss have all played a role in creating the situation that social and health care professionals confront when they get a call about a "self-neglecting" or an abused elder. Moving toward this aim of transparency in an elderly person's wishes and values requires that the caregiver (whether family, social worker, or other professional) becomes open and transparent so that he or she can discover what the elder most cares about, even if it cannot be easily articulated.

That said, we turn first to decisional capacity since the key question in almost all cases of abuse, neglect, and "self-neglect" involves the ability of the older person to make informed choices about his or her life. It represents the proverbial line in the sand—on one side of it, intervention can be justified even in the face of resistance or refusal; on the other side it cannot be justified. Hence, it bears a close examination. Commonly accepted features of decisional capacity include the ability to understand or assess the current situation, to evaluate the choices that are under consideration (including the risks and benefits), and to be able to communicate the choice to others (Dong & Gorbien, 2006). This definition—rational, individualistic and contextually detached—hardly seems descriptive of how many of us make decisions when we are ill or compromised in any way. Perhaps we discuss the situation with others or even leave the decision-making to our family or our physician. Yet, for the community-dwelling elder who has come to the attention of physicians, nurses, social workers or APS personnel, the standard model of decisional capacity retains a strong, if not absolute, hold. To determine decisional capacity, at a minimum, we need to ask if this person can rationally assess his or her situation, be fully aware of the risks and benefits, and have the option of good and meaningful choices. Given what we know about abused, neglected, or self-neglecting elders, this definition does not take situational complexities into sufficient account. Particularly for the abused or neglected elder, it is difficult to detach herself from the circumstances and people with whom she is enmeshed. In these complicated situations, it is unlikely that she can speak in what Meyers (2002) calls an "authentic voice" (see below for a fuller discussion). Depression and the accompanying feeling of worthlessness or fear of being a burden further challenge the likelihood that she can engage in authentic decision-making. Self-blame or embarrassment about how she is living or the choices she has made that contributed to her current situation can further hinder authentic choice (Bergeron, 2006).

Meyers (2002) describes an "authentic voice" as one that represents individuals' constructions of their "own self-portrait and self-narrative . . . that enables them to take charge of their lives" (p. 5). It means leading and giving an account of one's life, and it is achieved relationally (Meyers, 2002). Being "authentic" in this way means having a self that one recognizes as one's own. By contrast, both women in the preceding cases—Mrs. Chase and Mrs. Jones—might be speaking not in their own voices but from the cultural messages that uphold independence as the primary social value. To require that they give up that freedom would be to intrude upon their sense of self worth. Do they have freedom to depart from cultural scripts? While efforts to work with persons so that they can discover or recover an "authentic voice" might not give one license to interfere, those efforts can increase confidence that the ways in which these men and women are living are actual choices.

Currently, the thin concept of autonomy that dominates community care does not easily lead to discussions about voice or self and identity. So once a person is found to have the capacity to make decisions by the standards described above, she/he has the right to decide how she/he wishes to live, even if others find that way of life risky or even abhorrent. Much like refusing medical treatment, a "self-neglecting" or an abused older person may legally refuse any and all help. Yet, while we cringe at newspaper headlines about the elder found dead in her home surrounded by many cats and accumulated rubbish, or left impoverished by financial abuse at the hands of her son or daughter, we simultaneously uphold their rights to live without dependence on others, if that is their wish (Stevenson, 2008).

If that is their wish captures the dilemma that these situations create. "Their wish" may originate in the general social disregard for older women and their limited opportunities over a lifetime to develop what Meyers (1989) calls autonomy competency, essential for speaking in an authentic voice. "Their wish" may be based on the absence of basic support systems that make real choice possible; or, it may rest on a context and social/cultural forces that operate within that context to "simultaneously anchor and constrain an individual's freedom to decide and to act" (Marshall, 2001, p. 141). "Their wish" may rest on their vulnerability, a feature of the lives of many who have little or no control over what is happening to them. To say this is not to be disrespectful or ageist: it is rather to recognize that this condition of vulnerability so movingly described by Hoffmaster (2006) is part of all human life, and that it is more likely exacerbated as we age.

A further challenge to conventional ideas about decisional capacity is that of undue influence (Quinn, 2000). An older person like Mrs. Chase, for example, might refuse to do anything to change her situation because she defines herself primarily as a wife, a mother, or a grandmother, and so has internalized certain assumptions of what it means to be a "good" grandmother. These assumptions, rather than her own well-being, are shaping her ideas about what she should choose. When autonomy is understood relationally, it seems quite natural that one would make choices based on these important identity-conferring relationships—in this case, being a grandmother to Perry, her troubled but beloved grandson. She might worry, quite realistically, about who would do for her what Perry now does since community care is rarely adequate to meet needs. Having him living in her home, guarantees a minimum of company and help especially on weekends and at night. A narrative approach, which we will discuss further below, would help her to understand that there are other ways for her to help Perry, especially if the community has some resources to help him find a place to live and a job. That would, however, mean that she would end up living alone, a factor that would need to be discussed and weighed.

When social work professionals face these situations—whether they involve a perpetrator or not—they often report a feeling of dissonance between what they think respect for autonomy demands of them and their moral feelings. Underlying this dissonance is the commitment to care, to keep people from serious harm even when they appear to reject such help. It is this dissonance that may open a way to think more richly about abuse, neglect, and self-neglect and what autonomy, self-determination or beneficence means in this particular context. Once we face the limits of relying on conventional ideas about decisional capacity, which links back to speaking in an authentic voice as the most important determining factor in what is done, we can set aside the categorical thinking that forces a choice between self-determination and doing good.

Once we raise questions about the possible limits to authentic decision-making, it permits us to think not in terms of autonomy versus paternalism, but rather of how we can work with Mrs. Jones and Mrs. Chase so they can find a way to get what they most care about. Thus, we might ask what is good for a person like Mrs. Grace in the light of what she cares about (Kittay, 2006), especially in situations where what she cares about is elusive and difficult to achieve. Our commitment to honoring her autonomy might best be described as respecting the autonomy that is rooted in her identity and individuality, what Agich (1995) calls "actual autonomy." We are not honoring some abstract idea about her autonomy but rather an autonomy that would allow her to live in ways that confirm her identity. To honor abstract conceptions of autonomy would be easier "when effective protection would involve much more systematic and skilled intervention than is customarily offered to such people" (Stevenson, 2008, p. 30).

In an important way, narratives help us to move from an abstract commitment to autonomy-as-choice to actual autonomy as confirmation of identity and achieving what one most cares about. Narrative might facilitate an exploration of what meaning Grace Jones attaches to living in the way that she does. We might encourage her to tell a different story about her life that begins to repair an identity that has either been suppressed or tattered beyond recognition. These counter-stories (Lindemann Nelson, 2001) might begin a process of "imagining herself otherwise" (Mackenzie, 2000). Moral deliberation and decision-making thus involve constructing new images of oneself and one's relationships so that they support one's integrity. "Moral problems," Walker (2003) observes, "are points in *continuing* histories of attempted mutual adjustments and understandings between people" (p. 128). She thus reaffirms what we noted earlier: narrative understanding of moral deliberation "doesn't spurn general rules or broad ideals, but it doesn't treat them as major premises in moral deductions" (p. 128). Hence, we would not set aside our commitments to ensuring as much as possible an individual's self-determining action; but conversely, we would also not let it lead us to premature closure. We would invite complexity and complicating details, for that is the only way we, the older person, and in cases of abuse and neglect, the perpetrator, can come to understand what actions supports individual and group integrity.

In probable self-neglect situations like that of Mrs. Jones, we accept that a most basic moral responsibility is to assist her in understanding that what she most cares about might be best achieved if she accepts help to mitigate potential harms. It might even mean compromising short term autonomy to achieve longer term autonomy. For example, she might be convinced to reduce the amount of "stuff" that she has collected by negotiating an informal contract where she actively decides which of her possessions are core to her identity. If one accepts that the self is a self-in-relation, we might work with Mrs. Jones to see how respect for the relationship that she has with her daughter is something that she ought to consider. "An ethic of care requires respect for the integrity of the self, but the self as it is supported and maintained through relationships" (Kittay, 2006, p. 37). The transparent self, in Kittay's view, is sensitive to what the other cares about and in so doing moves "beyond the dichotomy of autonomy and paternalism" (p. 46). Even if we become incapacitated, Kittay suggests, we do not always lose the capacity to care about what we care about. Transparency has a core aim—to try to understand what the other person most cares about and then to work toward making that happen. This kind of empathic care transcends the paternalism-autonomy divide since its singular goal is meeting the good of another from that person's perspective. A contextually sensitive narrative and communicative approach, aided by transparency, expands the scope of what is considered morally relevant, and attends to emotional responses and to the lived experiences of persons. Furthermore, when a professional allows herself to be embedded in an elderly person's story, that professional can be a witness to the elder's suffering (Marshall, 2001), an important but often overlooked form of recognition.

Especially in cases of self-neglect, what the older person may care most about is avoiding becoming one more "old lady." Recall the wonderful, albeit painful, scene in Pat Barker's (1983) series of connected stories called *Union Street*, described in Chapter 10 of this book. Alice, no longer able to speak and barely able to get around as the result of a stroke, is low on coal and adds newspapers to her blankets to stay warm. She becomes incontinent. Her isolation increases because "it was difficult for them to believe that this slobbering, glugging thing that could not make its wants known was a human being" (p. 231). But she builds an internal defense against her son and the authorities who want to place her in a nursing home where she will be clean and safe. She knows that they see her as a risk to herself, a probable "case" of self-neglect. If one listened to her story, one might understand how Alice sees herself and what she most wants—to stay at home and to be recognized as a trustworthy confidante of the younger women. She finds a way, by being difficult, to preserve her identity. Similarly, if this is what

Grace Jones is doing, is there a way to address the situation such that she will accept some intervention while remaining the self by which she defines herself?

Likewise, a narrative approach would try to bring Mrs. Chase and her grandson Perry together so that they might mutually explore what their relationship has been over time and what they want from it in the future. Is it possible that Perry, because of his youth (or for some other reason) simply feels overwhelmed by his grandmother's needs? If so, might he be helped by more information and guidance? Does he feel that Mrs. Chase expects too much of him? While it seems that Mrs. Chase is not a "difficult" person, Perry might have some grievances that can explain his behavior. Together they might work out some boundaries about behavior, money and a commitment to stop his aggressiveness if he wants to continue living with his grandmother. Acknowledging that Perry might be incorrigible, we would then need to find ways to meet Mrs. Chase's wish for companionship, with other opportunities for social interaction; or we might limit his visits to times when other people are around. We would also try to find out more about the history of their relationship, in particular addressing Mrs. Chase's relationship with her daughter, Perry's mother. The use of a storied approach can deepen our understanding of both people and the history of this family's relationships. We might ask about cultural values, beliefs, and traditions in this family, since some behaviors may be acceptable in one family but not in another (Nerenberg, 2000). Mrs. Chase may have different expectations about care and how she defines and perceives abuse than the professionals involved in her care. Can they together reach a provisional agreement about how to ease her environmental threats? The professional could probe Mrs. Chase's values, trying to find some way to meet them while also lessening the danger that she might be seriously harmed. Walker (1993) describes this process as a "medium of progressive acknowledgment and adjustment among people in search of a common and habitable moral world" (p. 35) rather than blaming or contrasting beneficence against self-determination.

A narrative approach tries to give voice to each person involved. It assumes that older people in potentially life-threatening situations are vulnerable and that this vulnerability may impede wise decision-making. It takes seriously the issue of caregiver stress, which has often been singled out as a major contributing factor in neglect and abuse cases and considers the often intense emotional response that caregivers might experience when engaging in the most intimate kind of bed and body work with a mother or a father. When an adult child has responsibilities for bathing or toileting his or her mother, it elicits complex feelings that may lead to "unintentional" neglect and shame, often masked as anger on the part of the care recipient (O'Connor, 2003). Impatience with a parent who is cognitively declining can lead to neglect or even abuse (O'Connor, Hall, & Donnelly, 2009). Many caregivers may find it hard to enter into "the life and feelings of some very old people" who may be hard of hearing or suffer from dementia or depression (Stevenson, 2008, p. 33). These emotional complexities of caregiving are ripe for a narrative approach if we expect to repair damages done.

Narrative repair may also elicit recall of the past. Mrs. Chase may never have had to make decisions for herself and so may not have developed the necessary autonomy competency to do so (Meyers, 1989). She may require much more directed guidance from professionals than they are accustomed to giving. In cases of abuse and neglect, it is often difficult to see that current problems may have their origins in history as well as in the present. The older person, sadly, may have been an abusive parent when his or her caregivers were children and young adults; she/he may treat those who care for him or her with little to no respect, or be demanding and unconcerned for the welfare of others. At times, older persons have power over their caregivers because the caregivers are living in their homes.

In her work on the caring relationship, Joan Tronto (1993) includes responsiveness of the care recipient as one of the important elements of caring. Yet what if that responsiveness or reciprocity doesn't occur? And feminist philosopher Sara Ruddick (1999) reminds us about the virtue of gratitude, of trying not to ask for too much, of working with another to make life go as smoothly as possible. When the focus is almost entirely on the person *receiving* care, responsibilities to the care recipient are often shrouded. The Administration on Aging categorizes elder abuse as a rights issue (Nerenberg, 2000), which suggests pitting one person against another rather than attending to the relational aspects of care. We say this not to apologize for abuse and neglect but rather to suggest that it is often far more complicated than it appears on the surface. While abuse is certainly in part a rights issue, that is not all of the story.

Moody (1988) describes what he calls "negotiated consent" and suggests that taking the elder's refusal of help at face value is tantamount to abandonment. Yet, he further suggests that minimizing the problem might lead to the best possible outcome. Mrs. Chase would like Perry to behave differently, but she neither wants him to leave her house nor does she want to move. Perry apparently wants to stay with her. Both thus appear to want these living arrangements to continue. To make it work, they need to try to negotiate a resolution satisfactory to both of them, or at least as close to satisfactory as possible. At the end of this process, which might need to occur more than once, the hope is that a plan will have evolved that all can live with, even if it is not everyone's first choice.

We do not want to suggest that telling narratives, developing a complex understanding of decisional capacity, or fashioning a "transparent" self by professionals who work with the elderly can solve all the problems of neglect, abuse and self-neglect. That would be naïve at best. Rather, we draw this section to a close by noting that the ability to help a person realize what they most care about will be limited in many ways. The actual choices that are available might have no meaning to either Mrs. Jones or Mrs. Chase, so their capacity to decide matters little to the outcomes (Agich, 1990). To make informed decisions requires that there be real and meaningful choices, not merely choices. Bergeron (2006) notes that "victims need to see alternatives that mirror healthier versions of their current situations, producing a sense of comfort or security and hope that things may change without their losing the very foundation of their life-style and life-choices" (p. 91). Making the situation better, especially if there is a perpetrator, may, in some instances, be achieved by remedying the responsibilities that community care places on caregivers, as discussed in Chapter 7. Ethical responses then would range from efforts to transform the ways in which care is given in this country, to supporting a commitment to make available the resources necessary to permit the ongoing and supportive engagement that a narrative and communicative ethics calls for.

It is possible that the situation will remain intractable, no matter how probing the narrative becomes. Perry might be simply a callous young man who has bought into a sense of his own desert or to society's seeming disregard for old women like his grandmother. In this way, he is the victim of a society that leaves him feeling under-appreciated. There may be few ways to alter his behavior. In this case, if Mrs. Chase's cognitive capacities are intact, if she continues to refuse to bring charges against Perry, and if she refuses all other options, then there may be nothing left to do, a sad but unavoidable conclusion.

CONCLUSION

The problems associated with abuse, neglect, and self-neglect cannot be satisfied with a *pro forma* commitment to autonomy. If we as a society truly respond with alarm and anguish when an 86-year-old woman is found in her littered home, dehydrated and near death, then we must go beyond blame to change the situation. We must ensure that the case worker involved in the situation has the resources to help the elder engage in narrative repair of her identity, so that real choice becomes more likely. Similarly, such health and social service professionals should bring to bear the reflections and analyses of ethicists who are attempting to bridge the false division between autonomy and beneficence. Kittay's (2006) concept of the "transparent self" is one way for caregivers and professionals involved in elder care to understand and get for the elder what she or he cares about most, without distortion of those needs. Using narrative as a vehicle for social action is, we believe, an obligation.

We know that people are often unwilling to bring charges against an abuser, especially if that abuser is a family member. Further, as we have suggested, the demands of caregiving, especially for someone with dementia, are so strenuous that the caregiver may be driven to action in which she/he would not otherwise engage (Bergeron & Gray, 2003). When society and the state require that families (especially women) provide care, but do not offer basic assistance to do it well, then burn-out and its consequences are unsurprising, even if not excusable. In such cases, a more fully supportive system for "informal" caregivers could mitigate against the occurrence of such abuse and neglect (see Chapter 7).

In addition to alleviating the responsibilities of caregivers, which are only one (and probably not the most important) cause of abuse and neglect, each cause might call for a different ethical framework. We have argued for a relational autonomy approach, according to which we see the person and his/her abusers in the specific context in which the abuse takes place. We have also suggested that in the absence of good alternatives for the elder, continuing residence with the abuser might be not only her choice, but her best choice amongst an array of poor alternatives.

In cases of self-neglect, people who live by middle-class norms of cleanliness and order may be disturbed by the inability or unwillingness of "self-abusers" to do proper self-care. It may be particularly upsetting when an elderly individual can't easily get to his bathroom because of all the "things" that are in the way; or when she can't make a cup of coffee because the stove doesn't work. Yet, once serious cognitive difficulties and/or mental illness are ruled out and the individual refuses intervention, community providers, concerned neighbors, and sons or daughters often feel as if their hands are tied. They may feel that there is nothing to be done short of trying to persuade the person for whom they are caring to accept some help.

We have sought to introduce some morally rich ideas of what can be done to resolve such dissonance in order to bring the person closer to living in ways that honor what she or he has always cared about most. It is not simply "us" imposing cultural values on "them," but working together to find their voices and to learn what they most care about. Like Alice in *Union Street*, they undoubtedly have particular values and cares; it just takes time and effort to elicit them, and the resources of society to make the effort possible.

REFERENCES

Agich, G. (1990). Reassessing autonomy in long-term Care. *Hastings Center Report*, *20*(6), 12–17.

Agich, G. (1995). Actual autonomy and long-term care decision making. In L. B. McCullough & N. L. Wilson (Eds.), *Ethical and conceptual dimensions of long-term care decision making* (pp. 113–136). Baltimore, MD: Johns Hopkins Press.

Anetzberger, G. (2000). Caregiving: Primary cause of elder abuse? *Generations*, *24*(2), 46–51.

Barker, P. (1983). *Union Street*. New York, NY: Ballantine Books.

Bergeron, R. (2006). Self-determination and elder abuse: Do we know enough? *Journal of Gerontological Social Work*, *46*(3&4), 81–102.

Bergeron, L. R., & Gray, B. (2003). Ethical dilemmas in reporting suspected elder abuse. *Social Work*, *48*(1), 97–105.

Brody, H. (1994). The four principles and narrative ethics. In R. Gillon (Ed.), *Principles of health care ethics* (pp. 208–215). Chichester, UK: Wiley. Cited in Marshall, P. 2001. A contextual approach to clinical ethics consultation. In B. Hoffmaster (Ed.), *Bioethics in social context* (pp. 137–152). Philadelphia: Temple University Press.

Byers, B., & Zeller, R. (1994). Social judgments of responsibility in elder self-neglect cases. *The Journal of Psychology*, *129*(3), 331–344.

Connolly, M.-T. (2008). Elder self-neglect and the justice system. *Journal of the American Geriatrics Society*, *56*(52), S244–S252.

Dong, X. Q., & Gorbien, M. (2006). Decision-making capacity: The core of self-neglect. *Journal of Elder Abuse and Neglect*, *17*(3), 19–36.

Dyer, C., & Goins, A. (2000). The role of the interdisciplinary geriatric assessment team in addressing self-neglect in the elderly. *Generations*, *24*(2), 23–27.

Ernst, J., & Smith, C. (2008). Self-neglecting older adults in adult protective services: Characteristics and service use. *The Gerontologist*, *48*, 46.

Gibbon, S., Lauder, W., & Williams, L. (2000). Self-neglect: A proposed new NANDA diagnosis. *International Journal of Nursing Terminologies and Classifications*, *17*(1), 10–18. Cited in Iris, M., Ridings, J., & Conrad, K. (2009). *The Gerontologist*, *125*, 1–13.

Hoffmaster, B. (2006). What does vulnerability mean? *Hastings Center Report*, *36*(2), 38–45.

Holstein, M. (1995). Multidisciplinary ethical decision-making: Uniting differing professional perspectives. In T. F. Johnson (Ed.), *Elder mistreatment: Ethical issues, dilemmas, and decisions* (pp. 169–182). New York, NY: The Haworth Press.

Iris, M., Ridings, J., & Conrad, K. (2009). The development of a conceptual framework for understanding elder self-neglect. *The Gerontologist*, *125*, 1–13.

Killick, C., & Taylor, B. (2009). Professional decision-making on elder abuse: Systematic narrative review. *Journal of Elder Abuse and Neglect*, *21*(3), 211–238.

Kittay, E. F. (2006). Beyond autonomy and paternalism: The caring transparent self. In T. Nys, Y. Denier, & T. Vandervelde (Eds.), *Autonomy and paternalism: Beyond individualism and good intentions* (pp. 1–29). Leuven: Peeters.

Lindemann Nelson, H. (2001). *Damaged identities, narrative repair.* Ithaca, NY: Cornell University Press.

Longres, J. (1995). Self-neglect among the elderly. *Journal of Elder Abuse and Neglect,* 7(1), 69–86.

Mackenzie, C. (2000). Imagining ourselves otherwise. In C. Mackenzie & N. Stoljar (Eds.), *Relational autonomy: Feminist perspectives on autonomy, agency, and the social self* (pp. 124–150). New York, NY: Oxford University Press.

Marshall, P. (2001). A contextual approach to clinical ethics consultation. In B. Hoffmaster (Ed.), *Bioethics in social context* (pp. 137–152). Philadelphia, PA: Temple University Press.

Meyers, D. (1989). *Self, society and personal choice.* New York, NY: Columbia University Press.

Meyers, D. (2002). *Gender in the mirror: Cultural imagery and women's agency.* New York, NY: Oxford University Press.

Moody, H. (1988). From informed consent to negotiated consent. *Gerontologist,* 28(Suppl.), 64–70.

National Association of Adult Protective Services. (1991). *A national study of self-neglecting adult protective services clients.* Richmond, VA: Virginia Department of Social Services.

National Center on Elder Abuse. (2005). *Fact Sheet: Elder abuse prevalence and incidence.* NCEA, Washington, DC. Retrieved from ncea@nasua.org.

Nerenberg, L. (1998). Speaking the unspeakable: An interview with Holly Ramsey-Klawsnick. *Nexus,* 4(1), 4–6.

Nerenberg, L. (2000). Developing a service response to elder abuse. *Generations,* 24(2), 86–92.

O'Connor, N. (2003). When the helper needs help: A social worker's experiences in receiving home care. In M. Holstein & P. Mitzen (Eds.), *Ethics and community-based elder care* (pp. 122–131). New York, NY: Springer Publishing.

O'Connor, D., Hall, M., & Donnelly, M. (2009). Assessing capacity within a context of abuse and neglect. *Journal of Elder Abuse and Neglect,* 21, 156–169.

Quinn, M. S. (2000). Undoing undue influence. *Generations,* 24(2), 65–69.

Ramsey-Klawsnik, H. (1998). Speaking the unspeakable: An interview about sexual assault with Holly Ramsey-Klaswick. *Nexus,* 4(1). Retrieved from http://preventelderabuse.org/nexus/hrklawsnik.html.

Ramsey-Klawsnik, H. (2004). Elder abuse, neglect, and self-neglect. *Training Hand-outs,* unpublished material.

Rathbone-McCuan, E. (1996). Self-neglect in the elderly: Knowing when and how to intervene. *Aging,* 367, 44–49.

Ruddick, S. (1999). Virtues and age. In M. U. Walker (Ed.), *Mother time: Women, aging, and ethics* (pp. 45–60). New York, NY: Rowman & Littlefield.

Stevenson, O. (2008). Neglect as an aspect of the mistreatment of elderly people: Reflections on the issues. *The Journal of Adult Protection, 10*(1), 24–35.

Tatara, T. (1993). Understanding the nature and scope of domestic elder abuse with the use of state aggregate data: Summaries of key findings of an national survey of state APS and aging agencies. *Journal of Elder Abuse and Neglect, 5*, 35–57.

Tronto, J. (1993). *Moral boundaries: A political argument for an ethics of care.* New York, NY: Routledge.

Walker, M. U. (1993). Keeping moral spaces open. *Hastings Center Report, 23*(2), 33–41.

Walker, M. U. (1998). *Moral understandings: A feminist study in ethics.* New York, NY: Routledge.

Walker, M. U. (2003). *Moral contexts.* Lanham, CO: Rowman & Littlefield.

CHAPTER 11

Alzheimer's Disease and an Ethics of Solidarity

*Pray, do not mock me: I am a very foolish fond old man. And to deal plainly, I fear
I am not in my perfect mind. Methinks I should know you and know this man; yet I
am doubtful: for I am mainly ignorant what place this is, and all the skill I have
Remembers not these garments; nor I know not Where I did lodge last night. Do not
laugh at me; For as I am a man, I think this lady To be my child Cordelia*
—(King Lear, Act IV, Scene 7)

The Forgotten Daughter

*Emily, Nancy's daughter, was going through her mother's closet in the nursing
home room, looking for dirty clothes and putting in the clean clothes she had
brought from home. Her mother sat in the chair, rocking, and looking at Emily.
"What are you doing?" Nancy asked.
"Hanging up your clean dresses." Emily answered.
"Oh. You know, I have a daughter too, but she's younger than you. But you're
nice."
"Mom, I'm Emily."
"Why, how nice. That's my daughter's name too."
Emily paused as she was putting some soiled underwear in her laundry bag. It
had happened so often that she no longer cried. She felt there just weren't tears
left, not for this. Nancy glanced towards the hallway.
"Mom, that's me. Emily."
"Oh, no. I mean my daughter. . . . You know, my Emily used to come visit me,
but not anymore. How come? . . . I'd like to go home. Can you call my Emily
and tell her to come take me home?"*

This scenario is a common one, and highlights just one aspect of the onset of
Alzheimer's disease (AD). Over time, individuals with this disease tend to
lose bits and pieces of their past, until they reach the point, like Nancy,
where they may have difficulty even identifying family members. This
process is difficult for the individual with AD, but also painful for the
family members themselves. Consider Emily, who is lovingly caring for

213

her mother, yet who is increasingly becoming a mere stranger to Nancy. That her mother, the person to whom Emily's birth once meant the most, no longer remembers her is a loss of the most fundamental sort. Emily and her other family members must now decide how to interact with Nancy: whether they should constantly orient her to place and time, correcting her when she forgets her family members, or the date, or even where she is; or whether they should just accept her confusion and let her "live in the moment." Accepting the loss of a loved one's memories is especially difficult for family members given that those very memories are what link us to a common past and give context, meaning, and character to our lives.

Emil Kraepelin, the great German psychiatrist and nosologist, introduced the eponymous disease label in 1910. He did so based on a case that his friend and colleague Alois Alzheimer had encountered in 1906. In its initial framing, AD was considered a presenile condition since Frau Augusta D., Dr. Alzheimer's patient, was only 50 years old. This assumption—and hence the divorce between it and the more commonly known "senility" or senile dementia, though questioned on and off for many years, persisted until the 1970s when Robert Katzman (1976), in an article in *Archives of Neurology*, affirmed what by then was the accepted conclusion—there was no substantive difference between the neurofibrillary tangles and amyloid plaques in a 50-year-old and a 90-year-old. It was one disease, no matter the age of onset. This decision radically increased the number of people affected by this disease and contributed significantly to the birth of the AD "movement." Designed to call attention to this disease, Robert Butler, the first director of the National Institutes on Aging (NIA) chose AD as the centerpiece for the new institute. (For an account of this history see Ballenger, 2006; Fox, 1989; Holstein, 1997) The transition of AD from a little known pre-senile condition to a prominent biomedical condition is a historically significant move that has consequences for patients. In recent years, a cultural critique of the ways in which AD has been understood has evolved, leading to a renewed interest in how people experience AD, what it means to be a person, and the social and historical contexts within which disease is defined (Holstein, 1997).

More than three decades have passed since the NIA adopted AD as its primary disease focus. Today, the Alzheimer's Association is a major force in research and policy: public awareness about AD is rapidly increasing and scientific research is joined by work in the social sciences and the humanities. As it is diagnosed earlier and earlier, we are also privileged to have an array of first-person narratives that provide important insights about how individuals experience the disease (see, e.g., Snyder, 1999). Yet, while so much more is known about the brain than 30 years ago, AD remains something of a mystery.

There is no cure and much stigma that accompanies the diagnosis and progression of the disease, in part, because the losses that occur seem to erode what has been considered full personhood—some sense of past, present and future and the ability to live according to one's own values. Stigma places one at risk for shame and humiliation while the gradual ebbing of control over one's environment increases one's vulnerability. As one loses control, fear, even terror, results from the sense of losing one's grasp of essentials. With the emergence of "otherness" the person with AD is on the other side of a line between "us" and "them," a threat to possibilities for self-valuing. We name these features of AD because they are the source of many of the unique ethical problems that this disease creates.

First-person narratives have advanced our understanding of what a person with dementia experiences or the extent of self-awareness, but there are still deep gaps in our knowledge. What does it mean to forget what happened a moment ago or be unable to pay a simple bill in a restaurant or become lost in one's own neighborhood? While this is happening, the past seems as clear as if it were yesterday. Moody (1992) describes the experience as "shame, a loss of dignity in the eyes of others, a loss compounded by the fact that others adapt to the situation, get accustomed to the patients' incompetence, and finally come to consider the patient less of a person" (p. 44). Similarly, Herskovits and Mitteness (1994) see in the cultural response to AD, the marginalization and stigmatization that results when a "body" is aberrant. People with dementia fail the common social test of what gives individuals recognition as adults: mastery, productivity, self-responsibility, and cleanliness. This stigmatization often leads to isolation. But then what happens when there are moments of clarity, when the person sees quite plainly what he has lost and how people see him? What about suffering, of the person with AD and those who surround him or her? As we raise ethical questions about AD, it is important to recall these questions since, we suggest, an ethical response to AD must be grounded in the phenomenology, the experiences of the person as he or she loses much of the familiar world. These experiences also occur amidst multiple social relationships and arrangements that are ongoing and shift as others adjust to the changes in the person. If we are to ground ethics in the phenomenology of the person and because AD is, in many ways, a generic description for a variety of symptoms, it becomes quite clear that universal responses can have no place.

Furthermore, while it is the most common of dementias in the elderly, Alzheimer's is by no means the only such dementia. Parkinson's disease is another condition for which advancing age is a significant risk factor, and a significant percentage of Parkinson's patients suffer cognitive symptoms. Parkinson's dementia has subtle phenomenological differences from Alzheimer's. For example, we have noticed that many Parkinson's patients are self-aware of their cognitive deficits much farther into the progression of dementia than most Alzheimer's patients. Additionally, the brute biology of Parkinson's seems to differ from that of Alzheimer's. Instead of the plaques and tangles of Alzheimer's, Parkinson's involves a progressive failure of dopamine and dopamine receptors, making the appropriate communication by neurons impossible. And finally, the third major culprit is what is known as multi-infarct dementia. Here the dementia is a result of multiple, small strokes. Each stroke, a vascular blockage in the brain, is so small as to go unnoticed by itself. But with each of these very small strokes, brain tissue is deprived of blood, and hence of oxygen. While the brain may try to compensate for the lost tissue, it gradually becomes more and more difficult. And thus as parts of the brain erode, the respective brain functions that they hosted are compromised.

In the remainder of this chapter, we will explore the commonly accepted ethical norms and ideals surrounding AD, the areas that remain problematic, some conceptual developments that we might find useful in addressing AD, and a proposed moral framework for thinking about dementia.

BIOETHICS AND DEMENTIA: THE PAST

The lived experience of dementia has not been well understood by mainstream bioethics. Health law has done no better. First, as we have indicated (see Chapter 1) bioethics has been dominated by the acute care model, a model that misses many of the most fundamental moral struggles surrounding dementia. Second, in tandem with the law, bioethics has tended to divide us into those with sound, rational decisional capacity versus those without. In terms of the widely taught principles of biomedical ethics, that means that those of us with sound rational will are to be treated in accordance with respect for our individual autonomy (see Chapter 1). Those without sound rational will are then viewed through the lens of beneficence. Third, this framework tends to overlook the social context of caregiving. Family members, home care workers, institutional staff, and fellow residents in congregate living, are all marginalized by the caricature of the individual as an isolated decision maker (see Chapter 7). Fourth, this dominant bioethics framework carries crucial assumptions about what it means to be a person, to have an identity, and to have social and moral standing, in other words: to be of worth.

As noted repeatedly throughout this book, the ethical frameworks that may seem to grapple reasonably well with the occasional crisis in the acute care hospital miss much that is of great importance when we confront the community care, home care, or long-term care settings. (see Chapter 7). The acute care model focuses on the moment of crisis, and on decision making for the single intervention. Once that particular crisis is resolved, one way or another, deliberation and decision making revert from "ethical" struggles back to more technical medical management: the moral crisis passes and is over. In cases of dementia, the application of this kind of framework (in the 1970s and 1980s) resulted in a focus on supposed decisional crises, raising a number of decision-related concerns. For example, questions were raised about whom to recognize as the authorized decision maker in seeking to place someone with dementia into a nursing home, whether that person was the spouse, adult offspring, a close friend, or a state-appointed guardian. In considering advance directives for health care, the focus was on whether to attempt cardiopulmonary resuscitation (CPR), or withhold/withdraw feeding tubes should the individual no longer be able to swallow on her own. On a broader scale, given scarcity of resources, another question was how much society should set aside for the treatment and care of individuals with dementia.

We do not wish to pretend that such ethical crises are without moral importance. But in our conviction, almost singular attention to these acute care issues sadly detracts from the more mundane moral concerns that pervade the lives of those who suffer from dementia as well as their caregivers and loved ones. Some of these moral concerns are "decisional" in this traditional sense, such as whether an individual should continue to drive, or whether she/he can stay at home, even for just a little longer. But other concerns are much less about some singular decisional moment; rather they represent the fabric of our everyday lives. For example, we must determine how to negotiate a bath with someone who may be fearful and confused (Twigg, 2001), or what to do when an individual with dementia wanders, perhaps getting lost and/or disrupting the lives of others. As the case in Chapter 9 suggests, a common problem arises in determining what to do when two persons with dementia develop a sexual relationship with each other, but because of their dementia are relatively confused about their identities. Should we "protect" them from their decisional incapacity, or allow them to pursue their desires of the moment, however confused and "misdirected"? We must grapple with whether such a situation calls for explicit "consent," or whether tacit consent will suffice; and, in a relational vein, we must decide how to handle the adult children's objections to the relationship, even if the parents seem to be happy and flourishing.

Second, as noted, traditional bioethics and health law divides patients into one of two exhaustive categories: they are either competent or incompetent. When dealing with competent patients, the overriding concern is respect for individual patient autonomy; when dealing with incompetent patients, we revert to a substitute expression of autonomy, preferably an advance directive. Barring an ability to discern any prior relevant exercise of autonomy, we move to the principle of beneficence in an attempt to determine the "best interests" of the person in question.

Yet the lived experience of most dementias—Alzheimer's, Parkinson's, multi-infarct—is one of gradual, progressive loss. The individual, who because of alert family members, self concern, or an attentive physician, might be diagnosed very early in the course of dementia, is surely decisionally capable. For, at this early stage, there may well be some language deficit (loss of some words), or some short-term memory deficit; but such deficits would not seem to be major hindrances to significant choices about the overall goals of medical care, or identification of surrogate decision makers in case of future need. In the final stages of progressive dementia, it is also patently clear that the individual will be decisionally incapable. But it is difficult to determine when that transition from capable to incapable takes place, or when the "threshold" is crossed. Feinberg and Whitlatch (2001) argue that consistent decision-making concerning these types of issues can persist much farther into the course of dementia than we usually give credit.

This legal and bioethical divide reveals a presumption that there must be a definitive boundary, some line that is crossed that delineates a competent from an incompetent person. But such thinking is mistaken in at least two ways. First, decisional capacity should be understood as context-specific. We may not trust someone who is midway down the course of dementia to balance a checkbook and pay bills, but we may pay genuine heed to their value expressions concerning to what music they would like to listen; with whom they want to sit at dinner; what they do or do not eat; whether they remain at home or are institutionalized; or, more gravely, whether they would prefer to return to the intensive care unit in coming months, or to remain in the nursing home with the likelihood of death.

Furthermore, while this language of decisional capacity as "context specific" is helpful, we must still be cautious in that it persists in seeking a black-or-white, yes-or-no answer. In some sense, the strategy of focusing on task-specific ability "solves" the problem of the penumbra by addressing the questions in piecemeal ways. In short, by focusing on the trees, it is possible to avoid looking at the forest. Yet the real, lived experience of dementia is likely to have some truly gray areas of decisional capacity, and our intense efforts to contextualize in order to get a yes-or-no answer to a task-specific question may well distort the reality of the situation.

In a sense, what drives this desire to label an individual as competent or not, globally or for some context-specific task, remains the presumption that decision making is a highly individual activity. Yet, as we have argued in this book, that is a caricature of real decision making. Group process, especially here the deliberations of family and loved ones, is much more the norm. If we can move our thinking at least somewhat beyond the model of the isolated, insular, autonomous individual as decision maker towards acknowledging the important social aspect of decision making, then the pressure to find a black-or-white label (competent or incompetent) for the individual with dementia markedly diminishes.

Third, our popular conception of the independent, isolated, individual, autonomy-exercising agent also fails to adequately take into consideration the social structure of caregiving that care plans depend upon and affect (see Chapter 7). As an example, we might consider a patient—let's say Mr Habel—to be in the late-early or early-middle stage of AD. We may be relatively confident that, though we would not regard him as competent with regard to property (in a legal sense), we do think he has a sustained sense of self, given his adherence to enduring values over his lifetime. After a brief stay in the hospital for treatment after a fall, Mr Habel is insistent that he be discharged to the care of his daughter, rather than a nursing home. He emphatically refers to nursing homes as "hopeless hell holes," and refuses to even consider such a move. But framing the challenge in this way overlooks the daughter's situation: she has her own family—a husband and two children—who also need her care and attention. Mr Habel's daughter should have some chance at a life of her own; caring for her demented father at home could be more than a full time job in and of itself (see Chapter 7 for more on this). Thus, traditional bioethical frameworks, working from a conception of the individualized moral agent, are of very limited assistance in thinking through such socially contextualized challenges.

Fourth, perhaps the most damaging aspect of traditional moral frameworks is not so much how they direct us to make difficult choices, but how they lead us to regard those with dementia. Since the Enlightenment, there has been a profound emphasis upon rationality as the hallmark of human nature. This conception of the human as rational animal can be traced back at least as early as Aristotle, but it was eclipsed somewhat during the Medieval period. Since the Enlightenment, however, it has been a driving conception in Western moral and political thinking. This way of thinking can be most starkly seen in the work of Immanuel Kant. According to Kant, it is that we are a truly rational free will that qualifies us as members of the community of moral agents. Those who do not possess a developed, free, rational will are explicitly excluded from membership in the kingdom of moral agents (see Chapter 1).

In this modern view of humanity, those who are incapable of fully exercising rational, autonomous will are logically and inevitably marginalized. Lacking rationality, the basic defining feature of personhood, they are stripped of any true moral worth. We might pity them or have compassion for them, as we would for an injured animal, but on this view we cannot truly think of them as moral agents.

This devaluing of the individual with dementia is also a reflection of much of the more popular thinking of our culture. As we have argued elsewhere (see Chapters 3 and 4) many common features of the aging process are devalued by our culture, such that aging tends to socially marginalize older people to begin with. Even with recent efforts to focus on the positive features of old age (see Chapter 4), people with dementia are clear "failures," and so they do not fit into the current value system. With dementia, the devaluation and marginalization of the elderly on account of age is compounded by the conviction that with dementia comes an even worse loss: the loss of self. For, as our very reason erodes, and our memories become fragmented and riven with holes, we lose our very self. For example, sitting in the conference room of the nursing home, professional staff and family members oftentimes discuss the care plan of the resident as though she/he is not even present, though the resident may well be sitting at the table. Family members, in a variety of contexts, may sadly say, "That's not my mother," or "My father would never have done that."

Taken logically, this implies a fundamental alteration or loss of identity. Essential features that made this individual who they were are now absent, permanently lost. As the disease progresses, the individual can no longer remember his or her family members. He or she can no longer recall a professional career. He or she can no longer maintain social etiquette, can no longer converse intelligibly. The parts of the brain controlling inhibition have ceased to function. In some cases, individuals cannot even remember their own names. Viewed in this way, the individual with progressing dementia simply fades away, her personhood gradually dissolving, her identity eroding bit by bit. At some point, her body might become inhabited by some "stranger" whom her loved ones do not know; someone with quite different beliefs, tastes, commitments, and desires. It may seem as though the body eventually becomes a "shell," occupied by no one. No wonder dementia is so feared among us, especially amongst the elderly who are at greatest risk of developing it. Can there be any greater harm than to so utterly lose our very selves?

Such incredibly dark views are colored deeply, and darkly, by this prevailing idea of the individual person as defined by and co-extensive with individual rationality. Yet, as we have persistently argued, this conception of the individual person as an isolated, fully rational, self-determining, self-identifying project is a remarkable caricature. First, as persons we are far more than our rational intellect. Unlike the disembodied Cartesian thinking substance, a curious philosophical myth, our selves are *embodied* selves. We have feelings, emotions, tastes, desires, and yearnings. We are nurtured, and in turn nurture, in families and communities. Recognition of and care for the self need not be constrained into terms of the Rational Will. Recognition and care can be a loving caress of the hand, the brushing of hair, listening to the conversation of those we love, or just sharing some enjoyable music. Self-conception, identity, and self-esteem are all, to some degree, a social project (Agich, 1993; Basting, 2009; Gubrium, 1986; Lindemann, 2009). What happens then, as dementia progresses, is that we come to depend more and more on others to help maintain our identity. In the face of worsening dementia, the great burden and challenge for caregivers, families, and professionals is the work and loving care that preserves identity.

BIOETHICS AND DEMENTIA: NEW DIRECTIONS

If the bioethics of the past was overly framed by the acute care setting and the Rational Will, we can see a new trend emerging over the past several years that pays more heed to the whole person as a social being in a social context. First, critical theorists, including critical gerontologists, are pushing us to consider how much of our conception of dementia is a sort of biological given and how much of it is the result of social interpretation and framing (see, e.g., Baars, 1991). The historical narrative of "Alzheimer's Disease" is an interesting case in point. As noted above, until about a century ago, what was called "senility" was widely regarded as a normal part of the aging process. According to current statistics, while not every elder develops dementia, the longer one lives, the higher one's likelihood of developing it. In one sense, then, old age becomes a "risk factor" for dementia. By 1910, the diagnosis of senility was entered into Germany's medical lexicon as Alzheimer's disease. However, those who developed identical symptoms, except much later in life, were still thought of as experiencing "normal" aging, although "normal" aging, ironically, included "senility" (Ballenger, 2006; Holstein, 1997).

Further biomedical research suggested that the brains of the elderly with "senility" looked remarkably similar to those of younger persons with AD.

As such, thinking gradually moved toward considering "senility" as a medical condition. In recent decades, it became accepted to refer broadly to "senile dementia of the Alzheimer's type" (SDAT) (Fox, 1989, pp. 58–102). As pointed out by Holstein (1997), turning a common experience of memory loss into a medicalized, labeled disease has many consequences. Gubrium, for example, explores how the transformation of dementia into a "medical" condition, particularly with the name of Alzheimer's disease, significantly transformed how caregivers conceptualized and reacted to the being and behavior of those with dementia for whom they cared (Gubrium, 2000, pp. 181–203. See also, Robertson, 1991). Such medicalizing and categorizing can be helpful, providing goods such as increased resources for biomedical research, or the dissemination of effective practice guidelines. But there can be harmful or stultifying aspects as well: in this case, the medical narrative of AD may have in it some element of harm. In particular, the current medical narrative is one that emphasizes plaques and tangles and a steady, inexorable, degeneration of faculties. Similar narratives are told of Parkinson's and multi-infarct dementias. While this may be something of a stimulus to researchers, it bespeaks a bleak future to patients and families. Since the medical story focuses so heavily, nay, exclusively, on loss, it may be hard for patients, family members, or even professional caregivers to be open to recognizing capacities that may remain for human interaction.

Philosophy has also seen emerging trends in recent years. For example, the richer philosophical conception of the person that is seen in much feminist philosophy (Kittay, 1999; Mackenzie & Stoljar, 2000; Meyers, 1996) provides a way of comprehending personhood that can enrich the lives of those with dementia by reminding us of the many facets of personhood beyond mere Rational Intellect (see Chapter 2). Since the 1980s, feminist philosophy has emphasized the multifaceted nature of ourselves as persons, our nature as social persons in community, and a wider sense of community—including those persons who previously had been marginalized—and ethics as more of a fabric of care and relationships than as rational rules. All of these, as we can see, may have profound effects on how we understand, design, and participate in care for those with dementia.

Stephen Post has been an important contributor to the discussion of how to understand the person with dementia (Post, 2000a, 2000b). But in terms of truly extending our sense of personhood, Kitwood is an excellent example of scholarship that argues for a concept extending beyond the bounds of Kantian Rational Will (see, e.g., Kitwood & Bredin, 1992, pp. 268–287). Indeed, we can think of Kantian and post-Kantian moral theory as exemplifying the tyranny of rational intellect: one's moral status depends crucially upon one's rational ability. But the newer, and richer, concept of person acknowledges all the particularities of embodiment: that we feel physical, emotional, and aesthetic pain and pleasure, that we are spiritual, and that we are social and communal. We experience bonds of togetherness with others in our family and broader community. Admittedly, as dementia progresses, the individual will be less able to engage effectively in traditionally understood rational cogitation; additionally, memory may be adversely affected. Yet, as Kitwood points out, there are still ways in which we can connect with such individuals and not only show our care and sense of humanity, but also influence their behavior. Soothing someone's anxiety, sharing a seat in the warm sunshine, and caring touch, all express a warm sense of humanity (Kitwood, 1997). Having positive expectations of the person with Alzheimer's can often mean that the person with dementia meets those expectations, whether, it is setting the table or taking out the trash.

Those of us who have personally cared for a loved one as he or she experiences dementia know that this is a difficult experience, both for the individual and for the caregivers. It is hard to watch the emergence of chronic anxiety, fear, disorientation, and loss of memory in a loved one. It is difficult to be the object of verbal or, in some cases, physical abuse, behavior that arises from the disinhibition, anxiety and paranoia that come with advancing dementia. The biomedical disease model as well as the rationalistic philosophical model, by focusing on such losses, can blind us to the long-remaining possibilities of care and comfort.

PRACTICAL ISSUES

How can we best show our care for, our respect for, and acknowledge the dignity of, the individual with dementia? Let us first consider what our ideal vision might be, and then we will confront some of the challenges or obstacles that may stand between us and that ideal.

First, the individual with dementia is not a radically new, different person from before. Though her life will now become different that it had previously been, there is no small measure of continuity. What we mean to emphasize here is that the individual who now has dementia is not a socially and familially distinct individual from before, even though his or her life will become ever gradually quite different. Ideal care, therefore, will be care that does its best to sustain continuity of identity. This may take on various forms: frequent interaction with family and friends; pictures and storytelling to sustain social memories as long as practical; and the maintenance of routines that have helped shape the individual's life in the past. These kinds of concerns point to an environment of care that shapes itself to the individual's biography, and not the other way around. Routines and rituals, for example, can do much to ground our everyday living. For some people, it is the morning cup of coffee and the newspaper: a ritual that can be orienting and comforting even when it has become impossible to truly "read" the newspaper. Maybe there has been, for years, a late afternoon stroll each day before dinner. Or perhaps it is a particular television show on Sunday evening that defines the end of the weekend. Such seemingly simple things can be substantial threads in the fabric of our lives and identities.

Yet, when we become dependent upon others for daily care, especially in an institutional setting, the rhythms of our lives all too readily become dictated by the rhythms of the institution. That late afternoon walk becomes impossible because the few staff available are busy with other assigned duties at that time of day, such as preparing for dinner. The special Sunday dress becomes just another article of clothing in the closet from the staff point of view, or even worse, is lost to the communal laundry. The individual who persists in walking may be discouraged from doing so, for the sake of "safety" as well as the convenience of limited staff. In years past, this was carried so far as to apply the use of physical or chemical restraints to prevent the individual from walking or wandering when it was inconvenient for others. (Fortunately, that practice has been actively discouraged by the Nursing Home Reform Act of 1987.) In short, under the pressures of economic efficiency and bureaucratic regulation, care can be delivered to serve the institution's agenda rather than accommodating the needs of the individual resident.

Second, we are also called upon to intervene. One way to understand the ideal here has been described as "the least restrictive environment." Instead of caregivers directing and constraining the behavior of the individual, putatively for their own sake, we allow them as much freedom as is practical. But this, we must understand, is only part of the story. The "least restrictive environment" must be enacted so as to maintain reasonable standards of safety: We do not want to allow elderly persons with dementia to go wandering across the four lane expressway! We must not be so simple as to abandon individuals completely to their desires or preferences. The positive sentiment behind "least restrictive" is the ideal of providing an environment that facilitates individuals being themselves as much as possible. It means that individuals still live, as far as feasible, according to their own values, customs, habits, routines, and rituals. Yet given how dementia works, this may require not simply a hands-off approach, but instead an active engagement that facilitates meaning and personhood. Such engagement might include listening patiently as the person with dementia is speaking; it can include prompting engagement rather than allowing isolation. It should include programming that offers the stimulation of touch, taste, movement, and artistic expression. It should obviously include companionship. And it should all be done in terms of the person and the needs of the very individual person in need.

Even the principle of "the least restrictive environment" remains problematic. We suggest the addition that an individual with dementia be provided "an environment that facilitates individuals being themselves as much as possible." Consider the case of a woman who was adamant throughout her life of the value and virtue of marital fidelity, but who now no longer recognizes her husband. Furthermore, she has taken up a sexual interest in a fellow resident in the dementia wing (see Chapter 9). Is the "least restrictive environment" one that facilitates a relationship between her and the other resident with dementia? Or is it one in which staff and family deliberately steer her away from what would appear to be an infidelity of which she would herself disapprove? We do not think there is any easy, straightforward, universal answer here. These types of challenges will require integrated decision making involving family as well as staff. A variety of issues would need to be addressed, such as how the woman's husband and her children feel about the situation; how devoted the woman was to marital fidelity, and how she understood it, before her dementia; and whether interfering in this relationship would affect her present happiness, and make it overly burdensome for the staff. A discussion involving family and staff—weighing moral commitments against desire for happiness—is our best way to navigate such morally murky territory.

ADDRESSING COST

Needless to say, these sorts of ideals demand much caregiver love, time, energy, stamina, and money. For reasons of both family commitment as well as finances, much of this care, especially in early dementia, takes places at home where the care givers are largely family members. Particularly in our modern society, with much smaller nuclear families than in past generations, this burden can be concentrated on just a few select persons. An obligation, self-imposed by love and respect, may become an increasing emotional and financial burden upon the caregivers. Eventually, it becomes a burden that few modern families can bear if they are to remain healthy in the long term. An ethics of care and relationship requires that caregiver burden be recognized as part of the overall context. The care that any one individual "deserves" cannot be such that it destroys the very caregivers (or their families) themselves. An equitable balance must be found. While this is certainly true when only physical frailty is at issue, it is much more true when facing the additional emotional burdens that confront the family caregiver of someone with progressive dementia (see Chapter 7).

When caregiving takes place in the home, the financial costs of that care (in addition to the emotional costs) are often overlooked. But when an institution becomes the setting for care, financial costs become publicly visible. Indeed, quality institutional care of those with dementia is not inexpensive. Our society is deeply divided about where to assign those costs: some critics see it as a purely private matter, since the care of individuals is a family responsibility. Others, however, see not only institutional care, but also the home care of those with dementia as a social responsibility, meriting financial subsidy from society. The public policy that we have at present represents a somewhat awkward compromise between these opposing positions. Some states, such as California, have developed mechanisms to compensate nonspousal family members for some caregiving. Yet in many states, this remains a private financial burden. Concerning institutional care, about 8% of Americans carry long-term care insurance; the rest simply spend down resources to a poverty level and then convert to Medicaid coverage. As for public support for at-home, familial caregiving of persons with dementia, fears of abuse and fraud, plus a reluctance to pay for what is perceived as a family obligation, all come together to limit funds for family caregivers.

We think that an ethic of solidarity demands more: that individuals with dementia still deserve our care and consideration, even our respect. To be morally just, a larger social commitment to care is appropriate. Why should we be committed to this? That question leads us to the last part of this chapter, a reflection on the role of dignity in dementia and how ethically sensitive care might work to sustain it.

DIGNITY

One of the most frequently voiced fears that we hear from those who face dementia, as well as from their caregivers in the years that follow, is the loss of dignity. The concerns seem to be that as dementia asserts itself, we will gradually lose our dignity, being viewed and treated as a "lesser" person. These fears may trouble some people far more than the fear of losing a limb, being unable to drive, or being unable to walk. Indeed, for many people, the fear of loss of dignity may be even greater than the fear of loss of life. Perhaps the greatest moral challenge in caring for those with dementia, then, is how to do it in ways that bests shows and preserves dignity. This is both conceptually and practically challenging.

What does "dignity" mean in the face of dementia? In ordinary terms, the ravages of dementia seem to erode the very qualities that we associate with dignity, and to bring to the fore situations or characteristics that we associate with indignity. This perception is especially acute in our society because, as Post argues, we live in a "hyper cognitive" society, where ratiocination becomes the measure of human value (Post, 2000b, pp. 245–256). The individual early in dementia may be embarrassed by an inability to find the right word, for this brings the conversation to a halt, creating a socially awkward pause. There is the shame of not remembering the name of an important person, be it a daughter's husband, or a grandchild, and the shame some experience in being incapable of handling money, or of paying their own bills. As the disease progresses, there is the shame that comes with disinhibition, as the individual says or does things that are socially unacceptable, embarrassing to others, and thus, "undignified." And where is the dignity in becoming incontinent such that an individual's adult son or daughter must change him in the middle of the night, or at a restaurant on what was supposed to be a precious Sunday outing?

Dignity has, needless to say, become a seemingly thin notion in our postmodern, consumer society. Since having dignity seems to require that others should regard us as having dignity, the concept requires a social context. We must possess, or perform, something that qualifies us as having dignity in the eyes of the appropriate judges before we can truly be said to have dignity. But what is it that merits the ascription of dignity?

In the ancient world, a tradition emerged where dignity was recognized in certain individuals only by reason of unusual virtue, special capacities, or a special social role. In this tradition, dignity is a rare commodity, earned by a few. This conception of dignity has persisted through the ages, though in slightly varying fashions. It is evident, for example, in the work of Immanuel Kant (1785) mentioned previously in this chapter. Kant's argument was that persons have dignity insofar as they possess the capacity for autonomous rational free will. While certainly less elitist than the ancient theories, Kant's theory also leaves out many human individuals: children, people suffering mental illness, and, of course, people with dementia. Thus, by Kant's framework, individuals with dementia clearly lack dignity, because they are no longer capable of autonomous rational will. And, for Kant, we do not have any direct moral obligations to the demented, precisely because they lack dignity. For anyone who faces the erosive onslaught of dementia, such a moral framework is obviously of no comfort at all, but is instead a positive source of fear and anxiety.

A morally different way to conceive of dignity is to think of it not as something that one achieves or earns, but instead as something that one is born with. This has been a viewpoint of natural law theory and of certain religious traditions. But we fear that such views tend to leave ill-defined just what it is we are born with and what the consequent meaning of "dignity" might be. One of the more articulated examples of this view is the Roman Catholic tradition of human dignity, according to which one has dignity not through merit, but simply by being born human. What constitutes such a special human quality, according to the Church, remains quite vague: it cannot be DNA, for some individuals, such as children with Down's syndrome, would then be excluded. Nor is it a particular bodily form, since persons with congenital limb malformations would be excluded. Neither would this dignity rest on cognitive function, for the Church insists that even those who are without higher brain function still qualify as having human dignity. What does respect for that dignity then mean? This tradition has taken a vitalist approach: it is the life itself that has dignity and hence, must be preserved as an act of respect.

Harry Moody (Moody, 1998) argues that neither of these traditions works well for the elderly of today's society. Instead, appealing to a communicative ethic, Moody calls for the marginalized elderly to speak and have their voices heard:

> The appeal to dignity, more strongly, the insistent claim to dignity, points to something in us which is genuinely transcendent, something which reflects our freedom to call into question all social roles, to say out loud that I am something more than my frailty or my role performances or my buying power. At that moment, the passive victim rises up to say *You can't treat me this way*. The moment we speak those words, dialogue becomes possible and advocacy becomes inevitable. The outcome of the struggle is never certain, but this struggle for dignity emerges again and again through the course of history. It is a cry for justice as much as an affirmation of meaning.
> —*Moody, 1998, p. 37*

In an analogous way, Bruce Jennings has argued that even in the absence of linguistic-verbal ability, those with dementia can still "communicate," and thus, play their role in this communicative-dialogic process of creating identity and earning respect (Jennings, 2009, p. 425–437). As much as we applaud Moody's sentiment or admire the creativity of Jennings' argument, we feel that dementia makes it difficult and at some stage impossible for those with dementia to speak for themselves. The dialogue to which Moody and Jennings refer becomes impossible. The attempt to skirt this difficulty by creatively stretching the notion of what can count as sufficient "communication" can only succeed by effectively draining the concept of its very meaning.

The central difficulty is that all of these traditions and approaches see dignity as residing "in" the individual: by divine creation, by individual achievement, by individual capacity, or by the conferring of some special societal office. They all, to some extent, abstract from the individual. We find work such as that of Hilde Lindemann (2002, 2009) to be far more convincing and helpful in this regard. She emphasizes that identity and recognition are social enterprises, not simply the work of isolated individuals. By being social in nature—the cooperative work of many of us together—the sustenance of identity, and hence the possibility of dignity, is work that others can take on in ever increasing proportion as the individual becomes less able to contribute to this enterprise (Lindemann, 2009).

Consider the example of the dignity of an office holder more closely. One must refer to a judge as "your Honor," even if one thinks that the judge's conduct has left something to be desired. Even if the minority party in Congress disagrees vehemently with the policies of the sitting President of the United States, they are all expected to rise for the entrance of the President for the State of the Union Address. And in the military, one is required to salute a superior officer, not because one likes him or approves of his conduct, but simply because he is a superior officer. Note that we salute the dead of the military, even though they no longer have any capacities whatsoever.

In each of these cases, we invest these persons with dignity, and hence as deserving of respect, to some extent apart from their individual abilities. We believe that this offers one key to the question of dignity in the demented: those who are demented may no longer be capable of the character traits and behaviors that ordinarily garner respect and dignity, but as members of our society, we can choose in solidarity to recognize them as having dignity. Dignity is then not necessarily conferred by continuing, superior accomplishment—it can be conferred and sustained by us as a social act of solidarity.

Individuals with dementia are therefore no longer required to speak up and demand recognition, justice, or meaning: as a community, we can do that for them. We can step in and help maintain their identity, and sustain their dignity, when they are no longer able to take the lead in this by themselves. Such a way of thinking is, we believe, in harmony with Lindemann's (2009) analysis. It helps makes sense of a continuity of identity, even in the face of progressive dementia; and it helps to frame what we most deeply hope for when we think about the goals and nature of caregiving in the face of dementia.

Not only are we capable of doing this, we believe that it is at the core of what would constitute "good" care of persons with dementia. Bathing and feeding are, indeed, essential, as is maximally involving the individual in social activity, and providing physical stimulation and human companionship. But surely the goal of overriding importance, without which these other kinds of care miss the point, is the continued support of the identity, self, and dignity of the individual who suffers from dementia.

CONCLUSION

As long as we remain obsessed with rational capacity as the distinguishing marker of personhood, the ways in which we will conceptualize dementia, and thus care for those with dementia, will continue to depersonalize them. We will see them as embarrassments in our "hypercognitive" society, and we will hide them from view and skimp on the allocation of resources to them because of their devalued status. Care ethics and narrative ethics, as explored by theorists like Hilde Lindemann, can offer strategies for getting around this difficulty; but all of this rests upon reconceptualizing how we create and sustain identity and dignity. Understanding these as *social projects* rather than as tasks strictly for monadic, isolated individuals, is key to creating change, and to emphasizing our dignity and worth beyond our cognitive, rational capacities. In the end, dementia can remind us, even if painfully, of some of the many facets of being a human person: facets that an obsessive focus on rationality tends to obscure. This reminder can provide motivation and direction for the care of those who become affected by dementia.

REFERENCES

Agich, G. (1993). *Autonomy in long term care*. New York, NY: Oxford University Press.

Baars, J. (1991). The challenge of critical gerontology: The problem of social construction. *Journal of Aging Studies, 5*(3), 229.

Ballenger, J. (2006). *Self, senility, and Alzheimer's disease in modern America*. Baltimore, MD: Johns Hopkins University Press.

Basting, A. (2009). *Forget memory: Creating better lives for people with dementia*. Baltimore, MD: Johns Hopkins University Press.

Feinberg, L., & Whitlatch, C. J. (2001). Are persons with cognitive impairment able to state consistent choices? *The Gerontologist, 41*(3), 374–382.

Fox, P. (1989). From senility to Alzheimer's disease. *The Millbank Quarterly, 67*, 58–102.

Gubrium, J. (1986). The social preservation of mind: The Alzheimer's disease experience. *Symbolic Interaction, 9*(1), 35–51.

Gubrium, J. (2000). Narrative practice and the inner worlds of the Alzheimer disease experience. In P. J. Whitehouse, K. Maurer, & J. F. Ballenger (Eds.), *Concepts of Alzheimer disease* (pp. 181–204). Baltimore, MD: Johns Hopkins University Press.

Herskovits, E. J., & Mitteness, L. S. (1994). Transgressions and sickness in old age. *Journal of Aging Studies, 8*(3), 327–340.

Holstein, M. (1997). Alzheimer's disease and senile dementia, 1885–1920. *Journal of Aging Studies, 11*(1), 1–13.

Jennings, B. (2009). Agency and moral relationship in dementia. *Metaphilosophy 40*(3&4), 425–437.

Kant, I. (1785). *Grounding for the metaphysics of morals* (J. W. Ellington, Trans.) (3rd ed., 1993). Indianapolis, IN: Hackett Publishers.

Katzman, R. (1976). The prevalence and malignancy of Alzheimer's disease: A major killer. *Archives of Neurology, 33*, 217–218.

Kittay, E. F. (1999). *Love's labor: Essays on women, equality, and dependency.* New York, NY: Routledge.

Kitwood, T. (1997). *Dementia reconsidered.* London, UK: Open University Press.

Kitwood, T., & Bredin, K. (1992). Towards a theory of dementia care: Personhood, well-being. *Ageing and Society, 12*, 269–287.

Lindemann, H. (2002). What child is this? *Hastings Center Report, 32*(6), 29–68.

Lindemann, H. (2009). Holding one another (well, wrongly, clumsily) in a time of dementia. *Metaphilosophy, 40*(3& 4), 412–424.

Mackenzie, C., & Stoljar, N. (Eds.) (2000). *Relational autonomy: Feminist perspectives on autonomy, agency, and the social self.* New York, NY: Oxford University Press.

Meyers, D. T. (Ed.) (1996). *Feminists rethink the self.* Boulder, CO: Westview Press.

Moody, H. R. (1992). *Ethics in an aging society.* Baltimore, MD: Johns Hopkins University Press.

Moody, H. R. (1998). Why dignity in old age matters. In R. Disch, R. Dobrof, & H. Moody (Eds.), *Dignity and old age* (pp. 13–38). New York, NY: Haworth Press.

Post, S. (2000a). *The moral challenge of Alzheimer disease.* Baltimore, MD: Johns Hopkins University Press.

Post, S. (2000b). The concept of Alzheimer disease in a hyper cognitive society. In P. J. Whitehouse, K. Maurer, & J. F. Ballenger (Eds.), *Concepts of Alzheimer disease* (pp. 245–256). Baltimore, MD: Johns Hopkins University Press.

Robertson, A. (1991). The politics of Alzheimer's disease: A case study in apocalyptic demography. In M. Minkler & C. L. Estes (Eds.), *Critical perspectives on aging.* Amityville, NY: Baywood Publishing.

Snyder, L. (1999). *Speaking our minds: Personal reflections from individuals with Alzheimer's.* New York, NY: W. H. Freeman.

Twigg, J. (2001). *Bathing: The body and community care.* London, UK: Routledge.

CHAPTER 12

Beyond Rational Control: Caring at the End of Life

Priscilla Jones is 86 years old. She is a widow and lives alone in a mid-size city in the Midwest. She has been close to her grown children who live within 60 miles of her home. Her health had been remarkably good until she fell and broke her hip four years ago. This incident seemed to set up a cascade of other minor and major illnesses meaning that she has been in and out of the hospital 10 times over the course of four years. She is now in the hospital again. Her chart reads "failure to thrive." She is losing weight, is not interested in eating, and has a low grade fever—probably a bladder infection. Her doctor wants to insert a temporary feeding tube to build up her strength so that the infection can be cleared, perhaps paving the way for her to return home.

Since Mrs. Jones is very frail, sleeps a great deal, and seems disinterested in talking about anything, including her treatment, Dr. Davis meets with her 2 children and explains what she would like to do. They know their mother does not want to be on a ventilator or feeding tube if she has no chance of recovery, but this seems like an easy, temporary measure. Dr. Davis advises them to do it. They look at their mother, who seems so forlorn and alone, out of touch with everything around her. She smiles when touched and when she hears music but otherwise has few reactions to anything except pain, which they see on her face rather than hear in her words. Her children thought they would know what to do but they find themselves unsure, especially since Dr. Davis assures them that she still has some time.

Priscilla Jones is not an atypical person of 86. She was doing well, then suddenly took a bad turn. Her children love her and want to do what is right. Dr. Davis takes some time to explain her treatment recommendations, and frames the intervention in a positive light. It sounds very simple: a feeding tube is recommended just to make her strong again so that they can save her life. It is not "extraordinary" care the way Mrs. Jones' children understand that term. How could they not proceed with Dr. Davis' plan? Then again, that person lying in the bed is not the mother they have known all their lives. She seems to have given up, left them already. But what if clearing up the infection brings her back to her old self?

This kind of dilemma is familiar (see Kaufman, 2000 for an ethnographic account of a related situation). Mrs. Jones' children know the importance to her that her life end with continued recognition of what she values: being at home, surrounded by those she loves, with her pain under control, and her sense of self as intact as possible. It seems as if this wish is an elusive dream, and not because of anyone's bad intentions. Instead, like so many others, Mrs. Jones is in the hospital, touched by strangers with cold stethoscopes, with her worried children trying to decide what to do, if anything, to keep her alive. Like others, she is in pain. She has faced much treatment, perhaps more treatment than she wants, not only at the very end, but during the longer period of her multiple illnesses, each one treated as one more disease that is "fixable." Unlike many other patients, she has emotional support, although it is unclear how much of that comes from Dr. Davis, from whom she probably wants continued recognition and care (Marshall, 1995). She may feel isolated from the life around her, her humanness lost amidst the routines, structures and values of hospitals (Holstein, 1997a). She may worry that she will be a burden to those she loves and that her dignity will be compromised as she becomes "just a body" rather than a person (Howarth, 1998, p. 679). Thus, the reality of dying, especially for people who are old, is very different from the dominant ideal that upholds an image of dying persons freely rejecting "the use of medical technologies that prolong the dying process," managing their own pain, in their preferred environment (Kaufman, 2000, p. 1).

In what follows, we will describe efforts to "tame" death and then turn to a critical analysis of these efforts, particularly the focus on control as central to good care at the end of life. We will argue that its primacy rests on several problematic assumptions most significantly its individualistic, treatment specific, and decontextualized approach to the dying process that somehow erases the vulnerable, hurting self in favor of the rational, cognitive self. While hospice and palliative care are important to the kind of dying that many people seem to want, we will argue for a broader range of interventions that lessen the importance of individual treatment choices that ease the burden of decision making, and address the caring needs of patients and families. We again look to "bottom up" ideas directed at the still stubbornly resistant problem of easing the transition from life to death in ways that respect individuals and the significant relationships of which they are part.

In considering ways to reach this end, we build on the relational view of autonomy addressed in Chapters 1 and 2, which we find theoretically satisfying, but also find supported in research (see Hawkins, Ditto, Danks, & Smucker, 2005, for a good summary of this research). New research suggests that dying people, no matter how ill, continue to place importance on their relationships with their loved ones. As many of us think about dying we confirm our commitments to the people we love and who love us. Dying may not be the last bastion of control and choice, but rather a time to affirm the lifelong relationships that are essential to our identity. The more that families and others close to the patient can be relieved of the burden of decision-making, the more they can attend to their relationships, by talking, sharing music, or even rubbing lotion on their loved one's dry feet (see Morton, 1998). Such interactions may remind us of our embodied nature and the basic vulnerabilities and dependencies that inevitably come with it.

CHALLENGING ASSUMPTIONS

In the United States today, the primacy of patient choice, second only to pain control, has become "dogma in the clinical setting" (Drought & Koenig, 2002, p. 115). It is the foundation for advance care planning. This belief, despite evidence that it rarely works as anticipated (see Gillick, 2010; Silveira, Kim, & Langa, 2010 for an opposing view), rests on several problematic assumptions. It assumes that we can, and wish to, anticipate a time in the future when we are dying and that we can rationally make decisions based on a full understanding of the prognosis and the benefits and burdens of treatment options. It assumes that death is essentially subject to rational control, that people would "routinely, comfortably, and meaningfully confront and consider not just their own mortality but also the process of their physical decline and dying in an engaged and rational manner" (Drought & Koenig, 2002, p. 115). When appointing a proxy to make decisions for us, it assumes that we can tell them what we want in circumstances that we may be unable to anticipate and that they will be able to do what they understand we want in conditions of uncertainty and fear. It further assumes that it is about "us" only and not about us in the context of our relationships, which often have primacy over what we may want for ourselves. If we are in the hospital, it assumes that the familiar impulse to treat will be tamped down and that physicians will explain what our options are in such a way that our surrogates will understand that perhaps there are no real choices that will keep death at bay. It assumes that our physicians and others will help us to negotiate what are often gray zones between life and death (Kaufman, 2000). And, it assumes that our choices are unrelated to matters such as our insurance status or resource constraints. Many societal efforts to "tame" death are built on a foundation of these assumptions.

TAMING DEATH: TAKING CONTROL

Most of us will not die suddenly while engaging in our favorite activity, a wish that many people express (Howarth, 1998). Since death rarely comes quickly, the ability to manage the "mode, method, and timing" has become central in efforts to take control away from doctors and place it in the hands of patients and families. The commitment to such autonomous decision-making is now enshrined in law, in our thinking about the ethics of end-of-life care, and in community programs to encourage both discussions about death and the completing of advance directives. In this view,

> To be both a model American and a model patient, one must approach death rationally. A living will or a durable power of attorney should reside in one's chart along with a notation about one's code status. The model patient's doctor will know and honor her wishes; her surrogate will understand her values and perhaps her deepest notions about life and death, and if the time comes when she is unable to make decisions for herself, this surrogate will act in her stead. He will set aside his own needs and wishes and respect hers.
> —*Holstein, 1997a, p. 249*

These goals are not bad in themselves but they can divert attention from other matters of great importance like attentiveness and loving care during the dying process. A preoccupation with decision-making can push aside more relational concerns. The goal of autonomous decision-making can create unsettling confusion about what someone like Mrs. Jones would "really" want, and often pits family members against one another. Given the culture wars of recent years, understandings about withdrawing treatment, who decides when to withdraw, the basis for doing so, and how to review such a decision (Dubler, 2005) have also come under close scrutiny. When Congress passed the Patient Self-Determination Act (PSDA) in 1990, advocates assumed that it would bring the dying process into closer alignment with what people seemed to want. As the instruments to implement PSDA evolved (and often became more complex), individuals writing directives could note the kind of treatment they wanted or did not want so that their designated proxy could decide as they would have decided (substituted judgment). Considered less desirable was proxy decision making by the best interest standard, to be implemented if the proxy did not have a clear indication of the patient's preferences. Major advocacy efforts ensued with the express purpose of stimulating the use of advance directives.

In an effort to increase adherence to advance directives, about 15 states have implemented programs based on the POLST (Physician Orders for

Life-Sustaining Treatment) instrument. Developed in response to identified limitations with traditional advance directives (not available when needed; not transferred with the patient; not specific enough, and capable of being overridden by the treating physician), POLST was developed to complement durable power of attorneys (DPAs) and "to help ensure that patient wishes to have or limit specific medical treatments are respected near the end of life" (Hickman, Hammes, Moss, & Tolle, 2005). These instruments have the additional force of documenting physician's orders, a more powerful tool in the hierarchical medical setting than a designated proxy. They are also enforceable across settings. These instruments are intended for individuals who are suffering from advanced chronic illness, for whom the question, "would you be surprised if the patient did not die within the year" is a clear yes (Dunn et al., 2007; Hickman, 2005).

Other instruments, such as the Five Wishes, have been designed to motivate and structure a conversation about end-of-life care so that individuals and their families can discuss values and other important concerns about care. Efforts continue to encourage more people to prepare directives, to discuss their wishes with their designated proxy, and to assure greater attention to them in the clinical setting. Today, the focus is increasingly on the conversations that precede the execution of directives.

OTHER WAYS TO ASSERT CONTROL: HOSPICE, PALLIATIVE CARE, AND PHYSICIAN-ASSISTED SUICIDE

Cicely Saunders, the British physician who "invented" hospice care, offered an approach that eased people toward death by encouraging acceptance of the inevitable through conversation, support for the individual and his or her family, and a commitment to pain relief no matter the consequences. (In some cases, sufficient morphine to relieve pain can slow respiration resulting in terminal sedation or even death.) The first hospice in this country opened in Connecticut in 1975. In 1982, Congress passed legislation that provided Medicare funding for hospice care for those individuals who had six months or less to live; many private insurance companies followed suit. The person opting for hospice care, which was designed in part to counteract the medicalization of death, waived curative interventions in favor of comfort care. In exchange, hospice care made it easier for people to die at home; it provided assistance to families or other caregivers at the same time that it cared for the patient. For those people without caregivers, hospice units now exist in nursing homes and in step-down units in hospitals. Some also have in-patient facilities.

In her successful effort to have her husband, Tom, die at home, Eleanor Clift (2008), an American journalist, relied on hospice care. In her descriptions, one sees how hospice care can work—for Tom, hospice did what Cicely Saunders envisioned. He was not in pain and Eleanor had just enough freedom to continue her professional life while feeling supported during her husband's dying. Tom's case was an "ideal" one for hospice care. Also a journalist, he used his columns to chronicle his experiences with renal cell carcinoma (kidney cancer) that had metastasized to his bones and brain. He was a fierce fighter but also fiercely realistic. When he entered hospice, medicine had exhausted every known therapy that might have bought him more time. Both Tom and Eleanor knew—and accepted— that death was the only outcome available to him.

Hospice tends to work best for patients with cancer when prognosis is relatively reliable but even then, the decision to recommend and accept hospice care requires an acknowledgment by physician, patient and family that death is inevitable and relatively imminent. Yet, as research (Drought & Koenig, 2002) has suggested, negotiating that gray zone between life and death and confronting the fact that the death process has begun, is an expectation that often is more difficult than our best hopes and common assumptions anticipated. As a result, instead of the six months that insurance coverage supports, the average length of stay in hospice is 47 days. Yet, it does not work for everyone. In contrast to Tom, consider Suzanne, an intense and deeply committed scholar, who had stage four breast cancer. Suzanne summoned whatever energy she had left when a nurse suggested hospice care, shouting at her, "Are you trying to kill me?" She had hospice care for two days before she died in 2002. Suzanne's active rejection of hospice care is on a continuum with those who simply avoid the conversation. She, like many other people who are near death, was more concerned about living than facing her own dying (Holstein, 2002).

Palliative care carries many of the same commitments as hospice to providing comfort care to patients and assisting families throughout the illness continuum. It does not eschew treatments; it is not limited to the last six months of life; it focuses on treating and preventing suffering, and offers care in hospitals and nursing homes, where more than 55% of Americans die (Foley, 2005). Palliative care is particularly important because it can offer services to patients and families as illnesses progress and change. It is not reserved for the very end when, in some ways, the decisions may be simpler. Palliative care specialists "help people make tough decisions that are less about dying than about how they want to live at the end of their lives" (Brink, 2009, p. 2). Mrs. Jones and her children, one can imagine, would find such care an important guide for the decisions with which they must wrestle. Her children might hear the often unspoken words—that their mother is dying no matter what they decide to do. The problem, however, is the absence of specific reimbursement for palliative care services, which has limited its expansion. As a result only about 20% of American hospitals now offer such services (Foley, 2005).

AID IN DYING

Physician-assisted suicide (PAS) or physician aid in dying (www. compassionandchoices.org) is the last redoubt in the effort to tame death. While it is beyond the scope of this chapter to address in detail the contentious arguments this topic raises, we note some reasons for its growing prominence. For some people, it signifies a rejection of the "technicalization of medicine and death and the misery rather than the promise that technology is currently felt to offer" (Christakis, 1991, p. 27). Such fears apply particularly to deaths that occur in hospitals. For others, it is the last act of a person asserting the ultimate in control—choosing the time and place of his/her dying but doing so with knowledge and without violence (compared, e.g., to a shotgun blast). Yet, control, while important, may not capture what for many people is most significant: easing existential suffering, mitigating fears of being a burden, and ceasing the erosion of dignity (Angell, 1997).

Arguments for and against physician aid in dying tend to reflect very different perspectives. Arguments in support of it speak to the voice of experience, the narrative of patients who are near death. While some critics, like Callahan (2002) see the effort to choose the time and place of our own death as carrying autonomy to extreme limits, proponents see it as being more about containing suffering. Arguments in opposition tend to speak in a principled voice about physicians' obligations. It is the more detached view of the expert. We hear the patient's voice reflected in the account that Dr. Timothy Quill (1991), a Rochester, NY physician, gives in his description of how he helped his patient Diane, to die. Diane was suffering from leukemia, and was a long time patient, whom he had seen through difficult periods in her life. She was very aware of the terrible side effects of the treatment and decided that she did not want to go through it again. She was clear-headed and expressed her wishes more than once. Her disease was terminal. Dr. Quill provided her with information and a prescription for the medications she needed to take her own life. He was never indicted by a grand jury. For supporters of physician aid in dying, Dr. Quill is a model of how such assistance ought to be provided.

ADVANCE CARE PLANNING AND INDIVIDUAL CHOICE

As noted in Chapter 5, prior to every answer there is a question (Rein, 1983). The question that governs advance care planning is how medicine can return to patients (and/or their proxies) control over treatment choices. Ethicists, attorneys, and other advocates assume that patients want this control, which thus makes it the "problem" to be addressed. While advance care planning was never intended to "solve" the problems associated with end-of-life care, it gained immediate popularity in part because it fit so well with what was emerging as the individualistic and decontextualized bioethics paradigm (see Chapters 1 and 2). Thus, advance care planning not only rests on questionable assumptions about what patients really want and what is actually possible in a medical setting, but it also fails to consider variables such as the cultural and structural context in which care is provided. It does not confront the "feelings of mistrust and lived experiences of unequal treatment" (Murray & Jennings, 2005, p. S54) that so many people, marginalized by dominant society, face in the medical care setting. For those who lack access to mainstream medicine or simply do not trust it, the very idea of limiting treatment may appear to be either intolerable or quite simply, racist (Dula, 1994). As Dubler (2005), points out, in the New York City Bronx, patients are interested in accessing care, not limiting it. This fact might make any suggestions about limiting treatment suspect.

Older people differ in many ways when they consider issues related to the end of life. They may, for example, value shared rather than individual decision-making, which may render alien the national consensus about advance care planning (Hickman et al., 2005; Murray & Jennings, 2005). The assumptions that govern end-of-life care might prove the most difficult when nonwestern cultural approaches to decision making involve withholding diagnoses and prognoses from patients (Blackhall et al., 1995). Antipaternalistic commitments to the patient's right to know "may lead in some instances to a cultural paternalism that can psychologically injure patients from certain cultures" (Krakauer, Crenner, & Fox, 2002, p. 184), such as Korean- and Mexican-Americans (Blackhall et al., 1995). Sensitivity to such disparities in health care requires us to view the culture and practice of medicine from the margins rather than from the center.

Class may also matter. One of us (MH) met with about 100 maintenance men in an ethics workshop. These men worked for a large company that manages affordable housing for seniors and so they regularly encountered people who fell ill and died. One of the men brought up the subject of end-of-life care. In the course of the discussion, it became clear that not only did they not have advance directives, but that they had never heard of them and had no interest in discussing the topic of advance care planning. The very idea of talking about death was unacceptable to them.

There are other problems with the choice model. It elevates "rational and cognitive ways of knowing" over "emotional, psychological, and embodied experiences" (Drought & Koenig, 2002, p. 116). In the case of Priscilla Jones that opened this chapter, we need to ask questions about her bodily experience and not only her rational will. Focusing on choice elevates decision-making over virtues such as caring and love, devotion, solidarity, and attentiveness; it can deflect and distract, causing hand-holding to be replaced with hand-wringing (Holstein, 1997). It may inadvertently set up families in opposition to the person who is dying and assume they have no interests other than being a conduit of the patient's wishes (Arras, 1995; High, 1991). The individualistic focus thus fails to acknowledge that we die, as we live, within a web of relationships (Murray & Jennings, 2005).

Thus, it may be no surprise that fewer that 30% of Americans have done advance care planning; for those who have done such planning, physicians and/or surrogates often override their wishes (Hickman et al., 2005). Yet a recent publication (Silveira et al., 2010) documents that in a Michigan study, over 67% of people had directives that were honored in medical settings. This study, however, is retrospective, and focuses only at the very end when most people prefer comfort care. In an editorial comment, Gillick (2010) raises some important challenges to the conclusions that might be drawn from this study. More analysis is clearly needed. Yet it is fair to say that directives may help surrogates feel more comfortable with the decisions that they make; that in most cases unwanted care at the very end of life can be stopped, but that directives do not make end-of-life care better by being pain-free, emotionally supported, or comfortable (Teno, Grunier, Schwartz, Nanda, & Wetle, 2007).

When the expressed wishes of a patient are not honored, the cause is rarely ill will. Often it is because a patient's vague instructions make it difficult for doctors to resist the curative medical imperative (Kaufman, 2000). Sometimes it happens because, for older people in particular, seemingly simple treatment decisions (e.g., treating Mrs. Jones for a bladder infection) often trigger a cascade of further treatments. These interventions are effective in addressing specific pathologies when the person's body becomes frailer and weaker (Kaufman, 2000). Hence, physicians may not overtly reject a patient's expressed wishes; but the very process of deciding on treatment plans often involves multiple micro-decisions that are not addressed in directives (Kaufman, 2000). Priscilla Jones is a clear example of this problem: Directives may do well when in the final act but less well in the events leading up to that last act. In most instances, the "dying transition" is far less clear than in the celebrated court cases that are foundational to the American way of death.

We find it interesting that the standard upheld for surrogate decision-making—substituted judgment or choosing as the patient would have chosen if she/he could decide—may needlessly exacerbate these burdens. It has been clear for some years now, and a cause of considerable concern, that there is often little concordance between what patients say they would want and what surrogates think the patient would want (Hawkins et al., 2005; Lemay, Pruchno, Levinksy, & Field, 2004; Shalowitz, Gerritt-Mayer, & Wendler, 2006). Some reasons for this lack of concordance reside in the clinical setting. Prognosis is often uncertain and physicians propose single, seemingly modest interventions that surrogates find hard to reject (Kaufman, 2000). Situations change and attitudes of patients and surrogates may also change. We are bad predictors of what we might want at some future point, especially when we cannot know in advance the specific facts that we or our families will be facing in advance (Hawkins et al., 2005). What may seem intolerable at one point in our lives becomes tolerable at later stages or once we accommodate to what once seemed intolerable.

Yet, as it turns out, these concerns may be less problematic than the assumptions underlying advance care planning would suggest. While many surrogates appreciate having information about the patient's wishes, research has suggested that many people do not want to make individual treatment choices. A national study ranked fifth out of nine the wish to make such treatment choices (Hofmann J. et al., 1997, cited in Winzelberg, Hanson, & Tulsky, 2005). For many patients, defining broad goals of treatment was more important than making specific treatment choices. But perhaps even more significant, people wanted surrogates to do what they thought best and they wanted surrogates to take their own interests into account (Hawkins et al., 2005; Hickman et al., 2005). This empirical data reinforces our ethical commitments to relational autonomy and contextual care. When near death, people do not see themselves as surrounded by a wall of privacy designed to keep others from interfering with their choices. Instead their obligations to others continue to shape their lives, even when they can no longer actively engage in decision-making.

Yet, for some people, in some circumstances, planning well can help them achieve what most say they want even if they are hospitalized. We suspect that many of these people are comfortable with legal documents; they trust the medical care system, and are accustomed to exercising strong agency over their lives. Hence, it bears noting that this approach may be another graphic example of how the educated, middle class translates its wishes about end-of-life care into a universal assumption that does not hold up under scrutiny. The lens of privilege can assume universality when what it sees is rather particularistic. For this reason, we advocate, as we did in Chapter 4, for seeking understanding about how people in their different communities think about care at the end of life. Again, we suggest that by starting from the bottom-up, with what people *actually* want given their circumstances, we can achieve their best ends, rather than starting from a top-down, policy-based approach.

OTHER PROBLEMS: THE CULTURE OF MEDICINE

Ironically, cultural norms in the United States may romanticize the "good death" while seeing death itself as a failure, almost an obscenity. The culture of medicine reinforces this irony. Pauline Chen (2007), a liver transplant surgeon, reflects on mortality as follows: "Our professional fear and aversion to dying is the most difficult—and the most fundamentally human—obstacle to changing end-of-life care" (p. 217). Family members often feel abandoned by physicians who are both rushed and do not take the time to explain the patient's status and anticipated outcomes in a language that is free of jargon (Braun, Beyeth, Ford, & McCullough, 2007). Chen (2007) echoes this concern and calls upon physicians to accept "the honor of worrying—of caring, of easing suffering, of being present" as "our most important task ..." (p. 218). This task, however, may be the most difficult for the curative culture of medicine to realize. Medical students are now exposed to more training in end-of-life care than in the past, but that training is limited and the discomforts that result— reinforced by cultural resistance to talking about death—carries over into practice. Medical students learn little about care when cure is no longer possible, or when "cure" leads to a series of untoward and negative consequences for both the patient and his/her family, or when "cure" of one organ system does nothing to make the person more whole (Chen, 2007; Gillick, 2006; Kaufman, 2000). Training does not prepare physicians to discuss with patients the limits of life-sustaining interventions and they are not observed or supervised if and when they do hold such conversations (Lo, 1995). The chief of geriatrics at an academic medical center once unhesitatingly affirmed, "Talk to my patients about dying? No way, that I can do that" (personal communication). While this view may not be dominant, it reflects a common resistance to acknowledging that death is near while reminding us that physicians are not immune from fears about dying. Commenting on the SUPPORT study, which was specifically designed to improve communication between medical personnel and patient, Bernard Lo (1995) observes that embedded practices are resistant to change even when such practices are the specific targets of a major intervention. Despite these efforts, there has been little improvement in communication, patients' preferences have not been followed (often they were not even known), and pain relief has not improved.

Medicine's success in curing successive diseases and thereby transforming acute conditions into chronic ones further complicate the dying process. As Joanne Lynn (2005) states, "Many elderly people are inching toward oblivion with small losses every few weeks or months," (p. S14) an observation that Sharon Kaufman's (2000) ethnographic study reinforced. Old age and chronic illness make it difficult to decide when dying begins. The inability or unwillingness to confront the question of when death is likely to occur means that curative and restorative treatments continue even when no one seems to want them (Kaufman, 2000). Exacerbating this problem is the medical system's reluctance to let people die of old age. Each "disease" can be treated separately and often successfully (Gillick, 2006; Kaufman, 2000). Thus, swallowing, can be "fixed" (a benefit) without any change in the elder's overall condition. Mrs. Jones' bladder infection can be cured but her system will not become less frail. This ideology of treatment marginalizes the cumulative effects of embodied frailty. It is hard to let a person die—or even to face the reality of the dying trajectory—when the intervention is by no means "extraordinary."

In part, this situation comes about because neither our society nor biomedicine has resolved a core question regarding whether aging is itself a disease. Whether or not aging is a disease, whether or not normal aging is pathological, and whether or not aging must inevitably lead to death are all issues that are questioned and debated (Caplan, 2004; also see Chapter 5). If such issues are not considered, then specific interventions will always be justified if they are divorced from an assessment of the person's overall condition and prognosis.

The "choice" paradigm heightens the complications physicians face when identifying treatment options. Given the common bias toward intervention, physicians may present the statistical odds of possible benefit even when, in fact, death is inevitable. Patients and families may translate that information into having the "choice" not to die. "The irony of the choice paradigm is that it seems to present a choice that does not exist—the choice not to die of a terminal illness" (Drought & Koenig, 2002, p. 115) as patients and families translate a statistical possibility of benefit into a choice not to give up and die. A persistent belief in the power of medicine to cure emerged in the years following World War II, when medical successes heralded an unlimited sense of possibility. The idea of fighting death developed its own internal logic: after all, death is the "enemy," as our multiple "wars" on diseases like cancer suggest. The battle analogy is an apt one; if there is one more treatment to try, then it is generally tried, often without adequate attention to the potentially negative consequences of treating an already critically ill patient who has little or no likelihood of recovery (Gillick, 2006). Families and patients often join physicians in this "war" against disease. The reasons are understandable, since for many medical conditions prognosis is uncertain and hope that once again the enemy of death can be defeated runs deep in all of us.

These factors are reinforced by the increased privatization of death, which limits our experiences with it until we personally encounter it. Today, while most people express a wish to die at home, close to 80% die in hospitals where death is simultaneously very public and very private. In a hospital setting, death becomes a medical rather than a human problem (Holstein, 1997). The alienation and privatization of death, especially given medicine's "boundless frontier," often seems to eliminate the patient from the ritual of dying (Guillemin, 1995). Patients are also absented from society at large and "if the process of dying is lengthy and requires long-term hospital treatment" even families may be less present (Howarth, 1998, p. 675). All these factors—the "wars" against disease; the ability to intervene in more and more complex ways to stave off death; the medical profession's commitment to cure and limited training in being with the dying patient; the problematic assumption that dying is a rational process that can be anticipated and planned for; and the privatization of death—all contribute to the difficulties we face in improving end-of-life care.

PROBLEMS: THE POLITICS OF DEATH AND DYING

While an extensive discussion of the politics of death and dying is beyond the scope of this chapter, it cannot be completely ignored. The battleground is a shifting one. Consider Terri Schiavo, a young woman in a persistent vegetative state whose husband, against the wishes of Terri's parents, wanted to disconnect her feeding tube. This infamous case focused on the narrow question of who makes decisions and on what basis, and on the broader question concerning the provision of nutritional support via a feeding tube. More recently, the battle erupted on another front when a legislative provision to reimburse physicians for having conversations with their patients about end-of-life care was translated into "death panels" and the threat that the government was endorsing "killing granny." Given that the culture wars over death and dying are seemingly self-renewing even as the issues change, we can anticipate that they will continue. As discussed in Chapter 6, while ethics can play a vital role in informing policy choices, the barriers are high: among the highest may be the increasing politicization of these contentious bioethical issues.

PROPOSALS FOR CHANGE

Clearly, there are no simple solutions. Given our challenge to the assumptions that underlie the American "way of death" and the evidence to support these challenges as revealed in practice settings and in empirical research, we turn now to our proposals for change. We start with a consideration of what is special about dying people and those who love and care for them. From there, we consider how advance care planning and the cultural and structural features of medical care settings would need to change to respond to these elemental features of being a person who is dying. As we argued in Chapter 4, if popular norms and values do not resonate with the people to whom they are meant to apply, they either marginalize those people or challenge their identity or sense of self worth. We think that the same is true with the central values associated with end-of-life care.

To return to Mrs. Jones, we note first that she is vulnerable (we thank Hoffmaster, 2006 for his sensitive account of vulnerability). She has virtually no power over her environment because of her great frailty. Her children, who may have no trouble making decisions in day-to-day life, are also vulnerable. They need to rely on Dr. Davis and perhaps several interns and residents to help them make sense of what is happening to their mother. Yet, these providers don't really know Mrs. Jones, so they might see her bladder infection as something that is simple and "fixable," an interpretation that is unsurprising in the curative world of American medicine. Even if the children have a good idea of the conditions that their mother would find intolerable, they are not sure if in this situation the feeding tube meets those criteria. Denial is also at play: Maybe she really can get better. Uncertainties of this sort and fears of vulnerability in a society that values independence and control even at the end of life can make a struggle over making decisions easier than seeing what Mrs. Jones might need at this moment in her life. Hoffmaster (2006) notes that, "a familiar strategy for fleeing from fear and discomfort is to become task-oriented. Rather than focusing on the person for whom a task is being performed, focus on the task itself"

(p. 42). Vulnerability is the antithesis of individualism and control, the hallmarks on which efforts to improve end-of-life care rest. Further, it is unlikely that Mrs. Jones' rational self is central to her experience at this time; rather it is the fact of her bodily decline that is central and that fact makes her almost totally dependent upon others. Neither vulnerability nor dependency has a recognizable place in American bioethics and hence they cannot be central to how we think about care at the end of life. Though feminists scholars (see Dodds, 2007; Kittay, 1999) have placed dependency in the forefront of their thinking about human selves, this view remains a minority one. Yet, by placing vulnerability and dependency at the core of what it means to be human, we come to see how care, social commitments and context, which sustain us in our vulnerabilities, are essential and not contingent features of human life (Dodds, 2007). It also means that the ability to choose cannot be separated from material and social conditions. Once we see people in this light, we can understand why the individualistic and decontextualized assumptions that underlie such ideas as advance care planning are inadequate to the task of improving care at the end of life.

How then might these reflections about vulnerability and dependency inform our thinking about end-of-life care? We start with what might be the most radical solution: to take much of the decision-making out of the hands of individuals and families so that there is space for the feelings for which vulnerability calls (Hoffmaster, 2006). Research has confirmed that the original impetus for advance care planning is correct: most people opt for comfort care and not for doing everything (Silveira et al., 2010). As described above, research also suggests that most people are more interested in the overall goals of care than in specific treatment choices and that they often want to defer to their surrogates and even their doctors to make those specific decisions. We also know that the burdens of making decisions for another can be very great, especially if the outcome is death. Such burdens also interfere with the quality of caring.

When these features are combined with the problems identified in the medical care setting—for example, its hierarchical nature and its rational and curative orientation—we can see the foundations for a different way to structure care at the end of life. These institutions are not designed to give the support and attention that Mrs. Jones' children want and need. There are few, if any, opportunities to join the language of expertise with the language of experience, the very particularistic narrative of this patient and her "failure to thrive."

Joanne Lynn (2005) takes up the challenge by moving much decision-making out of individual control. She argues instead for "mass customization," which "aims to define manageable populations with similar needs and then engineers services that match the size of that population and its predictable needs" (S16). She identifies three trajectories: "long maintenance of good function . . . with a few weeks or months of rapid decline" leading to death (mostly as the result of cancer); slow decline in physical capacities punctuated by serious exacerbations, with death often coming rather suddenly (generally conditions like heart failure and emphysema); and "long-term dwindling of function, needing years of personal care" with death coming from "physiological challenge that would have been a minor annoyance later in life" (no single condition, although half the patients are cognitively impaired). With advances in prevention and treatment, the third trajectory will become increasingly common. Thus, for Lynn, caring at the end of life becomes an issue of systems design, which would automatically give people what they need in the absence of strongly expressed alternative wishes, rather than focusing on foregoing life-sustaining treatment or decision-by-decision choices. She outlines a series of steps that constitute a reform agenda designed to make the last of life as "meaningful and comfortable as possible at a cost the community can sustain" (p. S18).

We presume that surrogates take their responsibilities seriously and that this sense of responsibility makes the burden of deciding substantial. They may be more comfortable in addressing their responsibilities collaboratively and in the presence of identified pathways and predetermined default positions. If end-of-life care is focused on populations rather than individuals, with the foundational question of what needs dying persons generally have, and how we can design a health care delivery system that will meet those needs, then there is a chance that care can improve (Murray & Jennings, 2005, p. S54).

In some ways, this approach would treat end-of-life care similarly to how some hospitals treat abortion. It is not about individual choice but about hospital policy. Thus, an institution may adopt the trajectory approach that Lynn proposes and while it may be overridden, to do so, one would need ethics committee approval. This request could come from physicians, patients or families. If an override is not granted the care may not be paid for but it will not be denied. For clinicians, these approaches might lead to actions that are not their first choices but they are not necessarily integrity-effacing (Goodstein, 2000). There are a range of acceptable options that do not cross inviolable lines but reflect a diversity of morally acceptable alternatives. To live in such a world calls for the virtues of reasonableness, patience, and open-mindedness at a time when these virtues may be in short supply; and a process of "democratic deliberation" (Thompson, 1999) where the deliberators broadly reflect the diversity of the people who populate our health care institutions. Developing guidelines is itself a critically important process for which a community-wide discussion would seem to be essential (Callahan, 2002).

Yet, given norms in the United States that are so strongly committed to individual decision-making and choice, we believe it is unlikely that Lynn's (2005) recommendations will be adopted. What we like about her approach, in particular, is that it removes micro-managing decisions from individuals and surrogates so that attention can be focused on critically important needs that are not about decisions. While we think it is worth exploring this approach in a pilot study, we turn at this point to several more incremental recommendations.

The answer for some may come through better advance care planning—strengthening and improving documents while emphasizing the discussions that are prior to the signing of a directive and that continue as the person's condition changes. This approach involves intensifying efforts to have more people sign them while working in the medical setting to assure that directives are honored. POLST is one move in this direction. To improve advance care planning, well-trained personnel with standardized, visible forms (like POLST) that are actionable and timed are critically important (Hickman et al., 2005). So, too, are "ongoing evaluation and quality improvement" (p. S30). Gillick (2010), while critical of standard approaches to advance care planning, suggests that such planning can work more effectively if it is transformed "from the act of signing a form to a process that begins by clarifying the patient's current health status, moves to the elicitation of the goals of care, and then designates a proxy to work with clinicians in interpreting and implementing these goals" (Lo & Steinbrook, 2004 as cited by Gillick, p. 1240).

As we think of improving advance care planning, we also need to ask what we can learn from studies indicating that people often do not wish to exert control over specific decisions. With such studies in mind (see Hawkins et al., 2005), planning can focus less on specific treatment choices and more on the person's psychological, emotional, and cognitive needs, their families' embrace and, even for some, the preference to delegate decision-making to "loved ones or medical professionals" (Hawkins, et al., 2005, p. 108). Thus, one need is to find ways to incorporate a richer, more complex understanding of how individuals wish to express their autonomy even if, ironically, it means delegating decisions to others. Flexibility, more individualized styles of planning, and approaches that would suggest "how much authority patients want surrogates to have ... and to communicate a wider scope of values and goals ..". might ease the burden of responsibility and make patients feel more comfortable with advance care planning (Hawkins et al., 2005, p. 116). The goals of advance care planning would focus not only on the very end of life when ventilators or feeding tubes are at issue but it would consider "the many decisions affecting how patients live during the final stage of life" (Gillick, 2010, p. 1239). Training for medical personnel, social workers, and attorneys would also need to work toward loosening the "clear and convincing" standard of proof of what patients would have wanted. Certainty may come at a heavy price, isolating the patient and hindering realization of what he/she might find most important.

In rethinking advance care planning, we would also need to find ways to accommodate individuals and families who do not name a proxy and favor instead collective decision-making. No one should face unending treatment just because there is no evidence of advance care planning. We would need to work with families who never had a discussion with their dying loved one. State surrogacy laws can help here but, as Murray and Jennings (2005) point out, these procedural strategies evade the question, what "substantive standard should govern end of life care decision-making?" (p. S56). Yet, this autonomy-driven society has evaded the question of which standard to adopt. Research in the micro-communities of meaning that we described in Chapter 4 might be a good place to raise questions about possible substantive standards.

We offer several other recommendations. Continued development of palliative care services is important. Medicare and private insurance should adequately cover such services. Coverage should also allow for continuity of care so that one physician sees the patient through to the end. Patients may have the formal right to information but that right is not meaningful unless they have the ability to get that information in a timely and understandable way. To back up this physician support, it is important that medical schools, residency programs, and other educational programs do what Chen (2007) and Lo (1995) and others have recommended—teach end-of-life care, monitor how it is done and reinforce that teaching through mentoring. Given the communication and interpretative barriers that often exist between patients, surrogates and medical personnel, we further recommend that hospitals provide what, for lack of a better term, we are calling "interpreters." These individuals' responsibilities would include facilitating discussions between patients and/or families and the physician or medical care team so that jargon is reframed, statistics reinterpreted in lay terms, and communication enhanced. And, lastly, we recommend that a consensus panel or other deliberative group re-consider the ways in which the dominant approach to advance care planning can be modified. Modifications would be based on the growing number of studies that are documenting the problems with advanced care planning and the lack of concordance between their dominant goals and the values of the individuals to whom they apply.

CONCLUSION

We take for granted that pain relief is essential. We also have suggested that not all pain can be relieved and that suffering is inevitable. Even in the best of all possible worlds, pain and suffering are likely to accompany acute illness, chronic illness and the dying process. It is for this reason that physician aid in dying will not go away as a philosophical and political issue. We have supported hospice and palliative care as strong but under-utilized means of providing good care to both patients and family members. But we have been most critical of how the question about end-of-life care has been framed as one about patient control. From that challenge, we have examined—and found wanting—the related assumptions on which standard approaches to advance care planning have been developed. Such a model devalues the rational and independent decision-maker and not the vulnerable, often dependent, perhaps fearful and confused person and his or her surrogates who are also vulnerable and reliant on others. With our understanding of people as essentially relational, developing their identity and values from the contextual features of their lives, we take as essential the continuity of relationships and care as central to whatever chances for well-being remain for people nearing death.

Hence, we have proposed different approaches to advance care planning that start with a "bottom-up" understanding of what is important to people who may differ from one another in very important ways rather than starting from the ethical ideal of autonomy and control. We have called for a commitment of funding sources, hospitals, and physicians to being with patients and, if necessary, to be accompanied by an "interpreter" of medical language into more familiar language. In the most radical departure we have argued for removing many treatment choices from the hands of individuals and families as a way to step outside a task-orientation that the need to make decisions imposes. Such freedom can open space and time for expressing feelings and demonstrating love and care. This approach would still leave opportunities for discussion with family, friends and physicians of what was important to the patient because even a preference for comfort care may mean different things to different people. We favor it for a variety of reasons. Although, cultural differences would call for particular sensitivity, this approach acknowledges the dying trajectory and at that point ceases trying to "fix" even fixable pathologies. It does not force individuals and/or surrogates to interpret what they are being told about potential for benefit when they lack the expertise to do the assessment that is most likely needed. Relieving individuals and families of the minutiae of micro and macro decision-making frees them to rub lotion on dry feet and to do whatever else is wanted and needed to bring a life to a close. It permits them to focus on the significance of such a time without being diverted by the need to make choices that probably matter little in the end. It leaves no one person responsible for choosing or permitting another to die; thus the moral burden is shared.

REFERENCES

Angell, M. (1997). The Supreme Court and physician-assisted suicide—The ultimate right. *The New England Journal of Medicine, 336*(1), 50–53.

Arras, J. (1995). Conflicting interests in long-term care decision making: Acknowledging, dissolving, and resolving conflicts among elders and families. In L. McCullough & N. Wilson (Eds.), *Ethical and conceptual dimensions of long-term care decision making.* Baltimore, MD: Johns Hopkins Press.

Blackhall, L., Murphy, S., Frank, G., Michel, V., & Azeb, S. (1995). Ethnicity and attitudes toward patient autonomy. *Journal of the American Medical Association, 274,* 820–825.

Braun, U., Beyeth, R., Ford, M., & McCullough, L. (2007). Voices of African-American, Caucasian, and Hispanic surrogates on the burden of end of life decision-making. *Journal of General Internal Medicine, 23*(3), 267–274.

Brink, S. (2009). Bunny's last days: When living will isn't enough. www.msnbc.com. Retrieved on 2/27/2010. Reprinted from kaiserhealthnews.com.

Callahan, D. (2002). A commentary-Putting autonomy in its place: Developing effective guidelines. *The gerontologist 42,* special issue III: 129–131.

Caplan, A. (2004). An unnatural process: Why it is not inherently wrong to seek a cure for aging. In S. Post & R. Binstock (Eds.), *The fountain of youth: Cultural, scientific, and ethical perspectives on a biomedical goal.* New York: Oxford University Press.

Chen, P. (2007). *Final exam: A surgeon's reflections on mortality.* New York, NY: Vintage Books.

Clift, E. (2008). *Two weeks of life: A memoir of love, death, and politics.* New York, NY: Basic Books.

Christakis, N. (1991). Too quietly into the night. *BMJ, 337,* 326.

Dodds, S. (2007). Depending on care: Recognition of vulnerability and the social contribution of care provision. *Bioethics, 21*(9), 500–510.

Drought, T., & Koenig, B. (2002). Choice in end-of-life decision making: Researching fact or fiction? *The Gerontologist, 42*(Special Issue III), 114–128.

Dubler, N. (2005). Conflict and consensus at the end of life. Improving end-of-life care: Why has it been so difficult? *Hastings Center Report Special Report, 35*(6), S19–S25.

Dula, A. (1994). African-American's suspicion of the healthcare system is justified. What can we do about it? *Cambridge Quarterly of Healthcare Ethics, 3*(3), 347–357.

Dunn, P., Tolle, S., Moss, A., & Black, J. (2007). The POLST paradigm: Respecting the wishes of patients and families. *Annals of Long-Term Care, 15*(9), 33–40.

Foley, K. (2005). The past and future of palliative care. Improving end-of-life care: Why has it been so difficult? *Hastings Center Report Special Report, 35*(6), S42–S46.

Gillick, M. (2006). *The denial of aging: Perpetual youth, eternal life, and other dangerous fantasies.* Cambridge, MA: Harvard University Press.

Gillick, M. (2010). Reversing the code status of advance directives? *New England Journal of Medicine, 362*(13), 1239–1240.

Goodstein, J. (2000). Moral compromise and personal integrity: Exploring the ethical issues of deciding together in organizations. *Business Ethics Quarterly, 10*(4), 805–819.

Guillemin, J. (1995). Planning to die. In C. Weaver & A. Strauss (Eds.), *Where medicine fails* (5th ed.) (pp. 73–82). New Brunswick, NJ: Transaction Books.

Hawkins, N., Ditto, P., Danks, J., & Smucker, W. (2005). Micromanaging death: Process preferences, values, and goals in end-of-life medical decision making. *The Gerontologist, 45*, 107–117.

Hickman, S. (2005). Cited in Dunn, P., Tolle, S., Moss, A., & Black, J. (2007). The POLST paradigm: Respecting the wishes of patients and families. *Annals of Long-Term Care, 15*(9), 33–40.

Hickman, S., Hammes, B., Moss, A., & Tolle, S. (2005). Hope for the future: Achieving the original intent of advance directives. Improving end-of-life care: Why has it been so difficult? *Hastings Center Report Special Report, 35*(6), S26–S30.

High, D. (1991). A new myth about families of older people. *Gerontologist, 31*(5), 611–618.

Hoffmaster, B. (2006). What does vulnerability mean? *Hastings Center Report, 36*(2), 38–45.

Holstein, M. (1997a). Reflections on death and dying. *Academic Medicine, 72*(10), 848–855.

Holstein, M. (1997b). Alzheimer's disease and senile dementia, 1885–1920: An interpretive history of disease negotiation. *Journal of Aging Studies, 11*, 1–13.

Holstein, M. (2002). Facing death: An essay on Susan. *AAHPM Bulletin, 2*(3), 6–7, 9.

Howarth, G. (1998). 'Just live for today'. Living, caring, ageing and dying. *Ageing and Society, 18*, 673–689.

Kaufman, S. (2000). Senescence, decline, and the quest for a good death: Contemporary dilemmas and historical antecedents. *Journal of Aging Studies, 14*(1), 1–23.

Kittay, E. F. (1999). *Love's labor: Essays on women, equality, and dependency.* New York: Routledge.

Krakauer, E., Crenner, C., & Fox, K. (2002). Barriers to optimum end-of-life care for minority patients. *Journal of the American Geriatrics Society, 50*, 182–190.

Lemay, E., Pruchno, R., Levinsky, N., & Field, L. (2004). Predictors of patient preferences and surrogate perceptions: Implications for the inaccuracy of substituted judgment. *The Gerontologist, 44*, 524.

Lo, B. (1995). Improving care near the end of life: Why is it so hard? *JAMA, 274* (20), 1634–1636.

Lo, B. & Steinbrook, R. (2004). Resuscitating advance directives. *Archives of Internal Medicine, 164*(14), 1501–1506.

Lynn, J. (2005). Living long in fragile health: The new demographics shape end of life care. Improving end of life care: Why has it been so difficult? *Hastings Center Report Special Report, 35*(6), S14–S18.

Marshall, P. (1995). The SUPPORT study: Who's talking. *Hastings Center Report, 25*(6 Suppl.), S9–S11.

Morton, B. (1998). *Starting out in the evening.* New York: Berkley Books.

Murray, T., & Jennings, B. (2005). The quest to reform end of life care: Rethinking assumptions and setting new directions. Improving end of life care: Why has it been so difficult? *Hastings Center Report Special Report, 35*(6), S52–S57.

Quill, T. (1991). Death and dignity: A case of individualized decision making. *The New England Journal of Medicine, 324*(10), 691–694.

Rein, M. (1983). Value-critical policy analysis. In D. Callahan & B. Jennings (Eds.), *Ethics, the social sciences, and policy analysis* (pp. 83–112). New York, NY: Plenum Press.

Shalowitz, D., Garrett-Mayer, E., & Wendler, D. (2006). The accuracy of surrogate decision makers: A systematic review. *Archives of Internal Medicine, 166,* 493–497.

Silveira, M., Kim, S., & Langa, K. (2010). Advance directives and outcomes of surrogate decision making before death. *New England Journal of Medicine, 362*(13), 1211–1218.

Teno, J., Grunier, A., Schwartz,, Nanda, A., & Wetle, T. (2007). Association between advance directives and quality end-of-life care. *Journal of the American Geriatrics Society, 55,* 189–194.

Thompson, D. (1999). The institutional turn in professional ethics. *Ethics and Behavior, 92*(2), 109–118.

Winzelberg, G., Hanson, L., & Tulsky, J. (2005). Beyond autonomy: Diversifying end-of-life decision-making approaches to serve patients and families. *Journal of the American Geriatrics Society, 53,* 1046–1050.

CHAPTER 13

Aging and Disasters

Facing Natural and Other Disasters

Bryan Kibbe[1]

... So the day of the storm, we are just sitting down and listening to it. We didn't know really what was going to happen. The neighbors and all we were just kind of out on the porch. And all of a sudden somebody called us on the phone and said, "Y'all better leave, the levees is broke!" I didn't listen, I thought, "That fool don't know a thing." The levees were all the way out in the east, and it just don't flood here. So I said, "We're staying." We just kept on the porch talking and after a while somebody said, "The water is coming down Claiborne off the overpass?" What? "The water's just at Magnolia Street," which is just three blocks this way. We all jumped up and I said, "Margie, this sounds bad."
... Well I knew I didn't want to go in no helicopter, I thought, I'm not going. I refuse to go to the Superdome, because I remember the past in the Superdome. I said, "I'm not going there." First place, I can't stand up that much. I'm not crippled, but I got arthritis. Where am I going to go to the bathroom? I decided I'm staying home ...

This is the testimony of Miss Janine, 84 years old, widowed, and a resident of New Orleans since she was 17, as she describes her experience during Hurricane Katrina, which led to the deaths of 1800 people (as recorded by Croom et al., 2007).

While natural and human caused disasters are a tragedy for all, it is often the elderly who disproportionately suffer to a greater degree amidst them. In the first part of this chapter we will examine the ways in which catastrophic disasters of the 21st century have been a particular burden for the elderly. To

---

[1]Bryan Kibbe is a doctoral student in the Department of Philosophy, Loyola University, Chicago. He works in bioethics with a special interest in technology and its implications for human life.

this end, we strive to bring out the sense in which the elderly are a population of people susceptible to additional and compound harms during a major disaster. In the second section of the chapter we move to consider specific ethical obligations to the elderly prior to and during a major disaster. The two primary ethical obligations that we highlight therein are an obligation to responsible planning prior to a disaster taking place and also an obligation to promote and maintain effective communication and collaboration both in planning for and responding to a major disaster. In an effort to further specify these broad obligations, we introduce an ethics of place holding, which draws on the work of Hilde Lindemann (2002, 2009) and Iris Marion Young (1997) that helps to attune us to the subtleties of carrying out planning, communication, and collaboration that is meaningful for the elderly. In the final section we offer some concrete recommendations for future enlightened disaster planning that is attentive to the unique needs of the elderly in the midst of catastrophic disasters.

THE SITUATION

A catastrophic disaster is a natural or human-caused event that afflicts a specific geographic region and causes considerable loss of human life, extensive injury, and/or displacement from homes. While we may anticipate such events in their general form (i.e., a hurricane), the particular circumstances (i.e., the levees breaking during the Hurricane Katrina in New Orleans) make them unexpected and surprising to the people afflicted (Zach, 2009). Accordingly, when we imagine the events that this definition picks out, we would include things like typhoons, floods, mudslides, snowstorms, wildfires, terrorist attacks, tornados, hurricanes, tsunamis, bridges collapsing, earthquakes, heat waves, and cold waves. It has been the unfortunate fact that in the first 10 years of this 21st century, we as a global community, have collectively witnessed that all of these kinds of disasters take place, sometimes repeatedly, and often with devastating results to entire countries and regions of the world.

While catastrophic disasters have occurred throughout human history, it is, perhaps, helpful to consider some of the most horrific tragedies of the past decade (though by no means is it an exhaustive list). On September 11th of 2001, the United States faced a devastating terrorist attack that destroyed the twin towers of the World Trade Center as well as a portion of the Pentagon, and led to more than 2,600 deaths (The National Commission on Terrorist Attacks, 2004). During the summer of 2003, across Europe, particularly in France, a heat wave led to the death of approximately 15,000 people (Bouchama, 2004; Fouillet et al., 2006). In 2004, a tsunami struck southeast

Asia (India, Indonesia, Sri Lanka, and Thailand) and resulted in the death of more than 225,000 individuals, while maiming another half a million people (Brunner, n.d., "Tsunami Factfile"). During hurricane season in the United States in 2005, Hurricane Katrina devastated New Orleans and caused the deaths of 1,800 people, while displacing a million people from their homes (Brunner, n.d., "Hurricane Katrina"). In 2007, monsoon rains in South Asia killed more than 1,000 people, and displaced millions from their homes (Wax, 2007). In 2008, an earthquake in China caused substantial infrastructure failure, and about 70,000 people were killed (Chan, 2008). In 2010, we witnessed massive earthquakes in both Haiti and in Chile. While numbers still remain uncertain at this time, it appears that more than 200,000 people were killed in Haiti, where infrastructure failure was particularly acute ("Haiti's Situation Still Dire," 2010). It is difficult to even comprehend these staggering statistics, but then, they are not merely statistics; they speak about the tragic deaths of individual human beings who were grandparents, brothers, sisters, friends, spouses, mothers, fathers, sons, and daughters. As such, there are countless narratives, such as that of Miss Janine offered at the beginning of this chapter, that can be told and woven into this macroscopic view of the some of the worst disasters of the past 10 years.

One particular narrative that is relevant for our purposes here is that of elderly individuals, in general, amidst these catastrophic disasters. Nora O'Brien (2003) has observed that within the 24 hours following the September 11th terrorist attacks, "animal advocates were on the scene rescuing pets, yet abandoned older and disabled people waited for up to seven days for an ad hoc medical team to rescue them" (p. 1). One elderly woman living in the area surrounding the World Trade Center reported that many disabled elderly from her building found themselves in the lobby waiting for rescue along with many able-bodied young people, but when the buses arrived the younger people quickly got on the buses, leaving the elderly behind (Lagnado, 2001). She says, "We [the elderly] were down first. We were the last to be taken away" (Lagnado, 2001).

During the European heat wave, which killed nearly 15,000 people alone in France, almost 12,000 of those deaths were elderly individuals (defined as 75 years of age and older in the study) (Fouillet et al., 2006). Thus, nearly 80% of those that died during the heat wave were individuals over the age of 75. Amidst the European heat wave, a syndicated columnist, William Pfaff (2003), in a shockingly insensitive comment, wrote, "... The old people taken away during this European heat wave, like the 500 to 700 who died in the Chicago heat wave of 1995, were not, most of them, killed by heat. The time had come for them to die, and the heat eased their way. We should all be so fortunate ..." (p. A19).

When the tsunami struck Southeast Asia in 2004, among those displaced from their homes and in need of food and care were 92,000 people over the age of 60 (Mudur, 2005). Yet, many of these individuals failed to receive necessary food, care, or financial support because the specific needs of the elderly were not taken into account in dispensing relief aid (Mudur, 2005). In their report (2005) on the situation of the elderly following the tsunami, HelpAge International observed that when relief aid was distributed in often chaotic settings, the younger and stronger pushed elderly out of the way to obtain the limited supplies (HelpAge International, 2005, p. 7).

As many have observed (Elmore and Brown, 2007; Polivka-West, 2009; Rothman and Brow, 2007) the elderly only accounted for 15% of the population of New Orleans before the Hurricane Katrina, yet they constituted 70% of the nearly 1,800 deaths that resulted from the hurricane. Of the 53 nursing home facilities in the New Orleans area, 70% of them were never evacuated (Brunner, n.d., "Hurricane Katrina"). Included in that 70% was the tragic case of St. Rita's Nursing Home, where the owners and operators, Sal and Mabel Mangano, chose not to evacuate their population of frail elders, instead believing that they could weather the storm in place (Fahey, 2007). But when rapid flooding commenced, the staff and administrators were unprepared, and while able to pull some patients onto the roof, 35 patients drowned in their beds on the floors below (Fahey, 2007).

Although we have no definitive numbers yet about the tragic earthquake in Haiti, various groups and individuals (see Booth, 2010; "Haiti: Don't forget the elderly," 2010; Urbina, 2010) have already begun calling attention to the marginalization of the elderly in relief efforts. Some tentative numbers suggest that among the 1.2 million displaced from their homes by the earthquake, 7%, or 84,000 of those individuals are elderly (Urbina, 2010). One elderly Haitian man lamented, "It's as if everybody has forgotten us [the elderly], nobody cares, or maybe they really just do want us to starve to death" (Associated Press, 2010). In a recapitulation of some of the same problems that the elderly faced following the tsunami in 2004, relief packages are often poorly designed for the elderly. An aid worker from HelpAge International underscores this issue in Haiti by asking, "Does it really make sense to ask a 70-year-old to carry a 50-kilo bag of rice or to wait in line for two hours?" (Urbina, 2010). In another example of poorly designed relief aid for the elderly, early food packages provided soy-enriched bulgur wheat, but this proved difficult for some elderly individuals to digest, and forced cooks and caretakers to find food elsewhere (Booth, 2010).

A consistent narrative begins to take shape—the elderly represent a profoundly marginalized population amidst major disasters. From the highly developed world to the developing world, in rich countries and in poor ones, following natural and human-caused disasters, responses routinely overlook or under serve the elderly population. In some cases this problem manifested itself as a failure to effectively plan for rescuing large numbers of people who have special needs, or, following a disaster, to distribute aid in a way that respects the special needs of many elderly individuals. In other cases, there appeared a more explicitly ageist dynamic, where the needs and wellbeing of society's elderly, particularly the frail elderly, were ignored or denigrated, as was indicated by the comments of William Pfaff (2003). Thus, whether explicit or implicit, intentional or unintentional, recognized or not, there currently exists a perfect storm of factors that consistently lead to the marginalization of elderly individuals throughout the world, particularly during catastrophic disasters.

Thus far in this chapter, we have avoided using the term "vulnerable" to describe the elderly, although to all appearances this precisely describes the elderly amidst major disasters. While during nondisaster circumstances it is customary, and even helpful, to talk about the elderly in terms of their vulnerability to certain abuses, this simply will not suffice in the context of discussions about catastrophic disaster. Part of the very definition of a disaster is that it is not wholly predictable; various iterations of disaster can strike *any* group of people in *any* region of the world at *any* time. Thus, in thinking about and anticipating disasters, we must recognize that we are all vulnerable human beings. Accordingly, if we attempt to describe the elderly as vulnerable in the context of discussions about catastrophic disaster, we will not be picking out anything unique about their situation, since we are all vulnerable to catastrophic disaster. This can lead us to then ignore the special needs of elderly populations, as we mistakenly imagine that we are all vulnerable in precisely the same way. While it is true that we share a common human situation in the face of disaster, the elderly exhibit a unique situation over and above a shared sense of vulnerability during disasters.

Michael Kottow (2003) offers us a solution by distinguishing between vulnerability and susceptibility. All human beings, he argues, share in a sense of vulnerability, but some of those vulnerable individuals exhibit an increased susceptibility to harm. As he puts it,

> ... the vulnerable are intact but at risk, in the same way a fine piece of porcelain is unblemished but highly vulnerable to being damaged. The susceptible are already injured, they already suffer from some deficiency that handicaps them, renders them defenceless and predisposed to further injury; their wounds lower the threshold to additional suffering.
>
> —*Kottow, 2003, p. 464*

We think that this distinction adds an important insight into the situation of the elderly during catastrophic disasters. Not only are the elderly vulnerable to harm, but also they are, more especially, susceptible to harm. Even if all other things are equal during disaster, harms to the elderly will often result in more complex and extensive pain and suffering. However, there is a need to qualify Kottow's distinction slightly in order to make the best use of it.

It is possible to read Kottow as suggesting that an individual is either susceptible or not susceptible. This is a binary understanding of susceptibility in which the individual is all or nothing. As we discussed in Chapter 1, this disposition towards binary thinking has shaped the reading of autonomy. An individual is often understood to be either autonomous or not autonomous; the switch is, so to speak, "on" or "off." However, binary understandings applied to moral reasoning concerning human beings are often problematic because human beings are highly complex creatures that display a wide range of behaviors and characteristics across the space of their days, weeks, years, and lives. Instead, we have advocated for adopting an approach to autonomy that conceptualizes autonomy as existing on a spectrum of being more or less autonomous depending on certain formative skills and abilities that an individual is able to deploy at any given time. In similar fashion, we suggest conceptualizing susceptibility along a spectrum of being more or less susceptible to harm given certain axes of susceptibility. These axes of susceptibility point to distinctive characteristics that raise the potential for harm during a catastrophic disaster. The primary axes of susceptibility[2] are:

1. Physical impairments—a distinctive aspect of aging is the decline of physical abilities. This will often involve "impaired balance, poor exercise tolerance, decreased motor strength, and . . . [the loss of] The ability to walk, travel outside the home, eat, use the telephone . . ." or the performance of similar activities as one ages (Fernandez et al., 2002, p. 69). These features make it substantially more difficult for elderly individuals to avoid danger during a disaster, most notably in escaping falling objects or otherwise evacuating spaces, particularly if there is no electricity to power necessary assistance devices such as elevators or electronic wheelchairs (Fernandez et al., 2002).

---

[2]These axes of susceptibility are primarily informed by the general categories utilized in Fernandez's macro analysis of research studies regarding the elderly amidst disaster (see Fernandez, Byard, Lin, Benson, & Barbera, 2002).

2. Chronic illnesses—many elderly suffer from one or more chronic diseases such as arthritis, hypertension, heart disease, diabetes, and respiratory disorders that require careful management involving assistive devices, medications, and/or the support of health professionals (Aldrich and Benson, 2008). During a major disaster, the lack of electricity to power such things as respiratory assistance devices, or road closures that prohibit access to regular visits from health professionals or the opportunity to refill prescriptions can jeopardize the stability of an elderly person's chronic disease management, which can then lead to more acute complications (Aldrich and Benson, 2008; Fernandez et al., 2002; Mokdad et al., 2005). Additionally, when elderly individuals are evacuated without their medications or health records detailing prescriptions and treatment protocols, they can also suffer from complications involving the improper management of their chronic conditions.

3. Aid receipt—studies show that, following disaster, the elderly have a difficult time navigating complicated bureaucracies to request aid, or, because of a perceived stigma associated with receiving aid, do not request it at all (Fernandez et al., 2002). Consequently, the elderly tend to receive less aid than younger individuals (Fernandez et al., 2002).

4. Financial vulnerability—the elderly often lack the means to recoup financial costs suffered during a catastrophic disaster (Jenkins et al., 2007). As Fernandez et al. (2002) observe, "Elderly [individuals] have fewer opportunities and less ability to generate income, are increasingly reliant on Social Security benefits, and are more likely to live near or at poverty level than are the non-elderly" (p. 70). As a result, following a disaster, many elderly may suffer significant reduction in their standard of living (Fernandez et al., 2002).

5. Social isolation—where a spouse, partner, family member or friend can be a significant source of support during a disaster, the likelihood of living with another person decreases with age (Fernandez et al., 2002). This may substantially isolate individuals from their community, if they are known at all, or make them increasingly dependent on outside support from various aging network services. In either case, the lack of immediate support during a major disaster can significantly exacerbate a sense of helplessness among the elderly who are still living in their own homes.

6. Diminished sensory awareness—as age increases, sensory abilities decrease as well, often leading to reduced vision or hearing-impairment (Fernandez et al., 2002). Diminished sensory awareness can interfere with the ability to detect or hear warnings of approaching danger, and subsequently to avoid hazards (Fernandez et al., 2002).

7. Limited access to transportation—whether due to physical impairments, chronic illness, or diminished sensory awareness, or for any of several other reasons, many elderly people have limited access to transportation. Where they do have access, their physical condition may require special vehicles, such as those able to accommodate a wheelchair. Some elderly may rely on public transportation services that may not be working during a major disaster. The lack of access to functional transportation can foreclose the possibility of evacuation for many elderly individuals.

Importantly, the elderly population in any given region and throughout the world is not homogenous. Different individuals will experience varying degrees along these axes of susceptibility, especially as they age. Additionally, while outside this chapter's scope but addressed elsewhere in this book, considerations of intersectional identity along the lines of race, economic class, and gender will deepen the degree to which these primary axes of susceptibility are experienced by any individual, because, as Naomi Zach (2009) has observed, disaster magnifies already existing social inequality (p. 108).

This attention to intersectional identity alerts us to the fact that these axes of susceptibility are at least partially conditioned by social circumstances. As Simone de Beauvoir (1989) has observed, while it may be a biological fact that most females have less muscle mass and accordingly less raw physical strength than males, this fact is only significant in a society that chooses to put a priority on physical strength as the means to being admired or successful (p. 34). Similarly, in a society that values youth, physical strength, and independence, these primary axes of susceptibility by which the elderly often suffer additional harms will prove still more substantial. In this way, the degree of susceptibility that the elderly face amidst disaster should not be regarded as their responsibility alone. Susceptibility to harm is a burden that an individual bears, but which is created and sustained through the mutual interactions of that individual and the society they live in. Accordingly, there is no room for blaming the victim in this analysis of our ethical obligations to the elderly amidst catastrophic disaster.

In fact, despite the overwhelming attention thus far to the particular susceptibility of the elderly to harm during catastrophic disaster, they should not be consigned to the monolithic status of victims. Older people also display a proportional range of ability to be of service in responding to a disaster and assisting others (see HelpAge International, 2000). At the least, some older people will serve with others in performing common and necessary tasks during a disaster. Yet, beyond being just one more pair of helping hands and feet, the elderly also offer distinctive means of serving the population in virtue of their age and experience. Most notably, many of the elderly have already experienced traumatic events such as war, devastating natural disasters, or terrorist attacks. Thus, far from being only helpless victims, they bring their own memories and emotional repertoire to bear on present disasters in ways that can fortify a younger generation that has not lived through as many disasters. This will be a theme to which we return later in this chapter.

ETHICAL ANALYSIS

In order to take seriously the profound marginalization that the elderly individuals throughout the world experience during catastrophic disasters, we now consider our primary obligations to the elderly during major disasters. This portion of our discussion is not intended to identify all of our ethical duties or obligations during disasters in general, but instead those that most especially relate to the situation of the elderly. That said, we can observe two primary ethical obligations relevant to the elderly during catastrophic disasters: (1) we have an ethical obligation to prioritize and carry out planning for disasters, and (2) we have an ethical obligation to ensure effective communication and a commitment to collaboration between all those involved in responding to a disaster.

Catastrophic disasters, particularly natural ones (i.e., hurricanes, floods, wildfires, etc.), seem to be an inescapable feature of life on this world. To the extent that they are both inevitable and not wholly predictable, they will always involve tragic circumstances (loss of life, destruction of homes and belongings, etc.) that resist efforts to assign moral culpability. But to acknowledge this is not to say that any given catastrophic disaster is without its elements of moral praise and blameworthiness.

Part of what makes disasters so difficult is the often desperate lack or scarcity of necessary resources to rescue and repair all of the human lives and property that have been damaged by any given disaster. Scarce resources simply mean that there are insufficient resources (i.e., medical personnel, medications, transportation, etc.) to respond to everyone in need. Thus, governments, aid agencies, and individuals must make allocation decisions about how best to utilize the resources available. However, if not careful, it is easy to read the situation of scarce resources and the need for allocation decisions as an immutable given, and thereby an unavoidable feature of catastrophic disasters. The implication then is that we are to understand scarcity of resources on par with the impersonal and unintentional forces of disasters, particularly natural or accidental ones, thus making resource issues immune from efforts to assign moral culpability. But this would be too hasty.

Anticipatory planning can mitigate the extent to which resources are scarce during a major disaster. While all disasters involve an element of the unexpected, and will accordingly limit resources to some degree, if only in virtue of initial confusion and lack of immediate coordination, the situation is not entirely beyond human control, and, thereby, beyond the pale of moral assessment. Disasters in their specific contours can never be anticipated in their entirety; however, the persistent possibility of disaster, and the knowledge that particular types of disasters characteristically afflict certain regions of the world (i.e., hurricanes in coastal regions around or near the gulf of Mexico, wildfires in the western United States, and earthquakes in California), means that some degree of planning can take place. That is, as human beings who are vulnerable to catastrophic disasters, we need not merely respond to disasters when they occur, we can also plan for the reality that they will occur. To the degree that we can plan for certain disasters in their broad contours, we can also mitigate the extent to which resources are scarce amidst and following a catastrophic disaster. For instance, emergency responders can secure additional commitments from public and private sources to make vehicles available for transport when a disaster occurs. In this way, while scarce resources and the difficult allocation decisions that they precipitate will occur during catastrophic disasters, the degree to which they force and constrain rescue efforts can be reduced.

As human beings who are capable of planning for disaster, we have it within our power to at least potentially reduce the loss of life and damage to property through effective planning. Assuming that all human life has inherent worth and dignity, and where we are able to preserve it we should, then we must conclude that given the persistent reality of disasters, we have an ethical obligation to plan for them in such a way as to seek to mitigate or eliminate resource scarcity where it will lead to the loss of human lives. In this commitment to reduce resource scarcity through effective disaster planning, we can detect a secondary obligation to cultivate and maintain communication and collaboration between as many individuals, agencies, departments, and organizations as are necessary to save all those who have been stranded and/or maimed during a disaster.

Resource scarcity during a catastrophic disaster is often a function of time and place. While the immediate local government and emergency responders may be stressed and their resources stretched thin, higher and broader levels of response involving other levels of government, relief agencies, or neighboring communities can provide needed resources so as to diminish levels of scarcity. Hence, while disasters may precipitate a situation of limited resources, which hinders efforts to save human lives, it is not necessarily the case that the resources do not exist at all, but rather that they are "there" (i.e., elsewhere) and not "here." We will assume that when life-saving resources are available somewhere, those responding to the disaster are, at least, obligated to attempt to obtain them to the extent that their abilities and influence allow in any given situation. However, such an effort will be conditioned by already existing avenues of communication and relationships of support. Therefore, there is an ethical obligation to cultivate and maintain lines of communication and a sense of collaboration between multiple individuals, agencies, departments, and organizations so as to be able to make that attempt to contract the necessary resources. Importantly, as the ethical commitment to planning reveals, management of resources for saving human lives does not occur solely, or even principally, during disasters, and thus the commitment to communication and collaboration is as much an aspect of planning for disasters as it is during the response to any given disaster. More pointedly, where the commitment to communication and collaboration does not exist in planning for a disaster, it seems unlikely that it will spontaneously occur during a disaster. Thus, issues of communication and collaboration, like planning, attune us to what ought to happen prior to any given disaster and the moral space that opens up therein as a result.

As Zach (2009) has observed, when disasters occur, emergency responders commonly adopt a utilitarian principle of "save the greatest number of people" (p. 22). But such a principle ignores the prior susceptibility to harm that many individuals, particularly the elderly, then incur during a disaster through no additional fault of their own. A rule based on saving the greatest number of people is doggedly shortsighted in its inability to account for what takes place before and after a disaster. But, as we have strived to show here, human beings have the ability to exercise some degree of planning before disaster strikes, which takes into account the varying susceptibility of individuals to diverse harms during a disaster. Disaster forces alone do not dictate the success of our rescue efforts, but rather, through ethical commitments to planning, communication, and collaboration prior to a disaster, we can attempt to mitigate the degree to which any given community is tragically affected by disaster. In this way, Zach (2009) suggests that we adopt an alternative principle, "save all who can be saved" (p. 22). By emphasizing the rescue of all those who *can* be saved, this principle compels us to consider how preparatory efforts shape and influence who can be saved when disaster occurs. If we have failed to consider what resources will be needed to rescue everyone in a given area, we will have already, even before disaster strikes, foreclosed, or at least diminished, their possibilities of rescue. If our planning, for example, did not adequately account for people who were unable to board buses on their own, then, in practice, they would not be among those who could be saved.

This discussion is important for older people because it attempts to make morally significant the preparation for disasters. Through attention to competent planning, elderly people have the most to gain, since by the time a disaster strikes, emergency responders are often awash in a sea of vulnerable people and thus are unable to account for the specific susceptibility of the elderly to additional harms during a disaster. This relative blindness is the result of focusing largely on response to rather than preparation for a disaster. Ethical analysis of disasters, if it is to be significant in reducing the marginalization of the elderly must place an emphasis on the temporal space before disaster strikes when good planning, communication, and collaboration can be attempted and, hopefully, enacted.

As it is, though, there is often a tendency in disaster ethics (see, e.g., Johnstone, 2009 or Veatch, 2005) to focus too much on matters of triage at the expense of other important ethical considerations (i.e., what populations of people need to be named and addressed directly in disaster response plans). Triage means that when there are scarce resources, we adopt systems of ranking and evaluation to determine who will be saved when not all can be saved (see Kuschner et al., 2007; Pesik et al., 2001; Veatch, 2005). As can be easily imagined, triage often leads to tragic choices that entail the loss of some lives in order to save others. Such was certainly the case in New Orleans when Memorial Hospital, engulfed by floodwaters during Hurricane Katrina, required an evacuation. However, evacuation was slow and limited in terms of transportation; therefore, hospital administrators mandated a system of triage in which patients were ranked and prioritized to determine when they would be evacuated, if they were even assessed as being able to be evacuated (Fink, 2009). It eventually came to be that a number of frail elderly patients, who administrators decided could not be evacuated, were among the only people remaining in the hospital (Fink, 2009). At that point, a doctor, Anna Pou, and two nurses, Cheri Landry and Lori Budo, are believed to have administered high doses of morphine mixed with other drugs to at least four of the patients, which led to depressed breathing and eventually death (Fink, 2009). In 2007, Anna Pou was brought before a jury on charges of murder, but the jury ruled against indictment. The case captivated media interest, and underscored the difficult ethical situations that arise during disasters.

Indeed, this was a remarkable situation, fraught with ethical dilemmas. However, despite the tremendous media and judicial attention, it remains but one example in a larger consideration of ethical decision making in relation to disasters. As Pesik et al. (2001) observes, the act of medical triage itself requires prior thinking and planning to determine protocols in order for it to be done well (p. 642). Such considerations direct us once again to the larger act of planning for disasters, over and above merely responding to disasters. Importantly, attention to that larger ethical picture offers a better means to avoid a triage situation like that which occurred at Memorial Hospital in New Orleans. Triage with regards to medical treatment or evacuation makes it likely that the frail elderly will lose out consistently because a shortsighted view of the elderly fails to grasp their susceptibility to harm and need for special protections.

Disaster ethics can be shackled by the metaphor of lifeboat situations. Lifeboat situations are abstract thought puzzles used by moral theorists in testing the application of their moral system. Generally the puzzle involves an extreme case where the primary ethical dilemma is such that, while not all persons can be saved from impending disaster or death, some can be saved if a few are sacrificed. It then asks how a choice should be made, if there is even determined to be a choice at all. While generally used as abstract thought puzzles, catastrophic disasters often seem to involve the reenactment of these lifeboat situations. Thus, ethical analysis of disasters tends to be fixated on these kinds of cases, such as that of Memorial Hospital in New Orleans during Hurricane Katrina. But the application of abstract lifeboat situations to the real experience of catastrophic disaster is particularly detrimental to consideration of the elderly.

Simply put, whatever value lifeboat situations have in moral philosophy, they have extremely limited use, if any at all, during actual disasters. The abstract qualities of lifeboat situations, wherein people are represented simplistically and without any substantial narratives connecting them to one another and their situation, make them extremely difficult to apply to situations of actual disaster where narratives are essential elements (see our discussion of narrative ethics in Chapter 2). Therefore, whatever superficial similarities the experience of disaster may have to lifeboat situations, the rich narrative identities of all those involved in an actual disaster make a significant difference. Thus for instance, in our earlier case of Miss Janine, she was not just some generic body in the drowning lifeboat that was New Orleans during Hurricane Katrina. Instead, she was a woman who had previously endured the trials of evacuation to the Superdome, knew what evacuation entailed, was living alone, and had a profound connection to her home and the city of New Orleans where she had lived for more than 50 years. Moreover, as we have tried to show, the elderly, in addition to their own identifying narratives, are part of a broader narrative that involves their routine marginalization during disasters. Efforts to address that narrative of marginalization will not be made in the proverbial lifeboat, so to speak, or in the midst of an actual disaster. Instead, only by making important and ethically significant the preparation for disasters, where the specific susceptibility of the elderly can be addressed and remediated will we begin to take seriously our ethical obligations to the elderly during disaster.

It remains, however, to consider exactly how an ethical commitment to planning and communication in preparing for disaster can be brought to bear on the particular situation of the elderly amidst major disasters. As we have already argued, the abstract tools of traditional moral philosophy are inadequate for this situation. Instead, we need to strive to do moral philosophy on the ground, so to speak—an approach that we have recommended in several prior chapters. In planning for disasters, as in thinking about good end-of-life care or cultural norms for the third age, we have favored a "bottom up" rather than a top down way to think about ethics. Margaret Walker (2007) has similarly argued that moral philosophers must not act as though they exist over and above the moral plane, but rather they need to do moral philosophy within the moral plane of everyday existence, as we indicated in our general critique of traditional ethics in Chapter 1. In this vein, we turn to the critical appropriation of situated narratives and communities in order to focus our sense of ethical obligation to the elderly by means of a commitment to planning and communication prior to disasters. We adopt what we term an ethics of place holding, which draws from and synthesizes the work of Hilde Lindemann (2002, 2009) and Iris Marion Young (1997).[3]

In an especially interesting application of narrative thinking to ethical reasoning, Lindemann articulates what she calls "holding individuals in a sense of personhood" (Lindemann, 2002, 2009). By "holding," Lindemann means that through the narratives we tell about one another, we can responsibly or irresponsibly maintain a sense of recognition for one another as human persons (Lindemann, 2002, 2009). Lindemann discusses holding especially in cases where an individual may be severely physically and/or cognitively impaired, such that he cannot, on his own, articulate a narrative immediately recognizable as a personal one (Lindemann, 2002, 2009). In such cases, families and friends become instrumental in holding such an individual in personhood by telling stories to and about that individual that convey a sense of respect for her dignity as a person. Recently,

---

[3]Lindemann herself specifically gestures to this synthesis (i.e., Lindemann & Young) in her most recent work on holding persons in a sense of identity or personhood (see Lindemann, 2009).

Lindemann has brought this sense of holding to bear on the case of elderly individuals who suffer from various stages of dementia, though especially Alzheimer's disease (Lindemann, 2009). When our brains begin to fail us, we become increasingly dependent on caring others in our lives to help maintain our sense of personhood, that is, to hold us in our identities when we cannot do so all on our own. While the act of holding one another in personhood may be firmest when individuals are especially dependent, we ought to remember that, as many feminist thinkers have observed, the image of heroically independent individuals is a myth that runs contrary to the experience of dependence on one another that we all have as human beings throughout our lives (see our discussion in the chapters on Home Care and End-of-Life Care). Hence, holding takes place to varying degrees throughout an individual's life, though given our discussion about an older person's susceptibility to compounded harm, it is likely that holding may be more pronounced in old age.

Where Lindemann has sought to draw attention to how other people can help to hold us in our personhood through stories told by and about us, Iris Marion Young (1997) has emphasized the role that our dwelling places can have in holding us in our sense of personhood or identity. Conscious of the traditional injustices that have often been perpetuated against women in the home, Young (1997) presents a careful account in which she acknowledges the potential for abuses in the home, but then goes on to regard the home as assuming an invaluable and positive role in maintaining our sense of identity. As she observes, we structure our homes not in just any way, but rather in ways that reflect how we, as concrete and specific individuals, live, think, and remember. She remarks:

> The home is not simply the things, however, but their arrangement in space in a way that supports the body habits and routines of those who dwell there. The arrangement of furniture in space provides pathways for habits—the reading lamp placed just here, the television just here, the particular spices on the rack placed just so in relation to this person's taste and cooking habits.
>
> —Young, 1997, p. 150

As human beings, she argues, we are not merely brains or bodies alone, but our chosen and personally shaped environments become an extension of ourselves as well. In this way, the dynamic of homemaking, as Young observes, is immeasurably deep insofar as individuals use their dwelling places as means to preserve their identities (1997). But this is not to imply a static picture wherein the individual merely records personal tastes, memories, and preferences in or on the built environment; rather, the relationship between person and home is dynamic. Thinking and remembering happens between and amidst the physically embodied person and his carefully structured living space as though a conversation is taking place (Young, 1997).

Drawing Lindemann and Young together, we begin to see what we might call an ethics of place holding. This is an ethics that is deeply attuned to the ways in which we as human beings depend on one another and on our physical dwelling spaces to help us to tell, reinterpret, and retell stories about ourselves in such a way as to maintain our personhood or identity. But dependency here does not indicate anything abnormal or deficient; instead, it refers to our natural finitude and the extent to which brains or bodies alone cannot provide the kind of robust human experience that we all need and desire. While the act of place holding may become more explicit or firm at different points in one's life, such as during childhood or among the oldest old or frail elderly, it nonetheless remains a constant throughout life.

It is this kind of ethics that helps us to address the particular tragedy facing the nation of Haiti and its elderly population during the devastating earthquake in 2010. In Haiti, 50% of the population is under the age of 20, while only a small 3% are over the age of 65 ("Haiti," CIA Factbook). As a result, Haiti's elderly may be considered a "national resource" (Urbina, 2010). These few elderly individuals serve as the collective memory for a nation that has so many young who may not yet know that country's tremendous history (Urbina, 2010). Accordingly, in addition to being held in their own identities and personhood by caregivers and physical dwelling spaces, the elderly also hold the young in their sense of identity or personhood by maintaining a historical narrative. Yet, amidst the earthquake, which killed more than 200,000 people and maimed and/or displaced many more, it was the elderly, especially those with special needs, who suffered particularly deeply. Thus, despite their important role in anchoring the identities of other individuals and communities that together constitute the nation of Haiti, if special efforts are not taken to protect the elderly in their susceptibility to increased harms during a disaster, then they suffer substantially. An ethics of place holding highlights the extent to which the elderly are not just some population of people within the larger community of people, but rather that they are inseparably bound up in that community. The larger community depends on the elderly and the elderly on the larger community. This underscores the earlier insight that susceptibility to harm is a burden for an individual to bear, but is a product of the mutual relationship between any society and that individual.

This emphasis on place holding correspondingly helps us to specify our ethical obligations to plan for disasters and seek effective communication and collaboration with regards to the elderly. In particular, if there is an ethical obligation to plan for disasters, we must ask: how do we do so, especially with regard for the elderly? To answer that question, though, assumes that we are able to effectively identify those elderly who are susceptible to compound harms during a disaster. This will not be as simple as looking at census maps to determine who is over the age of 65 and, accordingly, in need of special considerations in the planning stage before disaster strikes. There will, at least, need to be some consideration of the level of susceptibility to harm given the axes of susceptibility noted above. But, as Lindemann and Young observe, we, as human persons, are more than discrete brains or bodies. Instead, the significant elements of our identities and sense of personhood are wrapped up in other people and in our dwelling spaces. Thus, the neat boundaries of individuals on a census map have little meaning in the actual experience of human life. Accordingly, assessment of an individual or population's susceptibility to harm along the primary axes of susceptibility will depend on not just broad assessment, but deep assessment. In this way, disaster planning that is sensitive to an ethics of place holding will seek to engage people and understand people where they are at, that is, where they are living and working. Nieli Langer (2004) has framed this in terms of meeting people, that is, planning with them for disaster, on their own turf. The significance of this is that these are not just random spaces within which people live and operate, but rather that they are important extensions of who they are and how they understand themselves. Thus, divorcing people from the context of where and how they live is to fail to engage with them in the fullest sense of who they are.

This may also help those planning for disaster to understand why many elderly, such as Miss Janine, resist evacuating their homes and abandoning their possessions when a disaster is imminent. Such objects and spaces are profound aspects of who an individual is, and, especially when the brain is failing, they may be tremendously important support structures in maintaining or holding someone in her sense of identity or personhood (see Campbell, 2007 for a similar observation). To abandon home and belongings may, in some cases, be tantamount to dying, insofar as the means to hold oneself in place as a person is lost.

This deeper approach would entail that, in order to interact with people where they are at, and, thereby, effectively draw them into disaster planning, attention to who interacts with and speaks about elderly individuals is an immeasurably important decision. In many cases, networks of support already exist. They involve nurses, doctors, spouses, friends, home health aids, neighbors, postal workers, family, social workers, pharmacists, and meals-on-wheels delivery persons, to name only a few. These are the people who frequently are involved in holding the elderly in their identities and sense of personhood. Consequently, they are a vital part of any disaster plan that strives to respect the equal worth and dignity of the elderly. Thus, a commitment to communication and collaboration before disaster strikes, and then, during a disaster calls for communication and collaboration done in the right way. An ethics of place holding helps to draw attention to those networks of care that are essential to the elderly during a disaster, and accordingly to the need to ensure that they are part of planning for and then carrying out coordinated rescue and relief efforts.

Finally, in considering the scope of good disaster planning and communication, an ethics of place holding further assists us in honing the extent of our obligation. If we are committed to elderly individuals not just as bodies or brains, but instead to their sense of self as it is spread across dwelling spaces, belongings, and human relationships, then we must display a similar commitment during and following disasters to repair and restore the elderly to their structured places. Good disaster planning, under the aspect of an ethics of place holding, avoids merely planning for the rescue of discrete individuals during a disaster because this is not all that individuals are. Instead, where individuals might need to be evacuated from the context of their day to day place holding structures during a disaster, the commitment to help them return and rebuild is part and parcel of treating them with dignity and worth. In this way, where the elderly have often suffered additional harms in trying to obtain financial aid or basic necessities following a catastrophic disaster, an ethics of place holding qualifies our understanding of what it means to effectively plan for a disaster. Planning for a disaster involves not merely planning for the immediate response to a disaster when it happens, but also to the efforts at repair and restoration following the disaster.

In this manner, an ethics of place holding applied to disaster planning and response may involve a stronger commitment to elderly individuals than current legal standards afford. For instance, at present in the United States, the *Robert T. Stafford Disaster Relief and Emergency Assistance Act* precludes providing federal funding following a major disaster to for-profit nursing home facilities, which, nonetheless, account for more than two-thirds of the long-term care facilities in the United States (Polivka-West, 2009, p. 6; *Robert T. Stafford Act*, 2007). An ethics of place holding, though, reveals that there is an ethical obligation to help repair and restore the elderly in their structured places following a major disaster, irrespective of whether that involves a for-profit or nonprofit facility. Legal standards are not sufficient in determining our ethical obligations. Instead, an ethics of place holding, by revealing these deeper ethical commitments to the elderly, is essential in shaping and directing current and future legislation so that it more and more respects the dignity of every individual human being.

RECOMMENDATIONS

So far in our discussion we have tried to show that the elderly have often disproportionately suffered during catastrophic disasters. This is due in part to the fact that the elderly, over and above being vulnerable to disasters, are also susceptible to compound harms during any major disaster. Their susceptibility to harm is especially determined by seven primary axes of susceptibility: physical impairment, chronic illness, aid receipt, financial vulnerability, social isolation, sensory awareness, and access to transportation. Any of these axes of susceptibility can also be further accentuated by the magnification of social injustices perpetuated during major disasters along the lines of race, economic class, and gender. In considering ethical obligations that any society might have to its members during a disaster, two obligations become especially relevant to the elderly: (1) an ethical obligation to conduct responsible planning prior to a disaster striking, and (2) an ethical obligation to cultivate and maintain lines of communication and collaboration between all those necessary to rescue everyone stranded or injured by a disaster. In order to further specify these obligations, though, we introduced an ethics of place holding drawing on the work of Hilde Lindemann (2002 and 2009) and Iris Marion Young (1997). This ethic attuned us to the ways in which human persons or identities are distributed across and amidst embodied communities and in physical dwelling spaces, and, thereby, the specific efforts needed to address the elderly in effective disaster planning and communications. In addition to the broad commitments to planning and communication, as informed by an ethics of place holding, we now attempt to offer some concrete recommendations for future enlightened disaster planning and response that is aware of and seeks to address the unique situations of many elderly individuals during major disasters.

Three central features of any attempt to engage in disaster planning that is conscious of the elderly will be (1) identification, (2) integration, and (3) contingency.

IDENTIFICATION

The elderly, as such, have not been identified and addressed in broad-spectrum disaster plans (Polivka-West, 2009). Future disaster plans, particularly those at the city/regional and national governmental levels, need to address this susceptible population (O'Brien, 2003; Polivka-West, 2009). But, merely identifying all those over the age of 65 in disaster plans will not be enough. Given tools like the axes of susceptibility, efforts will need to be taken to assess the specific nature and degree of any elderly persons' susceptibility to additional harm during a disaster. In order to accomplish such a task, much more information than currently exists at the broad level of a national census will need to be solicited. To do this, those individuals and agencies that help to hold the elderly in their identities through narratives and respect for their physical dwelling spaces will be essential sources of support (Elmore and Brown, 2007; Polivka-West, 2009; Saliba et al., 2004). Accordingly, enlightened disaster plans will not stop at the level of providing general transportation or medical care to injured, elderly persons during disasters. Instead, they will seek to provide transportation that accounts for elderly individuals with a wide range of physical disabilities (especially people in wheelchairs), and also medical care that is responsive to acute injuries suffered during the earthquake along with care that addresses the chronic illnesses that many elderly have, and thereby also their needs for certain medications and treatment protocols (O'Brien, 2003; Polivka-West, 2009). Further, identification of the elderly in their susceptibility to harm will also entail understanding their relationship to the physical space in which they live, think, and remember. Therefore, disaster plans must not take lightly an elderly person's commitment to sheltering in that place where they are able to maintain a sense of identity (Campbell, 2007). This could then entail a renewed commitment to helping individuals or nursing homes or assisted living communities to "harden" and resist the impending disaster forces (Polivka-West, 2009). If evacuation were necessitated, planners might anticipate creating a separate shelter for the elderly population where their needs can be carefully addressed and a sense of place and identity can be approximated (Aldrich and Benson, 2008).

INTEGRATION

If these efforts to identify and make meaningful the full range of an elder's susceptibility to harm during a disaster are to be successful, the massive influx of information that results will need to be processed and communicated among the key individuals, agencies, and levels of government involved in responding to any given disaster. While technology cannot solve all of our problems, trends in recent technological innovations do offer some ways forward for disaster planners. The practice of adopting a common electronic database within which all those involved in the care and rescue of persons during disasters can deposit and access information about specific disaster plans and needs is pivotal. One example of this recently has been the Virtual USA project that attempts to assimilate the specific, "on the ground," data of local emergency responders into a common data pool that can then be accessed by multiple individuals, agencies, and departments during a disaster ("Secretary Napolitano ... ," 2009). Such efforts will crucially hinge on there being both a commitment to share information between the already existing network of disaster planners and first responders, as well as encouragement of still broader circles of people being allowed to share information and take part in the disaster planning. Notably, this will entail the efforts to integrate the aging services network into current disaster planning and response before, during, and after disasters.

CONTINGENCY

The best disaster plans do not attempt to address every possible thing that could happen or go wrong during a disaster; costs and human finitude simply make such efforts impossible and even unwise in light of other important aspects of human life (i.e., attention to funding for education or environmental waste cleanup) that deserve attention. Instead, the best disaster plans anticipate a certain amount of unpredictability during any given disaster and allow for thoughtful adaptation and modification as circumstances change. For instance, it is likely that, at times, primary lines of communication between people responding during a disaster will fail—perhaps communication technologies simply stop working, perhaps people forget previously agreed upon protocols, and/or perhaps the data needed to rescue and treat injured persons goes missing or is damaged. In any case, it is essential that disaster plans incorporate a commitment to redundancy, which involves uses of multiple communication technologies, repeated instructions through different individuals, agencies, and departments, as well as remote backups of vital information (Aldrich and Benson, 2008; O'Brien 2003; Polivka-West, 2009). An example of this, especially pertinent to the frail elderly, is the use of electronic medical records. While paper medical records are especially vulnerable during major disasters (particularly those involving fires and flooding), electronic medical records offer a means to maintain consistent medical treatment of an elderly individual with health problems across multiple providers and in multiple times and places, as is likely to be the case during a major disaster evacuation.

Additionally, in spite of comprehensive disaster planning and communication, it is likely that some resources will remain scarce during a disaster, and some degree of triage will be an inevitable feature of certain disaster responses (at least during initial response stages). Aware of the tendency of the elderly to be penalized by triage systems, disaster planners ought to develop clear protocols for triage *prior* to a disaster occurring. Without stipulating what these may be, we endorse guidelines suggested already by Kuschner et al. (2007) who is drawing on the "fair process model" articulated by Daniels and Sabin (see Kuschner et al., 2007, p. 18). Ethical triage ought to be guided by (1) transparency, (2) stakeholder engagement, (3) public dissemination of reasons that drive decision making, and (4) flexibility to modify decisions as new information emerges (Kuschner et al., 2007, p. 18). To this end, issues of triage are not more important than other issues we have sought to bring attention to in this chapter, but rather are one more component, among others, of better disaster planning and response.

Undoubtedly, these recommendations are incomplete, but they represent at least the beginning of a more robust and enlightened commitment to planning for and responding to disasters with the unique needs of the elderly in mind. To be sure, the elderly have been routinely overlooked amidst major natural disasters, and, accordingly, often represent a disproportionate amount of those killed, maimed, or dislocated. Yet, as we have tried to show throughout this chapter, the ability to at least mitigate some of the damage suffered by the elderly during catastrophic disasters is not beyond human ability. In our ethical commitment to planning and communication prior to, during, and following a major disaster as informed by an ethics of place holding, the space is opened up for positive and significant change that honors the inherent dignity and worth of all human life.

REFERENCES

Aldrich, N., & Benson, W. F. (2008). Disaster preparedness and the chronic disease needs of vulnerable older adults. *Preventing Chronic Disease, 5*(1), 1–6.

Booth, W. (2010, March 13). Old and poor in Haiti suffer mightily after the quake. *The Washington Post,* A06.

Bouchama, A. (2004). The 2003 European heat wave. *Intensive Care Medicine, 30*(1), 1–3.

Brunner, B. (n.d.). *Hurricane Katrina: A disaster and its catastrophic aftermath.* Retrieved April 10, 2010, from InfoPlease via http://www.infoplease.com/spot/hurricanekatrina.html.

Brunner, B. (n.d.). *Tsunami Factfile.* Retrieved May 10, 2010, from InfoPlease via http://www.infoplease.com/spot/tsunami.html.

Campbell, J. (2007). On belonging and belongings: Older adults, Katrina, and lessons learned. *Generations, 31*(4), 75–78.

Chan, E. (2008). The untold stories of the Sichuan earthquake. *The Lancet, 372*(9636), 359–362. Retrieved May 10, 2010, from Elsevier.

Croom, C., Jenkins, P., & Eddy, A. (2007). Miss Janine's story: Deciding to stay. *Generations, 31*(4), 8–9.

de Beauvoir, S. (1989). *The second sex.* New York, NY: Vintage Books.

Elmore, D. L., & Brown, L. M. (2007). Emergency preparedness and response: Health and social policy implications for older adults. *Generations, 31*(4), 66–74.

Fahey, C. J. (2007). Ethics and disasters: Mapping the moral territory. *Generations, 31*(4), 61–65.

Fernandez, L. S., Byard, D., Lin, C., Benson, S., & Barbera, J. (2002). Frail elderly as disaster victims: Emergency management strategies. *Pre-Hospital and Disaster Medicine, 17*(2), 67–74.

Fink, S. (2009, August 25). The deadly choices at Memorial. *The New York Times.* Retrieved from LexisNexis Academic.

Fouillet, A., Rey, G., Laurent, F., Pavillon, G., Bellec, S., Guihenneuc-Jouyaux, C., et al., (2006). Excess mortality related to the August 2003 heat wave in France. *International Archives of Occupational and Environmental Health, 80*(1), 16–24.

Haiti's situation still dire, despite progress. (2010, April 15). *UN News Centre.* Retrieved May 10, 2010, from http://www.un.org/apps/news/story.asp?NewsID=34376&Cr=haiti&Cr1=

Haiti: Don't forget the elderly. (2010, March 12). *Integrated Regional Information Networks (IRIN).* Retrieved April 10, 2010, from http://www.irinnews.org/Report.aspx?ReportId=88403

Haiti. (2010). In *The world factbook.* Retrieved April 10, 2010, from https://www.cia.gov/library/publications/the-world-factbook/geos/ha.html.

HelpAge International. (2005). *The impact of the Indian Ocean tsunami on older people.* London: HelpAge International. Retrieved April 8, 2010, from http://www.helpage.org/Resources/Researchreports.

HelpAge International. (2000). *Older people in disasters and humanitarian crises: Guidelines for best practice.* London: HelpAge International. Retrieved April 10, 2010, from http://www.helpage.org/Resources/Manuals.

Jenkins, P., Laska, S., & Williamson, G. (2007). Connecting future evacuation to current recovery: Saving the lives of older people in the next catastrophe. *Generations, 31*(4), 49–52.

Johnstone, M. (2009). Health care disaster ethics: A call to action. *Australian Nursing Journal, 17*(1), 27.

Kottow, M. (2003). The vulnerable and the susceptible. *Bioethics, 17*(5&6), 460–471.

Kuschner, W., Pollard, J., & Ezeji-Okoye, S. (2007). Ethical triage and scarce resource allocation during public health emergencies: Tenets and procedures. *Hospital Topics: Research and Perspectives on Healthcare, 85*(3), 16–25.

Lagnado, L. (2001, December 12). Hidden victims. *The Wall Street Journal,* A1.

Langer, N. (2004). Natural disasters that reveal cracks in our social foundations. *Educational Gerontology, 30*, 275–285.

Lindemann, H. (2002). What child is this? *The Hastings Center Report, 32*(6), 29–38.

Lindemann, H. (2009). Holding one another (well, wrongly, clumsily) in a time of dementia. *Metaphilosophy, 40*(3&4), 462–474.

Mokdad, A. H., Mensah, G. A., Posner, S. F., Reed, E., Simoes, E. J., & Engelgau, M. M. and the Chronic Diseases and Vulnerable Populations in Natural Disasters Working Group (2005). When chronic conditions become acute: Prevention and control of chronic diseases and adverse health outcomes during natural disasters. *Preventing Chronic Disease, 2*, 1–4.

Mudur, G. (2005). Aid agencies ignored special needs of elderly people after tsunami. *British Medical Journal, 331*, 422.

O'Brien, N. (2003). *Emergency preparedness for older people.* ILC Issue Brief, January–February. New York, NY: International Longevity Center.

Pesik, N., Keim, M. E., & Iserson, K. V. (2001). Terrorism and the ethics of emergency medical care. *Annals of Emergency Medicine, 37*(6), 642–646.

Pfaff, W. (2003, August 22). Europe's heat wave. *Boston Globe*, A19. Retrieved March 21, 2010, from News Bank: Access World News (0308220017).

Polivka-West, L. (2009). *Statement of LuMarie Polivka-West before the U.S. Senate special committee on aging.* Retrieved April 10, 2010, from http://www.ahcancal.org/advocacy/testimonies/Testimony/StatementHurricaneDisasterPreparedness.pdf.

Robert, T. *Stafford Disaster Relief and Emergency Assistance Act*, Pub. L. No. 93–288, as amended, 42 U.S.C. 5121–5207 (2007). Retrieved May 10, 2010, from FEMA via http://www.fema.gov/about/stafact.shtm.

Rothman, M., & Brow, L. (2007). The vulnerable geriatric casualty. *Generations, 31*(4), 16–20.

Saliba, D., Buchanan, J., & Kington, R. (2004). Function and response of nursing facilities during community disaster. *American Journal of Public Health, 94*(8), 1436–1441.

Secretary Napolitano unveils "Virtual USA" information-sharing initiative. (2009, December 9). Retrieved April 26, 2010, from http://www.dhs.gov/ynews/releases/pr_1260375414161.shtm.

The Associated Press. (2010, January 21). Haiti's dying elderly say 'nobody cares'. Retrieved March 20, 2010, from http://www.msnbc.msn.com/id/34969140/ns/world_news-haiti_earthquake/.

The National Commission on Terrorist Attacks Upon the United States. (2004). *The 9/11 commission report: Executive summary.* Retrieved from 9 to 11 Commission via http://www.9-11commission.gov/report/index.htm

Urbina, I. (2010). Earthquake's burdens weigh heavily on Haiti's elderly. *New York Times*, A4.

Veatch, R. (2005). Disaster preparedness and triage. *The Mount Sinai Journal of Medicine, 72*(4), 236–241.

Walker, M. (2007). *Moral understandings* (2nd ed.). New York, NY: Oxford University Press.

Wax, E. (2007, August 5). South Asia floods displace millions, spark fears of widespread disease. *The Washington Post*, p. A16. Retrieved May 10, 2010, from LexisNexis Academic.

Young, I. M. (1997). *Intersecting voices* (House and home: Feminist variations on a theme). Princeton, NJ: Princeton University Press.

Zach, N. (2009). *Ethics for disaster*. New York: Rowman & Littlefield Publishers.

CHAPTER 14

Bringing It All Together

Our purpose in writing this book is to challenge, with the intent of modifying, current thinking and practice about ethics, aging, and old age. As should now be clear, ethics and practice are bound together. Our ethics are realized in our practices, in the simple gestures of everyday life and in those moments when we experience great uncertainty about what actions are right or good. While many tend to think of ethics as a set of binding rules about what we may or may not do, that view, while not entirely inaccurate, is also limited. A generous understanding of ethics welcomes many sources of moral knowledge, does not silence the emotions and moral sentiments, and appreciates the storied nature of our lives. Yet it also grasps that thinking ethically involves complex skills of listening, hearing, proposing, questioning, testing, and reflection. Thus, the richer our moral knowledge, the broader our life experiences, and the stronger our moral courage, the greater the likelihood that we will bring a complex repertoire of ethically informed approaches to our work and scholarship. These features of the moral life would also suggest that "doing" ethical work is a collaborative enterprise, since each person brings his or her own array of knowledge, experience, and skills to the conversation. The goal of all this is to ensure that we do not overlook possibilities that are morally acceptable, and often morally desirable.

Hence, we are committed to an ethics that is broad and deep, and that tries to understand people realistically: as flawed individuals, neither saints nor sinners, who are engaged in trying to live a worthy life. To this end, we began by addressing what we see as a fundamental problem in aging and ethics: the adoption of the same autonomy-based ethic that grounds the broader practices of medicine and bioethics. Indeed, we largely fault philosopher-bioethicists for propounding this conception of the "rational, autonomous man" that governs how we view and treat older people, and that informs our expectations of them. As we have indicated, the paradigmatic autonomous, rational individual who is free from impediments, including physical ones, is not well suited to addressing the ethical issues that arise in the context of aging and old age. While that image of individualistic and rational agency, which has attained almost mythic proportions, probably describes few of us, it is particularly problematic in old age. Rather, as we have argued, we need to acknowledge the deep and basic nature of human dependency, and the degree to which we all need one another in order to "survive and thrive" (Kittay, 1999, p. 107).

Indeed, the ability of elders to survive and thrive has motivated the writing of this book. We worry that many will not thrive, and that some may not even survive, under current conditions of economic insecurity, persistent ageism, chronic illness, and the cultural disenfranchisement that many elders experience. Some older people may find old age to truly be their "golden years"—a time of freedom, economic stability, and emancipation from the demands and expectations that often plague the young. Yet this scenario describes only the most privileged elders in our society. In our view, any approach to aging and old age that is worthy of attention will consider it from the perspective of the worst off: those who are struggling, who cannot afford to "beat" aging, at least temporarily, by cosmetic surgery, and who cannot enjoy their freedom in retirement because their incomes are inadequate to maintain even a good diet much less travel the world. It is to these people that we direct our attention, in order to ensure that they, too, can enjoy the virtues that may come with old age (Ruddick, 1999).

While we are particularly concerned with older people who are not "successfully" aging by current definitions of that term, we also emphasize that ethical problems associated with end-of-life care, Alzheimer's disease, cultural disenfranchisement, or physical detriments affect people whether they are rich or poor, male or female, or black, white, or brown. They are often more extreme and harder to address for elders who live at the margins, but they exist quite broadly. Despite efforts in recent years to recast the aging experience into a predominantly positive one, to be old in this country today and in probably many other parts of the world, is still to experience devaluation, especially if one suffers from stigmatizing diseases such as Alzheimer's (Herskovits & Mittteness, 1995; Luborsky, 1995). Devaluation threatens feelings of self-worth, which in turn is an impediment to speaking in one's own voice and thus acting as a moral agent. As discussed in several chapters in this book, in many ways today's dominant ethical norms reinforce this cultural devaluation by calling upon, and even expecting, people to be what they often cannot be (and may not even want to be)— that is free, independent, and in control.

To respond to what we see as both an insufficiently rich concept of ethics and the heretofore limited range of issues that have been considered ethically important, we have explored a very different, and some might find, challenging, framework for thinking about aging and ethics. By appealing to feminist ethics, narrative theory, and communicative ethics, we have tried to make a case for rethinking how we see and treat those who are aging or old. In doing so, we join other practitioners and theorists (Agich, 2003; Held, 2006; Holstein & Mitzen, 2003; McCullough & Wilson, 1995; Moody, 1992; Walker, 2007) who are unsettled by the current liberal, autonomy-based approach that blends out much of the gender, class, and race inequality and that overlooks the unique life moment that marks old age.

Beyond questioning the dominant paradigm rooted in a "thin" concept of autonomy, we have broader social concerns: to contribute to a change in the approaches and attitudes upon which we base our cultural thinking, education, community practices, and policy-making. While we do not pretend that fixing one's categories or shifting one's theoretical moral framework will *necessarily* lead to social change, we believe that such change will be unnecessarily limited without some deep rethinking about how we address aging and ethics. Hence, this book raises questions about the theoretical frameworks now in place for thinking about aging while it simultaneously considers how different frameworks that are rooted in social justice concerns might lead to different belief systems and practices. As we have argued, bottom-up approaches will serve us better than the top-down ones that have been put into practice.

Take, for example, our account in Chapter 4 of the attempt to rethink categories of aging and old age by appealing to concepts of successful aging and civic engagement. As we have argued, these concepts are inadequate to fill the space that many are now calling the "third age" because they do not reflect many old persons' lived experiences. While the intentions of these movements are good (to resist narratives of relentless loss and decline) their top-down application, and the fact that they reflect the experiences of only the most-privileged older people, make them poor candidates for a normative conception of a "good old age." For this reason, we have argued for a more contextual approach to such matters, starting from the reality that most older people *do* experience some degree of decline and loss. As Sandra Bartky admits,

> ... I see old age, for the most part, as a series of losses. There is the loss of one's social or professional networks; the loss, if one lives long enough and if there is one, of a life's companion; the loss, if one is unlucky, of motility, or sight or hearing or the control of one's sphincters; the loss of one's home, if illness requires moving in with an adult child or else removal to a nursing home; inevitably, there is the loss of life in death.
> —*Bartky, 1999, p. 61*

Bartky, a feminist philosopher, is using her own experiences and perhaps those of friends and colleagues to reflect more generally about old age. Along with other feminist philosophers, she is quite willing to acknowledge the losses associated with old age. By contrast, scholars like Gullette who identify with age studies argue that decline narratives that begin in middle age are primarily socially constructed and should not thus be publicly discussed, especially in an already ageist society. We have argued that a robust account of aging and ethics must take account of all experiences. While we do not accept that old age is wholly a cultural construct, we believe that how society responds to the changes that occur in old age is socially constructed and so can be changed. Thus, admitting to experiences of decline should not entail risk for individuals, and this is where we see the importance of changing the way we frame our thinking about human need and aging. If we radically alter our thinking about what it is to be human such that we no longer equate full human persons with autonomy and independence, we go a long way toward making it possible for *everyone*, not just our elderly population, to ask for help. While one may be better able to appear as the "Kantian autonomous, rational man" during one's younger years, the appearance is fleeting and misleading: no one is truly autonomous in the traditional philosophical sense, and we are all the better for it if we conceive of autonomy in relational terms (Mackenzie & Stoljar, 2000; Meyers, 1997).

Yet, despite the arguments laid out in this book, readers might object that they are not at fault for the problems faced by older people because these problems are not the work of individuals, but are brought about by cultural patterns and structures of inequality and ageism. Accountability for these patterns and structures is virtually impossible to determine, because they are diffuse and controlled by no one in particular. Like Iris Marion Young (2007), however, we deny this "liability model" of responsibility, which relies on direct interaction between the wrongdoer and the wronged party. Rather, like Young, we take a social connection model as the grounds for better understanding the responsibilities at stake for bringing about change for older people. According to Young's social connection model,

> ... individuals bear responsibility for structural injustice because they contribute by their actions to the processes that produce just outcomes. Our responsibility derives from belonging together with others in a system of interdependent processes of cooperation and competition through which we seek benefits and aim to realize projects. Even though we cannot trace the outcome, we may regret our own particular actions in a direct causal chain, and we bear responsibility because we are part of the process. Within this scheme of social cooperation, each of us expects

justice toward ourselves, and others can legitimately make claims on us. Responsibility in relation to injustice thus derives not from living under a common constitution, but rather from participating in the diverse institutional processes that produce structural injustice.

—*Young, 2007, pp. 175–176.*

A liberal framework, which endorses a sort of liability model of responsibility, is insufficient for understanding the complexity of relationships between people, both young and old. Our agist beliefs and practices connect us across generational divides, as well as across lines of race, class, educational status, gender, and sexual orientation. Given that we are "all in this together," so to speak, we are each responsible for bringing about the changes necessary to make a robust old age possible for current and future elderly citizens.

In the past 25 years, ethics as seen through the prism of age has become part of the professional and public conversation. Yet, new ideas—some more than two decades old—do not transfer easily into practice. There are many reasons for this gap. The public policy chapter addressed the lack of a social view that places care central to a just society (Tronto, 1993). It also explored the damages wrought by the neoliberalism agenda and the resulting risk to society. The new version of the welfare state forces us to ask whether there is any interest in responding to the continued deprivation that people of all ages experience. Our picture of the relational self can serve as a powerful counterweight to the ethic of "going it alone." Contrary to recent denunciations of socialism, human connections and the need for collective responsibility are fundamental, and not a much-maligned "ism."

Professionals, who may be interested in testing the ethical approach that we advocate, face difficulties that we recognize as real. Often they work within a commodified setting, where time is money and evaluations and/or contracts are based on tasks accomplished. That makes, for example, the slower, intensive process of narrative re-storying and the effort to dissolve the barriers between autonomy and paternalism so that professionals and elders can work together toward a common goal problematic. These obstacles are reinforced by codes of ethics, especially in social work, which are prescriptive or evidence-based practice, which can limit freedom to test new ideas. The organization of work, including bureaucracies and hierarchies arrangements, further constrains moral risk taking.

Traditional social work ethics is deeply committed to self-determination. With professionalism threatened from many directions, a more flexible, often ambiguous and particularistic approach to ethics seems out of reach. Hence, the familiar reliance on principlism is understandable. That approach was initially designed for busy professionals who had little time or interest to grapple with theory (Beauchamp & Childress, 1979). Yet, as we have argued, particularly in long-term care, that shorthand approach to ethical analysis is undermining much that is ethically important to people with physical and cognitive limitations. The possibilities for deliberation, which requires time, a safe place for discussion, equality of participants, moral imaginings, and courage to say the nonconventional, are usually beyond the capacities of the underfunded long-term care environment (Holstein, 2010).

If these problems can be addressed, even if slowly at the start, we would urge an ethics of solidarity that unfolds at multiple levels at the same time. People can talk together in informal groups in their own communities or in larger groups via the internet. These explorations can raise many questions, including what commitments a caring and just society ought to make toward its most vulnerable members. This commitment will make it possible for care, compassion, and concern to be the virtues that mark each encounter with another person who needs care while assuring that equal attention is paid to the demands of justice for caregivers both paid and unpaid. If our moral identity is always in process, evolving through and with our relationships as feminist ethics suggests, then our moral practices as helping professionals must rest on ongoing dialogue and interpretation so that we do not adopt ethical norms and values that sabotage what may be important to the older people for whom we care.

Questions abound and, although we have tried to address many in this book, there are many more remaining. If we think of ethics in terms of human flourishing and support of human capabilities (Nussbaum, 2000), a broad vision is essential. If we think about social obligations to assure economic and other forms of security, then our ethics must support a vigorous political agenda—both on a broad national scale and more locally—that would target the changes for which we argued in several chapters. We need, for example, to be as concerned about the institutions and power structures in hospitals as we are about the physician–patient relationship or the fact that the person has or has not executed a durable power of attorney for health care.

As we have tried to show in this book, a comprehensive view of ethics and aging would deepen our concerns about the phenomenological and moral aspects of embodiment and the normative aspects of cultural ideals. Indeed, this would become as important, if not more important, than the lack of concordance between an elder's wishes for end-of-life care and a surrogate's sense of what these wishes might be. The latter, however, has received far more attention than the former. When we think about our moral obligations to the person with Alzheimer's disease, we need to be as concerned with preserving whatever elements of identity and individuality remain as we are about moving him/her from home to a more protected environment. We need to be as concerned with the gestures of everyday life as with major treatment choices.

We note here what we did not address in the book but that would be part of a fully comprehensive account of ethics and aging: We did not address the issue of cultural diversity, which adds a layer of complexity to the differences among older people that we have already discussed. We have not looked at the ethical issues that arise in multigenerational households, especially when grandparents are caring for grandchildren. Nor have we looked at the ethical implications of a health care system that separates health and social care that is often the root cause of excess hospitalization, which not only has cost implications but also personal ones. We have not considered managed care, which may or may not become the dominant form of Medicare-provided services in this country, nor have we looked at the recurring question of age-based rationing.

In the public policy chapter, we outlined what we see as a normative foundation for policy that respects the ethical vision we proposed. We did not, however, explore the question of whether or not changes in the life course and overlapping needs of different age groups might call for a different approach to policy that is not age specific (Achenbaum & Cole, 2007; Hudson, 2005). While we recognize that argument, we are convinced that in the contemporary political environment, to yield to an age-neutral policy would most likely harm the people who rely on the public sector for their safety net. There are far more of these people than the optimistic scenarios that we addressed in Chapter 4 would suggest. This fact, however, does not mean the question is undeserving of ethical analysis.

RETHINKING PHILOSOPHIES OF AGING

We look, therefore, to a richer morality about living as we age despite agist and other negative attitudes. As we have indicated, many ethicists (Hoffmaster, 2006; Kittay, 1999; Lindemann, 2006; Parks, 2003; Walker, 2003) have expanded the subject matter of ethics to include issues of exploitation and oppression in all its forms and have recognized that dependency and vulnerability, as facts of life, call for moral analysis. We suspect, however, that gerontologists will be resistant to elevating vulnerability and dependency as central features of human life, descriptive categories that they have spent many years trying to overturn. This problem is particularly interesting because it reflects the often different goals and sensibilities of people working in different disciplines. Thus, before closing, we want to explore this claim in somewhat greater depth in an effort to bridge these differences. Most significantly, if we think in terms of mutual dependency throughout our lives rather than independence (except, of course, for babies and children, and the seriously impaired), then we recognize that we all need the material, social, and economic support to allow us to grow and develop. We further recognize that we never stop needing this support. If we assume instead that we are all independent, then we need not worry about attending to the conditions that make our lives together possible (Dodds, 2007). The "dependency critique," as Chapter 2 suggested, offers instead a way of thinking that calls for a collective commitment to providing the necessary foundation so that all people can survive and thrive (Kittay, 1999). It further helps give assurance that people whose dependency leads them to require the active and direct help of others are not anomalies. They thus merit more than charitable support. By acknowledging the universality of dependency, we also ensure that the person providing care is not an anomaly. If we accept that we are all vulnerable to conditions around us, we are forced to adopt a more generous understanding of social welfare commitments that are now under threat. This approach, we suggest, is another way of acknowledging that we are relational selves whose way of life is made possible by the ongoing support of the material and the social world. It reinforces Tronto's (1993) political argument for an ethics of care and challenges neoliberal thinking that marginalizes the role of the state and the public sector. We thus invite skeptics, who are committed to social justice, to think about the political power such an analysis can have and how it might be used without undermining efforts to reverse the decline and loss paradigm.

Diana Meyers (1997) invites us to welcome what she calls heterodox moral perceptions. What we do not see, she says, can "camouflage social ills and thwart critical moral reflection" (p. 197). If we fail to notice some act or situation as morally problematic, we will neither think about it nor seek to change it. In Chapter 4, we noted that one objective of the "productive aging" thread in formulating the "third age" was to reverse images of the aging population as burdensome by showing the degree to which they were productive, including the many hours of "free" care provided to older relatives. Conventional moral perception would affirm that this view indeed made sense. Yet, once we apply a different perceptual filter, the picture changes. It would see that it involves exploitation of women, who by their labor are making significant contributions to the state at a considerable price to themselves. Thus, rather than using these women to demonstrate that older people are not a burden, we would point out that this is hardly free labor. It is simply a transfer from the public to the private sector. If we are concerned about gender justice, we would ask what society should do so as not to exploit this productive labor. Similarly, it would suggest that these "third-age" normative expectations value a certain kind of subjectivity, which is largely dependent on health and relative affluence. That image of the self, and the self-worth that accompanies it, is thus quite fragile. As Kittay (2006) has pointed out, by linking a moral commendable life to independence, we all live at the brink. Sometimes heterodox perceptions lead to anger and sometimes to a pained recognition that there is much we cannot change. But many things are capable of change and we hope that this book has at a minimum stimulated your heterodox moral perceptions and that you will continue to notice and question what seems to be taken for granted.

None of what we have suggested in this book is meant to denigrate the important gains that have been made over the past 25 years. Serious attention to end-of-life care means that fewer people suffer from intractable pain or have unwanted treatments foisted upon them. Despite the persistence of biases about old women (Parks, 2000), decision-making is increasingly a shared enterprise. The concepts captured in the terms confidentiality, dual relationships, safety and risk, and conflicts of interest have become central to the common language of health and social service professionals. So have the ethics of principle that we have consistently challenged.

As we think we have made clear, we do not intend this criticism to mean the principles have no value. Instead, we have argued that they are guides and not end points of thinking (Walker, 1993). We need to be alert to not letting our thinking become ossified so that we have little flexibility to respond to the specifics of different situations and different people. We also need to remember how setting principles into sharply defined oppositional categories such as autonomy and beneficence or paternalism, with the first half of these opposites preferred, can impede one's ability to work with elders to help them discover their authentic voice. These distinctions dissolve when the goal of our ethical engagement is not to honor autonomy or to impose our will to make the elders safe but rather together to understand what they most care about and together work toward that end.

In closing, we return to where we started. We re-emphasize that a critical perspective involves a [polygamous] marriage of different disciplines, an openness to empirical research and multiple sources of moral knowledge, attention to context, an appreciation of the seminal role that seeing ourselves as relational selves provokes, and the importance of narrative and communicative discourse as essential to our ethical understanding of aging and old age. Narrative is hard work but it is the best we can do if we are to recover or discover who we are and what matters to us. Our final words return us to our call for passionate scholarship, the rejection of a privileged perspective, and the reliance in whatever ways are available to us to hear and listen to voices from the margins. Passionate scholarship "does not aim for control or domination, nor even for certainty but for the freedom to pursue questions, to challenge assumptions, to hear and respect a multitude of voices, and to take engaged critique as a long term commitment" (Holstein & Minkler, 2007, p. 26).

REFERENCES

Achenbaum, W. A., & Cole, T. R. (2007). Transforming age-based policies to meet fluid life course needs. In R. Pruchno & M. Smyer (Eds.), *Challenges of an aging society: Ethical dilemmas, political issues* (pp. 238–368). Baltimore: Johns Hopkins University Press.

Agich, G. (2003). *Dependence and autonomy in old age: An ethical framework for long term care.* New York, NY: Cambridge University Press.

Bartky, S. (1999). Unplanned obsolescence: Some reflections on aging. In M. U. Walker, (Ed.), *Mother time: Women, aging, and ethics* (pp. 61–74). New York, NY: Rowman & Littlefield.

Beauchamp, T., & Childress, J. (1979). *Principles of biomedical ethics.* Baltimore: Johns Hopkins University Press.

Dodds, S. (2007). Depending on care: Recognition of vulnerability and the social contribution of care provision. *Bioethics, 21*(9), 500–510.

Gullette, M. M. (1997). *Declining to decline: The cultural combat and the politics of the midlife.* Charlottesville: University of Virginia Press.

Held, V. (2006). *The ethics of care: Personal, political, and global.* New York: Oxford University Press.

Herskovits, E., & Mitteness, L. (1995). Transgressions and sickness in old age. *Journal of Aging Studies, 8*(3), 327–340.

Hoffmaster, B. (2006). What does vulnerability mean? *Hastings Center Report, 36*(2), 38–45.

Holstein, M. (2010). Ethics and aging: Retrospectively and prospectively. In T. Cole, T. Ray, & R. Kastenbaum (Eds.), *A guide to humanistic studies in aging: What does it mean to grow old?* Baltimore: Johns Hopkins University Press.

Holstein, M., & Minkler, M. (2007). Critical gerontology: Reflections for the 21st century. In M. Bernard & T. Scharf (Eds.), *Critical perspectives on ageing societies* (pp. 13–26). Bristol, UK: Policy Press.

Holstein, M., & Mitzen, M. (2003). Self, society, and the "new gerontology." *Gerontologist, 43*(6), 787–796.

Hudson, R. (Ed.). (2005). *New politics of old age.* Baltimore: Johns Hopkins University Press.

Index

Note: n = footnote